NORFOLK
SOUTHERN

VIRGINIA

*A Commonwealth
Comes of Age*

Photo Research by Edith Jeter
"Partners in Progress" by bj Altschul,
   Mark Dorfman, Deborah Geering,
   Roland Lazenby, and Andrew Pitzer
Introduction by James A. Bacon, Editor,
   Virginia Business

Produced in cooperation with the
Virginia Chamber of Commerce
Windsor Publications, Inc.

VIRGINIA
A Commonwealth Comes of Age

Lisa M. Antonelli

Windsor Publications, Inc.—History
Books Division
Editorial Director: Teri Davis Greenberg
Director, Corporate Biographies: Karen
    Story
Design Director: Alexander D'Anca
Staff for *Virginia: A Commonwealth Comes
    of Age*
Manuscript Editor: Amy Adelstein
Photo Editor: Lynne Ferguson Chapman
Assistant Director, Corporate Biographies:
    Phyllis Gray
Editor, Corporate Biographies: Brenda
    Berryhill
Production Editor, Corporate Biographies:
    Una FitzSimons
Senior Proofreader: Susan J. Muhler
Editorial Assistants: Didier Beauvoir,
    Thelma Fleischer, Alyson Gould, Kim
    Kievman, Michael Nugwynne, Kathy B.
    Peyser, Pat Pittman, Theresa Solis
Sales Representatives, Corporate
    Biographies: Wade Emmett, Diane
    Murphy, John Rosi, Jerry Thomas
Layout Artist, Corporate Biographies: Mari
    Catherine Preimesberger
Art Director: Ellen Ifrah
Designer: Tanya Maiboroda

Library of Congress Cataloging-in-
    Publication Data
Antonelli, Lisa M.
    Virginia: A Commonwealth Comes of
    Age. An Illustrated History. Bibliography: p. 460
    Includes index.
    1. Virginia—economic conditions.
    2. Virginia—Economic conditions—
    Pictorial works. 3. Virginia—
    Industries—History. 4. Virginia—
    Industries—History—Pictorial works.
    I. Virginia State Chamber of Commerce.
    II. Title.
    HC107.V8A65 1988
    330.9755—dc19 88-5702
    ISBN: 0-89781-235-2

Windsor Publications, Inc.
Elliot Martin, Chairman of the Board
James L. Fish, III, Chief Operating Officer
Hal Silverman, Vice-President/Publisher

*Previous page: A barge crosses Chesa-
peake Bay. Photo by Cameron Davidson. Courtesy, Southern Stock Photos*

CONTENTS

"*The Reward of Industry*," *a fitting slogan for the state of Virginia, was the motto adopted by tobacco manufacturers D.C. Mayo and Company in Richmond for this early label. Courtesy, Virginia State Library*

ACKNOWLEDGMENTS

There are many people whom I would like to thank now that this book is finished. I first would like to thank the ones nearest to my heart, family and almost family who suffered every word before it was written, for their love and support at times when I barely was lovable. I also would like to thank the venerable Virginius Dabney, for his suggestions and, retrospectively, for all his marvelous writings. Other friends like Lewis F. Powell III, Stuart Shelton, and Stephen Gill lent their professional support, and for this I would like to offer heartfelt appreciation.

There are other folks—the librarians of the Virginia State Library and of Hampton University, and Marty Callaghan and Bob Lewis of Virginia Polytechnic Institute and State University, to name just a few—without whom my research would have been much longer and more laborious. I also would like to thank my editors, Karl Stull for his faith in hiring me, and Pam Schroeder and Amy Adelstein who waited patiently while I stuttered on the computer.

Lastly, I would like to thank James Bacon, who not only provided encouragement but who also illuminated my arduous path with his insights, always a step ahead of me and yet behind me at the same time. To Jim, to those already mentioned, and to Jonathan, Christian, Marc, and Taylor, to Sara and Ginny, I dedicate this book.

This primitive method of taking tobacco to market in Virginia was employed in the early 1800s. Courtesy, Valentine Museum

INTRODUCTION

When Ms. Antonelli asked me to write this introduction, I asked myself: Does Virginia really need another history book? After reading her work, the answer became obvious. The pace of economic change in Virginia has accelerated to such a rate that any historical survey written more than 10 years ago is already out-of-date. In the past decade, Richmond has grown into a major corporate center with some dozen Fortune 500 and Service 500 companies. With the naval buildup of the 1980s, Hampton Roads has become a key component of the nation's military-industrial complex. Most significantly, Northern Virginia has evolved from a bedroom community of the nation's capital into a high-tech mecca on the scale of Silicon Valley and Boston's Route 128.

An old maxim warns us that those who are ignorant of history are doomed to repeat it. In the case of Virginia, the admonition might be restated: Those who are ignorant of history may be tempted to deviate from it. Clearly, Virginians have been doing something right—not just in the past 10 years, but the past 200. Despite the legacy of slavery, which hindered the modernization of the agricultural sector, Virginia was a leader in the commercial and industrial revolution of the early nineteenth century. Although the Civil War and its aftermath destroyed 250 years of accumulated wealth and saddled the state with a debt burden that might intimidate most countries, the state's economy has consistently outperformed the nation's for most of the twentieth century. By

the mid-1980s, the average per capita income nudged past the national average.

Looking back, we see old patterns repeating themselves. Ms. Antonelli's narrative, for example, reminds us that antebellum Virginia owed its tremendous economic growth to the expansion of the canal and railroad networks, financed in good measure by the state government. In taking the lead in funding multibillion-dollar improvements to Virginia's highways, ports, and airports, the state can call upon a long tradition of activism.

As a wide range of Virginia industries, from textiles to furniture, wilt under the pressure from foreign competition, it is worthwhile to recall the birth of the colony as a plantation economy tied into the global economy. Dependent upon a single cash crop, tobacco, Virginia was far more vulnerable to the vicissitudes of overseas markets than it is today. Virginians, unlike their fellow Americans in many other states, are accustomed to seeing themselves as part of a larger international economy.

Finally, as Virginians debate the propriety of a state policy that encourages foreign investment, it is helpful to recall that Northern and European capital has funded much of the state's economic growth for most of the past century. After the Civil War, British and Northern capital repaired the railroad lines, reopened the banks, reinvigorated the war-torn industry and pioneered the development of the coalfields. In the 1930s, when the rest of the nation was

Aluminum is one of the products of Virginia manufacturing. Photo by Robert Llewellyn

wracked by depression, Virginia avoided the worst effects by encouraging the influx of new industry and jobs.

The title of this book, *Virginia: A Commonwealth Comes of Age*, is aptly chosen. In the late 1980s, Virginia stands on the threshold of regaining the economic leadership it demonstrated before the Civil War. There is a maturity to Virginia's economy found only in a handful of other states. Northern Virginia has become a hotbed of technological innovation; the region is a dominant player in the realms of telecommunications and systems integration, two of the key industries of the twenty-first century. Richmond has emerged as a major regional financial center; Virginians have developed the institutions for mobilizing capital to finance the expansion of their home-grown industries. Hampton Roads is living up to its potential as the best deepwater port on the East Coast; through this door, Virginia is assured a prominent and growing role in international trade. Remarkably, Virginia has few liabilities. Pockets of economic hardship still can be found in the Southside and in southwestern mill towns, but these communities have shown remarkable resilience. Virginia is one of the few states in the country to have increased the total number of manufacturing jobs since the depths of the 1981 recession.

Virginia controls its own economic destiny to a degree it never has before. An obvious indicator is the state's growing prominence as a major corporate center. The ranks of Fortune 500-size companies have been swelled in recent years by astounding success stories such as those of James River and Ethyl Corporation. With the ongoing consolidation of the railroad industry, two of the nation's leading railroad companies— Norfolk Southern and CSX Corporation— have set up their headquarters here. And as outsiders discover the virtues of Virginia's business

climate, major firms such as Mobil, Mohasco and WearEver-ProctorSilex have begun relocating their headquarters in the state.

The vitality of Virginia's economy extends beyond the boardroom. While preserving its AAA bond rating, the state is funding massive improvements to its transportation infrastructure, particularly for roads, but for airports and harbors as well. State universities are making the shift from centers of higher learning to incubators for high-tech research and development. The rate of new business formation—especially in such exotic fields as fiber optics, biomedicine, software, satellite communications, and robotics—has never been higher.

Virginia may never regain the brilliance of the late eighteenth century when its plantation-based aristocracy helped create a new nation and forge a new system of government. After all, as the largest and most populous of the 13 colonies, its influence in the formation of the United States cannot be overestimated. Virginia's borders and, to a lesser extent, its population are far more circumscribed now. Even so, a second golden age may be at hand. When it comes, it will be stronger and more broadbased than the last. No longer is the state fettered by the feudal mentality of slavery and sharecropping; no longer does its economy hinge on the fate of a single crop. Given its many indisputable assets, Virginia is destined to become a world-class leader.

James A. Bacon
Editor, *Virginia Business*

An agile construction worker moves with apparent ease along some high beams at a Virginia building site. Photo by Robert Llewellyn

VIRGINIA BUSINESS AND INDUSTRY: A CHRONOLOGY

1607: British settlers arrive at Jamestown.

1612: John Rolfe plants Virginia's first tobacco crop.

1619: First black slaves arrive in Virginia.

1716: Alexander Spottswood explores the western territories.

1765: British-imposed Stamp Tax sparks colonial unrest.

1785: General Assembly charters the Potomac Company and the James River Company.

1837: Richmond, Fredericksburg & Potomac Railroad reaches Fredericksburg.

1860: Virginia emerges as the top tobacco manufacturer in the U.S.

1863: Virginia's western counties join the Union as the state of West Virginia.

1865: Richmond, the South's greatest industrial center, burns to the ground.

1870: Virginia rejoins the Union.

1871: Virginia sells its interest in railroads, paving the way for consolidation of state railroads by private interests.

1871: General Assembly passes the Funding Act, agreeing to pay the state debt in full.

1881: Norfolk & Western Railroad officials choose Roanoke as its link-up site.

1882: Readjusters push through the Riddlebarger Act, reducing Virginia's commitment for total payback of the state debt.

1883: The first coal shipment from the mines of Southwest Virginia arrives in Norfolk.

1886: Chesapeake Dry Dock & Construction Company receives its charter.

1887: The nation's first centrally operated overhead trolley debuts in Richmond.

1903: Maggie L. Walker establishes the country's first black-owned bank.

1920: Virginia's per capita wealth is the greatest of the Southern states.

1927: Virginia surpasses all other states in rate of industrial development.

1929: The U.S. stock market crashes.

1939: Virginia's economic recovery is complete, with market highs in production of rayon yarn, nylon, cellophane, and coal.

1952: Virginia State Ports Authority is created.

1968: Newport News Shipbuilding and Dry Dock Company becomes the state's largest manufacturing employer.

1980: Coal export boom draws ships from around the world to Hampton Roads.

1983: Center for Innovative Technology is established in Fairfax County.

1985: Fairfax County is selected as the site for the Software Productivity Consortium.

The wealth generated by tobacco grown in the Virginia colony created a class of prosperous planter merchants, wholly dependent on slave labor for the preservation of its privileged lifestyle. Courtesy, Virginia State Library

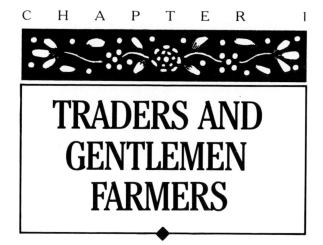

TRADERS AND GENTLEMEN FARMERS

On December 20, 1606, three ships carrying 100 men and 4 boys set sail from England to seek riches in the New World. After a wearying four-month voyage, the band touched shore at Cape Henry, then sailed into the Chesapeake Bay and up the James River. Finding a well-guarded peninsula with a suitable anchorage, the adventurers built a stockade and began sowing wheat, laying out a garden, and planting fruits and vegetables. They named their outpost Jamestown in honor of James I, King of England. From this base Captains John Smith and Christopher Newport launched explorations in search of the Northwest Passage, the fabled sea route to Cathay.

Inspired by tales of the Spanish conquistadors, these English adventurers sought trade and plunder. They had not come to settle a new land, but to discover quick riches—and to repay the investors in the London Company, the corporation financing their expedition. But even a hardened soldier of fortune like Smith, who had escaped enslavement by the Ottoman Turks and had roamed the steppes of Muscovy, was struck by the land's unspoiled beauty. "Heaven and Earth never agreed better to frame a place for man's habitation," he wrote back to England.

Virginia was the name given this uncharted territory. As Smith and his companions sailed up

the estuaries of the Chesapeake and pushed overland in search of gold, the appellation seemed ever more appropriate. The virgin land was a patchwork of meadows, marshes, and woodlands. Thick green forests rose from the moist, dark soil of lowlands. The trees were wide and tall, far more magnificent than anything in England. Groves of walnut, ash, beech, and oak sprouted amid seas of reedy grasses. Fields of flax, sorrel, and parsley grew wild. And the riverbanks, enriched by alluvial deposits, appeared most hospitable to farming.

The crops planted at Jamestown quickly took root and game was abundant. The woodlands were flush with deer, foxes, beavers, and raccoons. The marshes supported a multitude of swans, geese, and ducks. Wild turkeys, many as large as 40 pounds, dwelled in the woodlands. For a time it seemed the colonists would never go hungry.

But the illusion of a newfound paradise did not linger long. The would-be swashbucklers preferred searching for gold to toiling on the meager four-acre farm. Although the colonists built up their stores of maize by trading with the Indians, relations with the natives were often unfriendly. Damp, muggy vapors hovering over nearby marshes seemed laden with disease. The long voyage had taken its toll—16 lives had been

Captain John Smith was in the party that founded Jamestown, in the area that would become the state of Virginia. From Cirker, Dictionary of American Portraits, *Dover, 1967*

lost crossing the Atlantic—and by August, more began to die. Dysentery and malaria took some lives; Indian attacks claimed others. Too exhausted to farm or hunt, many simply starved. By November all but 38 had died.

The London Company rescued the colony from extinction by dispatching more ships with supplies. By late spring, 500 new settlers were boarding ships bound for Virginia. Beset by plagues, bad weather and travel hardships, 100 died en route. The survivors arrived in Jamestown too hungry and sick to work. Virginia's dry summers had stilted the crops. Crows had damaged the maize before it ripened. The colony's food supply was already low when the 400 arrived.

Pitching camp on the banks of the Elizabeth River and on the lower Powhatan, many settlers survived by eating from the oyster beds and scrounging berries, nuts, and roots. During what became known as the "Starving Time," a few were reduced to cannibalism. The hungriest of the community dug up the body of an Indian killed by settlers and ate it. Later one man was executed for killing, salting, and consuming his wife. By the spring of 1610, Virginia's population had dropped to 60.

Salvation came in the form of two more London Company ships. But within two weeks the new acting governor, Sir Thomas Gates, found the situation hopeless and decided to abandon Jamestown. The colonists had set sail for home when an approaching rowboat brought word that three more ships from England were carrying provisions and another 300 men. Once again the colony was saved. In late September 1611, 350 men led by Governor Sir Thomas Dale laid out a small fortified settlement 15 miles below the falls of the James River and named it Henrico, in honor of King James' eldest son Henry, the Prince of Wales. The English had planted themselves on American shores to stay.

The repeated expeditions were expensive, however, and the colony yielded nothing of value in its early years. For all its virtues Virginia had no silver deposits to mine, no Indian empires to plunder. Far from providing a trade route to the Orient, the Chesapeake proved to be a dead end. Jamestown was not the Elysian field the pamphleteers spoke of so glowingly back home.

Perennially short of cash, the London Company twice issued additional stock to resuscitate the venture. To counteract the perception in England that Virginia was a doomed colony, the company launched a campaign to entice more settlers. Pamphleteers—the mass media manipulators of the seventeenth century—extolled the wonders of the New World without mentioning such inconveniences as pestilence, starvation, and hostile natives. They wrote of natural abundance and of fortunes to be made. In London the popular play "Eastward Hoe" depicted Virginia as a paradise where gold was more plentiful than England's copper, and where natives plucked rubies and diamonds from the landscape.

Once across the Atlantic, the new colonists learned differently. There was no gold; there were no gems. Even pragmatic schemes, such as a plan to raise silk, failed to take hold: rats ate the silkworms sent to the New World. The soil was ill-suited to rice, and there was little demand in England for the sassafras, beads, and pitch that the colony did manage to export. French

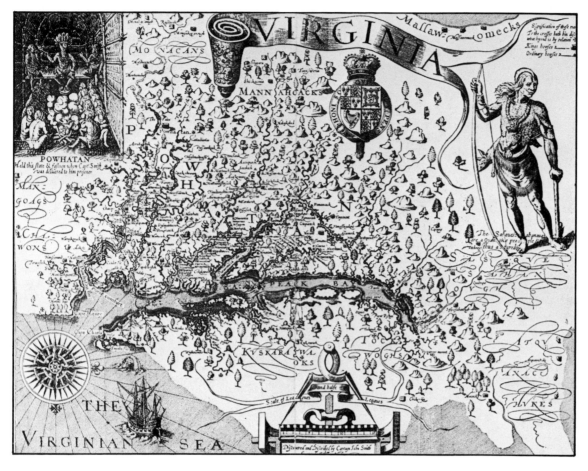

In May 1607, soon after landing at Jamestown, a party of colonists proceeded up the James River until its progress was halted by the falls at the future site of Richmond. One of Powhatan's villages was located nearby, and the inhabitants came down to the riverbank to greet the explorers. John Smith's 1608 map of Virginia, shown here, includes the "Falls" near the upper left corner. Courtesy, Maryland Historical Society

wine-dressers, recruited to cultivate vineyards in Virginia, boasted that the colony's grapes were large, plump, and superior to the product of their native Languedoc. But Virginia's first wine shipments arrived damaged in England and were poorly received.

Nothing could hide the fact that the London Company—the first financial venture associated with Virginia—was a financial disaster. The company had transplanted 5,000 colonists to the New World, but three-quarters of them had died. It had invested 200,000 pounds but failed to pay a single cash dividend. The company was broke and its investors demoralized. In 1624 King James revoked its charter.

Despite all its failures, the London Company had succeeded in planting a permanent settlement on a hostile foreign shore. While private investors were unwilling to put any more of their capital at risk, the English monarchy saw value in the colony. The small island nation looked with envy upon the Spaniards and the Portuguese, whose American empires spewed out gold, silver, pearls, sugar, and tobacco, making them

among the wealthiest nations in Europe. The English envisioned their own colonies producing valuable commodities that could be obtained only at great risk and expense from other nations.

The Crown saw another advantage to maintaining the Virginia colony: it would ease the pressure of excess population at home. In the early seventeenth century, England's ruling class sought a dumping ground for the island's human "refuse." The economy was growing, but not fast enough to accommodate the swelling ranks of England's poor. Peasants were being squeezed off communal land by the enclosure movement to make way for large herds of sheep. Thousands went jobless. A census of Sheffield in 1615 revealed that 775 of its 2,207 residents relied upon some form of charity.

A young man who owned no land and was not apprenticed in a trade or profession was destined to a life as an agricultural laborer. The annual wages of a rural worker in 1618 were eight pounds, eight shillings and nine pence; women made less as domestics. Even when both husband and wife were employed, they could

Governor Sir Thomas Dale, with a party of 350 men, founded the second settlement in Virginia, below the falls of the James River, and named it Henrico. Courtesy, Virginia Museum of Fine Arts, Richmond

The Spaniards had acquired a taste for smoking tobacco from the Indians, and the practice had spread to Europe. In the seven years before 1622, England imported an average of 60,000 pounds of West Indian tobacco annually; an equal amount may have been smuggled into the country. The first Virginia leaf, adopted from local Indians, was considered vastly inferior to the Spanish variety and sold for less than a third the price. But in 1612 John Rolfe introduced West Indian tobacco plants into the colony. Virginia tobacco soon gained a reputation as the equal of Spanish.

Tobacco's yield per acre was high, and when properly cured, it did not spoil in transit. Compared to other commodities, its shipping weight was low, therefore economical. Where grain fetched two shillings, six pence per bushel on the London market, Virginia tobacco brought three shillings per *pound*. No other product came close to generating the same return on investment, and it was not long before Virginians were devoting themselves utterly to the cultivation of the "sotweed." By 1619, the colony shipped home 20,000 pounds; by 1628, exports reached 500,000 pounds.

Efforts by the London Company and the Crown to diversify the economy through the production of wine, iron, and silk grass failed miserably. So passionate were the colonists in their cultivation of tobacco that they neglected to plant enough grain to feed themselves. To make sure the colony fed itself, the London Company demanded that land rents be paid in the form of grain for a common store: two and one-half bushels for every tenant and each of his servants. Governor Dale also prohibited farmers from planting tobacco in their private gardens until they had sown two acres of grain. Settlers even had to be prohibited from growing tobacco in the streets of Jamestown.

But tobacco gave the colony the economic base it had lacked. A small farmer could send tobacco valued at 100 pounds sterling to the English marketplace and bring back clothing for six agricultural servants, two guns, ammunition, various tools, and other merchandise. These he

barely afford to maintain a family; the cost of shelter, fuel, bread, meat, and clothing was reckoned at more than 20 pounds. Such was the plight of the working poor. Thousands of indigents roamed the countryside begging, stealing, or joining bands of highwaymen.

Even if Virginia yielded little in the way of riches, it could serve as England's social safety valve. At home the impoverished were a burden to the parish authorities and a menace to orderly society. In Virginia, with its abundant land, the same rabble might become a source of productivity and wealth.

It is somewhat ironic that James I, who launched the Virginia colony by chartering the London Company, was among the harshest critics of the commodity that would prove to be its salvation. A man of no mean literary talent, James is best known for commissioning a new translation of the Bible. But he also wrote a book on witchcraft—and a treatise denouncing the "filthy weed," tobacco.

could trade profitably in Virginia for livestock, land, or other commodities. By the end of his second year, according to nineteenth-century historian Philip Alexander Bruce, such a planter would have an estate valued at 600 pounds sterling.

The profits from the tobacco cultivation enabled planters to expand production even more. Settlement extended rapidly as planters sought fresh soil—so rapidly that, in 1634, the General Assembly divided the colony into eight counties, each with its own administrative and judicial system. Springing up first in James City County near the Jamestown settlement, the tobacco culture spread along the waterways of the Chesapeake Bay and its tributaries. Between 1637 and 1640, tobacco shipments to England averaged 1.4 million pounds annually.

The emerging plantation economy discouraged urban development. Planters on riverfront estates rolled their tobacco in hogsheads down to river landings and loaded them directly onto sea-going ships. Merchant vessels plied their trade up and down the York, the James, the Rappahannock, the Appomattox, and the Potomac, stopping at each landing to drop off European goods in exchange for tobacco. Plantations became self-sufficient communities, and there was no need for ports or cities.

So addicted was Virginia to tobacco that the leaf became the colony's currency. Not only did colonists use it to transact business in England, they also employed it when settling accounts among themselves. Because coinage was in short supply, the authorities proclaimed a number of acts establishing a fixed ratio of tobacco to sterling in the payment of taxes, fees, quitrents, tavern rates, and ferry charges.

Tobacco brought a fragile prosperity, however. As production soared, prices plummeted. A royal proclamation banned Spanish shipments to England in 1625, in effect giving Virginia tobacco producers a captive market. And fearing the loss of revenues from duties and customs on the trade, the Crown even forbade cultivation in England. But prices kept falling. English merchants reexported the leaf to the Baltic countries,

and as prices slipped, England's less privileged classes began picking up the smoking habit as well. But increasing production far outpaced the growing demand.

For the next century and a half, prices would remain ruinously low, generally fluctuating between a halfpenny and three pence per pound. When harvests were bountiful, as they often were, prices plunged. When storms or Dutch warships sank the tobacco fleets, prices recovered. An occasional profitable year could not hide the reality, however, that tobacco had lost its appeal. In 1682 depressed prices sparked plant-cutting riots in New Kent, Gloucester, and Middlesex counties. Rioters managed to push up

Flowerdew Hundred Plantation, one of the earliest English settlements in the New World, is located on the south bank of the James River, 10 miles east of Hopewell, Virginia. Originally inhabited by Indians, Flowerdew was granted to Governor George Yeardley in 1618. The governor named the plantation for his wife's family, the Flowerdews of Norfolk, England. The settlement survived the Indian massacre of 1622 and became a thriving farm. According to records, a windmill was constructed on the plantation circa 1621. Courtesy, Virginia Division of Tourism

transactions. A century later the legislature tried to prop up prices by mandating the destruction of inferior grades and restricting the last date of planting tobacco to curtail production.

Most of these measures were ineffectual. But Governor Alexander Spotswood did help in 1713 by establishing an inspection system to standardize the grades of tobacco. The Warehouse Act provided for public facilities where planters could take their tobacco for inspection and grading. Licensed inspectors enforced minimum standards by opening hogsheads and destroying inferior quality leaf. The class and grade of tobacco were marked on the hogshead.

By standardizing tobacco as a medium of exchange, the Warehouse Act gave Virginia planters and merchants a profound advantage over their Maryland competitors. Maryland brokers began moving to Virginia where they could buy better, more uniform tobacco, though at a higher price. In 1747, Maryland was forced to adopt similar measures.

Changing trading patterns in the 1700s made the Warehouse Act more practical to administer than it would have been a century earlier. As settlers pushed into the rolling hills of the Piedmont, they moved beyond the reach of the coastal merchant ships who served the Tidewater planters. Loading tobacco into carts or rolling them in hogsheads, Piedmont farmers transported their crop overland to the entrepots that sprang up at the fall lines of the major rivers. To handle the traffic between land-bound planters and seafaring merchantmen, markets, warehouses, loading docks, and customs houses arose at fall-line towns such as Petersburg, Richmond, and Fredericksburg.

While some government edicts benefited Virginia's trade, others crippled it. A series of Navigation Acts between 1651 and 1663 required that colonial cargo be carried in English ships. Certain "enumerated products," including tobacco, could be exported only to England, even if the final destination was another country. Finally, colonial imports had to originate in England or be transshipped from there. These measures augmented royal revenues and benefited

King James I launched the Virginia colony by chartering the London Company. Ironically, he disapproved of tobacco, the crop that would be the colony's salvation. Courtesy, Virginia State Library

prices briefly by ravaging tobacco fields—even cutting their own plants—and smashing 10,000 hogsheads of tobacco, but the respite was only temporary.

Twenty-five years after the formation of the colony, the General Assembly embarked upon a series of futile price-fixing measures. A series of acts in 1632, 1639, and 1640 set a price level for tobacco and penalized its exchange at a lower rate. But the laws had little practical effect. With no central markets for the exchange of tobacco, there was no way to supervise the

English merchants at the expense of the Dutch, who generally offered lower shipping rates. But by driving up transportation costs and adding unnecessary middlemen, the Navigation Acts made Virginia exports less competitive in markets outside England and forced Virginians to pay higher freight rates, taxes, and commissions on imported goods.

Virginia was locked into a colonial economy, its interests subordinated to those of the mother country. Parliament discouraged manufacturing in the colonies, so that most exports were raw materials. Tobacco remained the major money-maker, though declining prices encouraged Virginians to diversify into grain, forestry products, iron, and furs. About 1740, for example, one merchant ship departed for Great Britain with 304 hogsheads of tobacco, 9,600 staves, 1,200 feet of plank, and 21 bales of deerskin. Virginians also supplied provisions to the sugar plantations of the West Indies. One typical cargo consisted of 764 bushels of corn, 60 barrels of pork, 10 of beef, 7 of tallow, and 3 of lard. Virginia conducted a smaller trade with the New England colonies, particularly Boston.

From the earliest times, Virginia's economy was tied into the world economy. Probing far into the interior, the Chesapeake Bay and its

Not only did the Indians teach the colonists how to grow corn to feed themselves, they also taught them how to cultivate tobacco. In 1612 John Rolfe followed their example and planted a crop at Varina, just below the future site of Richmond. Others followed suit, and the popularity of the "noxious weed" in England soon convinced the colonists that money grew, if not on trees, then on tobacco plants.

tributaries linked Virginia with the Atlantic Ocean and all the territories along its rim. Events on other continents reverberated with profound effects in Virginia: the increase in tobacco consumption in Europe, the creation of new markets in the West Indian sugar plantations, the growth of the African slave trade, the industrial revolution in England, and the wars with the Dutch and French.

Only toward the middle of the eighteenth century, as settlers pushed far inland, did a significant number of Virginians tear themselves away from the influence of the global marketplace.

An abundance of land and shortage of labor made living conditions for immigrants much better than back in Europe. Virginia offered small farmers and free laborers a chance to earn a better living and provided more political representation than the average person enjoyed almost anywhere else in the world. This remarkable society, however, was marred by the extensive use of slavery and the total disregard of the rights of blacks, both African-born and American-born.

The spread of tobacco cultivation created an insatiable demand for labor. Planting the seed, tending the crop, harvesting the leaves, and curing the tobacco were laborious tasks—ones that the sons of the English gentry who immigrated to Virginia in search of easy fortunes were hardly willing to undertake themselves. Unlike the Spanish conquistadors, however, Virginia planters could not turn to the indigenous population for labor. The Powhatan Confederacy was no Aztec or Inca empire; the Indians were few in number and unaccustomed to hard agricultural labor. Planters could, and did, pay the passage of Englishmen across the Atlantic in exchange for seven years of labor. But as soon as their commitments were fulfilled, the servants were lured to the frontier by the prospect of land.

In 1607 the colony's servants were indentured to the London Company. They received passage and sustenance while clearing and working the land for the company's profit. Once the servants had earned their freedom, the company allowed them to rent three acres of land in return

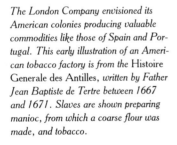

The London Company envisioned its American colonies producing valuable commodities like those of Spain and Portugal. This early illustration of an American tobacco factory is from the Histoire Generale des Antilles, *written by Father Jean Baptiste de Tertre between 1667 and 1671. Slaves are shown preparing manioc, from which a coarse flour was made, and tobacco.*

for a month's service every year and a donation of corn to the common store. In 1618 Sir Edwin Sandys, treasurer of the London Company, agreed to a superior inducement: an outright grant of 100 acres of uncleared land. To those who footed the bill for settlers to cross the Atlantic, he gave a 50-acre "head right" per immigrant. Seventeenth-century English reckoning associated land with wealth, and the offer enticed many to settle in Virginia.

The granting of head rights commenced a regular commerce in servants. Planters imported labor both to cultivate land and to acquire it. Traders sending ships to Virginia to pick up tobacco increased their profits by loading the bottoms with servants and selling them at the docks. Initially the London Company was discerning as to whom it admitted to the colony. But by 1621, as the need for labor grew, it became less discriminating. Overpopulated parishes in England happily sloughed off their charity cases, mostly young men over 15, for the cost of clothing and transportation to Virginia.

The Crown used the opportunity to dump convicts sentenced with the death penalty. These felons were not necessarily all thugs and murderers; some 300 crimes were punishable by death under British law at the time. One petitioner, for example, begged the authorities to release a certain John Throckmorton if she paid for his transport to Virginia. His crime: theft of a hat. Nonetheless, the colonials were none too happy about receiving criminals into their midst, and the practice of transporting felons to Virginia instead of to the gallows ended in 1642.

At times the commerce in servants degenerated into a sordid white slave trade. Perpetrators in seaport towns lured youngsters to their homes, altered the children's appearances, and sold them to sailors bound for Virginia. Even adults were shanghaied. In one such case, Robert Person, a Yorkshire drover visiting Smithfield, drank too much and was guided aboard a ship which, he was promised, would take him home. He awakened at sea. In another incident, Mary Cooper was told that she would

Tobacco even grew in the streets of Jamestown. From Heimann, Tobacco and Americans, McGraw-Hill Book Company, 1960

readily find work in Virginia which, she was assured, was a small town a few miles from the Thames. Another account tells of a guileless Elizabeth Smalridge accompanying a soldier on board and being sold into bondage on the spot.

Not all indentured servants were of humble origin. Many were like Adam Thoroughgood, who ignored his social connections in England and came to Virginia under indenture. Thoroughgood went on to acquire a great deal of

land in Princess Anne County and eventually rose to high office in the colony. Another indentured servant, Elias Nuthall, used part of his father's estate in England to buy his freedom.

Between 1634 and 1704, some 1,500 to 2,000 indentured servants arrived in Virginia annually. In 1671 Governor Sir William Berkeley reported that the roughly 6,000 servants in the colony accounted for about 13 percent of the population. Nearly all were male and worked as

Tobacco, an ideal crop for the young colony of Virginia, provided the economic base that was sorely needed there.

agricultural laborers; a few were apprentices learning marketable trades, and a handful were women who worked as domestics.

Indenture contracts, and later the law, provided servants some protection from abuse by their masters and guaranteed certain necessities. By custom, servants were allowed free time at night, part of Saturday, Sunday (the Sabbath), and all English holidays. Some beneficent planters allowed favored servants to grow their own

tobacco for sale. Often these servants invested profits in livestock or cash crops to build a base for their own farms when they received their freedom.

A standard contract provided that a servant be given a pair of shoes, three barrels of corn, and farming tools at the end of his indenture. Landowners often tailored the indenture contracts to suit their own needs and those of the servant. John Talbert's 1680 indenture, for instance, stipulated that his master teach him the shoemaking trade in exchange for an extra year's servitude. Other indentures forbade gambling, marriage, or fornication. As free persons, servants often became landowners themselves, sometimes hiring servants of their own. Many rose to prominence in colonial society. Seven of 44 burgesses in the 1629 General Assembly, for example, had been servants only a few years previously.

Freed indentured servants gave rise to a class of small landowners. By the time of Bacon's Rebellion in 1676, there were 4,000 farms. Unlike in England, land was not concentrated in the hands of a few earls and squires. The average land patent in Virginia was less than 500 acres; only a few estates were larger than 1,000 acres.

Planters acquired land in many ways. Governors were empowered to grant land to soldiers, colonial officials, and others for meritorious service. Sir Thomas Dale, for example, received lands worth 700 pounds sterling. The London Company also offered subpatents to private associations purchasing several shares. These associations transported families and servants to work as a unit to develop large tracts. Martin's Hundred and Smith's Hundred developed from the earliest-known subpatents.

In the seventeenth century the most common form of land grant was the "head right." Under this system, hundreds of landowners received grants for financing the transportation of settlers to the colonies or for completing their seven-year indentures. By 1619, records show, private planters had footed the bill for 660 of the 811 servants in the colony.

Governor Alexander Spotswood (1676-1740) established an inspection system in 1713 that standardized tobacco grades. From Cirker, Dictionary of American Portraits, Dover, *1967*

Anyone paying the cost of transporting emigrants—about six pounds sterling—was granted 50 acres of land per head. Some planters created enormous tracts of land this way: between 1618 and 1623 the London Company granted 44 patents to colonists who had brought over 100 persons or more.

Given the abundance of land, most free persons settled quickly on their own farms. By the end of the seventeenth century, the number of indentured servants was dwindling. Indentures expired continually and land speculators were opening up vast frontier tracts, offering immigrants an alternative to servitude. Yet plantation acreage was expanding, and the demand for labor was greater than ever.

Desperate for labor, planters turned to slavery. Black African slaves were cheap to maintain. They ate mush, vegetables, and maize bread and did not require as much clothing as English servants. They adapted well to Virginia's hot, humid summer climate. And most important, once slavery was established, planters did not have to recruit a whole new work force every seven years. For slaves, servitude usually lasted a lifetime.

Blacks were first introduced to Virginia in 1619 when a Dutch ship arrived with 20 Africans. The evidence suggests that they were treated as indentured servants. Of the 300 blacks in Virginia three decades later, many had completed their terms of indentured service and were free persons. One of the earliest, Anthony Johnson, settled on the Eastern Shore, owned his own land, and was among the colony's early slaveholders. It was not until 1662 that the General Assembly mandated that all non-Christian servants be held as slaves for life.

There were only 2,000 blacks in Virginia by 1671, about 5 percent of the population. But English and Dutch traders landed slaves on Virginia shores in increasing numbers. Obtaining slaves became easier, too, as Virginia developed trade with the West Indian sugar plantations. The sugar planters paid for food and stores with rum, molasses, and slaves. Through imports and natural increase, the slave population increased to 23,000 by 1715. Compared to the harsh conditions of the West Indian sugar plantations and the South Carolina rice fields, working conditions in Virginia were relatively benign. Virginia planters took the view that slaves were valuable property.

Slaves participated in every aspect of the growing agricultural economy: dairy farming and animal husbandry, as well as planting and harvesting every crop. While female slaves had few occupational options outside domestic or agricultural labor, planters employed many male slaves as craftsmen or artisans. Some became skilled in the production of metal and wooden tools.

Although slavery inhibited the social and economic mobility of blacks, it did not preclude it. Some blacks were freed after serving lengthy terms of indenture, others after their masters died. Like white servants, many were allowed to cultivate small tracts for food or for profit; some even purchased their own freedom from their masters. There is evidence that hundreds of free blacks—either freed slaves or their offspring—prospered as small farmers.

But the white majority was uncomfortable with the idea of free blacks. In the mid-seven-

Deep-water ships moored at a Virginia plantation landing take on a cargo of cured tobacco. From Heimann, Tobacco and Americans, *McGraw-Hill Book Company, 1960*

teenth century, the General Assembly passed a number of laws defining slave status along racial lines and restricting the legal rights of blacks and slaves. In 1640 slaves lost the right to bear arms. In 1662 mulatto children of slave women were declared to be slaves by birth, the same as children born to black slave families. A later law provided that the slaves of owners who died intestate would be resold by the county courts.

Even when laws existed to protect slaves, they were often ignored. If a slave died from a beating, the murderer usually went unpunished. Authorities tolerated the killing of fugitive slaves and condoned harsh corporal punishment for minor offenses. Hog stealers, for example, were whipped for the first offense. Recidivists had their ears nailed to a pillory, then had them cut

from their heads. Tagged as rebels, earless slaves commanded a lower price on the market.

Understandably, planters feared slave rebellions. To prevent insurrections they passed ever stricter laws. In 1680 the General Assembly strengthened its earlier law prohibiting slaves from bearing arms or assaulting their masters. Slaves were forbidden to leave their plantations without a written certificate of permission. The plantation economy that had blossomed under a slave system was now a captive of the class tensions it produced.

In 1673 young William Byrd married Mary Horsmanden, the daughter of a Cavalier officer who had fled to Virginia during the Puritan regime of Oliver Cromwell. Byrd had inherited a rich estate near the fall line of the

James, as well as a significant store of goods his uncle had used in trading with the Indians. In time Byrd would accumulate one of the greatest fortunes in colonial Virginia and establish a dynasty worthy of his native England. But he owed his success to more than a handsome inheritance and a well-chosen marriage.

Living on his plantation in the manner of an English lord, Byrd developed a trading network that extended from Virginia to London, Boston, the West Indies, and the Indian country of South Carolina. Byrd bought and sold tobacco, differing from his fellow planters only in the tremendous scale of his transactions. He imported slaves and indentured servants, and supplied his neighboring planters with many of the English goods they desired. From New England merchants he acquired earthenware and Madeira wine. From Barbados he imported rum, slaves, and molasses. In a letter to an agent in the Indies, for instance, he ordered 4,000 gallons of rum, 5,000 pounds of muscovado (unrefined sugar), 6,000 pounds of sugar, and 10 tons of molasses. Byrd also made his plantation a center for commerce with the Indians. His traders traveled hundreds of miles south to the land of the Cherokee and the Catawba. In exchange for cloth, kettles, hatchets, guns, ammunition and, of course, demon rum, they brought back furs, deerskins, rare herbs, and minerals.

Byrd was the quintessential eighteenth-century Virginia aristocrat. He made money from working the land in the manner of the old English aristocracy, yet he did not disdain commerce. Like Byrd, members of the emergent Virginia aristocracy were far more concerned with a man's worldly success and his accomplishments than with his genealogy.

Noble birth and inheritance certainly did not hurt a settler's efforts to enter the ranks of the colonial elite. But breeding was no guarantee and a humble origin no barrier. Many of Virginia's leading citizens had commenced their New World careers as indentured servants; oth-

Despite his social connections in England, Captain Adam Thoroughgood came to the New World under indenture. He acquired a good deal of land in Princess Anne County, Virginia, and rose to high office in the colony. His house, built as early as 1636, still stands in Virginia Beach and is maintained by the Adam Thoroughgood House Foundation. Courtesy, Valentine Museum

"Westover," in Charles City County, was built about 1730 by William Byrd II, planter, author, and colonial official. An example of Georgian architecture, the house remained in the Byrd family until 1814. Courtesy, Virginia Division of Tourism

The College of William and Mary, founded in 1693, is the second-oldest institution of higher education in the U.S. Courtesy, Virginia State Library

ers had been merchants in the Old World. Some merchant planters tapped their connections on both continents and set up stores on their plantations. These aristocratic retailers normally offered only necessities, but a few provided a variety of goods from cotton to calico, candlesticks to cowbells. One such merchant planter, Jonathan Newell, extended his trade over a four-county area as well as overseas.

Constant transatlantic travel was impractical in this era of sailing ships, so Virginia planters normally engaged English sales agents for their tobacco in London. Under this consignment system, planters relied on these agents to sell their produce for a profit and ship back clothing, foodstuffs, and other goods unavailable in Virginia. Although the system opened up trading opportunities abroad, it had its drawbacks. There was a 12- to 18-month lag time between a planter's purchase order and the delivery of goods. And the profitability of a planter's season was at the mercy of his agent's business acumen and personal taste in selecting trade goods to send back to Virginia.

Nontheless, by the beginning of the eighteenth century, the planter merchants straddled a vigorous, fast-growing society. In 1700 Virginia's population stood at 63,000. Although the number of inhabitants was no larger than that of a single large London parish, the colony spread over an area as vast as England. By midcentury, Virginia was home to nearly 250,000 people. Williamsburg, the capital since 1699, was a bustling town with a palace for the royal governor and one of the few colleges in the New World, William and Mary, named for King William III and Queen Mary.

By 1670, the Indians had ceased to be a threat, and planters no longer felt compelled to cluster together for self-defense. Free to settle anywhere, they spread out, each living upon a tract of land. Small farmers lived in isolation with a handful of servants or slaves. Although the wealthiest planters lived in baronial splendor, their resemblance to the lords of England was superficial at best. The old ties of feudal obligation and privilege had been replaced with a capitalist ethic. With the exception of slaves, who were treated as outright property, persons entered into free and voluntary agreements with one another.

Despite the multiplicity of laws, taxes, and tariffs designed to exploit the wealth of the colo-

nies for the benefit of the royal treasury and a few privileged English merchants, the Virginia planters enjoyed a rare prosperity. They lived in fine plantation houses filled with imported furniture and handsome prints. Silver, a symbol of wealth, was used liberally at social occasions. Orchards of apples, peaches, plums, pears, cherries, and figs surrounded the plantation houses; and many planters indulged in the aristocratic pursuit of gardening. The riverfront homes at Yorktown were so elegant that one British visitor compared them to those of London's exclusive St. James's district.

Left: Members of Virginia's planter class frequently assumed positions of responsibility in the government. This engraving of Patrick Henry by William S. Leney is based on the portrait of Henry by Thomas Sully. Henry served as governor of Virginia from July 6, 1776, to June 1, 1779. Courtesy, Valentine Museum

Below: "Tuckahoe," in Goochland County, was built about 1712 by Thomas Randolph, who had acquired the tract in 1710. It was the first plantation to be fully established above the falls. Courtesy, Valentine Museum

Above: "Berkeley," at Harrison's Landing on the James River, was built in 1726. It was the birthplace of Benjamin Harrison (1726-1791), a signer of the Declaration of Independence and governor of Virginia. His son, William Henry Harrison, was elected ninth president of the United States. Courtesy, Valentine Museum

The planter merchants adopted many mannerisms of the English ruling class. Often sending their children to England for schooling, the Virginia gentry placed great value on the Greek and Latin classics. They entertained one another with lavish parties, dinners, and dances. Horse races, usually informal affairs held on a cleared plantation field, offered another break from the routine of tobacco planting. Gambling was popular among the gentry, and Virginians were not picky about the sport: horse racing, cockfights, dicing, ninepins, cards. It was not unusual to bet tobacco by the ton. Those caught cheating were sentenced to time in the stocks.

Members of the Virginia gentry aspired to prominent office for reasons of prestige and self-aggrandizement. The colonists had been granted

considerable autonomy, and those with wealth routinely assumed positions of responsibility. The planter class dominated the government, holding seats in both the House of Burgesses and the Virginia Council, and the county courts. It was common for one individual to hold several positions. Richard Bland, for example, served on his county's court and in the House of Burgesses, and held the prestigious title of colonel in the militia.

Planters were only too happy to serve in administrative positions. The salaries provided a welcome source of income, and fringe benefits could be significant. As in Europe during this era, most people regarded appointment to government office as an opportunity for self-enrichment. For example, Alexander Spotswood, a royal governor admired for his efficient governance, did not hesitate to use the power of his office to pass legislation benefiting his interests in land speculation.

Yet these same Virginians exhibited far more concern for the common welfare than most ruling classes. Their attitudes toward individual rights and the need for countervailing powers in government set the tenor not only for Virginia, but also for an entire nation. It is incredible that an aristocracy so few in number could produce leaders and thinkers of the stature of George Washington, Thomas Jefferson, James Madison, Patrick Henry, and John Randolph. Built upon a traffic in " the filthy weed," eighteenth-century Virginia produced a golden age the likes of which has rarely graced the pages of history.

Left: The wheat harvest from "Berkeley" was shipped to Richmond, a booming industrial, commercial, and retail center early in the antebellum period. By the 1850s, Richmond had become the second largest flour producer in America. Courtesy, Valentine Museum

John Rolfe

The infant settlement of Jamestown had its share of bold, adventurous leaders. But John Rolfe more than anyone else deserves credit for saving the colony from an early demise. By marrying the daughter of an Indian chief, he ensured peace with the hostile natives. And by experimenting with tobacco, he discovered the commodity that would prove to be the colony's economic salvation.

The colony's first few years were precarious. The settlers had skirmished with the Indians, and war was an ever-present threat. Efforts to export silk, sassafras, glass beads, soap-ash, and pitch were miserable failures. Without a strong export commodity, Virginia seemed unable to generate any earnings for the London Company. Once the corporation ran out of cash and credit,

there would be an end to the ships replenishing the colony with provisions and eager new settlers.

The son of an old, wealthy English family, Rolfe had little experience in farming. He was, however, a heavy smoker, and he had an eye for opportunity. The colony's frequent warring with the tobacco-growing Indians disrupted what might have been a profitable

trade, so Rolfe decided to grow his own leaf. Indian-grown tobacco was strong and bitter—unpalatable to any English consumers but those transplanted to Virginia with no other source of smoke. The English preferred tobacco produced by the Spanish colonies in the Caribbean: the Orinoco, Trinidada, and Varinas varieties. Rolfe believed that it was possible to cultivate the same high quality, pleasant-tasting tobacco in Virginia and sell it for high profit in England.

Through trading, Rolfe collected enough of the popular Spanish seed by late 1611 to begin experimenting the following year. He first planted the Trinidada seed. From the clearing of the land to the curing of the leaf, he produced the first crop entirely through his own labor.

As the tobacco grew taller, Rolfe became enchanted by an Indian princess held captive by Governor Sir Thomas Dale. The daughter of the powerful chief Powhatan, she was named Matoaka. But the charming Indian princess is better known by the nickname given her by the settlers: Pocahontas, meaning "playful person." Rolfe met her in the presence of a chaperone, and she counseled him in the Indian method of tobacco cultivation.

In the spring of 1614 Rolfe drafted a letter to Dale requesting permission to marry Pocahontas. In the letter he wrote that his request had no foundation in "carnall affection," but rather in "the good of this plantation, for the honour of our countrie, for the glory of God, for my owne salvation, and for the converting [the heathen Pocahontas] to the true knowledge of God." Dale granted permission, and the couple was married. Their union began a period of uninterrupted peace with the Indians that lasted until the death of Powhatan in 1618.

Of Rolfe's first tobacco harvest, a small amount spoiled. Of the remainder, Rolfe gave some to friends for testing, smoked his share, and shipped four hogsheads to a London merchant to sell on the market. Rolfe and his compatriots found that the tobacco smoked well and that it had a strong, sweet aroma. Still, Rolfe thought he could improve it. Before word of its reception

in England had reached Virginia, he secured some Orinoco seeds from Caracas, Venezuela, which he crossbred with the Trinidada seeds for a second planting.

Meanwhile, Rolfe received the news that his first shipment had fetched from five to eight shillings per pound on the market. Although less than the high price of Spanish tobacco, this signaled that Rolfe's was a competitive product. Rolfe continued his experiments in hopes of producing a superior tobacco, "one that thriveth so well that no doubt but after a little more trial and expense in the curing thereof, it will compare with the best in the West Indies."

His second shipment was small: 2,500 pounds. But by the next year, Virginia tobacco had caught on in the English market. Rolfe and Pocahontas had been invited to London on royal tour in 1616. Pocahontas never returned; she died of influenza at the age of 22. Rolfe returned alone to Virginia, leaving their young son to be raised in England. He eventually remarried and died in the early 1620s.

Rolfe laid the groundwork for Virginia's progression from a floundering quasi-military outpost on the edge of the New World to a vigorous agricultural community. Tobacco became Virginia's leading industry, providing the impetus to clear the wilderness and generate the wealth that created the colony's planter aristocracy. Through John Rolfe's efforts, Virginia's first successful commerce was established.

Left: The marriage of John Rolfe and Pocahontas. Courtesy, Valentine Museum

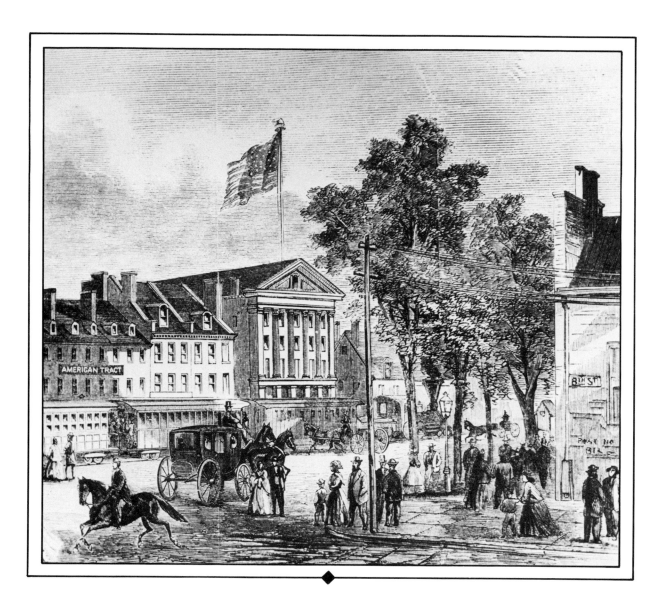

*Incorporated in 1834, the Richmond,
Fredericksburg, and Potomac Railroad
sent its first train north from Richmond on
February 13, 1836. The depot, shown
here as it appeared in 1865, was located
at Eighth and Broad streets. For many
years there was no central depot for all the
railroads converging on Richmond; passengers and freight had to be moved by
foot or by wagon from one rail line to
another many blocks away. From*
Harper's Weekly, *October 14, 1856*

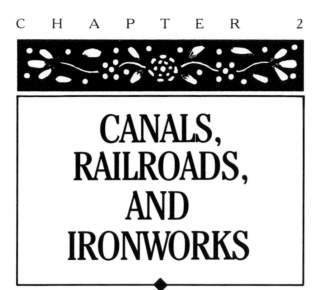

CANALS, RAILROADS, AND IRONWORKS

By 1700 Virginia had developed from a small military outpost into a vibrant provincial society. Representative governments in Williamsburg and the counties gave settlers a voice in their own destinies. The College of William and Mary instructed students in philosophy, mathematics, and Greek and Latin literatures. Even the arts had a place in the life-style of the aristocracy, which emulated the English ruling class in everything from fashions to sports. Indeed, the first play ever produced in the American colonies, *Ye Beare and Ye Cubb*, was enacted in Accomack County in 1665.

In the colony's first century, Virginians were reluctant to move beyond the lands of the Tidewater. Colonists were tied to the Chesapeake and its tributaries, which nourished an economy based on overseas trade. Having eliminated the threat of Indian attacks, they enjoyed a comfortable life-style within their own civilized boundaries. Settlement beyond the fall line, where Indians still roamed and where there were no expedient connections to the world marketplace, seemed a frightening prospect.

The first large-scale effort to settle west of the fall line inspired few to follow. About 1700, several hundred French Protestants seeking escape from Louis XIV's Catholic monarchy settled in Manakin, 20 miles above the falls of the James River. But the Huguenots were merchants and artisans, not farmers. They lacked the agricultural skills necessary to make their community self-sufficient. Many settlers moved to other communities where they could engage in the trades they knew.

But there were compelling economic and political reasons to expand to lands west of the fall line. Tobacco cultivation robbed the soil of nutrients necessary to yield a marketable product, forcing farmers to move on to fresh lands. As yields on the old lands declined, planters had no choice but to find virgin soil. Royal governors also were concerned about the intrusion by the French into the lands beyond the Allegheny Mountains—lands that the London Company charter of 1608 claimed for Virginia.

In 1671, as an expedition ordered by Governor Sir William Berkeley was preparing to explore the Great Lakes region in search of a passage to the Northwest, the French governor of Canada was making peace with the Indians near Lakes Superior and Huron in an effort to lay claim to their lands. Berkeley, like governors to come, believed that the British could win the

Concerned by the French settlement of lands beyond the Allegheny Mountains, Governor William Berkeley ordered an expedition to explore the Great Lakes region in search of a northwest passage. He encouraged Virginia colonists to move to the Piedmont, the valley and lands to the west of the Blue Ridge Mountains. Courtesy, Valentine Museum

tlements were not enough to guard against French interlopers.

With the double-barreled threat of French encroachment and agricultural disaster, Virginia's government liberalized the land grant system to stimulate westward expansion. In 1701 the General Assembly voted to disallow taxes on western lands to entice settlers to the new frontier. The next year the Virginia Council agreed to permit outright purchase of land at a price of five shillings per 50 acres.

Eastern farmers abandoned their homes in search of fresh, fertile soil, leaving the countryside dotted with rotting houses, weed-choked gardens, and fields overrun with wild growth. Anxious to beat the French to a stake of the western lands, Governor Alexander Spotswood persuaded the General Assembly to build a fort on the Meherrin, a branch of the Rapidan River. In 1714 he oversaw the settlement of a dozen German miners and their families there, and named the settlement Germanna in honor of the settlers' motherland and Queen Anne. It was the first major outpost in the Piedmont to thrive.

Two years later, Spotswood led a dozen men up the Rapidan from Germanna. In the course of their 400-mile expedition, the explorers discovered Swift Run Gap in the Blue Ridge, a byway through the mountains. When the group returned to Williamsburg, Spotswood launched a campaign to alert Virginians to the seductive lands of the west. With much fanfare he initiated the Order of the Golden Horseshoe, bestowing each of his fellow explorers with a gift of a small golden horseshoe embedded with precious stones.

Land speculation became a new avenue to wealth. Grasping the opportunity to claim as much property as possible, Spotswood acquired 3,000 acres around Germanna. Within a short time he owned so much land in the valley of the Rappahannock—25,000 acres—that he could not afford to pay the quitrents. At Spotswood's instigation the Assembly exempted western settlers from all taxes and asked the Crown to relieve landowners of all quitrents for ten years. When Brunswick and Spotsylvania counties

territorial struggle with the French if Virginia colonists moved to the Piedmont, the Valley, and the lands west of the mountains. It was the beginning of a bitter struggle that would culminate in the French and Indian War.

The only settlers in western Virginia were German and Scotch-Irish immigrants. Leaving Pennsylvania in search of religious freedom, they had trekked south, settling in the Shenandoah Valley. Among them were skilled tanners, potters, tinsmiths, and wagon makers. With their knowledge of agriculture—which included methods more advanced than those of the eastern planters, such as crop rotation, deep ploughing and use of fertilizer—they depended little on imported manufactured goods. But their small set-

were created out of these western lands in 1720, Spotswood had the boundaries drawn to include all the property on which he could not afford to pay quitrents. Confident that the King would indeed permit the exemption from quitrents, he quickly snapped up another 60,000 acres in the county named for him.

Land speculators made money by subdividing their properties and selling smaller tracts to settlers. In 1728 Governor Sir William Gooch appealed to the Board of Trade in England to grant large tracts to speculators who promised to settle western regions. Brunswick County, where few large grants had been made, was sparsely settled, he noted, while Spotsylvania with its expansive tracts was populous. Agreeing, the board relaxed the stipulations attached to land patents. Under the new system, landowners had only to settle one family per 1,000 acres over a period of years.

The liberalized system of grants and a peace treaty with the Iroquois in 1722 combined to spur western settlement. Speculators such as William Byrd II and Robert "King" Carter made tremendous profits by selling off tracts to eager farmers at reasonable prices. Settlers

Left: Governor Robert Dinwiddie (1693-1770) was active in the cause of westward expansion. From Cirker, Dictionary of American Portraits, *Dover, 1967*

snatched up land so quickly that the government permitted owners or their agents to transfer land titles on the spot, relieving purchasers of the need to travel to Williamsburg to handle the paper transactions.

In 1730 Carter obtained grants for approximately 63,000 acres in the Shenandoah Valley. In 1736 William Beverley was granted 118,491 acres near Staunton, which he called Beverley Manor. In dire need of money, Beverley hired Captain James Patton as his agent to attract buyers. Remembered as "the foremost man of the western section of the colony," Patton built his reputation on his involvement in the settling of that region.

Carter and Beverley also opened up to settlement land in the Northern Neck, a vast acreage stretching to the mountains, which became known as the Fairfax Proprietary. Acting as official agent for the sixth Lord Fairfax, Carter claimed certain lands in the northern Shenandoah Valley where settlers were beginning to stake out farms, arguing that the region was part of the Fairfax Proprietary, the boundaries of which had never been fixed.

A lordly brouhaha ensued. Lord Fairfax came to Virginia to claim his land, and the Brit-

Below left: Robert "King" Carter was an early land speculator in Virginia who made tremendous profits during the rush to settle the colony. From Cirker, Dictionary of American Portraits, *Dover, 1967*

ish Board of Trade appointed commissioners to survey it. Meanwhile, Pennsylvania settlers steered clear of the disputed zone, fearing that later adjudication would allow Fairfax to reclaim it. It took more than a decade and a half for the commissioners to reach a decision. In 1745 they confirmed that the contested land belonged to Fairfax, entitling him to collect quitrents on six million acres covering the entire Northern Neck and a swath of land stretching across the mountains into present-day West Virginia. Exempted from the Fairfax Proprietary were those lands granted to settlers by the government prior to the dispute.

While legal quarrels discouraged settlement of the Northern Neck, most of the Piedmont and the Valley was rapidly being populated. By 1749, settlers had pushed into what is now the Roanoke Valley and as far into Southwest Virginia as present-day Bristol. Adopting Spotswood's strategy, Governor Gooch encouraged Pennsylvania settlers to populate the Virginia frontier as a way to strengthen the buffer against the French in the Ohio Valley. Jacob Stover was notable among these settlers. A Swiss from Pennsylvania, Stover applied for a grant of 10,000 acres in the central Shenandoah Valley. Governor Gooch denied his request on the grounds that Stover offered no tangible assurance that he would be able to settle the land with the required number of families. Dissatisfied, Stover appealed directly to King George II, presenting a long list of names, all of whom he was sure he could settle on the land. King George approved Stover's land request, none the wiser that the list was composed of dogs, horses, livestock, and any breathing mammal to which Stover could ascribe a human name.

Two Pennsylvania Quakers, Alexander Ross and Morgan Bryan, acquired grants totaling 100,000 acres just north of Winchester. Under their auspices enough of their coreligionists settled in the northern Valley that, by 1738, Quaker meetings were a well-established feature of the area. Benjamin Borden, a New Jersey promoter, brought in more than 100 families in 1737, extending his title to a half-million acres

near Lexington. With the help of these Northern emigrants and others like them, Winchester was settled in 1730; Staunton in 1748; and Draper's Meadow (now Blacksburg) in 1750.

As Pennsylvania settlers moved south, prominent Virginians formed syndicates to acquire extensive tracts beyond the Blue Ridge and even the Alleghenies. As the frontier pushed west, they reasoned, they could sell their lands for significant profits. James Patton, John Buchanan, and John Preston formed the Woods River Company in 1745 and received a 100,000-acre grant near the New River, a tributary of the Ohio. Patton received a personal grant of 125,000 acres. By the end of the year, the area around present-day Blacksburg and Radford was filling with pioneers. The next year the Pulaski area had been surveyed and divided into tracts.

In 1749 a group of Northern Neck speculators, including Thomas Lee who had served as an agent for Lord Fairfax, formed the Ohio Company. In return for a 200,000-acre grant stretching across the Alleghenies, the company pledged to build a fort in the Ohio Valley to protect settlers from the French and Indians. The company further promised to win the Indians as allies by underselling competitive French fur traders.

On the very same day the Ohio Company received its grant, the Loyal Company, consisting of Albemarle County landowners including botanist and physician Thomas Walker, was granted 800,000 acres in Southwest Virginia on the condition that the company survey and settle it within four years. But the plans of both the Ohio Company and the Loyal Company would be thwarted by the outbreak of the French and Indian War.

When Governor Robert Dinwiddie arrived in 1751, he immediately became active in the cause of westward expansion. By the next year he had convinced the Ohio Indians to permit Virginians to build forts on the Ohio River. Dinwiddie then commenced to grant lands to settlers who promised to protect Virginia's ever-advancing frontier.

The French, too, were pushing into the Ohio Valley, first erecting a fort on the south side of Lake Erie, then marching overland to French Creek, a tributary of the Allegheny River, where they constructed Fort LeBoeuf. As the settlements of French and Virginians moved headlong towards one another, conflict was inevitable. Virginia, with some help from England and little from its sister colonies, undertook a war to force the French out of the Ohio Valley. After several less-than-glorious campaigns, the English captured the French stronghold at Fort Duquesne four years later.

After the last cinders of war had died, however, the treaty drove a wedge of resentment between Virginians and the mother country. When England wanted to keep the western lands from the French, she encouraged Virginia colonists to risk their money and their lives to settle there; once the French had been driven out, Virginia's interests were sublimated. Against Virginians' strong protests the Crown sealed a pact with France's former Indian allies—whose last-minute change of sides had made it possible to take Fort Duquesne. The Proclamation of 1763 officially prohibited Virginians from staking claim to land beyond the Alleghenies that they had fought to keep for the British.

In practice the proclamation had little binding force. Virginians who had settled the land more than a decade before were ordered to abandon their homes, but many stayed. Unable to obtain clear titles to the land west of the mountains, many new settlers ignored the paperwork and became squatters, moving across the mountains in violation of the act. Meanwhile, in order to protect their investments, land company speculators pressured government officials to extend the boundaries set by the 1763 agreement. With the Treaty of Fort Stanwix in 1768 and the Treaty of Lochaber two years later, lands were opened as far west as the Kentucky River and as far south as modern Bristol.

The compromises which overrode the Proclamation of 1763 were a short-acting balm. Having incurred an unprecedented public debt by the end of the "Great War for the Empire,"

On June 7, 1776, Virginian Richard Henry Lee declared to the Continental Congress that the colonies should be "free, independent states." From Cirker, Dictionary of American Portraits, Dover, 1967

England imposed a Stamp Tax on its colonies in 1765. The act aggravated a tension that had existed between the colonists and the mother country since the previous century, when Governor Berkeley's refusal to allow elections for a new House of Burgesses between 1660 and 1673 had inspired Bacon's Rebellion. The oppressive Navigation Acts were still in force, and Virginians had good cause to feel they had been shabbily treated after the French and Indian War. The colonists were tired of having their interests subordinated to the government in London.

A third Virginia Convention, held in Richmond from July 17 to August 26, 1775, committed the colony to war. In December 1775 Governor Lord Dunmore's forces were defeated at the Battle of the Great Bridge near Norfolk, and Dunmore fled to his ships. Although Dunmore would sail for England the following year, the British were to return to Hampton Roads several times before their final evacuation of Portsmouth in August 1781. Meanwhile, the burning of Norfolk in early January 1776 led to increased trade at Richmond and other river ports.

On June 7, 1776, Virginian Richard Henry Lee declared to the Continental Congress

Virginia statesman Thomas Jefferson was governor when Benedict Arnold's British contingent marched on Richmond late in the war. Jefferson and other officials barely escaped the city, which was set on fire. From Cirker, Dictionary of American Portraits, *Dover, 1967*

bacco. Governor Thomas Jefferson and other officials barely escaped, and many state and county records were lost.

By May, Britain's General Lord Charles Cornwallis had reached Virginia from the Carolinas. He was unable, however, to defeat the American army in Virginia under Major General Marquis de Lafayette. On October 19, 1781, the British surrendered at Yorktown.

All elements of Virginia's population were affected by the war. Two blacks from Henrico County, Adam Armstrong and Humphrey Blaine, fought in the Continental army. James Armistead Lafayette, a slave from New Kent County, served as a spy; a forager for the British army, he frequented Cornwallis' headquarters. James Armistead Lafayette gained his freedom by legislative enactment in January 1787 and eventually was rewarded a small pension for his patriotic service.

Women also greatly aided the war effort. Besides making the soldiers' uniforms, some were employed at the Westham foundry, eight miles from Richmond. Anna Marie Lane of Richmond, who "in the garb and with courage of a soldier performed extraordinary military services and received a severe wound at the Battle of Bermantown," was granted a military pension after Yorktown.

Independence had its price. Although Virginia won freedom from Parliament's odious taxes and trade restrictions, the colony's economy was still bound closely to England. English mercantile firms were not about to forget the old debts that Virginia planters and merchants had accrued before the war. And Virginia's methods of combating postwar inflation proved troublesome. When the new Commonwealth called in paper money for exchange at one-thousandth of its face value, debtors were hard put to pay up. In some cases taxes had to be suspended; no one had the money to buy auctioned lands of delinquent taxpayers.

Agriculture, too, suffered after the war. Occupying troops had bought great quantities of wheat and bacon; when the soldiers left, the demand for these products plunged.

that the colonies should be "free, independent states." Congress deliberated less than a month before passing Lee's motion on July 2. Two days later Thomas Jefferson's Declaration of Independence proclaimed the colonies' intentions to the world.

Until 1780, Virginia's direct contact with the war was largely through the troops she supplied for the Continental army. Suddenly, then, the war turned toward Richmond as the British sought to disrupt the tobacco trade and supply munitions depots. Marching from Westover, a British contingent led by Benedict Arnold set fire to the town's industry and confiscated its to-

The former colonists also discovered the disadvantages of departing from the English mercantile system. They lost their privileged status as sole suppliers of tobacco to England and of flour and meat to the English colonies of the West Indies.

Invading troops had destroyed vast acreages of crops. Slaves had deserted their masters and joined the British, leaving plantations insufficiently staffed. Many planters were forced to turn to wheat. Tobacco was still a viable commodity, but it would never again be King Tobacco.

Meanwhile, other changes confronted the Commonwealth. Virginia was dividing into two cultures, two ways of life.

In the 1750s eastern Virginians had enjoyed the blessings of civilization. The women followed London fashions: swishing hoop skirts,

hair piled high, and ornaments of feather and ribbon. Gentlemen replaced their wigs with powdered hair tied in braided pigtails. Knee breeches were still the style, and cocked hats had become quite the fancy.

In contrast, the wear of the west was that of the pioneer. Women's frocks were of the plainest homespun, woven from flax, wool, wild nettles, and buffalo hair, supplemented by the occasional materials hauled overland at great expense. Fashionable accoutrements were expensive, unnecessary, and even a hindrance to the hardy workday life on the frontier.

There was no plantation economy west of the mountains. Working small tracts of land, settlers raised their own wheat, vegetables, and livestock. Wildlife was both manna and menace: elk and bears provided food and clothing; but wolves threatened the livestock that provided the

The colonies won their independence when the British surrendered at Yorktown in 1781. Shown here is Yorktown's celebration of its centennial in 1881. Courtesy, Virginia State Library

hides, milk, meat, and wool needed to survive. Trade with eastern communities was nearly impossible. The mountains created a natural barrier, and there was no money. Early settlers relied on a barter system, trading furs and skins for necessities brought in on horseback from the Tidewater. In the frontier society, settlers crafted what they needed for themselves, importing only a few necessities from the east, or went without.

As the eighteenth century progressed, towns arose around courthouses and trade centers. Acting as magnets for artisans, merchants, and businessmen, these towns became the seedbeds of new enterprises. Abundant salt, iron ore, coal, and timber supported several burgeoning industries. Farmers found new markets for their wool and wheat. In time the west lost its rough frontier edge and developed its own vibrant, self-sufficient economy—one that would find a firm foothold in the world marketplace once canals and railroads connected it to the eastern ports.

The western lands (including those now part of West Virginia) were rich in natural resources. Silica and clay supplies around Morgantown, Wheeling, and Wellsburg enabled local artisans and merchants to make a living in glassware and pottery.

Working small tracts of land, western settlers raised their own wheat, vegetables, and livestock for home consumption and nearby markets. This farmhouse in Goshen Pass, shown in 1922, is in sharp contrast with the plantation homes of eastern Virginia. Courtesy, Valentine Museum

Salt-making operations had begun in 1797 when Elisha Brooks erected a salt furnace at Malden on the Kanawha River. Salt, used both as a flavoring and a meat preservative, was a vital element of the local economy. The first facilities were crude contraptions that pumped brine from the earth through large hollow logs. Using this primitive method, Brooks produced about 150 bushels daily, which he sold for 8 to 10 cents per pound.

In the early 1800s David and Joseph Ruffner introduced iron drill bits and tubes of twine-wrapped wood strips to drive through rock. They extracted enough brine to produce 25 bushels—more than 1,200 pounds—of salt in a day. Adding the horse-powered mill, the brothers increased production even more.

Landowners up and down the Kanawha sank wells and built furnaces. By 1815 there were so many furnaces in the area—52—that it became known as the Kanawha Salines, churning out 2,300 to 3,000 bushels of salt a day. With other improvements, like steam power, the production of Kanawha Valley salt makers reached 3,200,000 bushels in 1846.

As well as providing a major source of employment, salt making sparked a demand for coal when salt makers began substituting it for

Isolated from the eastern regions of the Old Dominion, the settlers in the western and central Piedmont regions developed new markets for their produce. Western towns arose near courthouses and trade centers. Here farmers are shown bringing their tobacco crops to market at Drake's Branch in Charlotte County about 1890. Courtesy, Valentine Museum

By the early 1800s western settlers had shown they were self-sufficient. However, they had to reach larger markets if their enterprises were to prosper. Because the General Assembly did not support improvements to roads or river ports, and because the links between the James and the Kanawha and the Potomac and the Ohio seemed to take forever, a schism grew between the east and west. These buggies crossed the Jackson River on their way to Clifton Forge in western Virginia, circa 1880. Courtesy, Valentine Museum

wood. The Germans had been mining coal in western Virginia since Spotswood's settlement at Germanna, living off the demand of local markets. Drawing on the vast supply of iron ore, a multitude of ironworks sprang up in the Monongehela Valley around the turn of the century. Wheeling Iron Works would become an industry leader by 1835, producing 1,000 tons a year in bar, sheet, hoop, and boiler iron. These activities gave rise to other industries, which turned the iron into stoves, grates, nails, and other products.

By the early 1800s, settlers no longer had to create their own fabrics; they could buy them from local manufacturers. Farmers took wool to mills and had it processed; fulling and carding mills broke, carded, and wound wool into rolls.

One of the first factory owners, Robert Marshall, charged 10 cents a pound to process plain wools, 12 cents a pound for processing and dyeing. For every eight pounds he demanded a surcharge in butter or clean hog's fat.

As settlers built homes, the forests of the Alleghenies provided the timber. Wood fueled the iron furnaces, and when the byways to the east were opened, lumber became a major export. And as they raised crops, western farmers discovered the advantages of distilling spirits. Resourceful farmers used surplus corn and rye to make whiskey, their apples and peaches to make brandy.

Western settlers had proven that they could live independently of the east. But if their enterprises were to prosper, they had to reach larger markets. That meant they had to reduce the cost of overland transportation, which doubled the cost of imported goods and made the export of basic products almost prohibitive.

In the east, improved roads, bridges, and ferries made it relatively easy to transport produce to the James and other rivers. In the west, the river ports were distant, serviceable only by poor roads that were impassable in bad weather, dusty and bumpy in good weather. In essence, the government had supported the settlers in their move west, then left them stranded and isolated. In time this was one of the issues that would polarize the eastern and western counties of Virginia and inspire the western portion of the state to break away in 1863.

The schism between east and west first became evident in the war debt issue at the 1784 session of the General Assembly. Prior to the Revolution, Virginia planters had piled up debts totaling 2,300,000 pounds sterling by importing manufactured goods worth more than the tobacco they exported. Thomas Jefferson, for example, owed firms in Glasgow and London 10,000 pounds sterling. In the Treaty of Paris of 1783, negotiators for the American colonies accepted the responsibility of repaying these debts. But Virginians refused to cooperate.

Representing western Virginia, James Madison declared that Virginians should feel honor bound to repay the debts. Eastern representatives to the legislature, led by Patrick Henry, felt that repayment of the debt would be ruinous to Virginia's economy. Supporting Henry, a majority of legislators defeated Madison's resolution. The issue remained unsettled until the 1790s, when the United States assumed responsibility for the colonies' debts under the Jay Treaty. Virginians' debts accounted for almost half the total.

It was not the only time Madison and Henry would square off. Madison's faction objected to taxes which had to be paid in tobacco or in hard money. Western Virginians produced little tobacco, and they had little money. Valley delegates also opposed Henry's proposal to issue more paper currency on the grounds that it would

Virginian James Madison, who served in the state legislature between 1784 and 1786, led the faction that believed Virginia should repay England for debts accumulated before the war. Madison was later elected the fourth president of the United States. From Cirker, Dictionary of American Portraits, *Dover, 1967*

reduce their buying power in Maryland and Pennsylvania where many Valley Virginians traded. On this count, the westerners won.

But discontent continued to mount. In 1816 the western counties called for a convention in Staunton to discuss a lengthy list of grievances, some political, some economic. Although the white population west of the Blue Ridge exceeded that of the east, westerners formed a minority in the General Assembly. And although the General Assembly had created a separate fund for internal improvements and created a board of public works to assign money to worthy projects, trans-Allegheny Virginians claimed that the monies were not sufficient.

These issues were finally addressed in the Constitutional Convention of 1829-1830 held in the capitol in Richmond. The western Piedmont and the Shenandoah Valley were granted more seats in the legislature, although the trans-Allegheny region came away with less. Suffrage was extended to leaseholders and householders as well as landowners, and the eastern-dominated Privy Council was reduced in size, though it retained the right to appoint county sheriffs and justices of the peace. The General Assembly also held firm in its right to elect the governor rather than submitting the question to popular vote. Delegates representing the counties of modern-day Virginia voted to ratify the constitution; delegates from west of the Alleghenies voted solidly against it. The debate between east and west was far from over.

Efforts in the 1830s and 1840s to improve east-west transportation failed to meet the westerners' expectations. Improvements on the James and Potomac rivers moved goods cheaply downstream to market. But the promised links between the Potomac and the Ohio and between the James and the Kanawha seemed to take forever.

The census of 1840 incited westerners further by revealing that the white population of the trans-Allegheny region was 271,000—about 2,000 greater than the combined white populations of the Valley, the Piedmont, and the Tidewater. Yet the western counties had only 10 of the 29 members of the state senate and 56 of the 134 delegates. When the legislature of 1844-1845 refused to permit the Baltimore & Ohio Railroad to extend its line up the valley along the Kanawha—a measure that would have opened western Virginia to the port of Baltimore—angry representatives from 13 western counties coalesced to block any and all appropriations for transportation improvements in any other parts of the state.

Virginians called another Constitutional Convention in 1850 to address western grievances once more. The Constitution of 1851 granted suffrage to all whites and allowed the governor, judges, and county officers to be elected by popular vote. It abolished the Governor's Council, allocated money to establish a school system, and awarded seats in the House of Delegates on the basis of population. Regional tensions lingered, but the new constitution did buy 10 years of relative peace.

Realizing that a vigorous commerce benefited everyone, easterners were more willing to concede on issues of transportation. Without convenient access to Virginia's eastern ports, the trade in western wheat, iron, and salt might be diverted to New Orleans via the Mississippi. The advantages of transportation improvements were evident as early as 1784, when George Washington wrote to Governor Benjamin Harrison after a visit to the tramontane region. Virginia, he advised, should bring the rich region between the Great Lakes and the Ohio River into its economic sphere by taking immediate action "to preclude western inhabitants from being seduced into trade" with other regions. A growing commerce would compensate the Commonwealth "for any trouble and expense we may encounter to effect it."

Early the next year the General Assembly chartered the Potomac Company and the James River Company; George Washington was made president of both. The Potomac Company assumed the task of improving navigation on the Potomac and connecting it, by waterway, to the Ohio River. The James River Company was to build a canal from Richmond along the banks of the James to the river's headwaters to the west.

Two years later the General Assembly approved the creation of the Dismal Swamp Canal in conjunction with a similar act passed by North Carolina. The canal would enable North Carolina farmers to ship lumber and agricultural products from the Elizabeth River through Albemarle Sound to Hampton Roads 50 miles away. Tied in with improvements to the Roanoke River in 1826, the project made it possible for Southside farmers to send tobacco and grain from the Roanoke River area to Norfolk.

By 1795 the first leg of the James River Canal was complete. Improvements on the main bed of the James enabled farmers as far west as Lynchburg to float their products downriver to Richmond. Disappointed with the James River Company's slow westward progress, however, the state took it over in 1820, ultimately extending the canal to Buchanan at the foot of the Alleghenies, 196 miles from Richmond. Here construction was abandoned; funds, supplied by the state and the cities of Lynchburg and Richmond, had petered out. Nevertheless, the canal was an immense success. Freight barges carried coal, lime, iron, and grain downriver to Richmond.

On the journey back west they took flour, tobacco products, and manufactured goods. By 1841, 110,000 tons of freight moved along the James River Canal.

The Potomac Company had a slower start, completing its first canal around the Great Falls of the Potomac in 1802. By 1808 the canal had opened up markets as far inland as Port Republic in Rockingham County. The company eventually relinquished its charter to the Chesapeake and Ohio Company—a joint project of the U.S., Maryland and Virginia governments—to qualify for an injection of federal funds. But the project failed to benefit producers in the tramontane region, and Virginians lost interest as construction began inching towards Cumberland, Maryland.

Fifty-foot-long canal boats, pulled by horses or mules trudging along a parallel towpath, plied both the James and the Potomac rivers. While stagecoach lines offered transport between Alexandria, Richmond, and Petersburg, and well-kept turnpikes connected various parts of the state, many travelers in the 1840s preferred the smooth, leisurely ride of the packet boat. On the 36-hour trip from Richmond to Lynchburg, passengers could dine and sleep on board. After dinner, men clustered on deck to enjoy smoking, conversation, and spitting into the river without having to aim for a spittoon. Ladies read, played backgammon, or chatted before retiring to sleeping compartments separate from the men's. The 1845 fare: $5.27.

Before Virginia's canal system was complete, railroad fever swept the state. The Commonwealth issued some $37 million worth of bonds for internal improvements during the pre-Civil War era; more than $18 million was invested in railroad stock, half of that in the single decade of the 1850s.

This woodcut from an Anderson and Company photograph shows a canal boat being pulled by mules along the parallel towpath. The James River and Kanawha Canal system successfully opened transportation westward from Richmond to Buchanan in the Allegheny Mountains. Richmond in 1870, with its many churches, mills, and factories, is in the background. Courtesy, Valentine Museum

Left: In 1787 Virginia's General Assembly, in conjunction with North Carolina, approved the construction of the Dismal Swamp Canal. Courtesy, Valentine Museum

Below left: North Carolina and Virginia farmers used the Dismal Swamp Canal to transport their lumber and agricultural products along the Elizabeth River through the Albemarle Sound to Hampton Roads. Courtesy, Valentine Museum

Facing page: The Great Dismal Swamp is neither a swamp nor dismal; it is actually a 102,000-acre peat bog located in the Tidewater region of Virginia and North Carolina. Discovered in 1650 by William Drummond, the Dismal Swamp supports a wide variety of unique plant and animal life. A large part of the refuge was owned by George Washington, Patrick Henry, and other prominent Virginians. Courtesy, Virginia Division of Tourism

For all the millions it spent, Virginia failed to construct a unified rail system. New York, Pennsylvania, and Maryland developed long railroads linking eastern metropolises with emerging commercial centers in the west. In Virginia a rail system connecting Hampton Roads with major inland cities might have made Norfolk the greatest seaport on the Atlantic seaboard. But the fall-line cities—Richmond, Alexandria, Petersburg—stood in the way of a comprehensive system. As each city strove to carve out inland markets, the state ended up with a profusion of short railroads.

The Richmond, Fredericksburg & Potomac Railroad—still in operation and the only U.S. railroad to operate more than a century under its own name—was chartered to build a rail line between Richmond and Washington. Construction was plodding. The line reached Fredericksburg in 1837. Interrupted by war, the line did not reach Washington until 35 years later.

Construction proceeded at a much more heated pace to the southeast. To siphon off some of the traffic developed by the Dismal Swamp Canal, the Petersburg Railroad Company built a rail link to Weldon, North Carolina, in the 1830s. Concerned by this peril to their port, Norfolk merchants put their money behind the Portsmouth & Roanoke Railroad Company, also bound for a Weldon terminus. With a significant head start, the Petersburg Railroad Company developed the market first; revenues in 1839 amounted to $131,000. A perennial laggard, the Norfolk company logged only $73,000 the same year. Plagued by poor construction and high maintenance costs, the Portsmouth & Roanoke eventually folded.

In the 1840s some Norfolk investors applied for a charter to build a rail line from Norfolk to Petersburg. Fearing the loss of waterborne commerce, the river port staved off approval, but the legislature approved the charter the next year. Under the leadership of young William Mahone, the Norfolk & Petersburg line was completed in 1858. Mahone pushed Norfolk ahead in the fight for port trade by coordinating rail schedules with steamship lines running from Norfolk to Baltimore, Philadelphia, and New York. He ensured west-east freight traffic by coordinating his railway's schedule with those of the Southside Railroad and the Virginia & Tennessee lines.

Similarly, rivalries between cities slowed the development of the Richmond & Danville Railroad. Chartered in 1838, the company took almost 10 years to raise the necessary capital. Promoters tried to stimulate interest in Richmond, but merchants were afraid that the railroad company might select a different eastern terminus or that a railroad might harm the James River Canal trade. Overriding the objections, the Richmond City Council bought 2,000 shares. Two months later the state government purchased 1,800 shares.

The city of Petersburg tried to derail the project by refusing to allow the Richmond & Danville to lay tracks beneath one of the Petersburg line bridges. Forced to tunnel under the bridge, the company encountered additional expense and delay. Construction was not quite complete by the Civil War. Even so, the Richmond & Danville would serve as one of three lifelines to the capital of the Confederacy, carrying troops, food, and supplies.

While hindering everyone else's railroads, Petersburg had developed three of its own by the 1850s and was working on a fourth. For years, however, the city refused to allow the railroads to connect. Instead, each railroad maintained separate stations. To switch lines, freight had to be unloaded and carted across town to a different station. The crosstown traffic generated a lot of business for Petersburg merchants.

Rivalry with Baltimore spurred Alexandria to join the railroad competition. Reaching inland with the Baltimore & Ohio Railroad, the much larger Maryland city threatened to infringe upon Alexandria's traditional markets. Scraping up capital, Alexandria merchants chartered the Alexandria & Harper's Ferry Railroad in 1847. The plan was to open much of western Virginia by linking up with the independent Winchester and Potomac at Harper's Ferry.

But after 20 years of petitioning the General Assembly, the Baltimore & Ohio received permission to extend its tracks across Virginia territory. Not only did the railroad siphon off the western trade that Alexandria had hoped to tap, it also snatched up the Winchester & Potomac in 1848. The Alexandria to Harper's Ferry project collapsed without the first shovel ever being put to the earth. But other projects—the Southside Railroad, and the Virginia & Tennessee—succeeded. By the time of the Civil War, Virginia could boast 1,800 miles of track.

Blessed by river transportation and abundant natural resources, Virginia entered the industrial era as early as the 1790s. The west parlayed salt, iron ore, and coal into lucrative industries; the east did the same with tobacco, iron, and its own coal. Norfolk shipbuilders used Allegheny timber to craft tall masts for sailing ships. Richmond processed wheat and tobacco

from the Piedmont and points west, creating valuable export products. The union of east-west commerce proved profitable to the entire state.

Although tobacco no longer ruled the agricultural economy, it provided a cornerstone for the state's industrial development. By the 1820s, Virginia factories were processing one-third of all U.S.-grown tobacco, exporting leaf products to Europe as well as to Northern states. By 1860, Virginia was the country's number one tobacco manufacturer, with 252 tobacco factories centered mostly in Richmond, Petersburg, and Lynchburg.

Flour, with its higher value, surpassed tobacco as the state's leading product. By 1861, 1,383 Virginia mills, representing a capital investment of around $6 million, ground grain from several states. Richmond was the largest producer, but Petersburg and Alexandria had significant industries as well. Before the war

Iron manufacturing, begun in 1622, grew in response to the need for large and small machinery. Iron works such as Tredegar, established by Joseph Reid Anderson, made Richmond the South's only important antebellum manufacturing center. Courtesy, Library of Congress

Mills such as the Rexrode Grist Mill near Blue Grass, Virginia, were built along major waterways. Located on the south branch of the Potomac River's south fork, the mill, owned by Ray Rexrode, is 100 years old. By the 1860s, flour surpassed tobacco as the state's leading export. In 1861, 1,383 Virginia mills were grinding the grain. Courtesy, Virginia Division of Tourism

Jewish immigrants, fleeing the German Revolution of 1848, rose to prominence in Richmond as retailers and merchants. They built a synagogue on Eleventh Street near Marshall Street in 1848; Beth Ahaba, pictured here, was built on the same site in 1880. Courtesy, Valentine Museum

Virginians exported flour as far away as South America.

Settlers had found numerous iron deposits in the state. By 1856, Virginia had 88 charcoal furnaces for smelting iron and 60 forges for molding it into nails, tools, and other utensils. Virginia led the Southern states in iron manufacture. Iron working created a demand for the coal mined at the Chesterfield pits south of the James River. By 1860, Virginia also was one of the South's leading coal-mining states, producing the fuel for the local iron industry and for gas manufacture throughout the Atlantic seaboard.

Cessation of trade with England during the War of 1812 encouraged domestic manufacturers

to replace imported goods. Twenty-two cotton mills arose around Petersburg, Richmond, Wheeling, and Lynchburg. Eighteen textile factories—many in western Virginia where merino sheep were raised—produced carpets and other woolen textiles. Smaller industries included paper mills, potteries, and furniture plants which made use of the state's great abundance of pine, oak, walnut, and maple trees.

Petersburg and Alexandria were prosperous cities by any standard, but nothing could compare to Richmond, one of the most affluent cities in the nation. It led the state in flour milling and tobacco manufacture. Its iron foundries ranked among the greatest in the country, and coal mining in its outlying districts made Virginia a leader in coal production.

Richmond stood at the economic center of the state, the beneficiary of superb transportation facilities, cheap waterpower, and accessible natural resources. At the fall line of the James, Richmond was an oceangoing port; at the terminus of the James River Canal, its commerce reached deep into the interior. By the mid-nineteenth century, the city was a major railroad center as well. Tapping the waterpower of the James, Richmond was a natural location for textile and flour mills. With coal mined in its suburbs and iron in its hinterlands, the city possessed the resources to support a vigorous iron industry. Few communities could boast of such a propitious combination of geography and natural resources.

Entrepreneurial talent migrated to Richmond, a city of opportunity. Among the developers of Richmond's flour mills were industrialists from Spain and Scotland. An influx of Northern capitalists joined the foreigners, adding to the reservoir of business talent. Newspapers heralded the arrival of several transplanted Northern businesses, such as a "looking glass manufactory" from New York and a hat manufacturer from Baltimore. The city also attracted a number of Jewish immigrants, who rose to prominence as local retailers and merchants.

Richmond expanded rapidly along the riverfront as droves of people arrived in packet boats, stagecoaches, and private carriages. Taverns with names like Hogg's, The Swan, and The Bird in Hand served politicians, doctors, clerks, and the ever-present tradesmen. Developers paved streets and laid sidewalks. Merchants erected stores and warehouses. Pioneer industrialists and their families built great brick mansions and fine churches.

The municipal authorities were hard pressed to keep up. One out-of-state visitor wrote that Richmond was dirty and that its streets were "narrow as well as crooked . . . full of hogs and mud." But to Richmonders enthralled by the prospect of imminent wealth and success, the conditions were like the emperor's new clothes: no one seemed to notice. A half-dozen years after assuming the distinction of state capital, Richmond sprawled across an area of two square miles. Eighteen hundred people, half of them slaves, inhabited 280 houses. Within four years the population doubled.

As houses and factories sprang up, real estate values climbed daily; by some accounts, prices matched those of New York. Land-hungry speculators swept through the town, marking cornfields and thickets for streets and lots. Samuel Mordecai, an eyewitness, described the frenzy this way: "Not one buyer in 20 purchased with the intention of building or even of holding longer than until the second or third installment should fall due, when, according to the auctioneer's assurance, he would double his money."

With the Panic of 1819, the bottom dropped out of the real estate market. Everyone dumped their property; everyone, that is, but those cool-headed capitalists with the nerve to purchase land while prices were in free fall and the patience to wait for economic growth to resume. At the bottom of the market, many speculators and small-scale entrepreneurs went out of business. The collapse blew away the speculative froth, but Richmond was a city of substance. Those who held out were amply rewarded.

Industry suffered little in the panic. Richmond's tobacco, iron, coal, and flour businesses had taken firm hold. The canal fed Richmond's port trade, drawing cargo from Virginia's interior for transloading onto vessels bound for ports around the world. Extensions of the canal in the 1830s and 1840s and the construction of railroads kept Richmond's docks in a state of constant activity.

Richmond had few peers as a manufacturing center. The city produced ceramics, beer, musical instruments, coaches, soap, and candles. And Richmond industrialists took the lead in transforming the tobacco industry. Traditionally, people had smoked tobacco; in the early 1800s, plug, or chewing tobacco, was all the rage.

Marketed under such charming brand names as Darling Fanny Pan Cake, Little Swan Rough and Ready, and the ever-popular Negro Head, plug enjoyed a booming popularity. One foreign visitor suggested that the national emblem should be the spittoon rather than the eagle.

The production of plug involved a lengthy process of stemming, flavoring with licorice, moistening with olive oil, and curing for 30 days. The stems were used in snuff, so there was little waste. By 1819, 11 tobacco manufacturing plants in Richmond were turning out plug tobacco and snuff as well as the kind used for smoking. Eventually, Richmond would employ 2,000 workers in some 52 tobacco factories, processing five million pounds of leaf a year.

Coal mining put Richmond at the forefront of another industry vital to America's industrial revolution. Coal had been mined commercially in nearby Midlothian, just west of Richmond, since

Rocketts Landing was the waterfront extension of Richmond east along the James River. A depot area for steamboats and other sailing vessels, Rocketts was the point of arrival and departure for many travelers to and from Virginia. Courtesy, Valentine Museum

1735. The region's bituminous coal, prized for its purity, produced heat, and gas for lights; it fired iron forges and powered locomotives.

Coal deposits were found on both sides of the James. Seams on the southern banks were reported to be extraordinarily ample in places: 25- to 50-feet thick. Seams on the northern bank, a mere seven- to eight-feet thick, were generous by any other measure. By 1822, Richmond was exporting 42,000 tons a year of coal produced in Chesterfield, Henrico, and Goochland counties. By 1826, the volume of Richmond-mined coal had increased to 79,000 tons. Exports peaked in 1833 when the Chesterfield Railroad began hauling coal. Although Pennsylvania soon surged ahead as the nation's leading producer, Richmond's industry continued to thrive.

The coal industry greatly stimulated the local economy. "At the Chesterfield coal mines, a space less than a quarter of a mile square yields

Following the Revolutionary War, Richmond expanded rapidly. Northern capitalists and foreign industrialists built warehouses and stores, elegant houses and churches. St. Peter's Catholic Church was built in 1834 at the corner of Eighth and G (now Grace) streets. Courtesy, Valentine Museum

annually about a fourth of a million dollars," observed a visitor in a letter to the *Richmond Enquirer*. Industrialists made significant profits from their mining operations. Landowners pocketed profits from their royalties. Hundreds of workers found employment in the mining camps a few miles outside the city. Furthermore, the mines generated revenues for local railroads, and supported an industry geared to manufacturing steam engines and rail cars.

Most significantly, the abundance of coal stoked the fires of a vigorous iron industry. David Ross, a Scottish immigrant, pioneered the iron industry with his mill across the river from the capitol. In 1809 Philip Haxall built his own ironworks on the site. Haxall's operation included a nail factory, as well as a rolling and slitting mill. Four other ironworks were quickly established, the most prominent of them being the Belle Isle Rolling and Slitting Mill and the Nail Manufactory.

These foundries all would be eclipsed in the 1830s by the famous Tredegar Iron Works. Joseph R. Anderson, a West Point graduate, commenced his business career as a commercial agent and ended it as owner of Tredegar, the largest ironworks in the South by the 1850s. Tredegar produced locomotives, rails, and later, cannons used by the Confederate army.

Two families dominated Richmond's powerful flour-milling industry: the Gallegos and the Haxalls. By 1831, Philip Haxall ran a conglomerate of businesses, including an iron mill, a plaster-grinding mill, a sawmill, a blacksmith shop, and a corn and gristmill. Two years later his gristmill was grinding out 200,000 bushels of wheat a year. Haxall's mills were gutted by fire twice before the Civil War. Meanwhile, the Gallego flour had gained an international reputation. The nine-story building dominated Richmond's business district, grinding 300,000 bushels a year until it burned in 1830. Both Haxall's and Gallego's would be rebuilt to become even bigger producers than before.

In the 1850s Richmond mills drew from the wheat fields of Virginia, Georgia, Ten-

nessee, and North Carolina. Producing a half million barrels a year, Richmond industrialists supplied markets as far away as California and South America. Until Minneapolis took the lead in later years, Richmond was considered the flour-milling capital of the country.

Although Virginia was never a major cotton-producing state or a leader in the textile industry, Richmond did support several wool and cotton mills. In 1833 P.J. Chevallie's Richmond Woolen Manufactory turned out 9,000 yards of flannel per week until destroyed by fire in 1853; the Virginia Woolen Mills, located two blocks away, picked up its business. The Richmond Cotton Manufactory was born during the embargo of 1808 when it was deemed patriotic to buy homemade goods. The company was reor-

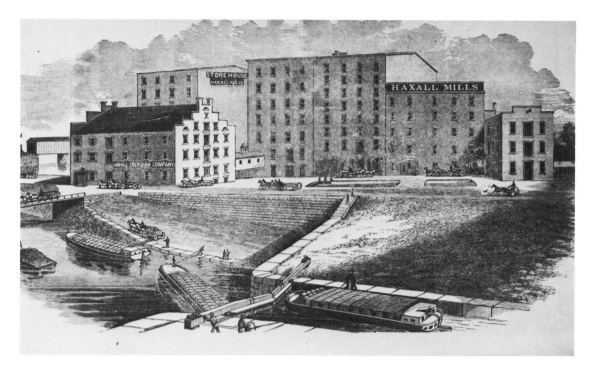

With the extension of the James River and Kanawha Canal westward along the James in the 1830s and 1840s, and the building of the railroads at the same time, wheat shipments poured into Richmond from the western sections of Virginia. Philip Haxall built his mill along the canal, and from 1809 until 1894 the property passed from father to son. This engraving of the Haxall Mills was published in 1888. Courtesy, Valentine Museum

In existence from 1798 to 1924, Gallego Mills helped to make Richmond one of the world's greatest flour centers in the antebellum era. The large brick building housing the mills was located on the east end of the turning basin of the James River and Kanawha Canal. Courtesy, Valentine Museum

This panoramic lithograph of Richmond was made shortly before the Civil War, in 1852. Courtesy, Valentine Museum

ganized in 1838 as the Richmond Cotton Manufacturing Company. Under new management it employed nearly 200 laborers to run its 3,776 spindles and 80 looms, which digested 1,500 pounds of raw cotton a day.

After the Civil War, Richmond would be tainted by its reputation as the capital of the Confederacy, a bastion of masters and slaves, moonlight, and magnolias. The reality could not have been more different. Richmond was in fact one of the most dynamic centers of industrial capitalism in America. As the city transformed the economic landscape of Virginia, it also added a few new twists to the "peculiar institution," slavery.

In search of labor, Richmond's industrialists did not hesitate to use slaves to supplement their white work force. Although tobacco manufacture was prospering, the old plantation system was on the decline and slaveholders only too happy to find a more remunerative employment for their property. Some landowners trekked with their slaves to the cotton fields of Alabama

and Mississippi. Others moved to Richmond. In an industrial setting the traditional relationship of master and slave broke down.

A handful of industrialists purchased slaves outright, but most hired slaves under contract from their owners. As factory workers, slaves enjoyed unprecedented freedom. Some received room and board with their factory jobs, giving them an opportunity to live free from their masters. Some simply made their own housing arrangements. As city laborers, factory slaves had the opportunity to earn extra money by working overtime, enabling some to buy their freedom.

Richmond was a melting pot of immigrants and natives: free and slave; Catholic, Protestant, and Jew. This bustling city on the James was a center of commerce and manufacture—and finance. Once, tobacco had been the only currency of the land; as industry grew, so did banks. The first, the Bank of Richmond, was chartered in 1792 but never became firmly established. In 1804 the Bank of Virginia set up headquarters

in Richmond. With $1.5 million in equity capital, it grew to the point where it established branches in nine cities.

By 1860, Richmond was a golden town. Five years later it would be a blackened ruin. As the eighteenth century progressed, several towns appeared in the western districts, usually centering around the county courthouse. Winchester was established in 1752. Within three years a small cabin was erected to serve as the courthouse, a necessity in a town where German and Scotch-Irish inhabitants didn't always mix well. As historian Samuel Kercheval notes, the Germans taunted the Irish on St. Patrick's Day by parading the effigy of the saint and his wife with strings of Irish potatoes around their necks. On St. Michael's Day the Irish returned the honor, exhibiting a mock St. Michael bedecked with sauerkraut. Riots often followed.

With the approval of the General Assembly, Stephensburg officially became a town in 1758, with Lewis Stephens, son of the founder, acting as surveyor. Four years later Jacob Sto-

ver's son Peter laid out Strasburg. Settled principally by Germans, their language was commonly used in those towns until the nineteenth century. Staunton, established in 1761, was settled primarily by the Scotch-Irish.

That same year, the General Assembly established Woodstock, the first large town in the west. Woodstock was settled—also by Germans—on 1,200 acres, 96 of which were divided into half-acre building lots. Streets and five-acre "out-lots" took up the rest of the area. In 1762 Mecklenburg, later called Shepherdstown for its surveyor, Captain Thomas Shepherd, was settled primarily by German mechanics, which proved to be somewhat prophetic: 22 years later James Rumsey would construct his first steamboat there.

Lexington was established in 1778, on a tiny chunk of land only 1,300 feet long and 900 feet wide, to give the new county of Rockbridge a place to hold its courts. Over the next three decades, more than a dozen towns would be established in the west.

On Saturday, April 2, 1865, while the Confederate army prepared to evacuate Richmond, military authorities set fire to warehouses over the objections of the city's civilian leaders. During the night, the fire spread through the city's business district, destroying flour mills, woolen mills, and the armory. This Currier & Ives lithograph shows the Confederate army and civilians fleeing the city south across the Mayo Bridge.

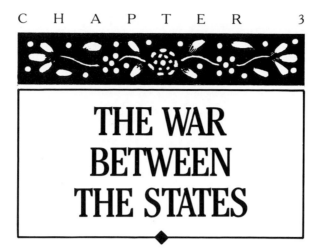

THE WAR BETWEEN THE STATES

In the words of Abraham Lincoln, the United States in the antebellum era was truly "a house divided." As the federal government exercised its powers to the advantage of Northern states, Southerners grew restive. They protested the use of federal funds to build canals and roads, which primarily benefited Northern capitalists and farmers. They were outraged by the "protective" tariff of 1828 which fed the North's industrial economy by eliminating foreign competition and threatened the overseas trade that buttressed the South's agricultural economy.

Overriding all other concerns was the issue of slavery. Although the debate took place on a lofty moral plane, the abolition of the "peculiar institution" would have profound economic consequences for the Southern states. First, it would wipe out millions of dollars in capital: in 1850 the average male slave was worth between $800 and $1,200 on the market. Second, abolition would undermine the plantation-based agricultural system which was built around gangs of slave labor. Without slaves the large plantations would be nothing but unwieldy chunks of land.

The North, where an industrial economy had no need of slavery, had grown increasingly intolerant of the institution. Sympathizers initiated the underground railroad in defiance of a federal law which demanded that fugitive slaves be returned to their owners. Tensions increased when Northern states refused to accept the U.S. Supreme Court's Dred Scott decision, which declared that slaves could be carried into non-slave states as property. *New York Tribune* editor Horace Greeley articulated the abolitionist sentiment when he wrote that the court decision deserved "as much moral weight as would be the judgment of a majority of those congregated in any Washington barroom." As Northerners continued to attack slavery and slaveowners, Southerners dug in their heels in the belief that it was each state's right to accept or reject slavery.

Virginia was a microcosm of the national miasma. Divided by sectional differences, the state engaged in debate over internal improvements and slavery, as well as free schools and political representation. Like the industrial Northeast, western Virginia's small-farm economy needed no slave labor. While 55 percent of the state's white population lived west of the Blue Ridge, only 13 percent of its slaves did. In the east, slaveowners held a majority in state government. A year before the war, 75 percent of the state legislators were slaveowners.

As early as the 1840s, western Virginians discussed the gradual abolition of slavery west of the Blue Ridge, and even of dividing the state. State-funded internal improvements, westerners

Eyre Crowe, an artist and friend of novelist William Makepeace Thackeray, accompanied the writer on his 1853 tour of America. On March 3 Crowe visited a Richmond slave market and made this sketch. From Eyre Crowe, With Thackeray In America, 1893

argued, had mainly benefited the eastern counties. Virginia's Constitutional Convention of 1850-1851 did little to soothe sectional strife. In return for concessions to the west on such issues as the franchise and legislative representation, the east exacted a provision barring the General Assembly from enacting an emancipation law. Although this act effectively closed the slavery debate, westerners remained dissatisfied. The institution of slavery had come to be directly equated with the east's political dominance.

Westerners, politically aligned with the North in their antipathy towards slavery, had become economically allied to the North through trade with Pennsylvania and Ohio. Major roads such as the Northwestern Turnpike, the Staunton and Parkersburg Pike, and the James River and Kanawha Turnpike connected western towns to Ohio River ports. By 1861, goods

in western Virginia were being shipped to Maryland markets via the Northwestern Virginia Railroad, terminating in Parkersburg, and the Baltimore & Ohio, extending to Wheeling. Promised improvements on the Kanawha, which would have facilitated east-west trade, were never made.

Tied by rivers, roads, and railroads to the North, western Virginians felt a greater sense of community with the cities of Pittsburgh and Cincinnati than with their brethren to the east. Virginians living on the far western fringes of the state resided closer to seven other state capitals than to their own. Given the difficulties in transportation, Richmond might as well have been on another continent.

Divided between Unionist and Secessionist parties, Virginia steadfastly straddled the fence as the United States careened toward Civil

War. Strong antislavery sentiment in the west precluded Virginia from siding immediately with the newly formed Confederate States of America. In February 1861 Virginia called for a peace convention in Washington. Northern states sent delegates with instructions to make no compromises on the issue of permitting slavery into the territories. The Confederate states sent no delegates at all.

Disheartened Virginians called for a special convention of distinguished citizens to determine the state's position. Virginians east of the Blue Ridge expressed secessionist sympathies; the people of the Valley supported a states' rights platform that tilted them moderately in favor of secession. Trans-Allegheny Virginia, however, was so strongly in favor of the Union that some western Virginians supported splitting

Settlers living in the far western regions of Virginia were tied by roads, rivers, and railroads to the North. Isolated from the eastern part of the state by mountains and inadequate transportation, they developed markets to the north and west. This photograph demonstrates the transportation problems faced by those western settlers. Courtesy, Valentine Museum

the state if the eastern counties insisted upon seceding. A newspaper article in the *Western Virginia Guard* urged readers to consider forming their own state. A writer for the *Parkersburg News* noted that "western Virginia, from its geographical position, must ultimately unite with the states in the Valley of the Mississippi," while an article in the *Wellsburg Herald* forecasted that the region would eventually become part of Pennsylvania. On April 4, after two months' debate, delegates voted 88 to 45 against secession, providing that the president refrained from using force to bring the Confederate states back into the Union.

As the Virginia debate drew to a close, South Carolina was preparing to take Federally held Fort Sumter by force. President Lincoln called for 75,000 volunteers, including three

regiments from Virginia, to subdue the rebellious state. To Virginians the call signaled clearly that the president would fight to force the Confederate states back into the Union. On April 17, 88 delegates voted to secede, and 55 voted against secession. Virginia became the eighth Confederate state.

One week later antisecessionist John S. Carlisle began garnering support for a convention. On May 13, 436 delegates from 27 counties met in Wheeling to discuss the future of Virginia's pro-Union western region. By 1862, the northwestern counties had organized a separate government. On June 20, 1863, the state of West Virginia was admitted to the Union.

As the Union and Confederacy commenced hostilities, the North appeared to have an immense advantage in population and indus-

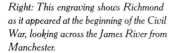

Right: This engraving shows Richmond as it appeared at the beginning of the Civil War, looking across the James River from Manchester.

try. The Union had 23 million people; the 11 Confederate states were inhabited by only 9 million, of whom 3.5 million were slaves who could hardly be counted upon to support the secessionist cause. Although the South had a predominantly rural economy, the North was far more capable of feeding itself. Southern acreage was tied up in cash crops, especially tobacco and cotton. So lucrative was the cultivation of cotton that the Deep South states actually imported grain from the North. Finally, the Northern states were far more industrialized. They possessed the economic base to manufacture the armaments of war and to keep some of the largest armies the world had yet known in the field.

General Winfield Scott, the recently retired commander of the Union's armed forces, believed that the best way to force the South to

Left: General Winfield Scott conceived a strategy which would force the South into submission by depriving it of much-needed supplies. From Cirker, Dictionary of American Portraits, *Dover, 1967*

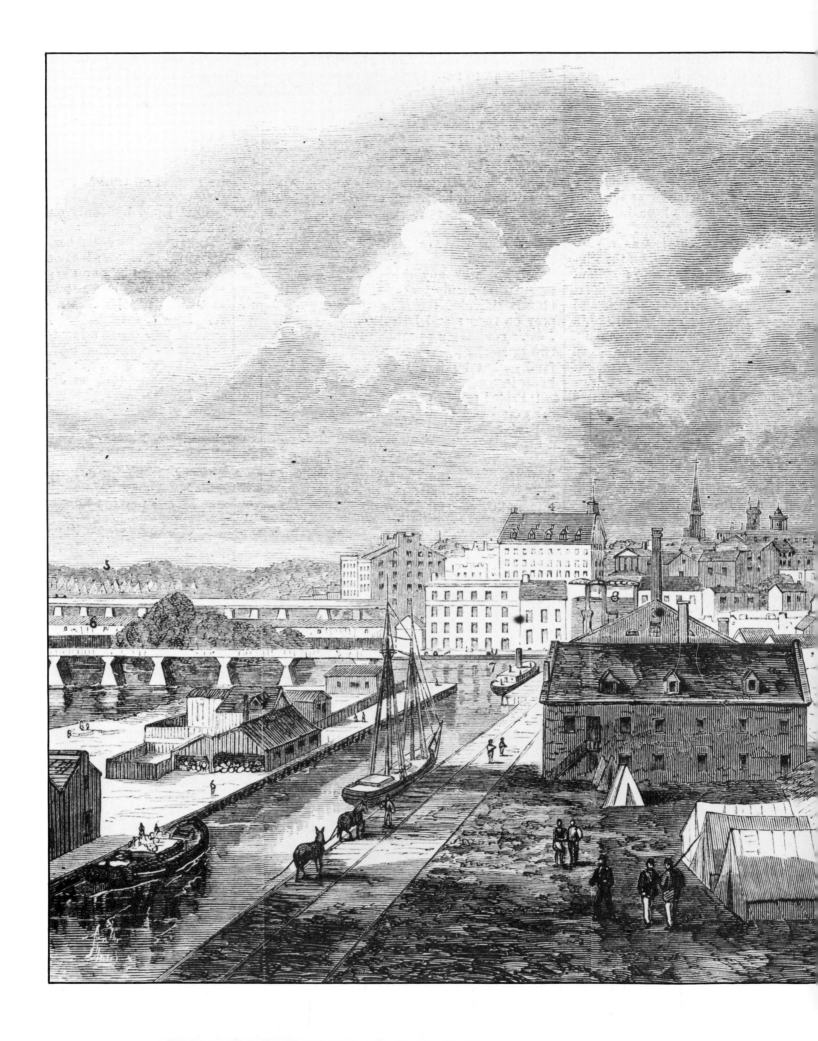

Left: Jefferson Davis was elected president of the Confederate States of America in February 1861. Davis moved his capital to Richmond in May 1861 after Virginia seceded from the Union. Courtesy, Valentine Museum

Far left: This view of Richmond from a west window in Libby Prison, at the corner of Cary and Twentieth streets, was published in Harper's Weekly in October 1863. Sketched by Captain Harry E. Wrigley, a Federal officer-inmate, it shows the Confederate capitol in the upper righthand corner and the city's important dock area in the left foreground. Courtesy, Valentine Museum

submission was to deprive it. By blockading the ports, the Union would cut the Confederacy's cotton and tobacco exports to Europe, prevent it from buying English and French armaments, and thwart efforts to import food. By controlling the Mississippi, the Federals also would cut off the main body of the South from supplies of Texas beef and grain. The strategy, designed to provoke hunger, hardship and, eventually, rebellion against the Confederacy, became known as Scott's Anaconda; like the powerful snake, it would squeeze the life out of the secessionists.

Although Scott's grand vision guided Union strategy in the long run, hot-blooded Union generals lacked the patience to wait for the South to slowly starve. They identified other targets that if captured would hasten the end of the war. Virginia was the one state in the Confederacy with an economy capable of sustaining the demands of mid-nineteenth century armies with their voracious appetites for supplies and their dependence upon railroads. Not surprisingly, Richmond was the premier target.

Not only was the city on the James the capital of the Confederacy, it was the South's only industrial center of importance. Richmond's

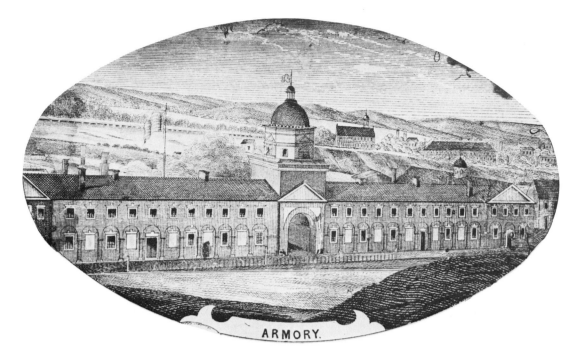

ARMORY.

Above right: This Harper's Weekly *engraving depicts the bloody three-day battle of Cold Harbor, during which the Northern army lost over 13,000 men and the Southern casualties numbered in the hundreds. After this battle General Ulysses S. Grant decided to lay siege to Richmond rather than attack it directly. From* Harper's Pictorial History of the Civil War, *1866*

ironworks, textile plants, and flour mills were vital to any enduring war effort. Not only were arms forged in Richmond, but niter, necessary to the manufacture of gunpowder, was also produced there. Additionally, with five railroad lines and a deepwater terminal on the James, Richmond was a major depot for supplies. Without Richmond as a base of operations, the South would have been hard pressed to field an army of sufficient size to oppose the North's massive Army of the Potomac.

A succession of Northern generals repeatedly struck at Richmond; Robert E. Lee repeatedly risked the destruction of the Army of Northern Virginia to prevent the city's fall. Many of the bloodiest battles in the Civil War—Fredericksburg, the Wilderness, Spottsylvania, Cold Harbor, Seven Pines, Petersburg, and the

Below right: After the Revolution, the government of Virginia sought a way to standardize the arming of the militia. An armory known as the Virginia Manufactory of Arms was built, and in 1802 it began producing muskets, rifles, pistols, bayonets, swords, and cannon. Eventually the supply exceeded the demand and the armory was closed in 1821. It was refitted with equipment and leased to the Confederate government during the Civil War, only to be gutted by fire in 1865. From Smith's Map of Henrico County, *1852*

Peninsula Campaign—were fought on the approaches to Richmond. When the city fell in 1865, the surrender of Lee's mauled army at Appomattox that same year was a mere afterthought.

Virginia offered many other tempting targets. Under the guns of the Union army in Washington, the port city of Alexandria was occupied early in the war. Norfolk fell soon afterwards, captured in a bloodless encounter by a contingent commanded by Abraham Lincoln himself. With Yankee ships patrolling the mouth of the Chesapeake Bay and soldiers occupying two of its major ports, Virginia was the first state to feel the squeeze of Scott's Anaconda.

Equally vital to the South's war effort was a reliable supply of salt. Without salt the South could not preserve the meat needed to feed the Confederate troops. Without salt livestock was vulnerable to a variety of diseases. Without salt Southern industry could not convert hides to the leather used in boots, horse tack, and shoes. Although some states set up their own works to extract the mineral from ocean water, mines near the southwestern Virginia town aptly named Saltville were the Confederacy's major source of

Above: General Thomas "Stonewall" Jackson saved the breadbasket of Virginia in his famous Valley Campaign. From Cirker, Dictionary of American Portraits, Dover, 1967

Facing page: On the morning of April 3, 1865, the capital of the Confederacy was a smoldering ruin. Its business and financial center had been torched as the Union forces approached Richmond. Gallego Mills, in the background, was back in operation within a year, but Virginia's economy would take years to rebuild following the war. Courtesy, Valentine Museum

Below: The White House of the Confederacy, designed by Robert Mills for Dr. John Brokenbrough, was occupied by Jefferson Davis and his family during the Civil War. Located at the southwest corner of Twelfth and Clay streets, the house also served as the headquarters for the commander of the First Military district after the Civil War. Courtesy, Valentine Museum

supply. Mining activity boomed in the mountain town, and loggers were kept busy for miles around supplying the wood used to dry out the blocks of salt. Recognizing the town's economic importance, Union forces launched sporadic raids against Saltville; the Confederates were equally determined to defend it. Saltville was so far from the major theaters of war, however, that it never became the site of a major battle.

The burden of feeding the Army of Northern Virginia fell largely upon Virginia, which had the most diversified agricultural economy of any Southern state. In 1863 the state legislature restricted the cultivation of tobacco in an effort to stimulate the production of corn and wheat. The

production of grain crops did increase substantially, but stores were pillaged by invading armies.

Yielding a great bounty of wheat, oats, and livestock, the Shenandoah Valley had considerable strategic value over and above its importance in protecting Richmond's western flank. General Thomas "Stonewall" Jackson saved the breadbasket of Virginia in his famous Valley Campaign. Southern armies in the Valley seemed to lead a charmed existence; in the Battle of New Market, young cadets from the Virginia Military Institute helped to rout a far larger Yankee force. But the North with its greater numbers eventually prevailed. Commanding an army

J. Becker sketched the surrender of the Confederate army at the Burkesville Station, Virginia, for Frank Leslie's Illustrated Newspaper. Many of the war's bloodiest battles were fought on Virginia's soil; the despair of the men and the devastation of the land is apparent.

of 35,000, Union General Philip Sheridan obliterated the Valley's economic usefulness by meting out the same treatment that General Sherman made famous in his march through Georgia. "I have destroyed over 2,000 barns filled with wheat, hay, and farming implements, over 70 mills filled with flour and wheat," Sheridan wrote. "I have driven in front of the army over 4,000 head of stock and have killed and issued to the troops not less than 3,000 sheep."

As invading forces ravaged Virginia's farm economy, Lee's army depended increasingly on the Carolinas and Georgia for food stores. But the line of supply was precarious. After years of warfare Virginia's railroad system was breaking down. Northern troops had torn up track, twisted rail, demolished bridges, wrecked the rolling stock, and burned stations at every opportunity. Unable to bring in sufficient

supplies from the south, Lee had to divert troops to eastern North Carolina and southwestern Virginia to forage for food.

The strains of war showed in the civilian economy as well. Runaway inflation inspired accusations of profiteering. A barrel of flour in October 1863 cost Richmonders an appalling $70; six months later the price had risen to $250 a barrel. Corn was $50 a barrel; sugar, $10 a pound; calico, $30 a yard. By February 1865, a dozen eggs cost $6. Confederate money lost its value as the government printed more and more notes without gold or silver backing.

Food, clothing, and medicine were so scarce that women took to the streets in protest. The most dangerous demonstration, known as the Bread Riots, broke out in Richmond in April 1863 when a band of 60 women shouting "Blood or bread!" stormed stores for bacon, flour, shoes, and other staples. Similar riots followed across the South.

With the blockade securely in place and half of the Confederacy subdued, only Richmond stood between the North and victory. On Saturday, April 1, 1865, Richmonders could hear gunfire from the south where the armies were clashing in the Battle of Five Forks. By 9:30 that night, Lee ordered his battered army to pull back from Petersburg, leaving Richmond wide open. As Union troops drew closer, Lee wired Confederate President Jefferson Davis

that there was no way to hold back the advancing army. Lee advised Davis to evacuate.

Richmond's bridges swayed under the weight of Confederate troops as they evacuated the city. The canal was brimming with packet boats loaded with fleeing townspeople. Trains heading for Danville—one car containing President Davis and his cabinet—were jammed to capacity.

By the morning of April 3, Richmond, once the South's most vibrant industrial and political center, was a smoldering ruin. Lee's

Lincoln's triumphal procession through the fallen Confederate capital of Richmond on April 4, 1865, was not greeted with universal enthusiasm; however, many inhabitants of the city were probably relieved to see the end of the long, bloody war. From Frank Leslie's Illustrated History of the Civil War, *1861-1865*

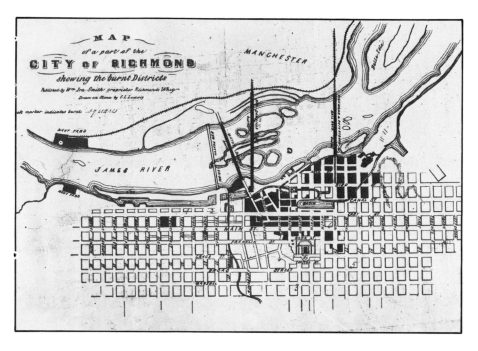

Most of Richmond's financial and manufacturing district was destroyed in the evacuation fire. This map shows the areas burned in some detail. From the Richmond Whig, 1865

surrender at Appomattox was only six days away.

The Civil War spread its devastation throughout the South, but nowhere else except Virginia had two mighty armies been locked in prolonged and destructive combat for four continuous years. Nowhere else had the economic underpinnings been so systematically destroyed. Invading armies had torn up railroads, turnpikes, and bridges. They had burned the cities and savaged the farms.

Virginia was picked clean. Troops had conscripted all the horses, burned the barns, stripped away the fences for firewood, foraged the hay, and slaughtered the cows, pigs, and sheep. Those few beasts not eaten on the spot were left to wander off through unfenced fields or to trample unguarded crops. An Augusta County resident described the area from Harper's Ferry to New Market:

> *There were no fences ... no cattle, hogs, sheep, or horses, or anything else ... fences were all gone ... barns were all burned; a great many of the private dwellings were burned; chimneys standing without houses, and houses standing without roof, or door, or window; a most desolate state of affairs; bridges all destroyed, roads badly cut up.*

The wholesale devastation of the war was exceeded only by the economic calamity of the Emancipation Proclamation. For all its evils, slavery had been the cornerstone of Virginia's plantation economy. Thousands of slaves ran to freedom during the war, leaving farms and plantations to founder. Although some slaves remained loyal to their former masters, Virginia's plantation economy was doomed. Until landowners could find a way to tap the labor of their former black servants, agricultural production would remain depressed.

Emancipation did far more than disrupt the plantation economy; it obliterated a significant portion of Virginia's capital stock. Where the North had invested in labor-saving machinery, the South had invested in slaves. Although slaves were in one sense a form of labor, they also represented a significant accumulation of capital. Planters could sell them for cash to the cotton barons along the Mississippi River or lease them

to labor-hungry industrialists in Richmond. By disposing of their slaves, Virginia capitalists could raise the money to forsake their moribund tobacco crops in favor of railroads and factories. But President Lincoln made that impossible with a stroke of his pen in 1863. Furthermore, emancipation undermined Virginia's tax base; much of the state's taxable wealth had been reckoned in the form of slave property.

Rebuilding Virginia's agriculture would be difficult enough without slaves. The decimation of the white work force made it nearly impossible. The war had wiped out an entire generation of men. Fifteen thousand Virginians had died; countless survivors were maimed.

Virginia would never recover the wealth and economic leadership of the antebellum years. Defeated, decimated, demoralized, and deprived of capital, the survivors had little with

which to rebuild. Even as the soldiers drifted home, the economy continued its downward slide. The wheat crop of 1865 failed miserably; the following year the yield was not much better. Tobacco cultivation withered. Confederate currency had lost all value. Confederate government war bonds were worthless, and even Virginia state bonds sold at a fraction of their face value. Land, the last vestige of wealth, plunged in price. Tracts that had brought $150 an acre before the war sold for $2.

Where war had stimulated the North's economy, it had devastated the South's. By one historian's calculation, the North's total wealth increased by 50 percent in the decade of the 1860s. In the South total wealth decreased by 60 percent. Virginia, once the most prosperous of states, would spend the next 120 years regaining the ground it had lost.

This scene, depicting the rebel soldiers taking an oath of allegiance to the Union in the State Capitol Senate Chamber in Richmond following Lee's surrender at Appomattox, was sketched by A.R. Ward. From Harper's Weekly, June 17, 1865

Joseph R. Anderson

Many years before people began talking about the "New South"—a land of industrial might where blacks and whites shared in economic progress— there was the Tredegar Iron Works. Under the leadership of Joseph R. Anderson, Tredegar put Virginia in the forefront of America's industrial revolution. Valuing economic efficiency over racial stereotypes, Anderson stood up to those who believed that blacks belonged in chains by giving skilled factory jobs to slaves. Later, during the Civil War, Tredegar produced the most sophisticated armaments of the mid-nineteenth century, enabling an overwhelmingly rural Confederacy to hold off the industrialized Union for four years.

Formed in 1836, Tredegar nearly failed at first. The Panic of 1837 and ensuing depression plunged the fledgling foundry into debt. In a desperate effort to save their investment, company directors recruited young Anderson to act as their commercial agent.

A West Point graduate and former army officer, Anderson had acquired a basic knowledge of ironwork in his native Rockbridge County before working as an engineer on the Valley Turnpike between Winchester and Staunton in 1836. When he joined Tredegar in 1841, he sought new markets. The depression had derailed railroad construction, so Anderson solicited the business of the federal government. Within a year the government had bought almost $90,000 worth of Tredegar iron in the form of chain cable, shot, and shell.

The next year proved more difficult. The navy blocked an order for 100 cannons when five pieces in the first delivery burst during test firings. As Anderson tried to persuade the government to continue its business with Tredegar, company officials became

meddlesome—unduly so in Anderson's appraisal—in the company's technical and business affairs. Chafing under their restraints the ambitious young agent proposed to lease the entire plant from the stockholders for five years at an annual rent of $8,000. The directors accepted the offer. Unencumbered,

Anderson continued rebuilding the business.

By December 1844, Anderson had regained the confidence of his federal customers and won new contracts. Soon Tredegar was back in full swing, turning out engines and boilers for navy frigates, heavy guns for the army, and the cannon upon which the reputation of Tredegar Iron Works would be built.

At the end of the five-year lease, Anderson bought Tredegar from the stockholders for $125,000; payments were to be staggered over six years. It looked like a solid venture. Virginia was back in the railroad business—eight railroads were chartered between 1846 and 1853—and it needed rail chairs, spikes, rolling stock, and locomotives. But Anderson had not anticipated competition from low-cost Northern and British rail manufacturers. He abandoned rail products and directed Tredegar's energies toward rolling merchant bar iron and rail chairs.

Narrow profit margins on the rolling mill operations made it difficult for Anderson to make his purchase payments. In 1853 he was forced to take in a partner; within two years he sold a three-fourths interest in the rolling mill and paid off the Tredegar owners. But through a series of financial combinations, Anderson reunited the Tredegar empire. By 1859—with the consolidation of the entire plant, including the rolling mill, and the formation of a partnership with the neighboring armory rolling mill—the Tredegar facilities became the South's largest ironworks, spreading over five acres along the James River.

Like several large factories of the times, Tredegar employed a great number of slaves. By letting slaves work in skilled jobs, Anderson undermined the slaveholders' contention that blacks were racially inferior. Fearful of where such innovations might lead and uneasy about the way Tredegar slaves came and went without overseers, newspaper editors fulminated about the threat to established society. Yet Anderson held firm. In 1847, when he assigned experienced blacks to work new furnaces, a large contingent of Tredegar's white employees staged the first major strike in Virginia's industrial history.

On May 23 Tredegar's white workers refused to work unless slaves were removed from skilled jobs. Anderson responded in a letter addressed "to my late workmen at the Tredegar Iron Works" in which he declared that the workers had just fired themselves. He ordered the strikers to leave the factories and their company-owned homes and then took them to court, charging that they had "formed an illegal combination in uniting to exclude slaves" from his factory. The case was dismissed, but the strikers were not rehired; in many cases slaves replaced them.

But it was Anderson's government liaisons, not his slave work force, that made Tredegar an industry leader. Between 1844 and 1860, the Tredegar works delivered more than 880 pieces of ordnance to the federal government. In 1861, as the Civil War heated up, Tredegar's contracts with the federal government were still in force; weapons cast for both the federal government and the Southern states lay side by side in the Tredegar foundries.

As the conflict escalated into full-scale war, Anderson chose his side. "Will make anything you want," he telegraphed the Confederate government, "work night and day if necessary, and ship by rail." Tredegar's 1,000-man labor force produced cannons, shells, gun carriages, naval machinery, experimental submersible vessels, and equipment for other arsenals. Notably, it also produced the armor that covered the CSS *Virginia* to stand against the USS *Monitor* in the first battle of the ironclads in 1862.

While the war effort and Tredegar fed each other, Anderson's factories were devastated by fire in 1863. Tredegar's machine shops were crippled and restoration took several months. Anderson swore that his factories would never be the victim of arson again.

As Federal troops advanced on Richmond in April 1865, Confederate troops were ordered to move through the city, setting fire to warehouses of tobacco and cotton and blowing up munitions arsenals and the powder magazine. Anderson called out his Tredegar Battalion to defend the ironworks. Armed with muskets, the militia held back the arsonists until they retreated. As Richmond burned to the ground all around, Tredegar stood ready to continue its work.

Anderson died in 1892, but Tredegar survived to serve armies to come. It made ammunition for the United States in the Spanish-American War, both World Wars, and the Korean conflict. The company also thrived in peacetime; before his death Anderson had rebuilt his ironworks into a profitable operation supplying the local market. Although the operation was moved from downtown Richmond to Chesterfield County in 1957, Tredegar—run by Anderson's descendants—continued producing metal products until it closed in 1987 after 150 years of service.

Facing page: Joseph Reid Anderson. Courtesy, Valentine Museum

Although Virginia's economy was severely damaged by the war, the market in Richmond seemed to be bustling on this day in 1868. The old First Market was located at Seventeenth and Main streets. From Harper's Weekly, *November 7, 1868*

A TIME TO REBUILD

As the veterans trudged home from Appomattox, they faced the challenge of rebuilding a shattered economy. The odds must have seemed every bit as daunting as that of holding off the Union army. One-seventh of the white male population had been killed or maimed, while most of the blacks had fled their plantations. Farms were gutted, cities burned. Money was worthless, and the state government was hobbled with debt. Perhaps most galling of all, Northern capitalists, flush with profits from a successful war, descended upon Virginia to buy up the state's patrimony. Although capital from the North and abroad (principally England) would help finance the monumental task of rebuilding, Northerners did not hesitate to use their financial clout and political influence in the General Assembly to subjugate Virginia's interests to their own.

The war had reduced Virginia's once-proud yeomanry and aristocracy to an economic underclass. Confederate and Virginia Treasury notes were no longer legal tender; wealthy Virginians, having loyally invested their savings in now-worthless Confederate bonds, were penniless. By one historian's estimate, the monetary losses of Virginians from the beginning of the war until the end of Reconstruction totaled nearly a half-billion dollars.

The economy was frustratingly slow in reviving. After Appomattox deathly deflation replaced runaway inflation. U.S. greenbacks were slow to replace the worthless Confederate currency. "It seems to be an established fact that nobody has got any money," recorded one *Richmond Times* writer, "and, therefore, if business is to go on we see no alternative but resorting to an exchange of commodities."

The state government was as poverty stricken as its citizens. With a mounting debt, Virginia had no money to rebuild the railroad tracks that had been ripped up or canal banks that had caved in. Although West Virginia had absorbed one-third of the state's land and 300,000 of its residents, it refused to assume any part of the prewar debt it had helped accrue, leaving a population of 700,000 destitute whites and 500,000 penniless black ex-slaves to shoulder the full financial burden.

For five years following the war, Virginia's agricultural economy, which provided sustenance to the majority of the population, was at a standstill. Emancipation had reduced the black labor force on white farms by two-thirds across the South. With no money to buy labor, tools, seed, or fertilizer, Virginia landowners were forced to take up the plow and till what little land they could on their own; the rest they left to grow wild. As their work force of former slaves sought opportunities elsewhere, the labor-intensive plantations shrank in size and number: between 1860 and 1870, the number of Virginia farms

larger than 1,000 acres dropped from 641 to 317.

As if the war's devastation were not handicap enough, successive droughts hindered the recovery of successful farming. Those with farm products to sell were equally disheartened to find their chickens might bring 25 cents apiece; their eggs, 8 cents a dozen. The total value of the state's farm produce declined each year betwen 1866 and 1869.

After reigning for two centuries, Virginia tobacco lost its preeminence in the marketplace. Cut off from their markets in the North and in Europe during the Civil War, Virginia tobacco growers had lost ground to their competitors. Without sufficient labor after the war, farmers were reluctant to plant the crop. In 1860 one-third of the nation's tobacco had been produced in Virginia; five years after the war the state supplied only one-sixth. Kentucky planters were raising a new leaf, white burley, that appealed to tobacco chewers because of its capacity to absorb flavoring. White burley was cheaper to produce; it didn't need fertilizer and it could be air-cured, a less-costly method than the fire-cure used to process the dark Virginia leaf. By 1870,

While farmers in the Midwest boosted productivity with combines and harvesters, Virginia's farmers were too poor and their farms too small to justify the cost of such equipment. Courtesy, Valentine Museum

Kentucky was producing three times Virginia's output.

Manufacturing also had sustained staggering blows. Abingdon, Wytheville, Bristol, and Richmond had been burned. Factories in Fredericksburg and Petersburg had been silenced by bombardments. Northern Virginia had become a blistered wasteland. A scarcity of capital made it difficult to rebuild; even if the factories had been running, Virginia's economy was too impoverished to provide much of a market. By 1870, factory output had still failed to reach prewar levels.

But not all was bleak. Banks quickly reopened their doors. Within two weeks of Richmond's great fire, First National Bank, headed by Hamilton G. Fant of Washington, D.C., was chartered and providing currency. Robert E. Lee was one of the bank's first customers. National Bank of Virginia and National Exchange Bank opened shortly thereafter. Within six months of Appomattox, 16 new banks had begun operations in Virginia.

The livestock trade was one of the first industries to revive, thanks to the rising demand for beef in urban centers around the country. Imme-

Above: Fredericksburg, heavily bombarded during the war, had to struggle to rebuild its factories in the aftermath. Courtesy, Virginia State Library

Facing page: Within two weeks of the Richmond fire, First National Bank, headed by Hamilton G. Fant of Washington, D.C., was chartered and providing currency. Courtesy, Virginia State Library

diately after the war, livestock was needed on the farms as well as for food, leaving little surplus for breeding. Responding to the growing demand, however, farmers in the northern Piedmont counties and the Southwest turned increasingly to raising livestock. By 1880, the number of cattle equaled prewar levels, and Southwest and Valley farmers were exporting beef to Europe. Horse breeding took hold even faster. Shortly after the war, Virginia ranked second only to Kentucky in turning out fine racers and hunters.

Wheat revived as the chief crop in the Southwest and in the Valley. As those regions prospered, producing 55 percent of Virginia's wheat crop, compared to 30 percent before the war, the number of farms and their cash values began to rise.

With the establishment of far-reaching rail transportation in the 1880s, farmers no longer had to limit production for home consumption and nearby markets. Rapid transit and cooled cars allowed farmers to ship produce to Northern markets and coastal ports for export. Blue Ridge farmers turned to fruit. The eastern slopes in Albemarle County became known for their peaches. Frederick and Clarke counties were the center of Virginia's burgeoning apple industry, which was generating revenues in excess of $1.4 million by 1899.

While the Southside's tobacco crop suffered from competition with North Carolina, farms around Suffolk grew such large quantities of peanuts that the small town became known as the "peanut capital of the world." Farmers on the Eastern Shore and along the western and southern borders of the Chesapeake Bay cultivated a wide variety of vegetables—potatoes, lettuce, spinach—for early sale in Northern markets. With the construction of the New York, Philadelphia & Norfolk Railroad in the 1880s, eastern Virginia produce could reach New York stands within 12 hours. Truck farms boomed in

Right: These western Virginia farmers are shown cutting their wheat in the "old style," around 1900. Courtesy, Valentine Museum

Below: The livestock trade was one of the first industries to revive after the war. Because of the influx of people from the rural areas to the urban centers, the demand for beef increased. Courtesy, Valentine Museum

the Chesapeake area, spreading over 45,000 acres and producing annual crops valued at $6 to $7 million.

As the demand for Virginia produce grew in the North, the agricultural system recovered. Despite valiant strides, however, the state's agriculture never regained the prosperity of its antebellum glory.

As Virginia farmers struggled to find new markets, they also were faced with devising a whole new form of agricultural production. The plantation system had become a dinosaur.

Seeking economic freedom as well as legal emancipation, slaves deserted the plantations in droves. With no prospect of restoring the old gang-labor approach to working the soil, many planters broke up their farms and sold off large chunks or leased it to tenants.

Under the new system landowners rented tracts of land to sharecroppers, mostly freed slaves, in return for one-third to one-half of the profits. The landowner supplied tools, seed, land, and shelter; the sharecropper provided the labor. The system benefited both tenant and

Among the manufacturing concerns destroyed during the evacuation fire were the Haxall-Crenshaw flour mills located at Byrd and Twelfth streets. By 1870, however, the mills had been restored to full production and the company's famous F.F.V. (First Flours of Virginia) brand of flour was again available. Courtesy, National Archives

Right: Peaches, grown in Albemarle County, became a successful Virginia crop after the Civil War. Photo by Robert Llewellyn

Left: Because of the introduction of rapid transit and cooled railroad cars, farmers in the Shenandoah Valley were no longer limited to production for home consumption and nearby markets. They shipped their apple harvests to northern markets and coastal ports for export. The apple industry was generating revenues in excess of $1.4 million by 1899. Courtesy, Valentine Museum

owner. Croppers enjoyed their own incomes and a measure of independence; landowners found a way to generate revenue from their land. Planters preferred sharecropping to hiring wage labor because the croppers were less transient than hired hands and had an incentive to see crops through to harvest.

Some sharecropping contracts were written, but most were verbal. Some agreements included perquisites for the sharecropper, such as "a peck of cornmeal or the equivalent in wheat flour each week, a house, and garden" as well as "materials for making & manufacturing their winter coats & pants & leather for their shoes..."

Addenda might give the sharecropper permission to raise "a pig, keep 6 hens and 1 cock," or otherwise add to their personal food stock.

As sharecropping took hold and landowners broke up huge estates into small tenant holdings, the number of farms in Virginia tripled. Average farm size dipped from 336 acres in 1860 to 119 acres in 1900.

Although sharecropping accomplished the essential economic function of keeping farms in production and providing a livelihood for Virginia's 350,000 former slaves, it represented a regression to a semifeudal condition. Sharecropping mired much of the state's agricul-

While the tobacco crop suffered from competition with North Carolina following the Civil War, farmers in southside Virginia began to produce large quantities of peanuts. This circa 1890 photograph shows farmhands picking peanuts in Surry County, Virginia. Courtesy, Valentine Museum

After the slaves were freed, landowners devised a new system of agricultural production. They rented tracts of land to sharecroppers, mostly freed slaves, in return for a share in the profits. Pictured here are sharecroppers picking cotton in Surry County. Courtesy, Valentine Museum

tural economy in a state of seemingly permanent backwardness. While farmers in the great corn belt of America's Midwest boosted productivity with machinery such as combines and harvesters, Virginians had little incentive to innovate. Sharecroppers were too poor to buy the machinery, and their farms were too small to justify the use of such equipment. Landowners had no reason to invest in labor-saving equipment because sharecropping agreements entitled them to only a portion of the profits.

Sharecropping also perpetuated the master-servant relationship between blacks and whites. Although the legal status of blacks improved immensely, subject to the willingness of local authorities to enforce the law, economically they were powerless. Although most whites were left destitute by the war, at least many of them still had their land. Although their fortunes had been wiped out, they might have access to borrowed capital. The former slaves had nothing to offer but their labor. There was no more wilderness to conquer in Virginia, no more frontier land to be granted to those willing to settle it.

Many ex-slaves remained on their plantations because they had nowhere else to go. Others tried following the Union troops home. Thousands drifted into the cities, looking for work. Many former slaves cherished the groundless hope that the federal government would carve up confiscated plantations and award them free land. Preying upon this belief, carpetbaggers peddled them pegs to mark off their 40 acres.

Whether living in the city or on the land, uneducated former slaves made easy victims. One sharecropper complained that his landlord took all the profits from a year's crops. Drought had killed off half the yield and that half, the landlord said, was the sharecropper's. Carpetbaggers hustled ex-slaves at every turn, selling them Confederate money, worthless knick-knacks, and lands to which they had no title.

In an attempt to protect former slaves from such exploitation, Congress established the Freedmen's Bureau to provide food, supplies, education, and shelter. In Virginia the bureau is-

The Freedmen's Bureau, a Federal agency established in the South to feed, protect, and educate former slaves, began operating in Richmond following the war. Schoolteachers came down from the North to instruct the blacks. The establishment of the Richmond Institute and the Richmond Normal and High School for the benefit of Negroes was a direct outgrowth of the bureau's activities. Courtesy, Harper's Weekly, *1865*

sued 178,000 rations before realizing that, at such a rate, funds would be exhausted before the ex-slaves had had a chance to adapt to their new way of life. It subsequently adopted a policy which denied aid to those who refused to work for fair wages.

During its five-year existence, the Freedmen's Bureau also attempted to protect blacks from other forms of exploitation. Any agent suspecting that a former slave had been denied fair treatment had the authority to fine or sentence the alleged offenders. In their zeal to reprimand the pettiest offenses, however, some agents ordered white farmers to ride great distances on short notice to answer such charges as "uttering offensive language." The agents also fed instances of racial abuse to the Northern radical press as evidence that Southern sentiment was both unrepentant and disloyal to the Union.

Although such tactics prolonged the disaffection of Southern whites, the bureau did fulfill many of its intentions. In addition to providing food and shelter for needy ex-slaves, it erected more than 200 schools and educated more than 50,000 blacks.

After rejoining the Union in 1870, the Commonwealth of Virginia plunged into a decades-long controversy over how to handle its prewar debt, a sum that totaled $45 million by 1870. The interest payments alone amounted to nearly $3 million, compared to the state's normal operating budget of about $1 million. If the state were to pay back its debt on schedule, however, it would be unable to meet obligations imposed by the new Underwood Constitution of 1869 to provide a free public education for its residents.

Although bondholders holding roughly a third of Virginia's debt lived outside the state—many of them in the North and in England—Virginia conservatives ardently supported total payback of the debt. Although some Southern states repudiated their antebellum debt, Virginians appealed to the ideals of honor and the state's unblemished fiscal record, arguing that failure to repay the debt in full would alienate potential Northern and foreign investors. Only by attracting outside interests, they reasoned,

could the economy resume its growth and the state generate tax revenues. Bankers, brokers, speculators, and railroad owners also supported the total payback, though their reasons were quite mercenary; the pledge would virtually force Virginia to sell its railroad stock. Eventually the debt issue became so entwined with railroad politics that the two became almost indistinguishable.

A key figure in both the debt and railroad controversies was Confederate war hero William Mahone. As president of three separate railroads in Virginia—the Norfolk & Petersburg, the Southside, and the Virginia & Tennessee—he wanted to secure legal permission to consolidate his roads. He received the support of representatives in Hampton Roads, Southside, and the Southwest, those regions that had the most to gain from unimpeded access to the coast and an increase in commerce through Virginia's own ports.

Mahone faced off against other railroad giants—most notably Baltimorean John W. Garrett of the Baltimore & Ohio. Garrett wanted to channel as much Southern trade as possible through the port of Baltimore. Controlling the Orange & Alexandria Railroad—Mahone's rival for Southwest trade—Garrett rallied allies around the state. Fearing that Mahone's railroad would reduce its canal-born trade with Lynchburg and build up the competing port of Norfolk, Richmond sided with Garrett. Lynchburg, which hoped to become profitable as a center for several railroads, wanted to be able to trade with Richmond, Norfolk, *and* Alexandria. The Valley, effectively serviced by the Orange & Alexandria, proffered like sentiment against Mahone's consolidation.

Mahone was just as motivated by self-interest as Garrett—he wanted to usurp some of the Ohio Valley trade from the Baltimore & Ohio. But he had the advantage of being able to tap the strong sense of Virginia patriotism by charging that "Baltimore gold" backed the opposition. The failure to consolidate lines running to Norfolk would allow other interests to consolidate rail lines running to out-of-state ports such as Baltimore and Philadelphia.

The industrialists courted lobbyists with greenbacks and booze. In the end Mahone prevailed. In 1870 the General Assembly granted him permission to merge his roads into the Atlantic, Mississippi & Ohio Railroad. It was a short-lived victory; within six years the railroad would be forced into bankruptcy.

Although Mahone won the consolidation controversy, he would not so brilliantly overcome the next issue. As bondholders clamored for redemption, the state government sought a means to pay them back. The state's heavy prewar investment in railroad securities offered one potential source of revenue. Northern industrialists, seeking access to the trade of the lower South, were eager to buy the Virginia roads. Sale of the state's railroad stock, it seemed, would be mutually beneficial.

Mahone would have been happy for the state to sell its interest in his three railroads—if he could afford to buy them. But he could not. Opening up the railroads to purchase by Northerners would allow interlopers onto his domain and would enable them to divert Southern trade to Northern ports. Mahone's bitter rivals, the Pennsylvania and the Baltimore & Ohio, supported the measure to allow sale of the state's stocks. A vicious legislative battle ensued. Both sides spent money liberally to buy votes, but

Mahone's dollars were wasted. Conservative members of the General Assembly supported the idea that anyone, regardless of origin, should have the right to buy or build a railroad as long as he did so without the state's money. On March 28, 1871, the state put its railroads on the auction block for anyone to buy.

The Pennsylvania Railroad secured interests in the Richmond & Danville and the Richmond & Petersburg railroads. The Baltimore & Ohio cemented its interests in the Orange & Alexandria, defeating Mahone in his quest to control access to western Virginia. Garrett's line then acquired the short Winchester & Potomac which, after 30 years' effort, had received permission to extend its lines to Baltimore, linking the Shenandoah Valley to that Maryland port as Mahone had predicted.

The Pennsylvania Railroad accessed Valley trade by building a line from Hagerstown, Maryland, through Front Royal and Waynesboro to the community of Big Lick near the Roanoke River. Later its residents would persuade the Pennsylvania road to join the Norfolk & Western—the result of the reorganization in 1881 of Mahone's Atlanta, Mississippi & Ohio—at their junction.

By early 1873, the Virginia Central ran all the way to the Ohio River. A few years later it became the Chesapeake & Ohio when California capitalist Collis P. Huntington assumed management. By the 1880s, another large trunk line had grown out of the Richmond & Danville. The parent company consolidated a number of short lines into a single, long system which provided a more direct route from Atlanta to commercial centers in the North. The company crashed in the 1893 depression but was reorganized by J. Pierpont Morgan as the Southern Railway Company.

Although Virginia would benefit greatly from the trade generated by railroads, it had surrendered its rail system to outside interests. By the 1880s, Northern corporations controlled rail transportation in the state.

The gentlemen planters of the antebellum era were mere specters in the General Assembly.

Confederate war hero William Mahone was successful in his bid to consolidate three railroad companies into the Atlantic, Mississippi & Ohio Railroad. Competition from other railroad lines vying for access to interstate and intrastate markets forced it into bankruptcy by 1876. Courtesy, Valentine Museum

In the Gilded Age, businessmen, industrialists, and financiers dominated the legislature. Issues of industry, finance, and the public purse supplanted those of agriculture.

The railroad sales failed to raise enough revenue to cover the state's debt. Because some companies paid for the railroad assets with unfunded bonds, Virginia gained little cash. Two days after approving the railroad sales, the General Assembly passed the Funding Act, also designed to facilitate payback of the debt.

According to the provisions of the Funding Act, the state issued $30 million of new bonds to retire the two-thirds portion of the debt that Virginia was prepared to assume. (The state abdicated responsibility for the other third, which legislators claimed was West Virginia's obligation; it wouldn't be until the twentieth century that West Virginia actually assumed the liability.) Payments on the new bonds, which yielded 6 percent interest, were stretched out over 30 years. The state guaranteed the interest with negotiable coupons which could be used to pay taxes, debts, or any other obligation to the state.

Although seemingly sound on paper, the Funding Act proved disastrous. As Virginians paid taxes with coupons, tax revenues dropped to less than half the amount needed to maintain public services and fulfill the debt obligation. As the state treasury fell into deficit, Virginians voted to replace 106 of the legislature's 132 members. The new Assembly voted to repeal both the Funding Act and the law providing for sale of the railroads. But the roads had been sold and Governor Gilbert C. Walker vetoed the measures. For years to come, conservative governors would stand firm against any legislation leaning toward repudiation of the debt.

Faced with the loss in tax revenue, the state government increased tax rates and cut expenses. Services, especially the school system, deteriorated sharply. In 1877, 127 schoolhouses closed down. In a desperate bid to restore the state's fiscal soundness, Culpeper delegate James Barbour crafted a bill modifying the terms of the debt settlement by restricting the amount of debt payment and funneling more money to the school

system. Of every 50 cents collected on property taxes, 25 cents would go to state operating expenses, 10 cents to pay against the debt, and 10 cents would be earmarked for schools. But the legislation was blocked by yet another governor, Frederick W.M. Holliday. By 1878, almost half the schools ceased to operate.

By 1879, the state treasury was on the verge of bankruptcy, and opposition to the Funding Act was reaching a fever pitch. Recognizing that the power of the Republicans was too scattered and disorganized to overcome the

"Funders," Mahone forged a new party to stand against the debt payers once and for all. Joined by Barbour, John S. Wise, John Massey, William E. Cameron, and state senator Harrison Holt Riddleberger, Mahone spent the summer and fall stumping for a reduction of the state debt.

Riding the current of mass discontent, the so-called Readjusters swept through the state. They garnered support by proclaiming to be people of ordinary birth, interested in helping the masses instead of the privileged few. This popu-

list party denounced foreign creditors as "vultures" and "shylocks" concerned only with accruing personal wealth. The new party contended that Virginia should not pay an interest rate that its people could not bear, that operating expenses should be met before money was sent to creditors in London or New York in payment of a debt of debatable legitimacy.

By election time, Mahone and his coalition of small-business owners, rural residents, and blacks who felt abandoned by the Republican party were ready to face the Funders, a party

The Underwood Convention, depicted in Frank Leslie's Illustrated Newspaper in February 1868, provided for a statewide system of public schools, establishment of a secret ballot, and changes in the tax structure. Blacks elected to the convention were (left to right) Hunnicutt, Snead of Accomac, Hodges of Princess Anne County, Lindsay of Richmond, and Morgan of Petersburg.

whose hallmark was privilege and old money. Mahone's organizational skills paid off at the polls: the Readjusters won the 1879 election by 82,000 to 61,000 votes. Replacing 56 of the 100 delegates in Virginia's House of Delegates and 24 of the 40 senators, they gained control of the legislature.

The Readjusters passed legislation scaling down the state's debt, repealing the poll tax, cutting the taxes on farmland and small business, raising taxes on corporations and corporate property, stabilizing mechanics' wages, and appropriating more money for public schools. Perhaps most important, the Readjusters changed the method of assessing corporate taxes. No longer were company officials permitted to appraise their own properties; state assessors determined the taxable value of holdings. The tax base soared: railroad and canal assessments rose from $9,876,306 in 1880 to $26,940,173

in 1881. By 1900, railroad and tax assessments reached a total value of $56,582,345.

In 1882 the Readjusters pushed through the Riddleberger Act to replace the 6 percent, 30-year bonds with 50-year bonds bearing 3 percent interest. The act also eliminated the practice of paying taxes with coupons. Readjuster policies relieved the burden of ordinary taxpayers and strengthened state finances. By the early 1880s, the Funders' deficit was replaced with a $1.5 million surplus. As Virginia trudged toward solvency, the question of who was to pay West Virginia's one-third of the debt remained unsettled. The debate between the two states continued until 1919 when the United States Supreme Court ruled that West Virginia was liable for $15 million in principal and accrued interest, payable over a 20-year period. The last payment was received July 1, 1939.

Right: A Norfolk & Western bunk car sits in the foreground of this view of Lynchburg, circa 1885. The city hoped to become a profitable railroad center by establishing connections with Richmond, Norfolk, and Alexandria. Courtesy, Valentine Museum

Above: Richmond was the only Southern city to have a major locomotive plant. The plant, started in 1865 as a farm machinery business, began locomotive production several years later. It continued its operations until 1927. This Chesapeake & Ohio Consolidation freight engine, the 350, was produced at the Richmond plant.

Left: James Barbour was a member of the Readjusters, the new political party formed in 1879 to work for the reduction of the state debt. From Cirker, Dictionary of American Portraits, *Dover, 1967*

In 1887 the Richmond City Council
agreed to replace mule-drawn rail cars
with an electric trolley system. This group
of men posed with the last horse-drawn
car on the Richmond to Manchester line
in 1886. Courtesy, Valentine Museum

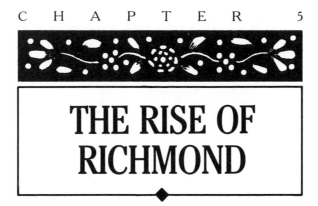

CHAPTER 5

THE RISE OF RICHMOND

The damage to Virginia's war-shattered industry went far deeper than torn-up railroad lines and burned-out factories. New track could be laid if the money was available, but the fortunes of most Virginians had been wiped out by emancipation, inflation, and unredeemable war debt. Factories could be rebuilt if the markets still existed, but a four-year blockade had taken Virginians out of the world economy. Worst of all, Virginia's entrepreneurial potential had been ravaged just as thoroughly as its farms and cities. Local businesses suffered a severe disadvantage competing against Northern industries bursting with profits and cash.

Immediately following the war, economic life was a struggle for economic survival. Jeremiah Morton, a prominent citizen of Orange County, wrote to a lady friend:

I was surrounded by every comfort which the world could afford—a delightful home and happy family of whites and blacks, an income of $30,000 annually, with a prospect of a yearly increase. The scourge of war has swept all from me, and at the age of 65, I stand a blasted stump in the wilderness of life.

Not only had the war shorn Virginia's business community of capital, it had also deprived them of the means to borrow. Collateral in the form of slaves, bank stocks, and savings was all gone. Money to finance new projects was unavailable except at extremely high interest rates. Wartime conditions had created a superficial demand geared to churning out war materiel as well as feeding and clothing thousands of soldiers. With peacetime those markets collapsed. In the brutal postwar economy, members of the old mercantile class resorted to manual labor just to survive.

Even so, there were opportunities. One Albemarle County farmer lost nearly $60,000 in property damages in the war. Selling his farm for $35,000, he paid his creditors in full, bought a stand for merchandising, and started a flourishing family business. An Orange County resident wrote to a friend that, although "under the new regime there cannot be the same pleasure" in farming, he planned to increase his operations and make more money.

As America's grain production shifted to the great wheat bowl of the Midwest and the Plains states, Virginia's flour milling industry never recovered. Yet some sectors of the economy performed handsomely. A decline in the cultivation of tobacco was counterbalanced by continued prominence in the processing of the weed; Virginians were instrumental in the development of the cigarette industry. Riding the great railroad boom of the late nineteenth century, iron and sawed lumber products as well surpassed prewar production levels.

Railroads were the driving force behind economic growth. In Virginia, railroad construc-

Virginia's railroads were nearly destroyed by the Civil War. In order for the economy to develop, Northern and Southern entrepreneurs invested money in reestablishing old rail lines as well as constructing new ones. Courtesy, Valentine Museum

tion kept dozens of local suppliers in business, reintegrated the state into a unified economy, and linked Virginia's industries to the larger world.

As it desperately funneled resources into the war effort, the Confederacy had cannibalized its rail system. Where poor maintenance failed to close the rail lines, Union raiders usually finished the job. In the spring of 1865, General George Stoneman's raiders ripped up railroad tracks and destroyed rolling stock all along the Virginia & Tennessee between Lynchburg and Petersburg. The Virginia Central had been almost completely knocked out; the Richmond & Danville, used by Jefferson Davis and his cabinet to escape advancing troops, had survived with only its rolling stock intact. Overuse and negligence had worn down the Southside Railroad as well. Rotting ties and general disrepair forced trains to travel slowly and caused occasional derailments.

When Richmond burned, the Richmond & Petersburg's bridge across the James River

went with it. The railroad's depot and workshops went up in flames; its books and records were reduced to ash. The same fate befell the records of the James River and Kanawha Canal Company when its general office and toll office ignited the same night. Scarcely a month before Appomattox, General Philip Sheridan's cavalry had trampled the canal's towpath and damaged locks from Scottsville to a point 30 miles west of Richmond. Locks were broken and canal boats burned, sunk, or taken over by former slaves for housing.

The canal system would never recover. Canal company officials tried to enlist outside capital to no avail. Northern industrialists wanted rail routes connecting their manufacturing centers to Southern markets and sources of raw materials; they had no use for a canal connecting Virginia communities to the sea. Besides, railroads had many advantages. Iron rails were less subject than canals to the whims of nature.

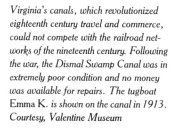

Virginia's canals, which revolutionized eighteenth century travel and commerce, could not compete with the railroad networks of the nineteenth century. Following the war, the Dismal Swamp Canal was in extremely poor condition and no money was available for repairs. The tugboat Emma K. *is shown on the canal in 1913. Courtesy, Valentine Museum*

Frequent floods damaged locks, dams, and tow-paths, periodically closing the canals. Freezes stopped traffic in the winter. Maintenance costs were frighteningly high.

Although the James River and Kanawha Canal Company reinstituted partial service by September 1866 and full service by mid-1869, the railroads usurped much of its business. Lynchburg was the only city of significance upriver from Richmond, and the promised connections between the James and the Kanawha—only 33 miles apart at their head-waters—were never made. The company cut its freight tolls steadily to attract more traffic, but the total take decreased yearly.

The Dismal Swamp Canal was in such poor condition that its company could not bor-row money. Revenues for the Rivanna Naviga-tion Company and the Roanoke Navigation Company steadily declined. On March 5, 1880, the James River canal company went out of busi-ness. The great canals that had revolutionized commerce and travel in the eighteenth century could not compete with the railroads of the nine-teenth century.

In contrast, railroad companies had no trouble finding financing. In the fall of 1865, President Andrew Jackson permitted railroad owners to reclaim their lines as long as they agreed not to press any damage claims against the federal government. The railroad managers could purchase equipment from the government, payable over two years at 7½ percent interest on the unpaid balance. Under these liberal repay-ment terms Virginians reestablished several railroads. Meanwhile, the General Assembly's much-debated decision to sell its rail stock encouraged an influx of private capital. North-ern businesses seeking to tap the resources of the South funded the construction of many new rail lines and integrated the short, unconnected Vir-ginia lines into larger rail systems.

The Civil War had rendered most of Vir-ginia's 1,800 miles of track useless. Concentrat-ing on rebuilding old lines rather than creating new ones, Virginia's railroad companies had built only 107 miles of track by 1870. But

railroad expansion accelerated soon afterward: the next 15 years saw nearly 1,000 miles of track constructed. By 1885, 32 railroads sprawling across the state maintained a total of 2,430 miles of track.

Gripped by railroad fever, railroad com-panies extended lines down the Peninsula, through the Eastern Shore, into the Valley, and across the Piedmont. In 1870 the Virginia & Kentucky, which spanned the 100 miles between Abingdon and Cumberland Gap, was consoli-dated with Mahone's Atlantic, Mississippi & Ohio, creating a line all the way from Norfolk to Tennessee. (These lines would become the Nor-

Confederate veteran James H. Dooley, who invested in railroads, real estate, and steel, rose rapidly in Richmond's postwar business world. In 1890 he purchased 100 acres of land to the west of Rich-mond overlooking the James River. His estate, Maymont, included an enor-mously expensive Victorian mansion and fabulous trees, flowers, and shrubs from all over the world. Courtesy, Valentine Museum

folk & Western Railroad.) Virginia Midland Railway Company joined the Lynchburg & Danville Railroad with roads between Lynchburg and Alexandria, creating a line from north to south through the state. Stockholders of the Virginia Central line even agreed to consolidate with the yet-to-be-built Covington & Ohio to extend service to the Ohio Valley. The consolidation was completed on August 31, 1868. On that day the Chesapeake and Ohio Railroad Company was born.

These consolidations and others opened the channels of commerce around the state. By 1880, an extensive railroad system crisscrossed the state, paving the way for a more vigorous commercial and industrial development. The Virginia Central linked the state's eastern and western markets while the Richmond & Danville tapped the trade of the Carolinas and Georgia. The Richmond & Petersburg Railroad tied into the coastal plains of the Carolinas, while the Petersburg Railroad traveled southward through the Carolinas and Georgia. The Alexandria, Loudoun, & Hampshire channeled trade from the Valley to Alexandria in competition with the Baltimore & Ohio's road from Harper's Ferry to

The Virginia Midland Railway Company joined the Lynchburg and Danville Road with roads between Lynchburg and Alexandria, creating a solid north-south passage through the state. This 1907 view of the Virginia Railway shows the line passing through Charlotte County, Virginia. Courtesy, Valentine Museum

Winchester. The Seaboard & Roanoke, an 80-mile line, brought goods from Weldon, North Carolina, to the growing Hampton Roads port of Portsmouth.

Three lines—the Virginia & Tennessee, the Southside Railroad, and the Norfolk & Petersburg—traversed the Southside to Norfolk, bringing cotton, corn, flour, fruit, peanuts, potatoes, tobacco, wheat, and lumber from far inland. Before the war three lines hauled Valley trade to port. The Winchester & Potomac took produce to Baltimore, while the Manassas Gap Railroad tied the Valley to the port of Alexandria. The Virginia Central ran from the Valley to Richmond. After the war damage was repaired, the only gap in the Valley was between Harrisonburg and Salem.

Towns and communities, new centers of trade, sprang up at railroad junctions. West Point, for instance, grew from a tiny town of 500 to a city of 5,000 after eight years of service by the Richmond & Danville Railway system. Briefly, before the trade shifted to Norfolk and Portsmouth with their superior ports, the town was the fifth greatest cotton-exporting port in the world.

Spurred by the railroads, Virginia entered a boom era. Developers carved fields adjacent to towns into lots. Weekly newspapers enlarged their presses to accommodate prospectuses inducing manufacturers to locate businesses in their circulation areas. Cities swelled in size as planters left their devalued lands in search of a better life. Former slaves flooded the cities, providing a ready supply of factory workers. An estimated 15,000 blacks came to Richmond after the war, doubling its black population. Although agricultural workers still outnumbered factory laborers, factory work commanded higher wages, affording an average annual income of $198 compared to $60 to $120 earned in the fields. Blacks working in skilled positions in the iron, tobacco, or flour milling industries were generally paid the same as whites. But because unskilled blacks worked for lower pay than whites, many earned less in a week than they had as factory slaves working overtime.

America had entered one of the most dynamic periods of economic expansion the world has ever seen. Virginia shared in that remarkable growth and prosperity. As early as its 1865-1866 session, the General Assembly approved charters for 44 new manufacturing and mining companies. The following year the legislature provided for the creation of another 39 firms. But the war-torn Old Dominion lagged behind many of its neighbors.

Before the war Virginia held a commanding lead as the South's most industrialized state, producing goods valued at $42 million. Tennessee was a poor second with $18 million. In 1870 Virginia was producing only $38 million, still falling short of its prewar output. In contrast, Tennessee's manufacturing had almost doubled to $34 million, and Georgia was not far behind with $31 million.

The ruin of Richmond, the leading antebellum manufacturing center of the old South,

A triple-decker railroad crossing was built at Seventeenth and Dock streets for the Chesapeake & Ohio, Seaboard, and Southern railroad lines in 1900. Eleven years later, these three steam locomotives were photographed at the crossing. Courtesy, Valentine Museum

accounted for much of Virginia's overall industrial decline. Before the war Virginia's capital was the thirteenth most important manufacturing center in the country; more than 300 manufacturing companies turned out an aggregate value of $12 million. But on the morning of April 3, 1865, the smokestacks lay in toppled heaps. Where factory exhaust had billowed, only wisps of smoke arose from the ruins.

Nine-tenths of Richmond's business district, 900 buildings, had been razed; 230 of the best business houses and their contents had been reduced to cinders. The fire had incinerated rolling mills, flour mills, and tobacco warehouses. Nine brokerage houses, more than 20 law firms, and every bank and saloon had been consumed by the inferno. More than two dozen groceries—and four-fifths of the food supply—were wiped out. When the Union army occupied the city, a third of the population was forced to rely on federal rations of codfish and cornmeal for sustenance. The lone silhouettes of the "Burnt District" were the granite customhouse, former headquarters for the Confederate government, and the Tredegar Iron Works, saved by Anderson's Tredegar battalion. Damage estimates ranged from $2 million to $30 million.

Citizens and occupying troops worked together to restore order. As the economy revived, Richmond became a city of contradictions, where hope glowed amid the ashes of desolation. As new buildings rose, garbage rotted in the streets. While some residents scraped together their resources to start anew, others robbed and burglarized. The Burnt District was said to be crawling with garroters, thieves, and pickpockets.

Because native Virginians had no capital, much of the new construction was fueled by Northern interests. One of the earliest infusions of greenbacks came from sutlers, army provisioners who followed Union troops into Richmond. Some opened stores on Broad Street, the temporary center of retail trade, while others leased lots in the Burnt District from local businesses which lacked the money to rebuild. In the early days of recovery, sutlers were practically the only

source of goods, although most moved on shortly for want of business.

The currency shortage eased with the opening of new banks, most of them established by Northern investors. Within two weeks of the fire, Hamilton G. Fant, a partner in a Washington business firm, and a group of his associates banded together to create the First National Bank of Richmond. As the largest stockholder, Fant became president of Richmond's first postwar bank. On May 10, only a month after Appomattox, First National commenced operations in the former customhouse.

Five days later the National Bank of Virginia, also backed by Northern investors, began operations in the same building. The next month the National Exchange Bank under the leadership of a German-born Washington resident opened its doors. The infusion of money accelerated the pace of rebuilding. The resulting building boom restored the capital to its former preeminence as a great commercial center.

Buildings were erected with great haste, so that many were shoddy structures. Ever mindful

After the war an estimated 15,000 blacks moved from rural areas to Richmond in search of work. These former slaves, posed beside the James River and Kanawha Canal circa 1865, were facing an uncertain future. The ruins of Richmond's business district in the background emphasize Virginia's war-shattered economy. Courtesy, Valentine Museum

Dunlop Mills, located on the south side of the James River in Manchester, survived the evacuation fire of 1865 but suffered financially in the early days of Reconstruction. The wheat crops of 1865 and 1866 failed miserably, and competition from the Midwest and Plains states hindered the recovery of Virginia's flourmilling industry. In 1902 the mill was purchased by Warner Moore and Company, and it continued to provide for domestic consumption until 1935, when it closed. Courtesy, Valentine Museum

Hamilton G. Fant and others banded together to create the First National Bank just two weeks after the evacuation fire, with Fant becoming its president. Completed in 1913, the bank's building at Ninth and Main streets is shown decorated in 1922 for a Confederate States Army reunion. Courtesy, Valentine Museum

Following the evacuation fire, buildings in Richmond's business district were erected with great haste. The city council outlawed wooden buildings in the area surrounding the state capitol, so iron fronts became a popular addition to the commercial district. Courtesy, Valentine Museum

Following the evacuation fire and subsequent rebuilding of Richmond's business district, scrap iron became a valuable resource. Bits and pieces, collected from vacant lots and battlefields, were resold to foundries, blacksmiths, and metal workers. This circa 1890 photograph was taken near Virginia and Dock streets and shows the one-story Southern Freight Depot and the Watkins-Cottrell building on 14th Street. Courtesy, Valentine Museum

of the recent fire, the city council outlawed wooden buildings in areas near the State Capitol. Likewise, the city banned lumberyards from the Burnt District, and merchants discouraged use of wood in new constructions anywhere in the commercial center. Brick was the material of choice. Iron fronts, used frequently in the North before the war, became a popular addition. Easily maintained with paint, the ironwork added ornamentation and strength, and allowed the installation of large windows for natural lighting and displays.

By October 1865, Richmond's *Whig* noted that at least 100 new buildings were being built in the business district alone. The boom furnished Richmonders with construction-related jobs and created a market for lumberyards, iron foundries, and metalworking shops. Scrap metal became a valuable resource, and junkyards profited from buying bits and pieces culled from vacant lots and battlefields around the city, then reselling them to foundries, blacksmiths, and metalworkers. Scrap metal became so profitable, in fact, that hawkers were known to rip out iron fences and pilfer iron stopcocks from gas streetlamps. One even stole the lead pipes from the kitchen of Richmond's Roman Catholic Bishop John McGill.

Richmond grew rapidly during its postwar renaissance. By 1867, the city's population had reached 38,710, and its corporate limits had doubled from 2.4 to 4.9 square miles. In the next four years the number of homes increased by 62 percent to 8,033 dwellings.

Ten years after the Civil War, Richmond's economy was again prospering. Large sailing ships could be found at the city docks and railroad lines traversed the James River. The business district featured the smokestacks of Tredegar Iron Works and Gallego Mills (left center). Five bridges spanned the James River, including the Mayo Bridge (directly below the Capitol). Courtesy, Valentine Museum

Commercial activity was facilitated by the rapid rebuilding of four of Richmond's five antebellum railroad lines: the Richmond, Fredericksburg & Potomac; the Virginia Central; the Richmond & Danville; and the Richmond & Petersburg. These roads, along with the York River line, which was restored later, reestablished Richmond as a leading transportation center. In both 1868 and 1869, more freight tonnage entered Richmond than Baltimore, Philadelphia, and Norfolk combined. Richmond ranked second only to New York in incoming freight tonnage.

As before the war, tobacco, milling, and ironworking dominated the city's industry, comprising 85 percent of the city's total manufactured product. These major manufacturers took longer than the small, retail-oriented businesses to reestablish their operations. It was two years before the Tobacco Exchange was reorganized and the Corn and Flour Exchange reopened. But by then Richmond was a town on the move.

Most heavy industry was situated in Shockoe Valley or along the river or the canal. Factories were rebuilt east of Shockoe Creek for accessibility to docks and railroad depots. Flour mills, dependent upon a source of running water, clustered along the river and on the canal basin. Large ironworks and rolling mills lined the riverfront at the western edge of the city.

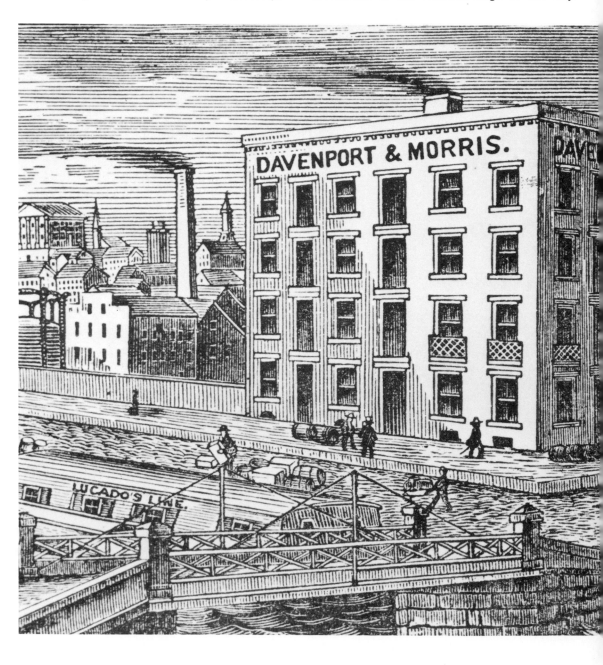

Blacksmiths, tailors, milliners, carpenters, and other small manufacturers dotted the downtown landscape.

Workers usually walked a mile or two to their jobs. While the omnibus provided crosstown transportation in horsedrawn cars, the fare was high. Within 18 months, however, horse-drawn railway cars were back in service along a short in-town route. The 10-cent fare was high but not prohibitive, and residents jammed into the stuffy railcars for the short ride around town. Three years later the street railway would carry travelers from various rail and steamship depots into the urban center. A westward extension of the line enabled city residents to travel to the country for a quiet weekend or a day trip at a reasonable price.

The number of manufacturers in Richmond doubled from 262 in 1860 to 531 by the end of the decade, though the total value of their manufactured product declined 15 percent. Factories and shops were smaller than before the war, employing only one-half the average number of workers per establishment. Population, on the other hand, had escalated 35 percent in the same decade, moving Richmond up a notch from 25th largest American city to 24th.

Of its 51,038 residents, 18,545, or 36 percent, worked in the labor force. Despite the revival of industry, the number of workers

Following the war, small retail businesses were quick to reestablish their operations. From 1874 to 1901, Davenport and Morris, wholesale grocers and commission merchants, operated in this impressive building at the intersection of Seventeenth and Dock streets in Richmond. Courtesy, Valentine Museum

Richmond's iron industry recovered quickly after the Civil War. Although a number of foundries forged rails, steam engines, and machinery, Tredegar retained its leading position. Courtesy, Valentine Museum

employed in manufacturing was 10 percent lower than the average for cities comparable in size. The number of employers involved in professional and personal services, however, was well above the national average. Only 311 Richmonders, or less than 2 percent of the population, worked on farms.

When the Panic of 1873 struck, the nation's economy dipped radically. The panic broke out with the failure of the New York financial house of Jay Cooke & Company in September and spread to Virginia not long after. Runs on Richmond banks occurred, and two small

banking establishments quickly went out of business. The ensuing depression cut short Virginia's commercial recovery. Richmond's resurgence in particular was slowed significantly as several railroads, banks, and factories were forced into bankruptcy or receivership. Several factories and small businesses closed.

In the fall of 1875 the Chesapeake & Ohio Railroad passed into the hands of receivers. Even the Tredegar Iron Works declared insolvency due to the bankruptcy of several of its Northern railroad clients. By the late 1870s, the effects of the panic were still visible in Rich-

mond. Many businesses had yet to recover and people were still jobless. As the depression began to wane, there were still approximately 175 applicants for every position on the local police force.

Recovery came with the new decade. The prosperity of the 1880s was reflected in real estate figures: in 1886, 400 houses were built; the following year saw 500 homes go up. In 1889 the figure increased to 600 new dwellings. Only one building and loan association had been established before 1880; seven were organized after 1886. But the boom was surprisingly frag-

ile. The city had lost its position as the South's leading industrial center to New Orleans, and its major industries were facing tremendous challenges.

While Richmond's three greatest industries—iron, tobacco, and flour milling—continued to dominate the city's economy, their progress after the Civil War was uneven. Iron was the only industry to increase its product value in the first five years after the war, but it encountered tremendous competition from the booming steel towns along the Ohio River Valley and the Great Lakes. The shift of tobacco production to

Kentucky and other states impeded the recovery of the tobacco processing industry. Similarly, the development of large, efficiently farmed wheat fields in the Midwest and the Great Plains also enabled Midwestern cities to supersede Richmond as a major flour milling center.

Yet none of these long-term trends were apparent in 1865. Immediately after the war the shared primary goal was to rebuild. Richmond's ironmaking industry, stoked by the demands of the railroad boom, recovered quickly. Within two years of Appomattox, more than a dozen foundries were forging rails, locomotives, steam engines, and machinery for a variety of purposes. By 1870, various iron foundries were producing goods worth approximately $3 million a year.

Tredegar Iron Works retained its leading position. That same year the 800 workers there accounted for a third of the city's ironworks production. The company had the advantage of possessing one of the few industrial plants to have survived the great fire. It also had the capital to quickly resume production. President Joseph Anderson had wisely forestalled payment on quantities of cotton shipped during the war. When the hostilities ended, Anderson and his associates were remunerated with $190,000 in greenbacks.

Tredegar was largely responsible for Richmond's rise to the status of regional center of the iron industry. Even after the depression of the 1870s, Tredegar expanded its operations to become the leading firm of its kind in the South. A visitor in 1870 wrote:

The Tredegar Ironworks, reconstituted since the war, if not the largest of its kind in the United States, execute an almost unequalled variety of work, not only making iron, but every kind of iron castings—from railway spikes to field artillery—with equal resource and success, and are carried on with vigour and activity, employing a thousand hands.

Ironmaking flourished throughout the 1870s, generating revenues of $5.5 million in 1872, surviving a depression drop to $1 million, and climbing again to $5.25 million in 1881. From there, however, Richmond's iron industry

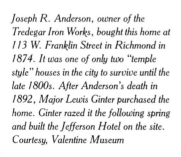

Joseph R. Anderson, owner of the Tredegar Iron Works, bought this home at 113 W. Franklin Street in Richmond in 1874. It was one of only two "temple style" houses in the city to survive until the late 1800s. After Anderson's death in 1892, Major Lewis Ginter purchased the home. Ginter razed it the following spring and built the Jefferson Hotel on the site. Courtesy, Valentine Museum

Lewis Ginter, tobacco magnate and philanthropist, came to Richmond from New York in 1842 and opened a home furnishings store which grossed $40,000 in 1860. After serving as quartermaster under General Joseph R. Anderson during the Civil War, he associated himself with a New York stock brokerage which failed. Ginter then returned to Richmond and entered into a partnership with John R. Allen. He is shown seated at the desk of Thomas Jeffress, a business associate, about 1890. Courtesy, Valentine Museum

began a slow decline. Although iron ore had been mined in Virginia since the eighteenth century, the state simply did not possess high quality reserves in quantities sufficient to sustain production levels demanded by the nation's roaring industrial economy. Richmond's coal reserves, too, proved to be inadequate. The nearby Midlothian mines were quickly depleted, driving up the cost of production. Meanwhile, cheaper coal was being mined at far less expense in the distant Appalachian coalfields. By the 1880s, shortages of locally produced coal and iron ore forced Richmond's foundries to seek sources

from other states; the cost of transporting the raw materials put Richmond at an enormous disadvantage compared to cities along the Ohio River basin. By 1890, Richmond's production had dropped to $4.25 million. By the turn of the century, Richmond's once-powerful iron industry was on a steady decline.

The war had thrown Virginia's tobacco industry into total turmoil. The manufacturers of tobacco products faced many of the same problems as their rural brethren, the tobacco planters. The Northern blockade had kept Virginia's darkleaf tobacco from reaching its profitable

markets in America and overseas; like her planters, Virginia's manufacturers had been supplanted by those of Kentucky, Ohio, and Missouri. Furthermore, the emancipation of slaves had created an inconsistent and unreliable work force in Richmond factories. The adjustment to paid labor would take time.

Before the war Richmond had been located at the center of the nation's tobacco belt. As cultivation spread, however, it became impractical for farmers to carry their product to the Richmond market. By necessity other centers of trade and manufacture in the leaf sprang up.

As farmers in the Piedmont, the Southside, and in North Carolina grew more of the popular new "bright" leaf, Richmond lost ground to Danville, then to Raleigh and Durham in North Carolina. Although more than three-fifths of the state's entire crop was brought to Richmond for inspection and sale at the Tobacco Exchange, the number of local tobacco factories dropped from 50 in 1860 to 38 a decade later; product value slipped from $5 million to approximately $4 million.

Still, tobacco remained Richmond's single most important industry after the war, employing nearly 4,000 hands in 1870. One of the most important postwar firms was Allen and Ginter, headed by Major Lewis Ginter, a New York native who had fought on the side of the Confederacy. Ginter sparked the Richmond industry in the mid-1870s when, observing the growing popularity of cigarettes, he employed 20 women to roll the new product. The Richmond-made cigarettes won wide acclaim at the Centen- nial Exposition held in Philadelphia in 1876. By 1881, cigarette manufacture in Richmond had risen from 3 million to 65 million a year. Ten years later Richmond firms were turning out 100 million a year. Cigarettes had become the most important element in the tobacco industry.

But Ginter missed a phenomenal opportunity to regain Richmond's former dominance.

The rolling cigarette machine, invented by James A. Bonsack in 1883, is pictured in the Allen and Ginter Tobacco factory about 1890. Bonsack had offered his invention to Ginter, who refused it. Bonsack then took the machine to James Buchanan Duke of Durham, North Carolina, who moved to the forefront of the cigarette industry by 1887. Courtesy, Valentine Museum

James A. Bonsack, a Lynchburg resident, invented a cigarette rolling machine and offered it to Allen and Ginter. The Richmond manufacturer tried the machine in 1883, but discarded it. Bonsack took his innovation to James Buchanan Duke of Durham, North Carolina. With the new contraption Duke promptly began outproducing and outselling his rivals, and soon

moved to the head of the industry. By the time Allen and Ginter adopted rolling machines in 1887, Duke dominated the industry. The Richmond firm subsequently merged with Duke's firm and others in 1890 to form a tobacco trust which would control 95 percent of the nation's cigarette market.

As the popularity of cigarettes grew, Lewis Ginter employed women to roll the new product, as seen in this circa 1910 photograph. Courtesy, Valentine Museum

Although North Carolina came to dominate the tobacco industry, Richmond remained a major player. In 1885, 74 million pounds of leaf came through the city's exchange; half was shipped off and half was locally turned into marketable products. By the early twentieth century, more than one-third of the total industrial capital invested in Richmond had been earmarked for tobacco manufacturing.

While the flour milling industry ranked second to tobacco in product value before the Civil War, it was the slowest to recover. With a scanty wheat crop and most of its mills inoperable, Virginia milled little flour in 1865. The Gallego and the Haxall mills, which had burned in the great fire, had to be rebuilt. The Dunlop operation survived physical devastation but was hurt by the wheat crop failure.

Eventually the wheat crop recovered and some mills resumed operation, but the trade in Richmond was slow to develop; the lack of storage facilities after the fire increased spoilage. Richmond merchants lost the business of many farmers in western Virginia who took advantage of the new railroad combinations, particularly the Baltimore & Ohio and its subsidiaries, to ship their wheat to Baltimore. Richmonders also found themselves unable to compete in their old export markets. Before the war they had run wheat to South America in fast brigs and along the coast on some 23 schooners. After the war Richmond businessmen had to hire foreign- or Northern-owned vessels, which ran up their transportation costs. Three years after the war's close, production levels of Richmond's flour mills were considerably lower than the half-million barrels a year produced before the war. In 1870 city mills turned out less than 200,000 barrels, of which only one-third was exported.

Despite the economic obstacles, a rash of fires, and unreliable waterpower, the flour milling industry managed to increase its postwar revenues to $3 million a year between 1881 and 1883. But competition from other wheat-producing regions proved insurmountable. Meanwhile, flour milling concerns in the Midwest used technological developments to gain a competitive edge over Richmond mills. California was another formidable rival, often shipping flour to the East Coast for sale at lower prices than those of Richmond's mills. After peaking in the early 1880s, Richmond's milling industry entered an irreversible decline. By 1887, flour production fell to $1.5 million, rose again to $2.5 million in 1892, then dove to less than $1 million in 1897.

By the turn of the century, only one of Richmond's three major mills survived. The Haxall-Crenshaw mill failed in 1891—after 100 years of operation—when its South American market disappeared. The Gallego operation passed into the hands of receivers. Only the Dunlop Mill, which served domestic markets in the South and the Southwest, continued operations.

As the mainstays of Richmond's traditional economy declined, the city developed other businesses. Following Reconstruction, iron,

As Richmond's industries stabilized the economy, improvements were made to the city. City Hall, located on the block bounded by Capital, Tenth, Eleventh, and Broad streets, was completed in 1894 at a cost of $1,440,000—almost five times the original estimate. Courtesy, Valentine Museum

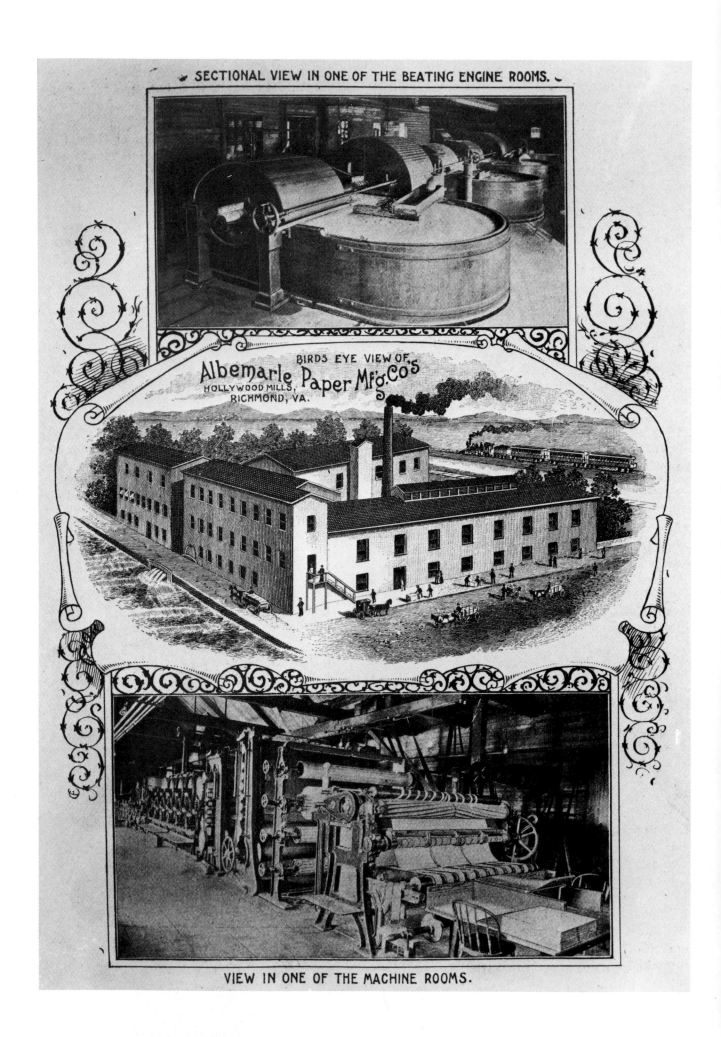

SECTIONAL VIEW IN ONE OF THE BEATING ENGINE ROOMS.

BIRDS EYE VIEW OF.
Albemarle Paper Mfg Co's
HOLLYWOOD MILLS,
RICHMOND, VA.

VIEW IN ONE OF THE MACHINE ROOMS.

flour, and tobacco accounted for 89 percent of the city's total manufactured products. The contribution of the big three dropped to 63 percent by 1880, and to 43 percent a decade later.

The building boom created a heavy demand for construction materials. Brickmaking was one of the earliest secondary trades to become a major industry. The city produced more than 13 million bricks a year in the 1870s. Other factories turned out stoves, wagons and carriages, boxes, soap, plywood, farming tools, and barrels.

Fed by six railroad lines, Richmond attracted a number of other industries: lumber, chemical fertilizer, paper products, and flavoring extracts. Thirteen confectioners and 20 bakers kept Richmonders supplied with sweets. The Southern Fertilizing Company and Richmond Chemical Works turned out significant volumes of acids and fertilizers. The Richmond Cedar Works was the world's largest woodworking plant. Albemarle Paper Company produced newsprint in the same decade, then switched later to blotting paper, matrix, and filter papers. Of the numerous coffee and spice manufacturers, the C.F. Sauer Company would come to be renowned for its Old Dominion Baking Powder as well as for its ground spices and extracts.

One important Richmond business, founded by Mann S. Valentine II, was based on a formula for beef extract. Produced initially on a small scale for the local market, the formula ultimately enjoyed renown on five continents. The Empress of Russia praised Valentine's Meat Juice after its use in the Russo-Turkish War. After President James Garfield was shot and wounded in 1881, he breakfasted on toast soaked with the juice. Explorers to the North and South poles considered the award-winning juice standard equipment.

Blacksmiths, wheelwrights, carpenters, shoemakers, tailors, milliners, and dressmakers occupied city storefronts, while "objectionable" industries—breweries, a tannery, a soap and candle factory, and the city's gasworks—stood on the outskirts of the city where their noxious odors and wastes were less of a nuisance.

Richmond was not hospitable to all industry. While dry goods merchandising expanded, cotton manufacturing was altogether abandoned. The two postwar mills, the Marshall Manufacturing Company and the Manchester Cotton and Wool Company, closed down by 1900. The Richmond-Virginia Woolen Mills, a small operation started in the 1880s, died after a few years. Shipbuilding and car manufacturing came and went quickly. Chartered in 1888, Trigg Shipbuilding Company constructed the South's first torpedo boat before being forced into receivership after 14 years. Kline Motor Car Corporation, producer of Stanley and White steamers, moved its operation to Richmond from York, Pennsylvania, in 1911, only to go out of business 12 years later.

Electricity came to Richmond in 1881 with the organization of the Virginia Electric Lighting Company. On the theory that competition would keep rates low and service high, the city council approved charters for two more companies. In 1884 the city became involved in the power business as well, replacing the city's gas lamps with electric streetlights and constructing a power plant the following year. Wires soon crisscrossed Richmond as the city provided electricity for streets and parks while private companies supplied power to private customers. But the arrangement failed to live up to the council's expectations. Believing that electricity was a natural monopoly, the council in 1890 chartered the Richmond Railway and Electric Company which bought out four other power and streetcar firms.

As Richmond's population topped 63,000 in 1885, the need for a more expedient means of travel became apparent. In 1887 the council agreed to replace the mule-drawn rail cars, which ran top speeds of three miles per hour, with an electric trolley system. Richmond became the first city in the nation to employ overhead trolleys powered from a central system. By 1890, eight streetcar companies traveled over more than 32 miles of track. As Richmond continued to grow, pedestrian viaducts were built, bridges were improved, and streets and sewers were extended.

Albemarle Paper Manufacturing Company's Hollywood Mills produced newsprint during the 1890s. Later the mills switched to blotting paper, matrix, and filter papers. In 1969, James River Corporation purchased Albemarle Paper Company and expanded it to produce not only specialty papers but also paper towels, paperboard packaging, customcoated films, and imaging products and pulp. From Richmond: City on the James, *1893*

Mann S. Valentine II founded the Valentine Meat Juice Company in 1871, and the business grew rapidly for several years. The meat juice can still be found in some U.S. pharmacies, but it is more readily available on foreign markets. Valentine (in the rear, center) is shown with some of his employees. Courtesy, Valentine Museum

But the city would not continue its reign as Virginia's undisputed leader in commerce and manufacture.

In the early 1870s Richmond was still the state's busiest port and rail center. But the city's upriver location, which had served it so well a century earlier, was now a disadvantage. Oceangoing trade was being conducted on much larger vessels than in 1800, and the trip up the undredged, silted-over channel of the James River made slow, tedious sailing. It was far easier for the big, iron-hulled vessels that predominated in the late nineteenth century to dock at Baltimore or Hampton Roads, both of which were well served by railroads.

As Richmond entered the twentieth century, its commerce had leveled off to a steady, unremarkable tempo. Tobacco processing remained a mainstay, while the paper and chemical industries contributed an element of stability.

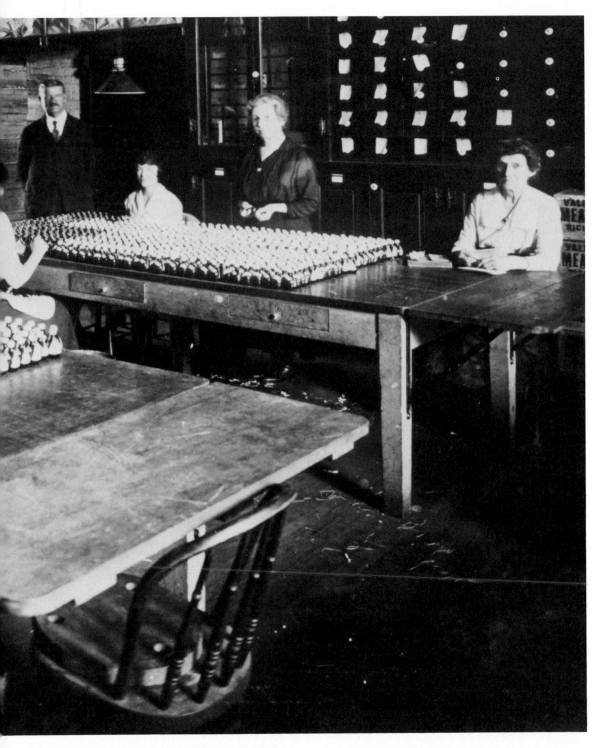

Its position as a major rail center increased with the coming of major railroads like the Atlantic Coast Line and the Southern Railway Railroad Company, and the city was recognized as a notable regional financial center when it was chosen as the headquarters for the Fifth Federal Reserve District in 1914. Yet the ironmaking and flour industries had all but disappeared, and competition with Norfolk had reduced Richmond forever to the status of a second-class port.

As worldwide economic forces turned against the port of Richmond, they worked to the advantage of the port cities of Hampton Roads. William Mahone's newly consolidated Atlantic, Mississippi & Ohio Railroad, which connected with Norfolk, funneled considerable Southside trade from Richmond to Norfolk. Later as the large, consolidated lines—the Norfolk & Western and the Chesapeake & Ohio—carried coal, cotton, and produce to port, they

In the 1930s dry goods merchandising expanded along Broad Street in Richmond. Thalhimers Brothers and Miller & Rhoads added onto their department store complexes to meet the demands of a growing population. This 1932 view of Broad Street, looking west from Eighth Street, shows the city's preparations for a Confederate States Army reunion. Courtesy, Valentine Museum

sought deep-water ports from which to export their cargoes. At Norfolk ships could transfer their cargo directly from dock to train and vice versa. Large freighters, too large to navigate Richmond's inferior channel, poured into Norfolk's harbors.

In 1881 Norfolk's exports totaled nearly $18 million, more than nine times Richmond's exports in the same year. As Norfolk's shipments rose, Richmond's plunged. The value of Richmond's imports between 1875 and 1880 declined from $575,000 to $40,000.

Produce and manufactured goods traveled the rails to Norfolk from all over Virginia and other Southern states. By 1874, the port ranked third in volume along the country's cotton exporting ports. Ten years later nearly a half-million bales a year would pass through the city, half of it bound for Europe.

In the late 1800s the Norfolk & Western began shipping millions of tons of the "black diamond" through Norfolk from the newly opened Pocahontas coalfields in Virginia and West Virginia. Between Norfolk and nearby Newport News, the cities of Hampton Roads would become the largest coal-exporting ports in the world.

The port activity created a wealth of jobs. Between 1880 and 1910, Norfolk's population tripled. When the Chesapeake & Ohio extended a rail line down the Peninsula, Newport News grew from a small fishing village to a vibrant town. Newport News Shipbuilding and Dry Dock Company, founded by Chesapeake & Ohio tycoon Collis P. Huntington, became the state's largest employer with 5,000 workers. In the 1890s the company began building ships for the United States Navy. Soon it was one of the country's major builders of warships and steamships.

Railroads created other commercial centers around the state to compete with Richmond. The linkup of the north-south Shenandoah Valley line and the east-west Norfolk & Western line created western Virginia's first full-fledged metropolis. The population of the village of Big Lick increased from 669 to 24,495 within 20 years. Roanoke, as the community was

Right: In 1899 William R. Trigg, a prominent industrialist, opened a shipyard in Richmond on the James River. Although it was at first successful, obtaining contracts for two U.S. Navy torpedo boats, the company began to struggle when Trigg's health declined. He died and the company went into receivership in 1902, never to return to full operation. Courtesy, Valentine Museum

Above: The paper and chemical industries contributed to the stability of Richmond's economy at the beginning of the twentieth century. The Standard Paper Company's mill, located at Hull Street and Canal in Manchester, is shown here. From Richmond: City on the James, *1902-1903*

Workers plowed the cobblestone streets so that Richmond's electric streetcar tracks could be laid. The new transportation system helped to create the city's suburbs by allowing workers to move beyond the traditional neighborhoods. By 1890 Richmond had eight streetcar lines. This photograph shows track construction near First and Broad streets. Courtesy, Valentine Museum

The Norfolk harbor was bustling with activity in 1912 when this photo was taken. In the 1870s Norfolk replaced Richmond as the state's commercial center. Railroad lines located there could transfer their cargo from train to ship with great ease. Cotton and coal became the two largest exports from the Norfolk area. Courtesy, Valentine Museum

renamed, also became a major center of heavy manufacturing, boasting the South's largest locomotive factory and a number of iron foundries.

No longer were communities slaves to the geography of coastlines and navigable rivers. As railroads probed into every corner of the state, they gave rise to numerous smaller centers of commerce and industry. The railroads opened up the coalfields of the farthest western reaches of Virginia: Pocahontas and Big Stone Gap became prosperous mountain towns.

The restoration of the Richmond & Danville Railway brought life to the textile industry that would make Danville one of the country's chief textile centers. Drawing upon the cotton and wool resources of the Southeast, Riverside

Cotton Mills arose along the banks of the Dan River in 1882. As the tobacco industry spread, Danville also became the world's largest market for loose-leaf bright tobacco.

Farmville, Bedford, Chatham, Lynchburg, Martinsville, and South Boston also became centers for handling tobacco. Like Danville, Petersburg's rail accessibility boosted its tobacco and textile industries. As early as 1885, five cotton manufacturers with an aggregate number of 26,554 spindles were operating there.

In the Piedmont, Lynchburg quickly renewed its antebellum reputation as a commercial center. The world's largest loose-tobacco market before the war, the city of seven hills rebuilt its tobacco industry within a few years. Shortly after the end of Reconstruction, a visitor to Lynchburg reported that the city's 35 tobacco factories employed "great numbers of negroes, men, women and children ... [who] earn good wages, work faithfully, and turn out vast quantities of the black ugly compound known as 'plug.'" Shoe and candy businesses grew into important enterprises in the new century. Ranking first in the Union in per capita income in 1850, Lynchburg was still one of Virginia's wealthiest cities for its size a half century later.

The small Piedmont town of Charlottesville, home of Thomas Jefferson's University of Virginia, had one substantial industry that predated the war: a woolen mill. Burned by Sheridan's army, the mill was rebuilt by businessman Henry Clay Marchand. Resuming operation in 1868, the Charlottesville Woolen Mills became one of the nation's leading woolen manufacturers and continued business until 1964.

The railroad boom extended to Northern Virginia as well. Alexandria, a busy port city on the Potomac, benefited from the extension of rail lines into the nation's capital. By the early 1870s, three rail lines traversed Fairfax County: the Washington & Ohio; the Orange, Alexandria & Manassas (later the Midland Railroad); and the Alexandria & Fredericksburg. While some industries such as brickmaking and lumbering took root, Northern Virginia remained largely rural, a magnet for well-heeled Washingtonians in search of respite. The resort at Wiehle—on the present site of the planned residential community of Reston—boasted a lavish hotel with bowling alley, tennis courts, and lakes. The surrounding woods were popular for horseback riding and hunting.

By the 1880s, Fairfax was becoming known as a bedroom community for Washington. Northern Virginia residents from Falls Church to Herndon commuted daily to jobs in the District of Columbia. The Loring Company made the first effort to promote Northern Virginia as a suburb rather than as an agricultural supplier to Washington. "Its nearness to the town of Washington ... renders it most desirable to persons employed in that city and wishing for a healthful country home," explained a company pamphlet touting the new community of Dunn Loring.

With its superior ports and its elaborate rail networks, Virginia had a well-developed industrial-agricultural economy by the turn of the century. In 1920 the value of Virginia's manufacturing had risen to $650 million. Although the state was still overwhelmingly rural, Virginia was no longer a plantation society; industrialists and financiers had totally replaced the planter-merchants as the leading entrepreneurs. Towns and cities with more than 2,500 residents, accounting for 18.3 percent of the state's population in 1900, had become hotbeds of entrepreneurial energy.

Nevertheless, Virginia was far from regaining its preeminence as one of the leading states of the Union. As was the case with the other states of the old Confederacy, the average income of Virginia's citizens trailed far behind the rest of the nation. None of Virginia's cities could compare to such bastions of capitalism as New York, Philadelphia, Pittsburgh, or Chicago. And to a degree never seen before the war or since, Virginia's economic destiny was controlled by outsiders. But by the turn of the century, the state had completed the vital task of repairing the war damage. Virginians were in a position to unleash their native entrepreneurial genius.

Coal mining and iron ore production brought thousands of families into the southwest region of Virginia. Mining opened up the land between Pocahontas and Clinch Valley for settlement. This coal mining plant in Pocahontas is pictured in 1974. Courtesy, Roanoke Valley Chamber of Commerce

*This 1946 photograph shows Water
Street in the Tazewell County coal mining
town of Pocahontas. The painted green
and white "company houses" were rented
to miners for $2.75 per month per room.
Courtesy, Richmond Newspapers, Inc.*

C H A P T E R   6

VIRGINIA'S "WILD WEST" BOOM TOWNS

America's westward expansion with its gold rushes, mining towns, gunplay, and intercontinental railroads has always captured the popular imagination. During the same period, from 1880 to 1900, Virginia's own west was booming as railroads drove deep into the mountains to exploit a vast wealth of timber and coal. To the newcomers Appalachia seemed an untamed land, and its ruggedly independent mountain folk were as alien to the brash nineteenth-century capitalists as were the Plains Indians. But unlike many western communities, which turned into ghost towns as the gold and silver ran out, Southwest Virginia's towns survived.

The sale and consolidation of Virginia's railroads gave rebuilding and expansion new impetus. As various roads extended into the hinterlands of the Old Dominion to tap vast resources of mineral wealth, the Southwest entered a period of boom growth. New towns sprang up at railroad junctions and at mining camps that were their destinations. Quaint crossroads sparked to life as prospectors and speculators came to chip their fortunes out of the land. Mountain towns like Clifton Forge, Pocahontas, Pulaski, and Covington blossomed along the rail lines probing into the heart of the Appalachians.

Roanoke showed the most remarkable growth during the period, exploding from the tiny hamlet of Big Lick with such speed as to earn the sobriquet, "The Magic City." In the early 1800s, Big Lick was nothing more than a settlement beside a spring, a stagecoach stop for Tennessee-bound travelers. By the 1870s, it had become a small center for trade, with a number of mills, stores, saloons, factories, and warehouses crammed into its one square mile; yet its population had yet to top 700. Despite the Virginia & Tennessee Railroad depot there, Big Lick was still mainly a way station for cargo and travelers bound for the California gold rush. Land sold for $30 an acre then, a fraction of what it would go for a decade later when one citizen claimed to have asked and got $50,000 per acre.

Roanoke might still be a mountain hamlet today had not a throng of farsighted citizens pooled their resources to solicit the attention of Norfolk & Western officials in June 1881. Seeking a site to link the Norfolk & Western with the Shenandoah Valley line, railroad representatives were combing the area between Lynchburg and Salem for such a location. When some of Big Lick's civic-minded citizens called a town meeting to discuss the future of their community, one resident suggested that the Norfolk & Western might take a harder look if a subscription of several thousand dollars were raised.

Clifton Forge was one of several mountain towns that sprang up along the rail lines in the late nineteenth century. Later, large plants for manufacturing iron and other products were located there. Courtesy, Virginia State Library

In a few hours the money had been raised. Reports vary as to the exact sum, but it is known to have been between $7,000 and $10,000. Railroad officials were in Lexington that evening, considering that town as a point of connection. The townspeople of Big Lick hastily dispatched a special courier to convey the bonus.

The courier rode into the night to Arch Mills where he handed off the papers to another rider who took the package to Lexington. The committee was in session when the bearer burst through the door. Impressed by the zeal of Big Lick's townspeople, Colonel U.L. Boyce, one of the chief movers in the railroad project, declared, "Gentlemen, this brings the road to Big Lick." The following February the Virginia General Assembly issued the city its charter, and Big Lick formally became Roanoke.

The town erupted with activity as people prepared for the coming of the trains. The Roa-

The western Virginia town of Big Lick exploded with the consolidation of the state's railroads. In 1881 citizens of the town solicited the attention of the Norfolk & Western Railroad, which was looking for a site where it could link up with the Shenandoah Valley line. This aerial view of Roanoke, looking southeast, shows Mill Mountain in the background at right and the American Viscose Corporation in the background at center. Courtesy, Roanoke Valley Chamber of Commerce

noke Land & Improvement Company, formed in August 1881, oversaw the purchasing and laying off of lots which sold at prices ranging from $100 to $500. Real estate soared as speculators snapped up properties. The town grew so quickly that real estate agents stopped relying on the survey-and-stake method of dividing lots and took to pacing them off, using boot heels as markers. Building materials were in such great demand that even the supplies of nearby towns were exhausted. As lumber piled up at intersections of newly graded streets, Roanoke was said to be "the most excavated place in the United States."

The speculators were not to be disappointed. Railroad employees would double Big Lick's population. The Norfolk & Western planned to move its general offices from Lynchburg, and the Shenandoah Valley Railway had similar plans for its Hagerstown, Maryland,

headquarters. A building craze ignited as hundreds of employees sought accommodations. In the town's first year, the Norfolk & Western and its subsidiaries erected more than 130 dwellings. A mill, 2 office buildings, 15 stores, and 7 homes went up on lots bought from the railroad. When Norfolk & Western official Frederick Kimball sought a new bank to process the railroad's financial transactions, Roanoke got its second bank. Kimball guaranteed subscription if city financial leaders could raise $25,000 locally. The money was raised and the First National Bank was chartered. When the first train rolled in on June 18, Roanoke was ready.

Industry blossomed with the coming of the railroads. The Roanoke Machine Works were operating by May 10, 1882, producing and repairing railroad equipment with capitalization of $5,000 and 1,000 employees. And the big Crozier Furnace was lit. A crowd gathered for that event. The first iron was drawn and declared to be of the finest quality. By 1883, Roanoke Gas Company was organized to provide for the burgeoning population. As brilliant gaslights replaced feeble oil burning lamps, Roanoke began to take on the appearance of a real city.

Workmen found ready jobs in a plethora of trades. As the labor force swelled, the building boom accelerated. Brick houses erected by the Roanoke Land & Improvement Company were the envy of the shop mechanics, while railroad officials and clerks purchased more lavish cottages near the Hotel Roanoke. Clever contractors built long blocks of brick structures and divided them into apartments.

Rapid growth had its problems. Roanoke residents, many of them fresh off the tenant farms of Virginia and North Carolina, clung to provincial habits such as tossing "the accumulations of both chamber and kitchen into their yards." Such methods of disposal combined with crowded living conditions to render Roanoke vulnerable to disease. Meanwhile, so busy were Roanokers with building, buying, and selling buildings that street construction took a backseat. After even the slightest rain, roads

became veritable quagmires, clogging up traffic and making a general mess of things.

With the frenzy of construction came hearty laborers who played as hard as they worked. Saloon owners, enjoying a boisterous business, stayed open all hours. As they sought to quench their thirst at the local saloons, day laborers often became overzealous in their pursuit of leisure. With great regularity, the town sergeant was forced to incarcerate rabble-rousers in the famed "calaboose."

Although prostitution houses would later become a problem, such transactions in the early days were confined to assignations at one of the city's several hotels. "Wenching, drinking and gambling" were considered normal pastimes. Men toted guns, even to work. A *Baltimore Sun* reporter noted, "At night, with the red light beacons of the bar-rooms all ablaze over the plank sidewalks, and the music of the violins and banjos coming through the open windows, the town suggests a mining camp or a mushroom city in Colorado."

By the end of its first year, Roanoke had grown to a bustling city with 63 merchants, 44 tobacco and cigar dealers, 17 liquor dealers, 12 factories—most of which were for tobacco— and enough real estate and insurance agents to defy enumeration.

The boom continued into the mid-1880s. Ravines were filled and hills leveled. Grazing land was graded for streets. According to the second report to the shareholders of the Roanoke Land & Improvement Company, the number of buildings rose from 119 in 1881 to 747 in 1883, including 2 office buildings, 54 dwellings and 6 stores. The number of saloons quintupled in the same period. Assessed value of real estate and personal property more than tripled to $1,079,012 between 1882 and 1883.

Some people came to town to stay, others just to visit. Roanoke quickly acquired the reputation of a convention town with 50 to 60 hotels and boardinghouses. The grandest dame of them all was the Hotel Roanoke. It exceeded all others in elegance with its barber shop and attached bathroom fully equipped with hot and cold

water, an elevator, a grandiose dining room seating 200, and gaslit chandeliers.

By 1883, Roanoke had evolved into a stable if somewhat raucous community, with a militia and enough schools, including two private schools, to educate its young. Several businesses were established which would last into the twentieth century, including a branch of the J.P. Bell Printery of Lynchburg, later nationally known as Stone Printing and Manufacturing Company. Rorer Iron Company was transporting 200 to 250 pounds of washed ore daily to the Norfolk & Western yards for shipment to Iron Town, Ohio. Electricity, telephones, and streetcars all came to Roanoke in the 1880s.

The new payroll became the lifeblood of Roanoke's economy. Tapping the resources of the Southwest, the railroad brought steady business to the town. In 1883, 65,675 bales of cotton passed through the city on their way to Northern mills, while 1,604 carloads of cattle,

sheep, hogs, horses, and mules came through on their way to various destinations. On June 21 of that year, 16 carloads of coal, the first of thousands, traveled through en route to Norfolk. After iron mining began just south of Roanoke, freight trains carried 200 to 250 tons of the brown hematite ore in a normal day's load. As tonnages mounted, the Roanoke Machine Works—having been purchased by the Norfolk & Western—prospered.

As the 1880s wore on, a recession settled on the country, and Roanoke's boom pace slowed. Unemployment became a serious problem and businesses suffered. Speculators who had bought unimproved real estate were forced to sell at sacrifice prices. A number of merchants closed their shops and moved on, leaving vacant stores and houses with "for rent" signs swinging on their doors. The machine shops were nearly dormant, except for repair work. Unable to find steady employment, mechanics left town to seek

Roanoke's industrial growth paralleled that of the Norfolk & Western Railroad Company. In 1941 the company had 7,000 employees in the Roanoke area with an annual payroll of $14,500,000. This photograph, taken from the cement stack at the powerhouse, looks west from the upper end of the railroad yards. Courtesy, Roanoke Valley Chamber of Commerce

work elsewhere. Widespread rumors that Roanoke was a pest hole for noxious fevers exacerbated the depression. Rail passengers could be seen closing windows as they passed through town to guard against contamination. Even the most successful, prominent Roanokers were caught by the disaster. Ferdinand Rorer, whose family predated the city, sold his Rorer Park Hotel for $30,000 and left town, "cleaned out." Former Mayor Marshall Waid lost his beautiful brick house and headed home to Waidsboro, never to return.

But Roanoke's energy quickly buoyed. In 1885 Mayor J. H. Dunston reported to city council:

With the New Year, the clouds have begun to break and roll away and flashes of sunshine to brighten the firmament of our city. Prices of produce have arisen to gladden the hearts of our farmers; orders are coming into our factories, which brightens the faces and keeps busy the hands of our mechanics; and relieves the pressure of shelves loaded with merchandise and gives pleasure and profit to our merchants. The increased demand for goods will soon act on our ener-

getic, enterprising young and indominable people; and the factories and enterprises which a short time ago nearly culminated, will be taken up again and carried to a successful conclusion, and our people who have so steadfastly stood by . . . will soon earn the reward of their . . . perseverance.

The recession had lifted. Spurred by a nationwide shift to standard gauge rails that enabled railroad cars to move between rail systems without cumbersome hoists, Roanoke's machine shops gained new business. Real estate and personal property values climbed to $3.2 million—

nine times the 1882 figures. City finances recovered as the tax base swelled. By 1886, Roanoke was back in the black: total receipts were almost $30,000, surpassing expenditures of $26,000.

Nineteen new land companies were chartered. The Hotel Roanoke added 52 rooms. Saloons, bawdy houses, and gambling houses proliferated. On November 22, 1889, the editor of the *Roanoke Times* wrote:

More internal improvements are needed but so many buildings are in the course of construction and so

The Hotel Roanoke was the finest establishment of its kind when it was built in the booming city of Roanoke. This was the hotel's lobby. Courtesy, Virginia State Library

Roanoke's remarkable growth and activity attracted investors from other parts of the country, who came to Roanoke to survey the situation. Airmail began in the city in 1934. This group ushered in the new service at Woodrum Airfield. The rate was six cents per ounce. Courtesy, Roanoke Valley Chamber of Commerce

many houses going up in the suburbs, the streets are littered with bricks, mortar, lathes, and building debris that cannot be helped, nor can sidewalks be constructed fast enough to keep up at once with the grading of the new streets.

Articles in Northern journals about Roanoke's remarkable growth and activity spurred investors from other parts of the country to come to Roanoke to survey the situation. By 1890, the city was enjoying a new wave of prosperity. Prospective buyers and potential investors from all over the country arrived in trains and in caravans of carriages. As full-page newspaper ads touted spectacular land buys, an average of five families moved to Roanoke daily. "The rush of vehicles to various parts of the city

is continuous and every agent seems to have all of the business he can attend to," noted the *Roanoke Times*. On a single day in February, real estate agencies reported sales of $150,000, while private sales exceeded $200,000. Prices soared. Property once assessed at $70 an acre brought $50 to $200 per front foot. Meanwhile, construction continued at a furious pace to meet the demand for homes and business houses. A million dollars worth of buildings were erected between 1890 and 1891.

As real estate mania took hold, investors snatched up bond issues for streets and bridges over the railroad but ignored the need for a new hospital. Local capitalists poured money into the construction of a railroad, the Roanoke &

Southern, to tie the city to Winston-Salem, North Carolina.

Between 1890 and 1891, 1,025 business licenses were issued to merchants, lawyers, doctors, house builders, real estate agents, and owners of various establishments. Census takers estimated the city's population as between 16,000 and 17,000.

In the Gay Nineties, a veneer of civility settled over the rough-and-tumble frontier town. The city managed to pave some of its roads with vitrified brick. Men still packed guns and patronized houses of ill repute, and professional gamesters still catered to the gambling crowd. But across town, gloved ladies held "tiddly wink parties" and "violet teas." The wealthiest citizens sank small fortunes into lavishly furnished private railroad cars, the ultimate status symbol.

The fever was spreading across the Roanoke Valley. With the completion of a dummy line to Vinton, lots there inflated in value. Speculators descended upon the village, making first payments with the intention of quickly unloading their purchases at a profit. Land companies like the Vinton Land, Loan and Building Company bought up hundreds of acres of grainfields and grazing lands for development. Skilled workers quit their trades and took up speculation. Vinton quickly outgrew its original boundaries. Across the valley, Salem burst into activity with the organization of a dozen or more land companies. Banks opened; ironworks, machine works, brick works, and mills were established. In Norwich rows of cottages were built to accommodate the laborers who flooded the area.

The Norfolk & Western consolidated its dominance in the local economy by purchasing the bankrupt Shenandoah Valley Railroad and absorbing the Roanoke & Southern line. By doubling the capacity of its freight station, the Norfolk & Western continued to feed the commerce of Roanoke and its adjoining settlements.

Roanoke's boom was one of the greatest explosions of vitality in Virginia's 375-year history, and the indisputable success story of the late nineteenth century—an era when eastern Virginia was still dogged by the legacy of the Civil War destruction, sharecropping, and the decline of iron, textiles, and grain milling. But there were limits to the city's growth. Iron reserves were meager, not sufficient to sustain a steel industry in the face of competition from the emerging Birminghams and Pittsburghs. Lacking access to rivers and ports, Roanoke remained on the periphery of world trade. Hemmed in by mountains, Roanoke could never realistically aspire to being more than a regional center of commerce. Inevitably, the boom lost its fizzle.

Some believed that a paralyzing snowfall, which suspended business, precipitated Roanoke's downward spiral. Others attested that the weakening of English investment and unwise currency legislation triggered the collapse. Whatever the reason, Roanoke was swept up in the Panic of 1893, an economic catastrophe that washed over the entire United States.

With money tight, several prominent citizens admitted an inability to pay debts. Some were forced to auction their holdings in order to pay taxes. In May 1893 the Roanoke Times carried full pages of advertisements offering properties for sale under deeds of trust. To ease climbing unemployment, the city council hired laborers to work on streets alongside chain gangs. Families petitioned the council for relief.

Despite the hardship, the Magic City fared better than other nascent metropolises across the country. Property values fell, and the days of easy money were gone forever. Fair-

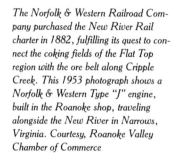

The Norfolk & Western Railroad Company purchased the New River Rail charter in 1882, fulfilling its quest to connect the coking fields of the Flat Top region with the ore belt along Cripple Creek. This 1953 photograph shows a Norfolk & Western Type "J" engine, built in the Roanoke shop, traveling alongside the New River in Narrows, Virginia. Courtesy, Roanoke Valley Chamber of Commerce

weather businesses packed up and left town, leaving a nucleus population of stalwart citizens to carry on the task of building a stable economy.

By 1895, depression had bottomed out, and citizens found cause for sober optimism. Real estate was cheap, and families were again moving to Roanoke. Houses could be bought with a $10-cash down payment. New houses were built and more were under construction. Some clever investors bought empty cottages in Norwich and moved them to more desirable sections of Roanoke for sale at a profit.

Merchants returned to steady businesses. Furnaces and factories resumed full-scale operations. The Norfolk & Western, which had passed into receivership, announced reorganization plans. The machine shops surged back into action with new orders. By February 1896, payroll at the shops had increased to $70,000. By the end of the year, every empty house was reoccupied and nearly every vacant store reopened.

A *Roanoke Times* editorial on New

Year's Day, 1899, greeted residents with a message of hope: "the New Year finds the city entering upon an era safely said to be better than anything in its history." Roanoke was back on its feet, striding confidently into the new century.

"It takes a railroad to bring progress and culture," wrote John Fox, Jr., author of *The Trail of the Lonesome Pine*, a turn-of-the-century novel set in Appalachia against a backdrop of clashing cultures: capitalism triumphant versus the primitive economy of the mountaineers. Before the coming of the trains, Southwest Virginia was a land of dispersed settlement and subsistence farming. Industry was of the most rustic sort, geared to local consumption rather than faraway markets. Although Northern states had been producing coal and coke for several years, the counties of Southwest Virginia remained a primeval forest. As the industrial revolution stoked the fires of growth all around, the richest coalfields on the face of the earth remained inaccessible, guarded by walls of mountains.

The existence of coal was no secret. In

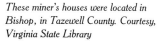

These miner's houses were located in Bishop, in Tazewell County. Courtesy, Virginia State Library

1750 both Christopher Gist exploring for the Ohio Company and the Loyal Company's Dr. Thomas Walker discovered the black rock in their travels through the Southwest. Walker even dubbed the area "the coal land." But, with seemingly limitless timber, local inhabitants saw no need to chip into the ground for fuel.

As early as 1852 Dr. George W. Bickley wrote of Tazewell County, "Coal exists everywhere, though wood is so plenty that it has not been used as fuel to any extent ... Coal has been found below, and in every direction around, and no doubt, exists generally through the county. When shall we have an outlet for this coal?" Twenty years later geologist J. P. Leslie reported to the American Philosophical Society on the nature of coal deposits in the Southwest: "It is good blacksmith coal and no doubt will make good coke." By the mid-1870s, a mining engineer reporting for the Virginia Board of Immigration declared the Southwest to be rich in valuable deposits of iron and coal.

But roads were poor, and the horse-drawn wagons were crude, laboriously slow, and uneconomical. As the industrial revolution increased the demand for coal—the boiler fuel of railroad locomotives, steamships, electric generators, and industrial plants; as well as raw material in the steel-making process—Northern capitalists turned their attentions to Virginia's Southwest. They had long been aware of the abundant resources in Virginia's wilds. When the county of Wise was created in 1856, the edition of the Philadelphia *Pennsylvanian* which carried the news sold out. A second edition was printed so that no interested party would miss the story of a new county in "the land of vast natural resources." A *Richmond Dispatch* writer noted the keen interest of outside capitalists: "The great resources of Virginia seem to be everywhere more highly appreciated than by herself." Indeed, as the 1880s progressed, a significant amount of capital invested in the Southwest would come from Pennsylvania and England.

As the railroads penetrated deeper into Virginia, investors plumbed the far reaches of the state for coal reserves and iron. In the early 1880s railroads running through Bristol in the Southwest transported primarily cotton and agricultural products. Ten years later coal had become the major commodity.

Mining camps and small towns like Coeburn—named for the Norfolk & Western's chief engineer—sprang up along the rail lines, providing humble if not sophisticated settlements for miners and their families. People flocked to the mining communities. Big Stone Gap, Norton, and Wise rapidly doubled in population, overwhelming the resources of local authorities to maintain order. Rowdies routinely shot the glass out of streetlights. Women were imported from Philadelphia to remedy the lack of eligible females. Promiscuous spending and reckless gambling were the hallmarks of the boom years across the Southwest.

As settlements grew, land prices inflated. Dazzled by unprecedented prices, longtime locals sold land and mineral rights for what seemed a fortune. In fact, they virtually gave their wealth away. Outsiders assembled huge tracts of coal reserves that would still be generating millions of dollars in annual royalties a full century later.

Far left: Frederick Kimball, chief operating officer of the Norfolk & Western, pioneered the railroad's move into the Pocahontas coal fields. Courtesy, Virginia State Library

Following the Civil War, General J.D. Imboden spearheaded the development of the coal reserves in southwest Virginia. A native of Washington County, he convinced several capitalists to invest in his Tansalia Coal and Iron Company, which later became Virginia Coal and Iron Company. Courtesy, Valentine Museum

A handful of coal men from Pittsburgh, the coal and steel capital of America's industrial revolution, spearheaded the development of Virginia's coal reserves in the winter of 1879-1880. At a dinner gathering, General J.D. Imboden, a former resident of Washington County, told his colleagues of the potential he saw for development of Virginia's mountainous southwest, which was about to be tied by rail to Bristol. Two guests offered Imboden $500 and expenses to examine the potential of the region for iron manufacturing. The expedition was a success.

Imboden returned bearing samples enough to convince the capitalists to invest in the Tinsalia Coal and Iron Company (later to become the Virginia Coal and Iron Company).

Tinsalia purchased mineral lands, including land at Big Stone Gap and in the Wild Cat Valley, and acquired a controlling interest in the Bristol Coal and Iron Company Narrow Gauge Railway. The first plans for the railway, which would become the South Atlantic & Ohio Railway, included an extension to Big Stone Gap.

Tracks were speedily thrown down, extending deeper and deeper into the mountain wilderness. In 1887, under a joint agreement, the Louisville & Nashville and the Norfolk & Western had begun laying tracks toward a connecting point in Wise County. Meanwhile, the South Atlantic & Ohio brought its first passengers to Big Stone Gap in May 1890. A year later, the Louisville & Nashville railroad also reached Big Stone Gap, while the Norfolk & Western brought life to the nearby town of Norton.

The 1890s found all three railroads converging on a point just north of Big Stone Gap for access to the rich mineral fields that lay beyond. "Gappers" had anticipated the boom. Even before the first train pulled into town, a development company advertised a great land sale, and competing purchasers deposited checks totaling three times the sum asked by the com-

The Norfolk & Western Rail Company was responsible for the operation of 144 mines in southwestern Virginia. The company located its shops in the city of Roanoke; in this 1936 photograph a locomotive is getting a major overhaul. Courtesy, Roanoke Valley Chamber of Commerce

pany. Land was auctioned at such a price that one old farmer who had sold his land for $100 an acre bought some of it back for $1,000 a lot. Taking advantage of the impending building craze, one Northern businessman recruited a corps of gunslingers from the Tennessee mountains to work in his brick plant at the Gap. These folks did not always mix well with the locals, and Virginia's Wild West often erupted in violence.

Analysts' reports commenting on the superiority of the coal deposits of the Southwest generated excitement in iron and coal circles around the country. Lots advertised in prospectuses and in metropolitan newspapers piqued interest. For

the August 1891 land auction, some 30 Pullman cars brought potential buyers from distant cities. The town's hotel overrun, speculators used the sleeper cars as living quarters. Small-time fortune hunters slept in tents. "Big Stone Gap, seat of empire," wrote the editor of the *Stone Post*. "Such will be unless an earthquake swallows it."

The only earthquake was one of cataclysmic change. Twelve different railroad lines were surveyed into the Gap in 1891. Laborers, engineers, surveyors, and coal operators found ready work. Shrewd investors and slaphappy speculators flocked in on stagecoaches, wagons, horses, mules, and even on foot. Real estate transactions

were conducted at the Grand Central Hotel, where newcomers slept eight to a room, paid a dollar a gallon for oil, and feasted on potatoes that cost 10 cents apiece. "Poker ceased," noted one magazine writer. "It was too tame in competition with this new game of trading in town lots."

An old iron furnace in St. Louis was dismantled and reconstructed at Big Stone Gap, initiating the production of iron. Coal companies bought more land and opened more mines. In the fall of 1892 the first shipment of Wise County coal was shipped out over the South Atlantic & Ohio Railroad. Three years later the Louisville & Nashville carried out Wise's first load of coke.

Before the coal boom Tazewell County had been nothing more than an agricultural community of 1,922 farmers, 10 doctors, 8 lawyers, 36 teachers, 22 merchants, "and a total of 91 persons engaged in non-productive callings," according to the 1850 census. In Tazewell the seed of the coal boom sprouted early. In 1872, believing that existing charcoal furnaces would eventually shut down for lack of blast, 26 investors, including William Mahone and Montgomery County delegate Gabriel C. Wharton, established the New River Railroad, Mining and Manufacturing Company for the purpose of developing the coal beds of the Flat Top Mountain region for production of coke.

The development of the Pocahontas coal beds brought thousands of miners and consumers to Tazewell County. Pocahontas coal, known for its superior quality, was specifically requested by the U.S. Navy as well as by premier transportation companies. This 1983 photograph shows a Norfolk & Western train carrying the high quality coal out of the Virginia hills. Courtesy, Roanoke Valley Chamber of Commerce

But local businessmen had little capital. Wharton and his associates looked north for cash support. Hearing of the great mineral riches of the Flat Top region, some Philadelphia financiers and promoters invested in the company. Their cunning reorganization schemes resulted in the formation of the New River Railroad. The Norfolk & Western absorbed the road in 1882 in its quest to connect the coking fields of the Flat Top region and the ore belt along Cripple Creek.

Norfolk & Western's chief operating officer, Frederick Kimball, pioneered the railroad's move into the Pocahontas fields, a basin containing the highest quality metallurgical coal in the world. Prompted by Professor J.P. Leslie's 1881 report of various coal showings in Southwest Virginia, Frederick Kimball set out to locate and examine the outcroppings. Using Leslie's maps, Kimball and his party moved throughout Tazewell's most isolated, inaccessible countryside, through Abb's Valley to Hutton—the future site of the town of Pocahontas. Before they dismounted their horses, Kimball and his accomplices could see a 12-foot-thick vein of coal. Kimball chipped out a few chunks with his knife and lit it. As the combustible rock burned, Kimball noted, "This may be a very important day in our lives." Thrilled with his find, Kimball rerouted the New River line through the Flat Top region to Pocahontas.

By the twentieth century coal mining dominated the economy of Virginia's far western edge. One hundred and forty-four mines were operating along the Norfolk & Western lines by 1905. This 1983 photograph shows one of the modern coal preparation plants served by the N&W system. Courtesy, Roanoke Valley Chamber of Commerce

After the Norfolk & Western purchased the New River Rail charter, it financed development of the area by organizing the Southwest Virginia Improvement Company. Capitalized at $1 million, the company held mineral rights to approximately 100,000 acres of land. Houses and other buildings were hastily constructed by the Crozier Land interests to accommodate the Norfolk & Western's growing labor force. It would be two years before the railroad extended its line west from Radford to Pocahontas; but by 1883, coal producers could ship directly to Norfolk.

Even before rail lines were complete, the Pocahontas fields produced 40,000 tons of coal. Within a year of its beginnings, the village of Pocahontas possessed a hotel, seven stores, and related facilities to serve 1,000 inhabitants. The town became the socializing center for miners from neighboring camps. "Almost every other building was a saloon," recorded one coal operator. "I concluded that Pocahontas was the toughest little town I had yet seen in my travels from Maine to Texas." Weekends were stained by shootings and "sudden deaths," as Pocahon-

tas was the chief liquor supplier for neighboring camps.

The development of the Pocahontas and Flat Top coal beds had brought thousands of miners and consumers to Tazewell County, establishing good markets for farm products that had previously been marketed only locally.

By 1890, the boom in the Southwest was climbing to a crescendo. Virginia miners produced 784,000 tons of coal that year, and total coal tonnage handled by the Norfolk & Western alone had long since topped one million tons. Virginia had risen from seventeenth to sixth place among U.S. iron producers since the beginning of the boom 10 years before. New furnaces were expected to increase Virginia's yearly output by more than 300,000 tons. But with the Panic of 1893, the surging economy began sputtering.

As the national economy slipped into depression, demand for coal and iron slumped. Coal mining was almost discontinued in the prosperous Pocahontas fields and in Wise County. Norton and Graham, at opposite ends of the Clinch Valley Railroad, became veritable ghost towns. The coke ovens at Pocahontas were

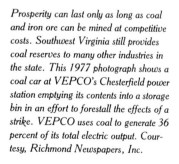

Prosperity can last only as long as coal and iron ore can be mined at competitive costs. Southwest Virginia still provides coal reserves to many other industries in the state. This 1977 photograph shows a coal car at VEPCO's Chesterfield power station emptying its contents into a storage bin in an effort to forestall the effects of a strike. VEPCO uses coal to generate 36 percent of its total electric output. Courtesy, Richmond Newspapers, Inc.

Coal and iron mining provide a livelihood for many in Virginia's southwestern region. Elsewhere, the iron and coal reserves have been mined out. This view of the Roanoke Valley from Mill Mountain shows the industrial area along Interstate 81. Courtesy, Roanoke Valley Chamber of Commerce

abandoned, save for hogs who had made their beds there. Promoters lopped off lots into small farms for sale. Many lots reverted to their original owners on deferred payments, and some landowners were forced to give up their lands for auction due to delinquent taxes.

By 1897, the depression was over and growth in Virginia's coal industry resumed. By the turn of the century, 39 mining operations were back in business, 25 of which were on Pocahontas land, and new ventures were started. The demand for high quality coal was so high that the Norfolk & Western got a premium $25 per acre on its leases. Pocahontas was buzzing again as 23 trains stopped each day to unload coal miners from neighboring coal camps. In the twentieth century, Pocahontas coal would maintain its superior standing, specifically requested by the U.S. Navy as well as by premier transportation companies like the Cunard Steamship line. By 1905, 144 mines were operating along Norfolk & Western lines, from Pocahontas to Clinch Valley, including the Tug River, Thacker, and Kenova districts in West Virginia.

By 1920, coal mining had consumed the entire economy of Virginia's far western tip. Mines were opened in Lee, Dickenson, Buchanan, and Russell counties. Farming was all but abandoned as the local populations with single-minded intensity devoted themselves to the extraction of the "black diamond." With the smaller volumes mined in Montgomery, Pulaski, Augusta, Botetourt, Bland, and Wythe counties contributing to Virginia's output of more than 12 million tons, Virginia ranked as one of the leading coal-producing states in the country.

Iron ore production also grew into the new century. In 1920 production totaled 320,109 long tons with a value of $1,227,601, while pig iron valuation equaled $16,086,946. Clifton Forge, Covington, and Pulaski had large plants for manufacturing iron and other products; similar plants were established throughout the Southwest. The total value of all mineral products mined and quarried in Virginia that year totaled $82,662,945, representing a 40-percent increase over the preceding year.

Prosperity built upon the extraction of minerals can last only as long as the mineral—be it coal or iron ore—can be mined at competitive costs. In Virginia, such prosperity has been fleeting. Only in the far Southwest, blessed by abundant reserves, does mining provide a livelihood today. Elsewhere the iron and coal eventually was mined out, and the local mineral-based industries shriveled. But the railroads, paid for by hauling coal, remained in place to ease the transition to a more stable economy.

Lacking land, capital, and an education, many Virginia blacks were forced to sharecrop. This circa 1890 photograph shows a mother and her son standing outside their cabin in Chesterfield County, Virginia. Courtesy, Valentine Museum

THE DUAL ECONOMY

Emancipation abolished slavery, but it did not end the economic and legal oppression of blacks. Lacking land, capital, and education, Virginia's blacks slipped into a subtler form of servitude: sharecropping. And outnumbered by whites who shamelessly wielded their political dominance to disenfranchise the former slaves, blacks were powerless to seek political redress. After Reconstruction and Jim Crow blacks could legitimately ask if emancipation were anything more than a polite fiction. For the thousands of blacks who swarmed the cities, unprecedented freedoms awaited. Yet freedom and opportunity were not to be confused.

Where slavery had forced blacks into servitude, post-emancipation discrimination almost as strongly enforced their subordination. While life's basic necessities had been provided under a system that simultaneously permitted harsh treatment, suppression, and hard work for little or no compensation, emancipation invited blacks to provide for themselves under an unwritten code that placed them at the lowest social and economical rungs of a society which defined racial equality in its own terms.

Faced with the challenge of surmounting or enduring the limitations placed on them through written as well as attitudinal codes of suppression, black Virginians forged their own economic structure. "Jim Crow" laws were intended to create separate societies, but they also created separate economies and insulated markets for black businesses. Banned from the political arena, blacks channeled their energies into the development of black enterprise.

Secret societies, initiated in the days of slavery, gave birth to mutual aid organizations which became the benefactors of black enterprises and the forerunners of black-owned banks and insurance companies. When blacks were restricted residentially, small vibrant communities sprang up with their own stores, banks, restaurants, and barber and beauty shops, catering to and patronized by black clientele. Ironically, "Jim Crow" laws created the conditions for the greatest surge of entrepreneurial energy in black Virginians' history.

Discrimination against blacks was not unique to the South. While Northerners verbally promoted black freedom and cursed the South for its oppression of blacks, they failed to enforce equality on their own turf. One black leader in Boston observed in 1860 that "it is ten times as difficult for a colored mechanic to get work here as in Charleston."

Given the prevailing attitude, emancipation proved to be no panacea. Blacks were no longer the property of another man, but their freedom was hemmed in by numerous legal restraints. Under the gun of Northern occupation troops, Southerners were somewhat tolerant of black political activity.

Little had changed for blacks by 1900. An unwritten code placed them on the lowest social and economic rung of society. Courtesy, Valentine Museum

The polls as well as seats on juries and even in state government were opened to blacks for the first time. Blacks voted and held office while whites who had served as officers in the Confederacy could not. In the 1870s and 1880s, blacks and whites mixed in the marketplace and traveled on trains with no segregation.

But white legislatures began undermining black freedoms as soon as they had the power to do so. Separation was enforced at theaters and on public conveyances. Mixed marriages were punishable with a $100 fine and a year in jail.

When federal troops withdrew in 1877, a new wave of "Jim Crow" laws was inaugurated. Hotels and restaurants usually enforced separate seating. Those hospitals, private establishments, and public buildings that permitted blacks enforced segregation. While blacks continued to vote and hold elective and appointive offices, many public facilities excluded them or limited them to certain hours.

By the turn of the century, racial sentiment was so strong that laws were adopted to enforce the discrimination already in practice. Every

to impose this "color line." For the next 60 years discriminatory laws tightened the noose of racism. Where state laws left leeway, local regulations took up the slack. Blacks were relegated to seats in the rear of streetcars and later buses, and to separate seating at theaters, restaurants, and parks. Signs specifying "White Only" and "Colored" appeared in profusion over drinking fountains and entrances to bathrooms, theaters, boardinghouses, and other public buildings.

The most damaging law restricted blacks' right to vote. By requiring voters to read and explain any section of the state constitution as well as to pay a poll tax, Virginia's white politicians virtually wiped out black voting power. When the registration books closed in 1902, only 21,000 of the state's 147,000 blacks of voting age were registered. When the poll tax took effect in 1905, less than half of those could afford to pay it. With the diminished strength of the black electorate, blacks had little hope of enacting legislation to ease their worsening economic plight.

The effects were far reaching. The General Assembly allocated disproportionate shares of funds to the education of whites. In the Southside counties, where school-age blacks were concentrated in 1915, only $1 per child was spent to educate blacks as opposed to the $12 per child spent on education of whites. Cities instituted their own plans for residential segregation. Richmond and Ashland, for instance, designated blocks as white or black according to the majority of residents. Citizens were forbidden to reside in any block "where the majority of residents on such streets as occupied by those with whom said person is forbidden to marry." Similar plans were mapped out in other cities.

Most effective in maintaining the suppression of blacks, however, was the unwritten code that limited their employment. In 1902 Richmond's city council threatened to block a white contractor from a job because he employed black mechanics. Virginia's larger cities excluded blacks from a majority of municipal occupations. Those who were able to secure

Southern state except Virginia had adopted a law applying to segregation on trains. After Governor J. Hoge Tyler awakened in his train berth to find black passengers above, opposite, and in front of him, Virginia likewise enacted a law forcing blacks to ride in separate rail cars.

Giving voice to the growing feelings of racism, the *Richmond Times* in 1900 called for segregation "in every relation of Southern life" on the basis that "God Almighty drew the color line and it cannot be obliterated." The Virginia Constitutional Convention of 1901-1902 attempted

Facing page: Stores, banks, restaurants, and movie theaters owned by blacks were easily accessible from this black residence, located at 612 North Third Street in Jackson Ward. In spite of residential segregation and employment discrimination, the black economy developed and thrived in Virginia's inner cities. Courtesy, Valentine Museum

Right: Sedley D. Jones displays samples of his goods outside his store at 726-728 North Second Street in Jackson Ward in this photo, circa 1905. Because of the restrictions on blacks, they opened their own stores, banks, and restaurants, catering to and patronized by black clientele. Courtesy, Valentine Museum

employment in skilled jobs often received less pay than their white counterparts.

The black freedman often fared worse as a free laborer than he had as a slave before the war. In 1860 hired-out slaves earned $105 a year plus rations and clothing; in 1867 freedmen working as laborers earned a flat $102 a year. In many cases skilled black laborers were denied union membership. Unions that did admit blacks sometimes negotiated separate contracts for whites. Other unions forbade promotion of blacks. The International Brotherhood of Blacksmiths, Drop Forgers and Helpers (AFL) would not allow black members to be promoted to positions as blacksmiths or as helper-apprentices.

However oppressive, residential segregation and employment discrimination were two of the primary factors in the development of a separate black economy. The desire to improve their

plight and upgrade their employment prompted blacks to start their own businesses and to hire other blacks.

Black residential communities provided the setting. Stores and businesses had a captive clientele in residents who were pleased to work, shop, and pursue entertainment in their own neighborhoods. Usually the business activity centered around one main street within the neighborhood. Second Street in Richmond's Jackson Ward had a number of hotels, restaurants, and movie houses, a law office, a tailor shop, and a bicycle and repair shop. Roanoke had its Henry Street; Norfolk, its Church Street; Portsmouth and Danville, their High Streets. These communities were microcosms of the white urban economy.

If residential communities were the seedbed for black economic development, churches were the fertilizer. For blacks the church was far more than a religious organization; it was the chief organ of social, religious, and economic exchange. At camp meetings, all-night shouts, and Sunday services, black ministers admonished their flocks to "save money," "get an education," "live within your means," and "buy homes." Worshipers were advised to pay poll taxes and to vote. It was at church that the former slaves and their progeny found the moral support and encouragement to help them make their own way.

After the Civil War, blacks left the white-run churches in droves to form numerous independent denominations. Some were direct counterparts of the orthodox religions their former masters had shared with them; others were offshoots or independent churches. Pastors were elected from field hands, coal miners, and former slave preachers. The separation was momentous.

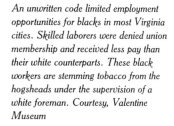

An unwritten code limited employment opportunities for blacks in most Virginia cities. Skilled laborers were denied union membership and received less pay than their white counterparts. These black workers are stemming tobacco from the hogsheads under the supervision of a white foreman. Courtesy, Valentine Museum

While whites excluded blacks from every other aspect of day-to-day life, blacks voluntarily withdrew from the white-dominated churches.

Church leaders were often great fund-raisers, leading drives and campaigns to raise money for their churches. The building and furnishing of a church was a sacred duty in which no expense was to be spared. Some preachers showed extraordinary entrepreneurial talents. One very popular minister was Bishop Daddy Grace. While other pastors solicited contributions for God's work, Bishop Daddy published a magazine and peddled a variety of products under his own label. "Freely you receive," he said, "freely you give." With the proceeds Bishop Daddy built a two-story, stone and steel church in Newport News for his following of 5,000.

Too poor to build new churches, many black congregations purchased churches vacated by whites. By 1900, expanding black urban communities encroached on white neighborhoods, stimulating white flight and driving down property values. "Segregation has been a boon to Negro congregations," observed one writer. "As Negro districts expand, white residents move away, and expensive church buildings go on sale at a fraction of their cost."

By 1930, 48 percent of Virginia's black urban residents as well as 62 percent of its rural blacks were regular churchgoers. Churches would continue to play a powerful role in the economic development of the black community, providing the foundation and the voice of civic reform.

Thomas Jefferson's wish to educate "every description of our citizens from the richest to the poorest" had yet to be fulfilled by the end of Reconstruction. Although education was theoretically available to every Virginian, higher education for blacks in the public system was virtually unknown.

Even before emancipation, schools for blacks existed in Virginia. And the Freedmen's Bureau had provided education for approximately 50,000 black Virginians. By 1880 Virginia had 1,256 black schools, staffed mostly by

In March 1878 the Reverend John Jasper, minister of Sixth Mount Zion Baptist Church in Richmond, Virginia, preached his "Sun Do Move" sermon which challenged Galileo's observations on planetary motion. So great was his oration that audiences almost unanimously agreed with him. Jasper preached this sermon to white and black audiences in Philadelphia, Baltimore, Washington, D.C., and throughout Virginia. Courtesy, Valentine Museum

white teachers. Yet it would be 45 years before Virginia would have its first accredited black public high school. In a state whose constitution provided for education for all, black Virginians found that their opportunities for advanced education were severely limited. White politicians denied that blacks needed education beyond the primary level. Eager to move ahead, blacks sought ways to provide further education for their own.

Missionary societies and other church organizations created schools to supplement public facilities which would provide higher learning for blacks. For instance, Norfolk Mission College, founded with the support of the United Presbyterian Church of North America, provided four years of Latin study, Bible courses, English, science, mathematics, history, home economics, and industrial arts. Tuition was 50 cents a month, charged only to those who could afford it. By the 1880s, Virginia had three institutions of higher learning for blacks.

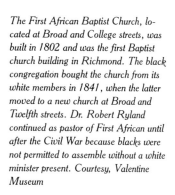

The First African Baptist Church, located at Broad and College streets, was built in 1802 and was the first Baptist church building in Richmond. The black congregation bought the church from its white members in 1841, when the latter moved to a new church at Broad and Twelfth streets. Dr. Robert Ryland continued as pastor of First African until after the Civil War because blacks were not permitted to assemble without a white minister present. Courtesy, Valentine Museum

In some cases the students themselves pitched in to raise funds for their schools. Students at Hampton Institute, chartered in 1869 to provide higher education for "young people without distinction of color," raised substantial amounts of money. When a $20,000 donation from the Freedmen's Bureau in the early 1870s didn't cover the cost of a building, the Hampton Institute Singers brought in another $20,000 through a performance tour of 500 concerts in seven states and Canada.

Schools were often built on land bought by community groups or donated by landowners. Churches, unions, lodges and other organizations generated funds for these black schools which were referred to interchangeably as "institutes," "colleges," and "universities."

A number of funds established by individuals in the North benefited Virginia's black students. The Slater Fund, the Jeanes Negro Rural School Fund, and the Phelps-Stokes Fellowship were just a few of the foundations dedicated to the education of blacks. Yet black schools would continue to suffer from underfinancing well into the twentieth century. As late as 1939, 62 percent of black public schools in Virginia had only one room and one teacher.

Even before the Civil War, blacks were active in a variety of businesses. Entrepreneurs were divided into two groups: free blacks who had accumulated through labor the capital to establish their own businesses, and slaves who

parlayed their plantation skills into marketable services. In some cases the proceeds of these efforts were used to purchase freedom. Larger cities with concentrations of blacks supported black-owned labor and service enterprises such as barbershops, restaurants, caterers, and undertakers. While undertakers stayed within color lines, black caterers were especially popular among the white well-to-do. Many survived the Civil War and its aftermath.

Reconstruction saw the expansion of black business into other areas. Butchers, clothiers, boot makers, mechanics, and draymen ran flourishing businesses. By the 1880s, the black entre-

preneur was no longer a rarity, and the barbershop and the pool room were no longer the only black businesses. Blacks competed in numerous areas of commercial enterprise, including building and loan and land improvement businesses.

Racial discrimination drove blacks together. Black neighborhoods became microcosms of the cities in which they existed, providing necessities as well as niceties to a clientele which would otherwise be forced to travel to distant business districts for goods and services. Blacks entered the commercial sector in increasing numbers. As early as 1890 black merchants

Blacks fill every available seat and crowd into the aisles to hear the sermon in this Harper's Weekly *engraving of the interior of the First African Baptist Church in Richmond. Courtesy, Virginia State Library*

numbered 1,068 in Virginia. By 1899, Richmond was one of only 20 cities in the country with 20 or more black businesses of considerable size. Three years later blacks in Hampton owned 20 mercantile establishments as well as 40 to 50 small shops.

By the second decade of the new century, black economic consciousness solidified. In 1913 the National Negro Business League, conceived by Virginia native Booker T. Washington, opened a chapter in Virginia. The league's stated objective was to encourage blacks to develop "their own resources, to establish more business enterprises among themselves, to patronize them for their own racial benefit . . ." Mottoes like "Share your trade with Negroes" and "Don't trade where you can't work" cemented segregation in business while bolstering trade among blacks. Businesses were encouraged to offer services and prices comparable to their white counterparts in an effort to draw trade.

Through the league, business leaders began to exchange ideas and to share knowledge of merchandising, office management, corporation financing, salesmanship, and advertising. "With the growth of the league," observed one black magazine writer, "ignorance and narrow-mindedness are disappearing." By 1919, black Virginians had three insurance companies, nine banks, and five building and loan associations capitalized at a total of $710,000 and gross resources of $407,487.

Black enterprise received extensive support from a black banking system which developed out of the secret societies of slave days. These mutual aid societies also formed the foundation for the life insurance business which would become the largest, longest sustained business conducted by blacks in the United States.

Dating back to the eighteenth century, benevolent societies provided for members in illness and in death from a treasury supported by an initiation fee and small periodic payments from each member. Like the tribal systems of Africa, these societies served as centers for social activities and religious worship. In the event of illness members were provided stipends; in death

After the Civil War, the Freedmen's Bureau opened schools for black children in Virginia. These schools met in black churches and homes, despite difficulties in obtaining adequate teachers and books. Courtesy, Valentine Museum

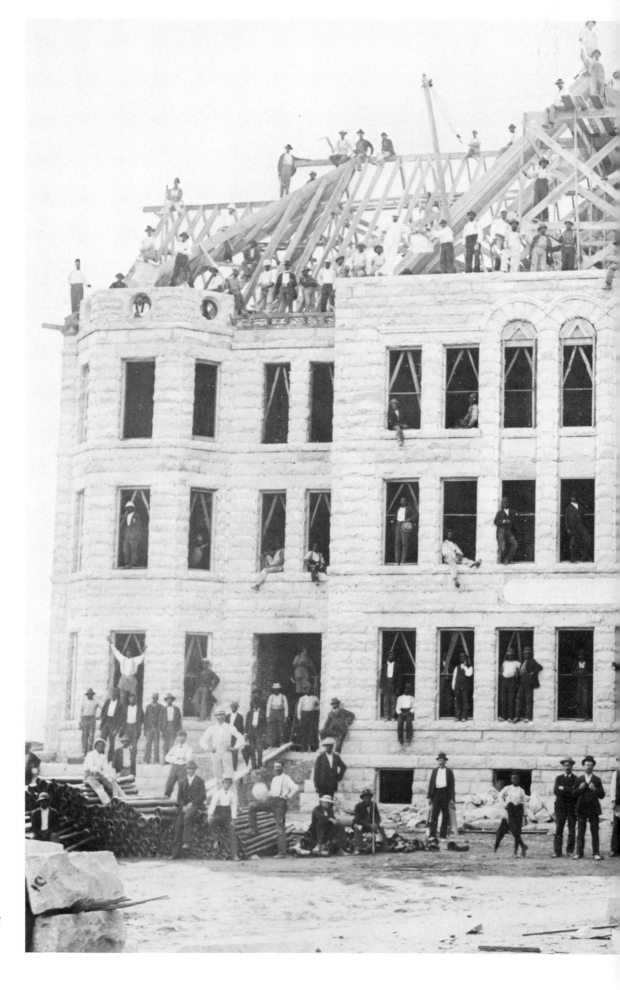

Virginia Union University developed from the Richmond Theological Seminary School for Freedmen, founded in 1865. Incorporated as the Richmond Institute in 1876, the school was moved from Lumpkin's slave jail to the Union Hotel, a former military hospital, in 1870. Soon after its merger with the Wayland Academy of Washington, D.C., construction was begun on Kingsley Hall, shown here. The building is still used by the university as a dormitory. Courtesy, Library of Congress

they were afforded decent, and sometimes lavish, burials. By the time of emancipation, more than 30 such orders existed in Richmond alone.

In the late 1800s, when a number of publications proclaiming blacks to be poor insurance risks caused several white insurance companies to cancel policies held by blacks, these mutual aid societies expanded their insurance offerings. Through this business many organizations amassed large sums of money which they reinvested in land and buildings. As the orders grew, they developed various commercial enterprises and subsidiaries. The Grand Fountain of the United Order of True Reformers that was organized in Richmond in 1883 eventually counted a bank, a weekly newspaper, a retirement home, a building and loan association, and a real estate agency among its subsidiaries.

Of the commercial enterprises in which these secret orders engaged, banking was the most significant. Early in the nineteenth century, society leaders loaned not only their own money, but also the savings entrusted to them by others. Military savings banks established during the Civil War offered blacks their first experience as a group with formal banking practices. After the war the Freedmen's Bank provided banking services to the black community, but its collapse in 1873 left blacks distrustful of banks.

As the black economy expanded in the 1880s, blacks realized the need for credit. Unable to secure loans from most white banks, they sought backing from their mutual aid organizations. Banks became a logical outgrowth for societies seeking investment opportunities. One of the first black banks was the Savings Bank of

Above: The Lancasterian School, based on the educational concepts of English Quaker Joseph Lancaster, opened in Richmond in April 1816. The school operated with only one teacher; older pupils assisted the younger ones. Underwritten by both public and private endowments, the school opened at its permanent site, Marshall Street near Fifteenth, in 1817. In 1871, after public education was established in Richmond, the building became the Valley School for Negroes. Courtesy, Valentine Museum

Facing page: Chartered as a normal and agricultural school, the Hampton Institute, in Hampton, Virginia, was among the first colleges for blacks. Courtesy, Virginia State Library

According to the 1900 Richmond city directory, there were two black-owned drugstores in the city that year. They were the Duval Street Pharmacy and the Thompson and Benson Pharmacy. In 1901 the directory listed George A. Thompson and John M. Benson as the proprietors of both stores. It is not known which of the two stores is depicted here, but it is probably the latter. Courtesy, Library of Congress

the Grand Fountain United Order of True Reformers, established in Richmond in 1887.

Once black banks opened their doors, aspiring entrepreneurs spurned by white banks had a new source of credit. Black banks would be the wellspring for economic development within the community. While one function of white banks was to boost circulation of money, black banks were inaugurated mainly to provide financial services to the black community and to serve as a depository for its money. By encouraging and assisting black entrepreneurs, banks inspired new confidence and spawned a variety of enterprises. By the early 1900s, Richmond, with its four black banks, was a major center of finance for black Virginians. The St. Luke Penny Savings Bank, chartered in 1901 under the leadership of Maggie L. Walker, still exists as the Consolidated Bank and Trust Company, the oldest black-owned and -operated bank in the country today.

By the 1920s, hotels, restaurants, bakeries, barbershops, and undertaking firms were common in the black marketplace. And black commercial enterprise had expanded into entertainment, newspapers, real estate, savings and loans, clothing, and confectionery establishments. These began to comprise significant segments of black commercial activity. In 1927 more than 70,000 black businesses across the country did a volume business of half a million dollars. Richmond was the self-proclaimed "Negro Business Capital of America"—although Atlanta and Durham, North Carolina, made the identical claim—leading the country in the number of black cooperative enterprises.

Blacks enjoyed the pleasures of success. Still excluded from white hotels and resorts, they patronized establishments run for and by blacks. The Rappahannock Hotel and the McGuire Hotel in Fredericksburg were at one time the largest black hotels in the state. And the Bay Shore Hotel near Fort Monroe, with its piazzas, pavilion, and pier, gained national acclaim, drawing patrons from as far away as Indiana, Alabama, and Georgia.

As the century wore on, the legal plight of blacks gradually eased. Although racism persisted, discrimination with legal sanction was on its way out. In 1929, two years after the U.S. Supreme Court ruled that residential segregation ordinances were unconstitutional, Richmond's city council voted to enforce segregation. Yet the U.S. District Court and the U.S. Circuit Court of Appeals each ruled against the measure. Twice the city sought a reversal by the U.S. Supreme Court; twice it was denied.

The black vote strengthened in 1931 when the Virginia Supreme Court of Appeals clamped down on the practice of purposely confounding prospective registrants, requiring electoral officials to be more conscientious in their choices of questions regarding the state constitution. By 1936, the greatest number of blacks since Reconstruction voted in state elections.

Although most white-owned businesses still hired primarily whites, blacks were no longer excluded from municipal jobs. In 1937 the city of Richmond listed 281 black employees on its payroll. In 1941 a federal requirement directed that "all contractors getting defense contracts" could not discriminate against anyone on the basis of race, creed, color, or nationality.

In 1940 Virginia ranked eighth in the United States in black population and third in the number of black businesses. While most black-owned retail businesses were confined to a half-dozen major categories—predominantly restaurants and general merchandise stores— there were nearly 1,000 black-owned stores in Virginia by 1930. By 1938, net sales of black retail businesses amounted to more than $5 million.

Black-operated beauty parlors were the state's fastest-growing business, numbering 300 in 1940. Restaurants were still a major factor in black economy across the state; nearly every town had at least one. Meanwhile, black areas in cities often had two or three for every other kind of business.

More than three dozen black newspapers had been established. The white journalistic community acknowledged the competition by initiating "special colored editions" distributed in black areas.

By the time Chief Justice Earl Warren delivered the Supreme Court's unanimous opinion in 1954 that segregation in public schools was unconstitutional, the era of "Jim Crow" was drawing to a close. Segregation in housing was no longer legal. In the 1960s, laws would be passed to phase out legal discrimination on every level. Ironically, integration would weaken the black business structure that had evolved out of necessity during the years of segregation. As blacks moved into the mainstream, racial loyalty to enterprises owned and operated by blacks diminished. The lines dividing black and white commerce gradually blurred, and Virginia's dual economy was obliterated.

Virginia native Booker T. Washington (1856-1915) conceived the National Negro Business League. A chapter opened in Virginia in 1913. From Cirker, Dictionary of American Portraits, Dover, 1967

Consolidated Bank and Trust Company, formerly the St. Luke Penny Savings Bank, was founded by Maggie L. Walker in November 1903. It is the nation's oldest black-owned bank. Located at 329 North First Street, the bank building was demolished in 1974 and replaced by a more modern structure. Courtesy, Valentine Museum

Maggie Lena Walker

... in twenty-five years, a small spiritless company of men and women is converted into a compact army; a dilapidated dwelling house is replaced by a magnificent office building filled with earnest and zealous workers ... Where once stood a residence, now stands a bank, and the once empty treasury, like the widow's oil, is being constantly increased. The once unknown school teacher becomes a national figure, and your Organization is favorably spoken of from East to West ...

—Reverend T.J. King, then pastor of Fifth Street Baptist Church in Richmond, at a Testimonial of Love in honor of Maggie L. Walker, November 30, 1924

Maggie L. Walker distinguished herself not only in Richmond's black community as a leader of remarkable business acumen, but also in the national business arena as the country's first black bank president and the first woman to hold such a position. As leader of the Independent Order of St. Luke, the founding organization of the first black bank in the nation, Walker transformed the order from an indebted fraternal society careening toward financial disaster into a thriving organization with numerous black-run subsidiaries. By the time of her death in 1935, Walker had emerged as one of this century's great black leaders.

Reputedly the illegitimate issue of a white abolitionist writer and a cook in the household of Union spy Elizabeth Van Lew, Maggie Lena Mitchell was pressed into work at an early age, helping her mother take in laundry to support the family after her stepfather was found murdered. Although her natural father wanted to send her to boarding school in Baltimore, Maggie stayed at home and attended Richmond Colored High and Normal School.

At the age of 14, Maggie joined the Independent Order of St. Luke. She rose quickly through the society's ranks, holding a variety of positions throughout her teen years. After graduating from high school in 1883, she worked as an insurance agent for the Women's Union and attended night classes to learn bookkeeping before returning to her alma mater as a teacher. Three years later she married Armistead Walker, Jr., the son of a locally respected building contractor, and left teaching to raise her family.

Maintaining her commitment to the Independent Order of St. Luke, Walker occupied every office in the organization. As national deputy, she formed councils throughout Virginia and West Virginia; she called for the formation of a juvenile branch of the Independent Order of St. Luke, a division which would grow to a membership of 20,000 during her lifetime; and she oversaw the growth of the society into a vibrant organ which provided revenues, cared for the sick, and buried the dead.

But as the order expanded, its assets diminished and membership flagged. When the society's secretary-treasurer resigned in 1899, the 1,080-member order had only $31.60 in the treasury and $400 in unpaid bills. Walker stepped into the position and assumed the burden of reversing the downward spiral. In March 1902, under her leadership, the *St. Luke Herald* began a publishing career that 25 years later would be acclaimed as one of the best association newspapers in the country. In November 1903 she created the St. Luke's Penny Savings Bank, which would eventually grow into Consolidated Bank and Trust Company, the nation's oldest black-owned bank. As president of the bank Walker customarily stood near the front doors,

welcoming customers. By 1927, membership in the order had grown to 100,000 and assets reached nearly $400,000.

Walker worked her financial miracle despite a series of personal tragedies. The second of her three sons died in infancy. A crippling fall in her late 30s eventually forced her into a wheelchair. One of her sons mortally wounded her husband, mistaking him for a prowler; eight years later that son died. Yet Walker steadfastly continued her life's work.

In addition to her service through the order, Walker made numerous contributions to the development of the black community. She raised money for humanitarian endeavors such as the creation of a school for delinquent girls near Richmond, a nursing home, and a community center. She also served as president of the Virginia NAACP.

In 1912 Walker formed the Council of Colored Women to raise money for various black-promoted organizations. She was instrumental in establishing a tuberculosis sanitarium for blacks at Burkeville and in providing support for the Colored Industrial School at Peaks. By 1927, the club had grown to nearly 1,000 members and had contributed more than $36,000 to black causes.

Until her death in 1935, Walker worked diligently. She had dedicated her life to furthering the progress of the black community. In recognition of her efforts, a Richmond high school was named for her and her home has become a National Historic Landmark.

...she, by whose energy and tireless efforts most of this has been accomplished, may smilingly exclaim, "These are my jewels," and rejoice that she heard and answered the call.

—Reverend T. J. King.

Maggie Lena Walker. Courtesy, Valentine Museum

Even the Great Depression did not halt the growth of the tobacco industry in Richmond. Pictured here is "Tobacco Row" on Cary Street near Twentieth. Courtesy, Dementi-Foster Studios

ROARING TWENTIES, WHISPERING THIRTIES

On the heels of World War I, America entered an age of peace and prosperity. It was the decade of good times, when "flappers," hounded by "parlor snakes," went to "speakeasies." It was a decade of conspicuous consumption, when grocers stocked caviar and pate de foie gras, when millions of Americans bought their first autos, stoves, refrigerators, and radios. Buoyed by unprecedented optimism, the economy rode a seemingly endless wave of euphoria. Stock market speculation became a national obsession; the average prices of common stock doubled. Hints of imminent economic disaster were drowned in the boisterous tide of the decade.

Along with the nation, Virginia roared with the twenties. Bridge parties, suspended during the war, were all the rage. Even the slightest occasion was an excuse for a party for which revelers donned togas, medieval garb, or other thematic costumes. Country clubs were on the rise, and in the horse country of Albemarle County hunt clubs were the choice of the gentry.

Shocked by corsetless females, racy theatrical performances, and moonshine liquor, ministers railed from pulpits about loose practices of the day. Meanwhile, many of the clergy joined their flocks in clubs like the Rotary and Kiwanis,

discarding their conservative attire for stylish business suits.

While the popular passions pandered to indulgence, Virginia's strict regimen of fiscal conservatism and efficient management of public funds stood the state in good stead. With his "pay-as-you-go" system of highway building and a reorganized tax system, Governor Harry Flood Byrd was building a surplus in the state coffers. Virginia's per capita wealth was the greatest of the Southern states. Her percentage of bank suspensions was among the lowest in the nation, while her automobile population and wholesale and retail trade volumes placed her in the top half of the 48 states. While 47 percent of Americans owned their homes, 51 percent of Virginia residents owned theirs. Between 1925 and 1929 Virginians enjoyed sizable increases in wages and salaries as industrial output rose approximately 50 percent.

Where the Civil War had devastated Virginia's economy, World War I had stimulated it. When the United States entered the war, the Hampton Roads area blossomed into one of the country's largest centers for shipping and shipbuilding. It was the site of the headquarters for the Atlantic Fleet as well as of the largest

Black soldiers form up ranks at Camp Lee during World War I. Courtesy, Virginia State Library

army supply base in the country. With a superior railroad system linking it to the rest of America, Hampton Roads served as a conduit for war materials, food, and soldiers to Europe.

The war-induced prosperity spread throughout the state. Virginians shipped thousands of tons of produce, tobacco, petroleum products, and seafood to other American ports. Mines spewed out coal as Pocahontas coal became the preferred fuel for steam-powered engines. Railroads upgraded their track to handle the inflated exports of the Hampton Roads ports. Munitions plants at Hopewell and at Penniman on the York River offered employment to thousands of Virginians, as did Newport News Shipbuilding and Dry Dock Company, which produced merchant and naval ships to transport American soldiers and supplies overseas. Camp Lee, with its facilities for 45,000 men, greatly bolstered commerce in Petersburg and Richmond.

Virginia's transition from an agricultural to an industrial economy was not painless, however. Glutted overseas markets pushed down prices, and lower prices shoved thousands of laborers off the farm. Meanwhile, wrenching changes in the tobacco and timber industries knocked out the props of two mainstays of rural and small-town Virginia. Nature also tormented the Virginia farmer in the twenties. A drought in 1922 was so

severe that car traffic ground dirt roads into powdery dust six inches deep. Three successive bad seasons virtually destroyed the apple and peach harvests of the rich Crozet orchard area. Insects, worms, tornadoes, and hail sabotaged Virginia's agricultural recovery. In 1929 gross farm income was 33 percent lower than it had been a decade before. Rural population and the number of farm acres in use declined as farmers looked to the cities for employment.

Meanwhile, as tobacco cooperatives bought out and consolidated smaller factories, the role of the small manufacturer diminished. Even before the war, Southside manufacturers were being eclipsed by the American Tobacco Company and Reynolds Tobacco Company across the border in North Carolina.

For more than 200 years, Virginians had eschewed the state's vast timber resources to make tobacco the lynch pin of its economy. Yet the lumber industry enjoyed success on a smaller scale. It is believed that a sawmill was in operation in the Old Dominion as early as 1608, cutting wood for the building of homes. Later, timber from the thick, green forests of the Piedmont would be used in shipbuilding and in the production of naval stores. Not until the late nineteenth century, when Northern forests had been depleted, were Virginia's forests industrially harvested.

In 1909, with a significant number of logging operations and large sawmills, Virginia's total production peaked with 2.1 billion board feet. By 1917, the lushest forests of the Coastal Plain and the Piedmont had been plundered, forcing loggers into the mountain ridges to meet the growing demand. The lumber industry thrived, especially as the number of furniture manufacturers increased. By 1930, Virginia's forests were severely depleted.

Large-scale lumbering operations were no longer possible except in virtually inaccessible areas like the Dismal Swamp. Large mills were replaced with small, mobile circular saws which were looked upon as the scavengers of the industry.

The overcutting that had occurred prior to World War I had a long-lasting effect. Ironically, the Great Depression with its low demand for timber helped save the industry by giving Virginia's forests time to rest and replenish. As demand resumed in the late thirties, Virginia's forests were green again and mills were back in operation. By 1942, 2,618 sawmills were turning out 1.2 billion board feet of lumber.

The abundance of Virginia's forestry resources was instrumental in creating what would become another major industry. As the tobacco industry faded, a handful of tobacco growers turned to the furniture industry. In 1902 John D. Bassett gave up tobacco speculating and put his full attention toward making the family sawmill into the Bassett Furniture Company. Four years later Tazewell County native Ancil Davidson Witten and North Carolinian Charles Blackwell Keesee founded the American Furniture Company. By the twenties, these two businesses had spawned six furniture companies, a cotton mill, and two textile and three lumber plants, as well as other smaller industries in the Henry County area.

The Martinsville-Henry County area enjoyed a burst of homegrown entrepreneurial energy the like of which was seen nowhere else in

Munitions plants such as the DuPont Powder Company in Hopewell offered employment to thousands of Virginians during the war. Courtesy, Appomattox Regional Library

"I'D WALK A MILE FOR A CAMEL"

At the turn of the century tobacco was still the leading industry in Virginia. As a result of anti-trust litigation, the American Tobacco Company divided into four firms—Liggett & Myers, R.J. Reynolds, P. Lorillard, and American Tobacco—all of which had plants in Richmond. During the Depression, tobacco cooperatives such as R.J. Reynolds and the American Tobacco Company, headquartered in North Carolina, bought out and consolidated smaller factories while maintaining their operations in Richmond. Courtesy, Valentine Museum

the state in the years between the two world wars. Local merchants, hungry for the employment and payrolls that such industry could provide, pledged backing for new companies, such as Hooker-Bassett and Stanley Furniture Company. By the early twenties, approximately 40 percent of Henry County's population was employed in the manufacture of furniture.

It was not long, however, before textiles came to rival furniture for preeminence in manu-

facture. Since the development of the rail system, millions of pounds of cotton rolled through Virginia, bound for the textile mills of the North. But by the early twenties, Virginia was making use of its cotton connection. In 1919 Chadwick-Hoskins Company of Charlotte, North Carolina, purchased the Martinsville Cotton Mills and boosted local employment. In 1925 William L. Pannill founded Pannill Knitting Company to manufacture underwear. By the end of its first

Virginia's lumber production peaked with 2.1 billion board feet in 1909. Twenty years later, the state's forests were severely depleted. Courtesy, Virginia State Library

The abundance of forestry resources in Virginia allowed for the development of furniture production as a leading industry in the state. Virginia's southern Piedmont area is second only to North Carolina in furniture production. Courtesy, Richmond Newspapers, Inc.

fiscal year, Pannill Knitting Company boasted sales of $207,000. All stock was locally held. In time, Pannill gave rise to Sale Knitting Company and Bassett-Walker Knitting Company. In later years the three knit mills would so dominate the production of fleeced knitwear that Martinsville would boast of being the "Sweatshirt Capital of the World." Martinsville was almost unique among Southern mill towns in hosting so many strong, locally owned firms.

Entire communities grew out of some mill operations. Marshall Field & Company purchased 25 separate tracts of land in Henry County to create its Fieldcrest Towel Mill. Fieldale, with its own grocery stores, post office, furniture store, theater, bank, and school, provided Fieldcrest's 300-plus employees with more than the basic necessities. Fieldale had no

charter and no statutes, no taxes except county property taxes, and no governing body; but when amenities like street repair or lighting were necessary Fieldcrest provided them. Like the 100-house village of Stanleytown, created by Stanley Furniture Company, Fieldale provided a convenient, self-contained residential community for its employees.

Thirty-five miles to the east, Danville, a textile center since the 1880s, had built a city around its Dan River Mills. At the turn of the century, 20 or more tobacco factories provided employment to its citizens. Dan River Flour Mills ground 500 barrels a day by 1913. In the twenties Danville buzzed with the construction of a municipal building, a Masonic Temple, a hotel, and a theater. In Roanoke to the north, textiles were affording similar security; the Viscose

Right: Between the two world wars, the Martinsville-Henry County area enjoyed homegrown entrepreneurial energy in the furniture industry. Local merchants pledged backing for new companies. The Lester Brothers plant, located in Martinsville, began its operations at this time. Courtesy, Richmond Newspapers, Inc.

Below: In 1906 Ancil D. Witten and Charles B. Keesee founded the American Furniture Company in the Henry County area. The American Furniture Company and other furniture plants in and around Martinsville made the city one of the largest furniture-producing centers in the world. By the early 1920s nearly 40 percent of the Martinsville-Henry County population was employed in this industry. Courtesy, Richmond Newspapers, Inc.

Danville, Virginia, a textile center since the 1880s, built a city around its Dan River Mills. This aerial view shows some of the mill buildings in the center and background. In 1963 the Danville plant employed about 9,800 workers, including 1,100 blacks. Courtesy, Richmond Newspapers, Inc.

Corporation, established in 1917, employed 70 more people at its "silk mill."

The revision of the Virginia tax structure under Byrd attracted new industries to the state. In fiscal year 1927, Virginia surpassed all other states in industrial development with an infusion into the state's capital of $265 million. Textile and chemical producers came in droves, attracted by the abundant water supply, labor supply, and good transportation system. Tubize-Chatillon Corporation opened a rayon plant at Hopewell, and Industrial Rayon Corporation opened at Covington. After the arrival of the E.I. du Pont de Nemours Company in 1929, with its rayon plant in the suburbs of Richmond and another in Waynesboro, Virginia became the leading state in the nation in the manufacture of artificial silk yarn. By 1930, Virginia was responsible for one-third of the country's—or, one-ninth of the world's—rayon production.

When the Depression hit, every industry would feel its effects—all except for one: bootlegging. Virginia's outspoken Anti-Saloon League began campaigning against the demon rum as early as 1901. When the league joined forces with the Women's Christian Temperance Union in their fight to control the sale and consumption of liquor, it convinced the General Assembly to tighten alcohol restrictions. As a result more than 500 saloons across the state closed.

By 1916, Virginia's "drys" had gained enough sway to institute statewide prohibition—three years before the Eighteenth Amendment prohibited the manufacture, sale, or transportation of liquor throughout the country. When nationwide prohibition nullified Virginia's One Quart Law (allowing residents to buy from out-of-state one quart of liquor, a gallon of wine, or three gallons of beer), bootlegging became big business.

Bootlegging was a "social crime" and a profitable one at that. Aspiring purveyors could buy a half-gallon of moonshine for three dollars or less and sell it for 20 cents per two-ounce shot, making more than 100 percent profit on the deal. Not everyone made or sold liquor, but nearly everyone bought it. Country club conversations often centered around how to contact one's bootlegger. Poor brewing or distilling techniques caused explosions, and loud booms commonly could be traced to closets or basements in the most respectable homes. Despite strong "dry" sentiment across the Old Dominion, many leading citizens had few inhibitions about violating the prohibition law.

Bootlegging knew no class distinctions. From the poorest to the wealthiest, Virginians illegally bought liquor. During the twenties, the "blind tiger"—where liquor could be purchased without seeing the seller—came into being. Speakeasies, which filled the function of saloons as well as many restaurants, were popular meeting places. Locked doors with peepholes replaced the swinging doors of saloons.

Business was conducted in backrooms, basements, or first-floor flats. In Richmond the heart of the bootlegging district was conveniently located several blocks west of its business district. Folks in Alexandria reportedly floated kegs of liquor in the river and tethered them to the shore. The Wickersham Commission reported that 99 percent of Franklin County was connected, directly or indirectly, with the illegal manufacture or distribution of "white mule." Jewelers and department stores all over the state featured stylish hip-flasks for personal consumption.

By the mid-1920s, raids on suppliers were routine. These were not all good-natured affairs. In many cases, especially in moonshine country, gunplay and bloodshed often accompanied the seizure of mountain stills. Headlines in the Charlottesville *Progress* told of "Another Killing in the Foothills of the Blue Ridge." Others were more sporting: "Over 29 Gallons of Christmas Cheer Poured Into Sewer At Police Station." In less volatile areas of the state, police bartered confiscated liquor on the sly.

With the Layman Act of 1924, which allowed the most strident measures, including entrapment, in the pursuit of a bootlegging arrest, liquor dealers invented numerous ploys to avoid being caught. One Roanoke purveyor used a trap whereby a mason jar was tilted for

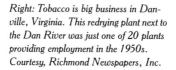

Right: Tobacco is big business in Danville, Virginia. This redrying plant next to the Dan River was just one of 20 plants providing employment in the 1950s. Courtesy, Richmond Newspapers, Inc.

Left: Bootlegging was all the rage in Virginia and elsewhere during Prohibition. Stills such as the one shown here began operating even in the most respectable places. Courtesy, Virginia State Library

emptying, then flushed with a stream of water. Some bootleggers outfitted their cars' exhaust pipes with contraptions that emitted thick smoke to blind pursuing officers.

Throughout Prohibition the courts were clogged with dry law violations. Penalties for bootlegging involved a jail sentence and a fine. Those found guilty were barely locked up before a spouse or a cohort was on hand to post bond.

After 17 years of Prohibition, Virginians joined the national tide for repeal. In a dual referendum in 1933, almost twice as many voted for repeal of both federal and state prohibition laws as those who cast their votes in favor of retaining them. Although illicit liquor trafficking did not cease completely, related killings and arrests dropped off significantly.

When the stock market crashed in 1929, Virginians thought it was a temporary setback. As the resulting depression seared America's economic landscape, Virginia staved off its harshest effects for two years. Buffeted by the financial stability of the Byrd Administration as well as by recent industrial development, Virginia rested on sturdy ground when the economy plunged.

The stock market crash failed to dampen Virginia optimism. With their own peculiar brand of hubris, Virginians considered themselves exempt from doom. Before leaving office Governor Byrd commented, "The close of the year 1929 sees Virginia facing a bright future. Never, probably in the long history of the Old Dominion has she faced a destiny more filled with promise." In an article entitled "A Billion Dollar Manufacturing State by 1930," economist James E. Ward wrote that: "this State is even now entering into an expansion of industrial activities on a scale never before equalled in its history."

As year-end statistics rolled in it looked as if the optimists might be right: Norfolk & Western announced 1929 to be its best year since 1926, with a net income of $11,059,571 over 1928. Roanoke's cost of living was the lowest in two years. Norfolk retail merchants noted that Christmas sales were up from the preceding year,

and a group of Richmond industrialists announced construction plans to the tune of $15 million for the coming year. But the national picture was ominous. Steel operations were running at 50 percent capacity; automobiles were being stockpiled; freight tonnages were sliding; and commercial failures were rampant.

The nation's somber mood was reflected in everything from farm prices to fashions. Ballroom dancing replaced the wilder dances of the Roaring Twenties. Stutz Bearcats and cries of "whoopee" died out. Gloom soon gave way to desperation. Banks closed. Bread lines grew longer, and able-bodied men sold apples on the street. It was an oft-repeated joke that when someone registered at a hotel, the clerk wryly asked, "Do you want the room for sleeping or for jumping?"

With low-bonded indebtedness and low taxes, Virginia was better equipped to face the Depression than other states. State finances were not overextended and the industrial expansion of the twenties provided a cushion. With major industries of high demand and necessity—tobacco and textiles—Virginia was less vulnerable to depression. An income well-balanced between agriculture, manufacturing, and trade was as hearty a defense as state officials could hope for.

Although it became apparent that the Depression was no passing phase in the economic cycle, Virginia weathered its earliest days admirably. Her industries were indispensable to the consumer: food, clothing, and cigarettes. (People didn't stop smoking; they simply bought cheaper brands.) Richmond's well-balanced economy and its stable tobacco industry buoyed that city. Lynchburg's sound banks and construction start-ups fueled her economy. In Norfolk, where the navy spent $20 million a year, conditions were also relatively stable. While banks around the country closed their doors, not one Norfolk bank closed.

A severe nationwide drought in the summer of 1930 seemed to be a harbinger of doom. Virginia's rainfall for the year registered at 60 percent of normal. In the Shenandoah Valley a 42-day dry spell ruined crops. Virginius

Dabney, then correspondent for the *New York Times*, noted: "The usually fertile Shenandoah Valley ... almost looked ... as if Sheridan had just finished his devastating ride through it." Dried-out grazing land in Northern and Southwest Virginia affected the livestock trade. And truck crops in the Tidewater were choked as well. The tobacco crop was the meagerest since 1876. Farmers feared the lowest crop production since the earliest figures recorded in 1860.

Yet Virginia's agriculture, like her industry, was better prepared to meet the Depression than other states. Crop diversity allowed for a balanced farm income. Proximity to eastern markets gave some stability to prices. With a high percentage of subsistence farmers requiring little or no income to maintain their exiguous existence, a great number of Virginia farmers would be little affected by the consequences of the crash. While farm tenancy posed problems in the tobacco-growing regions of the state, Virginia had the third-lowest ratio of tenants to farmers in the U.S. Furthermore, the state ranked sixth lowest in farms under mortgage. In fact, as economic conditions worsened, Virginians returned to the soil in great numbers to feed their families. Between 1930 and 1935 the number of farmers rose 16 percent.

As the stock market continued to plunge throughout 1930, manufacturing production nationwide dipped below 1928 levels. Although the lumber and flour milling industries suffered, Virginia remained seemingly aloof from the thunderous disaster. Industrial output dipped from $897 million to $814 million, a modest decline. And while the production value of tobacco declined slightly, the shipbuilding, fertilizer, and chemical industries increased the value of their output in 1930. Although unemployment in the Old Dominion rose to 50,000 that year, the percentage of those out of work was far lower than the national average.

The Norfolk & Western Railroad had a very good year in 1929, despite the national economic picture. Shown here is a passenger train on the main line circa 1930. Courtesy, Virginia State Library

Following the 1920-1921 organization of Virginia farmers into the Virginia Crop Improvement Association, the marketing of certified seed became a problem for the association's 500 members. As a result, the Southern States Cooperative was formed in 1923 to serve the farmers' seed requirements. The cooperative has since grown into one of the largest farm-related operations in the United States. Shown here are the feed mill and grain receiving station at First and Hull streets in Richmond. Photo by John Salmon

By 1931, Virginia began to feel the crushing weight of the Depression. Industrial output plunged 17 percent to $679 million, pushing up unemployment across the state. Even Norfolk, where shipping maintained a steady pace, declared that its rolls had doubled. During the first seven months of the year, unemployment in cities and towns rose 15 percent. The most extreme situations were in industrial centers or in the Southside tobacco region. The cities of Roa-

noke, Richmond, and Petersburg and the counties of Alleghany, Wise, Halifax, and Pulaski took the hardest blows. Half of Halifax's work force was unemployed, and coal production in Wise had dropped to three percent of normal levels, leaving hundreds of coal miners hungry.

Norfolk laid off firefighters, police officers, and garbage collectors. Several teachers were fired; others took salary cuts. A cutback at the Viscose plant in Roanoke affected 4,500 workers. In some areas college graduates were reduced to begging on the streets. Yet Virginia's 19 percent rate paled next to the nation's 30-plus percent.

By the next year, farm prices had dropped to one-half the 1929 figures, and farm cash income was the lowest in 26 years. Wheat sold for 50 cents a bushel, the lowest price in 132 years. Tobacco prices were hacked to $6.63 per 100 pounds, the lowest price since 1920. Prices were so low that farmers could not even meet production costs much less make a profit. Rather than market their crops at such a loss, farmers let them rot.

The state surplus, earmarked for new public buildings, went to meet immediate expenses. In Richmond the Social Service Bureau provided relief to 926 families. Three thousand Hopewell residents ate from a public dispensary. School children in the mountain

Left: President Franklin Delano Roosevelt revived the troubled American economy during the Great Depression by rushing through Congress a number of fiscal and social reform measures and setting up agencies to tackle the reorganization of industry and agriculture. From Cirker, Dictionary of American Portraits, *Dover, 1967*

Below: The West Virginia Pulp and Paper Company, located in Covington, is shown here. Courtesy, Virginia State Library

regions were fed at soup kitchens, and striking mill employees in Danville were near starvation.

Responding to cries of desperation, Governor John Garland Pollard cut state expenditures, which included a 10 percent reduction in his salary. The General Assembly approved a diversion of highway funds to schools and transferred the burden of road repairs to county governments. As a result of the latter, many unemployed Virginians were soon back at work repairing secondary roads. As the relief rolls grew fatter and tax collections shrank, Virginia looked to the federal government for help.

With Franklin Delano Roosevelt's inauguration the country had a New Deal. FDR's Alphabet Soup—which included the AAA, the FCA, the REA, the CCC, the PWA, the WPA, the FERA, and the NRA—fed the nation's hungry, including a quarter million Virginians.

Virginia farmers benefited greatly from the programs. Under the Agricultural Adjustment Administration (AAA), farmers were given acreage allotments and benefit payments in exchange for reduced crop production. By the end of its first year, the AAA had proven its success. With production down 13 million pounds, tobacco had doubled in price. Across the board, crop values, prices, and farm cash income had registered remarkable gains. Also of benefit to the farmer were the Farm Credit Administration (FCA), which coordinated all farm credit activities, and the Rural Electrification Administration (REA). The FCA reduced the number of foreclosures and helped stabilize farm income, while the REA provided electric power to small towns and family farms.

The Civilian Conservation Corps (CCC) and the Works Progress Administration (WPA) provided thousands of Virginians with employment. The Public Works Administration (PWA) was a major supplier of funds for relief in Virginia, providing millions of dollars for various projects, including construction of navy vessels, harbor improvements in Newport News, a hydroelectric plant for Danville, a sewer complex in Arlington, a public housing project in Rich-

mond, and waterworks for Lynchburg. In its first year of operation, the PWA approved $90 million worth of projects in Virginia.

The National Recovery Administration (NRA) aided industrial recovery by allowing businesses to administer their affairs with limited governmental supervision. Wage and hour standards were instituted and, in exchange for their acceptance, antitrust laws were suspended. Thousands of Virginia workers received wage raises, and State Drive Chairman Mason Manghum estimated that the NRA was responsible for the rehiring of 10,000 Virginians in its first three months.

By 1934, however, the NRA had outlived its usefulness. Consumers, industry, and labor decried the resulting high prices and the reluctance of business to recognize labor. Wage and hour violations were numerous; many employers had subscribed to the NRA's policies on paper but not in spirit. The NRA's code deficiencies as well as its lack of enforcement power laid the groundwork for its demise. In 1935 the United States Supreme Court declared the NRA and its wage fixing unconstitutional.

In Virginia the Federal Emergency Relief Administration (FERA) carried the brunt of relief appropriations, doling out more than $26 million around the state, primarily for school improvements, malaria control, airport projects, parks, and streets. While FDR's New Deal provided greatly needed relief, Virginia's relief rolls were smaller than those of almost any other state.

In 1933 the number of Virginians on relief declined noticeably: on a national unemployment census, Virginia showed the second lowest percentage in the country of people on relief. Employment across the state was up 20 to 25 percent. The value of manufacturing output climbed to $616 million, increasing the Old Dominion's percentage of U.S. manufacturing

With the opening of the E.I. du Pont de Nemours Company in Ampthill in 1929, Virginia became the leading state in the manufacture of artificial silk yarn. A year later, Virginia was responsible for one-third of the nation's rayon production. This aerial view shows the plant at Bellwood just south of Richmond. Courtesy, Richmond Newspapers, Inc.

production from 1.06 percent in 1929 to 1.62 percent. By 1935, Virginians had put their starving years behind them.

Virginia's economy was in many ways better than it had been before the Depression. In 1937 all manufacturing indices of 1929 had been surpassed. Virginia led the nation in increased value of industrial products. The value of manufactured goods in Virginia had increased 31 percent, while their value nationwide had decreased 11 percent over the same period. The state's per capita wealth increased 4 percent during that time, while the country's declined 20 percent. Wages and salaries were higher and more people were employed.

In 1939 the Census of Manufactures showed that Virginia was responsible for one-quarter of the nation's production of rayon yarn, nylon, and cellophane. Coal production reached a decade high with 13.2 million short tons. Tobacco, paper, and pulp products, furniture and metal machinery manufacturing, and automobile and railroad repair work were making similarly significant strides.

Virginia had weathered the painful years and emerged with a sizable surplus in its general fund and the lowest state and local debt per capita of any state in the country. A stable economy, plentiful work force, and good transportation system made the state attractive to new industry. Its favorable tax system, relatively low wage rates, plentiful raw materials, and good climate enticed businesses to settle in the state. Virginia was on the verge of its second industrial boom.

Between 1935 and 1940, 510 new manufacturing plants began operations in the state. A $500,000 silk printing and dyeing plant went up in Richmond; a $1 million insulation-board plant appeared in Jarratt; Franklin became home to a $2.5 million pulp and paper plant; and Pearisburg in Giles County was selected as the site for the $10 million American Cellulose and Chemical Company plant.

With industrial output up 44 percent over 1929 levels, Richmond was now the fastest growing industrial center in the country. Unlike most other industrial centers, Richmond had weathered the Depression well. The expansion of the tobacco industry buffeted the city from the harshest effects, as did the arrival of new businesses in the twenties.

The twenties had brought a flurry of business to Richmond. Southern States Cooperative, currently one of the largest owners and operators of farm-related industries, located its headquarters in Richmond. Harry Marks Clothing Company, later Friedman-Marks Clothing Company, began manufacturing its garments in the city in 1925. Two years later Southern Biscuit Company came to town. By the onset of the Depression, the E.I. du Pont de Nemours Company had opened a huge rayon yarn plant on the city's outskirts and Reynolds Metals Company acquired the Lehmaier, Schwartz & Company foil works.

Richmond became an important retail center. Ranking seventh in the South in retail sales in 1939, the city was responsible for 20 percent of Virginia's retail sales. The financial district grew as well. The 1929 Economic Census notes that 24 financial institutions and 21 insurance companies had made the city their headquarters.

Tobacco manufacturing boomed. The American Tobacco Company manufactured 100 million cigarettes a day at its two plants. Leggett and Myers and Larus and Brother expanded their operations. Philip Morris & Company, a firm of British origin, began manufacturing cigarettes in Richmond in 1929. By 1940, a third of all U.S.-made cigarettes were produced in the city.

Served by six railroads, two steamship lines, three inner-city transport lines and, after 1927, a major airport, Richmond was more than hospitable to business. In a decade the volume of Richmond's industrial output had increased 59 percent. The city had reestablished its position at the forefront of the nation's commercial development, ranking second among the country's 19 major industrial centers.

Except in isolated pockets, such as the homegrown furniture and textiles firms in Martinsville, Virginia did not owe its progress to entrepreneurial genius. The strength of the state's economy rested in its conservative governmental policies, low-cost labor, weak labor unions, low taxes—in sum, its favorable business climate. Virginians could take much comfort from their superior economic performance. But there were hidden weaknesses in the state's economic growth.

To an unusual degree Virginia's was a branch-plant economy; the important decisions concerning hirings, firings, expansions, and shutdowns were made in the centers of Northern capitalism. Virginia's economic growth also was tied to the unprecedented growth in the federal government. Northern Virginia became the bedroom community for federal employees in Washington; Hampton Roads owed its growth far more to military mobilization than to its natural advantages as a commercial center. Even so, while the rest of the nation was clawing its way out of the Depression, it was hard to argue with prosperity.

Inside the Philip Morris plant on "Tobacco Row," men operated the machines that loaded cigarettes into packs, which women then sorted into cartons. With machines to speed the work, some plants could turn out millions of cigarettes a day. Courtesy, Dementi-Foster Studios

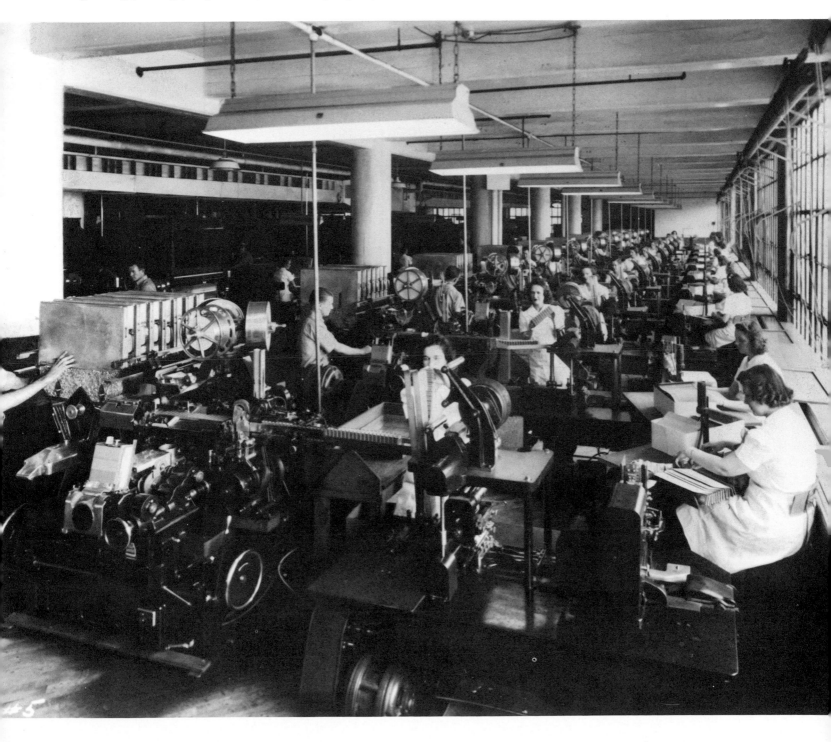

Newport News grew from a small fishing village to an industrial center with the founding of Newport News Shipbuilding and Dry Dock Company by Collis P. Huntington. The company employed nearly 5,000 workers. By the 1890s it began building ships for the United States Navy. This 1925 photograph shows the USS Virginia under construction. Courtesy, Valentine Museum

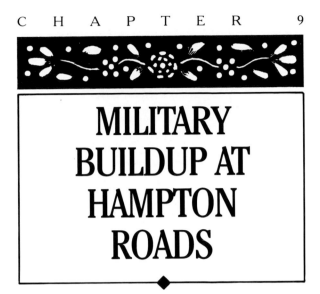

MILITARY BUILDUP AT HAMPTON ROADS

Since the settlers arrived in Jamestown in 1607, war has been the single most influential factor in the development of Hampton Roads. With each successive altercation, population and commerce jumped, pumped up by seamen, soldiers, dock laborers, and shipbuilders. Today Hampton Roads is Virginia's second largest population center, home to one of the nation's finest ports, a vigorous shipbuilding industry, and a vast military establishment.

The stretch of water at the confluence of the James River and the Chesapeake Bay is one of the finest natural harbors in the world. Not only does it offer superb protection from storms, it also permits access by ships with 45-foot drafts—all but the largest cargo carriers and oil tankers. By the mid-eighteenth century, ports had been established in Hampton on the peninsula and Norfolk on the south channel. Hampton Roads was thick with commerce during the Revolutionary War when Virginia's little navy patrolled its waters.

The ports of Hampton Roads survived the Revolution, only to fall subject to future battles. The War of 1812 had a shattering effect as the British blockade and the U.S. embargo in 1813 brought trade to a standstill. Counteracting the

negative effects of the war, the federal government strengthened fortifications and expanded the Gosport Navy Yard in Norfolk for the construction of heavy war vessels.

By the mid-nineteenth century, Hampton Roads had gained prominence as a major East Coast port. With the development of Virginia's rail network, produce from all over the state, as well as from North Carolina, came to Hampton Roads for export. Local boat builders averaged 1,000 tons of shipping a year. And the U.S. Navy continued to pump money into the area, spending an estimated $1 million a year on the navy yard alone.

The Civil War interrupted the region's growth. Federal troops burned the Gosport Navy Yard—by then the largest in the nation—before surrendering it to the Confederate states in 1861. The next year, evacuating Confederate soldiers burned it again. The ironclads *Virginia* and *Monitor* battled for control of Hampton Roads. Although the duel was a tactical draw, the *Virginia* withdrew, leaving the Northern fleet in control. Shut off from trade by the Northern blockade, commerce withered. By the war's end, Norfolk's docks, once the center of commercial activity, were frighteningly quiet.

RULES
For the Regulation of the Navy-Yard at Gosport.

IT being essential to the Public Interest, that the Officers, Workmen, and others employed in the Service of the United States, at the NAVY-YARD at GOSPORT, should conduct themselves with Order and Regularity in the execution of their several Duties, whereby the same may be carried on with Economy and Dispatch—I DO HEREBY ORDER AND DIRECT, That all Officers, Workmen, and others of every denomination whatsoever, employed therein, do conform themselves to the following REGULATIONS as a GENERAL RULE for their conduct.

OFFICERS.

Each Officer will receive from the Constructor, such Orders and Instructions, from time to time, as may be judged best for the Public Service, to which he must undeviatingly adhere: He will have such persons placed under his directions as may be deemed necessary; he will direct them in the performance of such parts of the works as he may entrusted with, which it will be his duty to forward by all the means in his power, and see that the same be properly and efficiently executed, at the smallest expence possible.

He will discourage those placed under his direction, from quarrelling, committing excesses of any kind, or absenting themselves from work. He will use his utmost endeavors to protect all public property placed under his charge, or otherwise disposed. It is expected, that he shall attend to the business of the Navy Yard in preference to any other whatever, and shall on no account absent himself therefrom, without leave, except in case of sickness, or other unavoidable cause. He will be careful to check each person under his direction, for the time he may be absent from his work; and observe those who shew an idle disposition; and in all cases to report transgressors.

ARTIFICERS, LABOURERS, &c. &c.

All persons on being entered in the Navy-Yard, will report their real Names to the Constructor and Clerk, that they may be inserted in the roll.

Such Wages will be allowed to each Workman or other person, as the Constructor may judge his qualifications entitle him to receive, which shall be paid on the Saturday of each week, (or as soon after as can be done) to himself, or the person who may be qualified to receive the same, as circumstances may be.

To each Workman who may be sent on board any ship or vessel to work, the same lying below Fort Norfolk, one quarter of a dollar per day, will be allowed him in addition to his Wages at the Yard; to those who may work on board any ship or vessel above that place, the same wages will be paid him, as if he had actually worked in the yard, and no more.

As soon as possible after his name has been entered on the roll, he will be placed under the direction of a Quarterman, or other Officer, as occasion may require, to whom he will apply for instructions respecting his work, &c. and from whose orders he shall in no wise deviate, (unless directed so to do by a Superior Officer) but in all respects he is to execute the same with diligence, care, fidelity, economy and dispatch.

The time of Daily Labour will be from Sun-rise until Sun-set: The commencement and termination of which will be noticed by Ringing of the Yard-Bell, as well as at Breakfast and Dinner; for the former three quarters of an Hour in Winter, and one Hour in Summer will be allowed; for the latter, one Hour in Winter and two in Summer: The Winter to be considered from the first of September to the first of May; and the Summer from the first of May to the first of September following. N. B. From Sun-rise to Noon is to be understood as comprising one half a Day's Work; and from Noon to Sun-set the remaining half—and he shall not at any time quit his Work, before the Bell rings for that purpose, without leave of his Officer, unless compelled thereto by rain or other unavoidable cause.

To perform his work in the best and most expeditious manner, he shall provide himself with such Tools as the officer placed over him may deem requisite for his occupation;—He shall not make use of Tools belonging to another person, without his leave, neither shall he conceal, injure, nor destroy them.

He shall not loiter at his work, nor set an example of idleness to others by unnecessary conversations or otherwise—He shall neither Game, Quarrel, give abusive Language, get Intoxicated, or insult any Person whatsoever within the Yard, nor when absent on Public Duty.

He is not to perform work for individuals during the hours of Work, without leave being first obtained; and it will be expected that he shall not leave his Work to perform Military Duty without leave (except in case of emergency) unless the Fine for absence shall exceed the amount of a Day's Work.

He shall not wilfully Waste, Destroy, nor Embezzle any part of the Public Property, nor suffer others to do it; and it is strictly forbidden to cut up any serviceable Timber, Boards, &c. for Chips—He is not to break the Fence of the Yard, or Enclosures, nor take off any Boards, &c. from the same, nor suffer others to do it, without leave being first obtained from the principal Officer at that time in the Yard.

In case of Fire happening in the Yard, or to any Ship of War, or other Public Vessel lying in the vicinity thereof, it will be required of him to use every endeavour in his power to extinguish the same, and preserve and protect all Public property that may in any wise be endangered thereby—And it is strictly ordered that no Fires shall be kindled in the Yard, but at such places as may be appointed for that purpose.

He will be accountable for such Tools, Implements, &c. belonging to the United States, as he may occasionally be furnished with, and in case they are lost, or wilfully destroyed, the amount of their value will be deducted from his wages.

If any Person finds himself insulted, or personally aggrieved, he is required to make his case known to the Constructor, or in his absence to the Superior Officer, who will take the same into consideration, and afford him such redress as circumstances may dictate.

As it may happen that Workmen and others, whose residence is distant from the Yard, may have occasion to quit their Work on Saturday Afternoons at an early hour, those will have the time noticed, and when the same shall amount to a Days Work, it will be deducted from their wages.

A PRINTED COPY of the preceding "Rules for the Regulation of the NAVY YARD," shall be hung up in the CLERK'S OFFICE, or some other conspicuous place, for the perusal of all Persons concerned; and no plea will be admitted of ignorance of any part thereof.

Given under my hand at the NAVY YARD, Gosport, this   day of   18

JOSIAH FOX, Navy Constructor and Superintendant.

NORFOLK: PRINTED BY WILLETT AND O'CONNOR.

Right: These are the earliest extant regulations for the Gosport Navy Yard, circa 1800. Courtesy, Virginia State Library

Below: The Gosport Navy Yard, shown here in a bird's-eye view, was burned twice during the Civil War—once by federal troops and once by evacuating Confederate troops. From Frank Leslie's Pictorial History of the War of 1861-62. Courtesy, Virginia State Library

Norfolk was a big cotton port by the mid-1870s. Courtesy, Norfolk Redevelopment and Housing Authority

Despite wartime starvation and suffering, the cities of Hampton Roads revived with a vigor not seen since the days before Jefferson's Embargo of 1807. By the close of Reconstruction, port activity had attracted thousands of tradespeople, shipbuilders, laborers, and others seeking work in port-related jobs. The populations of Norfolk and Portsmouth swelled to two and three times their numbers of a half century earlier.

Shipbuilding became the driving force behind the region's economy, employing some 7,000 workers by the turn of the century. The industry's first boom came with the Spanish-American War as the Gosport Navy Yard and the Newport News Shipbuilding and Dry Dock Company, a private company founded in 1866 by railroad magnate Collis P. Huntington, sped to build the U.S. fleet "Manifest Destiny."

Throughout history, wars shaped the economy of Hampton Roads. Its shipyards would bustle again with the outbreak of hostilities in Korea in 1950. Its naval and military installations would become a gateway to America's involvement in Vietnam. But none of America's military conflicts had quite the effect of the world wars.

With a vast harbor and railroad ties to the interior, Hampton Roads became the focal point of the United States' participation in World War I. The advantages of both ocean and rail traffic made the region the ideal site for the country's largest army supply base and the headquarters of the navy's Atlantic Fleet.

With every available local worker employed in the construction of military installations, agents scoured the nation for laborers. Lured by tales of sky-high wages, employment seekers came from all over the country to cash in on the building craze. "If you see any unbelievably wide-brimmed hat," noted the *Virginian Pilot*, "there is either a Texan or a Kentuckian under it."

Overseas and coastal trade burgeoned. Guns, food, and war materials from around the country funneled through Hampton Roads for export to Europe. To better handle the inflated wartime exports, railroads and port facilities were upgraded and expanded. In 1917, as the United States entered the war, exports from Norfolk and Portsmouth alone totaled nearly 11 million tons.

America looked to the shipyards of Hampton Roads to create the world's best navy. Shipbuilding sparked the local economy, employing thousands in the construction and overhaul of the nation's warships. Between 1917 and 1919, the payroll at Newport News Shipbuilding and

Dry Dock Company rose from 7,600 to 12,500, while employment at the Portsmouth Navy Yard reached 11,000. By 1918, employment at Norfolk Shipbuilding and Dry Dock Company had reached 20 times the level of two years before.

As war vessels, both foreign and domestic, sought its ports for repairs and rest, Hampton Roads thundered with activity. Hundreds of thousands of soldiers and sailors came to the Hampton Roads region during the war. For some it was a way station en route to a European platform. Others brought their families to put down roots. Still others came for a short leave, overtaxing filled-to-capacity housing. As the population ballooned, a housing shortage ensued. Servicemen were hard put to find living space for their families. Workers crowded into vacant rooms. Charges of profiteering were rampant. Finally the government responded with the emergency construction of a handful of residential developments.

To serve the booming war economy, private industry built new plants and expanded old ones. The American Chain Company, the British-American Tobacco Company, and Linde

Air Products began operations in Hampton Roads, as did E.I. du Pont de Nemours and Company, Virginia Coal and Navigation Company, and Standard Oil Company. The Chesapeake and Potomac Telephone Company doubled its exchange, adding 10,000 new phones to accommodate the skyrocketing population.

Just as war had quickened the pulse of the Hampton Roads economy, peace signaled a downturn. Although the volume of exports diminished rapidly, it was still 10 times larger than in 1914. Coal shipments fell, yet millions of tons of the fuel were dumped as waste each month over Hampton Roads' piers. Grain exports flourished and Hampton Roads was on its way to becoming the world's greatest tobacco port. Cotton, flour, starch, lumber, and livestock left the docks, bound for Germany, Italy, Great Britain, and Japan. While exports fell off, imports rose, constituting 15 percent of the port's foreign trade in 1928, compared to 4 percent a decade earlier.

Shipbuilding sustained the sharpest blow. Operating at top speed with 23,000 workers at the war's end, the industry suffered a direct hit. Three years later the Conference for the Limita-

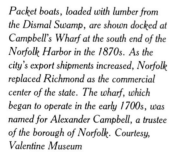

Packet boats, loaded with lumber from the Dismal Swamp, are shown docked at Campbell's Wharf at the south end of the Norfolk Harbor in the 1870s. As the city's export shipments increased, Norfolk replaced Richmond as the commercial center of the state. The wharf, which began to operate in the early 1700s, was named for Alexander Campbell, a trustee of the borough of Norfolk. Courtesy, Valentine Museum

tion of Armaments cut even deeper into the industry, promptly halting tens of millions of dollars worth of work in progress. Employment at the shipyards plunged.

The mere threat of war, however, was enough to reenergize Hampton Roads. In the 1930s President Roosevelt launched a major naval shipbuilding and improvement plan. The Hampton Roads shipyards began to hum again, preparing to rebuild the Pacific Fleet. Under the naval improvement plan, new construction employed 15,000 workers at Norfolk's naval base alone.

By 1940, unemployment in Hampton Roads was only 8.6 percent, significantly lower than Virginia's 9.5 percent rate and way below the country's 14.4 percent rate. The government was the largest employer, followed by retail and wholesale trade and services. Even before the war, with its 400,000 inhabitants accounting for only 15 percent of the state's population, Hampton Roads comprised 22 percent of Virginia's wholesale trade, 21 percent of its retail trade, and 25 percent of its total service receipts for 1940.

As the nation braced for war, the military presence expanded rapidly. The navy outgrew the Norfolk base and spilled east into Princess Anne County and west nearly to Williamsburg. By the war's end, the area's 10 prewar military establishments would number 26, and their personnel would increase seventeenfold.

The government spent more than $267 million constructing nonmanufacturing army and navy establishments and another $107 million on manufacturing plants. As with World War I the building boom of World War II drew thousands of workers from all over the country. This time growth did not stop until the entire Hampton Roads area was converted into a huge construction camp. The Camp Peary project alone brought 10,000 workers to a community whose inhabitants had numbered less than 3,000 before the war.

As war workers and military personnel poured in, the population soared. During the first two years of the war, some 28,000 families

moved to the region; by 1943, the civilian population alone had risen about 40 percent. During the war years the region's share of Virginia's inhabitants increased to 20.6 percent.

The construction boom failed to keep pace with the burgeoning population. People were pushed out into the streets. Rooms were rented in shifts. Landlords split their houses into several units and then divided them again, sometimes forcing several families to share a single bath. With a hospitable spirit some hotels agreed to reserve rooms until evening while servicemen and war workers looked for more permanent dwellings. A war housing program of more than 14,000 new dwellings was little help: 90 percent of the units were snapped up even before completion.

Transportation was so miserably overtaxed that some construction companies built on-site dormitories for their workers. Sailors commonly were seen piling atop streetcars or hanging onto the rear platforms. A local joke referred to a motorman who always succeeded in crowding yet one more on, not realizing that for every new passenger, one was shoved off at the rear.

By 1874 Norfolk ranked third in volume among U.S. cotton exporting ports. Ten years later nearly half a million bales a year passed through the city. This 1923 photograph shows a cotton field at the Robinson Farm in New Kent County, Virginia. Courtesy, Valentine Museum

Facing page: Pictured here is a giant crane in use at the Newport News Shipbuilding and Dry Dock Company. Courtesy, Virginia State Library

Left: Because native Virginians lacked capital following the Civil War, much of the new construction was funded by Northern interests. This engraving, sketched by T.R. Davis, depicts the rebuilding of the Burnt District of Richmond—the city's financial and commercial center. Courtesy, Valentine Museum

Below: Philip Rahm's Eagle Foundry, located on Cary Street between 14th and 15th streets, was one of 13 iron foundries operating in Richmond in 1860. Lithographed by W.H. Rease and published by T.W. Bovell, this advertisement shows the various commercial and domestic ironworks manufactured in the city. Courtesy, Valentine Museum

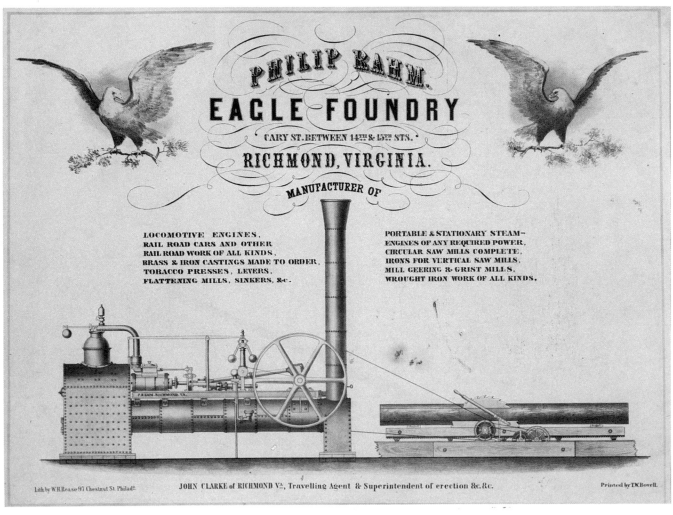

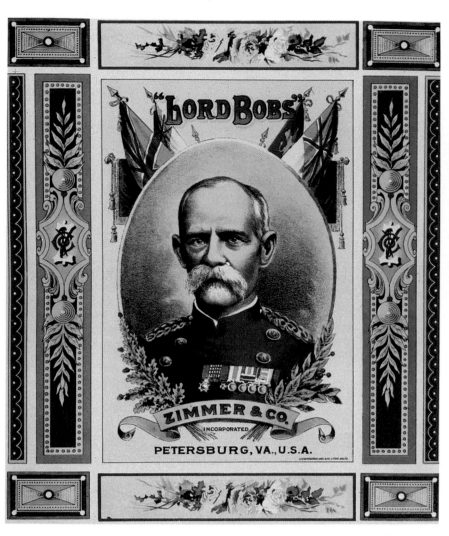

Virginia tobacco companies used a wide variety of colorful images to market their product. Shown here are advertisements and labels from several different companies. Courtesy, Virginia State Library

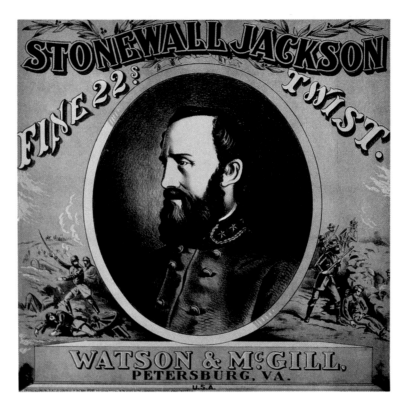

Facing page: Monticello, located just outside of Charlottesville, is an excellent example of Thomas Jefferson's architectural inventiveness. The home is a Virginia landmark and is open to the public. Photo by Sylvia Schlender. Courtesy, Nawrocki Stock Photo

Right: Isolated mountain farmers looked to Ed Mabry and his mill to grind meal long before transportation brought commerce to the Blue Ridge region. Photo by Carol Cotter

Below: The Jefferson Hotel, financed by tobacco magnate Lewis Ginter, opened in 1895 in Richmond. The design of the elaborate structure was based on the Villa Medici in Rome. Although the hotel burned in 1901, the Franklin Street facade was saved. The remainder of the building was reconstructed and the hotel reopened in 1907. Courtesy, Virginia State Library

THE JEFFERSON
RICHMOND, VIRGINIA.
WINTER SEASON
AMERICAN & EUROPEAN PLANS.
SUMMER SEASON
EUROPEAN PLAN EXCLUSIVELY.
ROOMS $1.50 PER DAY AND UPWARDS.

Right: This smiling gentleman in period dress welcomes visitors to colonial Williamsburg, one of the most popular tourist attractions in the state. Photo by Sylvia Schlender. Courtesy, Nawrocki Stock Photo

Below: Colonial Williamsburg is one of the largest and most comprehensive restored villages in the world. Here, some visitors enjoy a carriage ride. Photo by Mark Gibson

Above: The state capitol in Richmond, designed by Thomas Jefferson, was built in the late eighteenth century. The wings were added in 1904-1905. Photo by Sylvia Schlender. Courtesy, Nawrocki Stock Photo

Left: This impressive statue of George Washington stands in the rotunda of the state capitol in Richmond. It was sculpted by Jean Antoine Houdon, and is the only such statue of Washington taken from life. Photo by Mark Gibson

The Richmond skyline is shown by twilight. Photo by Everett C. Johnson. Courtesy, Southern Stock Photos

Right: Fredericksburg has a colorful history, and is a popular tourist attraction in Virginia. Many of the more than 350 original eighteenth and nineteenth century buildings in Fredericksburg's 40-block National Historic District are open to visitors. Photo by Audrey Gibson

Below: The old and the new Richmond are depicted in this photograph of some historic buildings reflected in the glass of a modern structure. Photo by John Salmon

Left: The University of Virginia is the chief center for graduate and graduate-professional studies in the state, and is one of the top 100 research universities in the country. The original buildings were designed by Thomas Jefferson, and the campus is widely regarded as one of the most picturesque in the country. Photo by Mark Gibson

Following pages: The revitalization of Norfolk's downtown area began with the Waterside, the $13 million waterfront marketplace, featuring more than 100 places to browse, shop, or dine by the water. Visitors can enjoy international cuisine and numerous festivals, including HarborFest. Courtesy, Virginia Division of Tourism

Above: Busch Gardens, an amusement park located in Williamsburg, offers rides, live entertainment, food, and shopping in an "international" setting. Photo by Paul Pavlik

Right: A tour boat plies the busy waters of Norfolk. Photo by Audrey Gibson

Facing page: The most extensive parks and forests in Virginia are west of the Piedmont. Shown here is Lewis Falls in Shenandoah National Park, which extends along the Blue Ridge from Front Royal in the north to the vicinity of Waynesboro. Photo by Mark Gibson

Right: Natural Bridge, located in Rockridge County, is one of the seven natural wonders of the world. Called the "Bridge of God" by the Indians, it supports a national highway today. Photo by Carol Cotter

Left: The Blue Ridge Parkway affords travelers some magnificent views, such as this autumn scene. Photo by Mark Gibson

Below: In the Shenandoah Valley, oak, hickory, and yellow poplar are the dominant hardwoods while white, Virginia, and shortleaf pine are the major softwoods. Over two-thirds of Virginia's total land area is forested and nearly all the wooded land can produce timber. Photo by Mark Gibson

Right: Shown here is the sun setting through the trees on Chincoteague Island. The island is known for its wild pony auctions, held there every July; ponies are brought over from neighboring Assateague Island. Photo by Paul Pavlik

Below: The scenic Shenandoah Valley was an important corridor in the early westward journeys of pioneers. Photo by Mark Gibson

This scenic farm is located in Augusta County, in the western part of the state. Farm income in Virginia is divided about evenly between field and orchard crops and livestock and livestock products. Photo by Everett C. Johnson. Courtesy Southern Stock Photos

Right: Throughout Virginia's colonial period tobacco dominated the economic, social, and legislative affairs of the state. The first crop of tobacco was experimentally grown in 1612 on John Rolfe's farm in Jamestown. The Danville Harvest Jubilee, held annually in October, features the World Tobacco Auctioneering Championship. Courtesy, Southern Stock Photos

Below: Virginia has evolved from an agriculture-based state into a post-industrial society with one of the country's most diverse economies. Still, farms like this one carry on. Photo by Robert Llewellyn

Above: This delicate rainbow was produced by the irrigation of some Virginia farmland. Photo by Sylvia Schlender. Courtesy, Nawrocki Stock Photo

Left: Corn, squash, and beans are grown on this truck farm in Floyd County. Truck farming is mainly on the Eastern Shore and in the Tidewater. Photo by Bob Shell/Shellphoto

Right: Before 1960 only about 16.5 acres of Virginia farmland were producing grapes. In 1986 almost 1,600 planted acres were producing American, American-French Hybrid, and Vinifera grapes. Wine production in the Old Dominion has increased to 280,000 gallons with a wholesale value of about $5.6 million. Photo by Carl Purcell

Below: Home canning of such farm goods as these ripe red tomatoes is still practiced after the harvest in rural Virginia. Photo by Bob Shell/Shellphoto

Above: Most Virginia poultry is raised in the Shenandoah Valley. Broiler chickens and turkeys are the most common types. Photo by Robert Llewellyn

Left: These eggs are undergoing testing to determine whether they have been fertilized. Photo by Robert Llewellyn

Right: Livestock and dairy farming predominate in the northern Piedmont. Shown here are some cattle at feeding time. Photo by Jim Pickerell. Courtesy, Southern Stock Photos

Below: A mother nurses her calf on a Shenandoah Valley farm. Photo by Robert Maust

*A Virginia farm is silhouetted against a
fiery sunset. Photo by Robert Llewellyn*

Facing page: The sculptures at the entrance to the Omni Hotel, which are lit in neon at night, are a familiar sight to motorists on Waterfront Drive in downtown Norfolk. Photo by Mark Gibson

Right: Situated between the Blue Ridge and Allegheny Mountains, Roanoke is the gateway to the Shenandoah Valley and is therefore the region's commercial center. Pictured here is Market Square in Roanoke. Photo by Audrey Gibson

Below: In the commercial apple orchards of Virginia's Shenandoah Valley, production totaled 455 million pounds in 1983. In recent years Virginia has ranked seventh in the nation in apple production. Photo by Ken Layman. Courtesy, Robert Maust Photography

Facing page: A worker oversees steel casting in Bristol. Photo by Bob Shell/ Shellphoto

Right: The Chesapeake Paper Company is located near Williamsburg. Photo by Robert Llewellyn

Below: Paper plants such as this one are common in Virginia. The James River Corporation, based in Virginia, has pulp and paper plants nationwide. Photo by Robert Llewellyn

*The North Anna nuclear power station,
located in Mineral, Virginia, began operations in 1974. Photo by Mark Mitchell.
Courtesy, Virginia Power*

Right: A technician examines sliced beets for their color. Processed foods are among the leading products in the state. Photo by Robert Lightfoot III. Courtesy, Nawrocki Stock Photo

Below: A welder creates a beautiful shower of sparks as he practices his craft. Photo by Robert Llewellyn

Right: This chemical plant is located in Norfolk; others are found in Portsmouth and along the Appomattox. Photo by Robert Llewellyn

Below: Shown here is a plastics manufacturing plant. Manufacturing is the chief source of income in Virginia. Photo by Robert Lightfoot III. Courtesy, Nawrocki Stock Photo

Shipbuilding recovered from its post-World War II slump with the advent of the nuclear age. In 1985, the Newport News Shipbuilding and Dry Dock Company employed 30,000 workers for the production of nuclear vessels for the navy. Photo by Robert Llewellyn

258

Right: Shown here is a view of Norfolk's bustling harbor. Photo by Carl Purcell

Below: This boat is getting a new paint job in dry dock. Photo by Paul Procaccio. Courtesy, Nawrocki Stock Photo

Above: Two architects review a blueprint for an addition to Monroe Hall at the McIntire School of Commerce, University of Virginia. Photo by Robert Llewellyn

Left: Virginia's nonagricultural work force has grown rapidly in the last several years, and the state's unemployment rate is among the lowest in the country. Photo by Robert Llewellyn

Facing page: Pictured here is strip mining on a hillside in Wise County, in south-western Virginia. Photo by Robert Llewellyn

Left: In recent years Virginia has ranked sixth in the nation in coal production. Photo by Robert Llewellyn

Below: During the late 1970s and early 1980s, the nation's energy shortage brought a sudden boom to the coal-mining industry in the southwestern part of the state. Photo by Jim Pickerell. Courtesy, Southern Stock Photos

Above: A Virginia coal sample is tested for sulfur. Photo by Robert Perron. Courtesy, Nawrocki Stock Photo

Right: This coal miner displays the dirt of a day's hard work on his face. Coal has consistently led the exports of Hampton Roads since mining began in southwest Virginia. Photo by Robert Llewellyn

Left: A freight train in Elliston heads for West Virginia. Virginia retains a large portion of its railroad trackage because it is an important link in Eastern Seaboard traffic and Deep South freight traffic. Photo by Bob Shell/Shellphoto

Below: Interstate 66 is shown during rush hour, where it passes through Vienna, in the Washington, D.C., area. The freeway crosses the northern part of the state, ending in Skyline Drive. Photo by Cameron Davidson. Courtesy, Southern Stock Photos

Right: The great fisheries of Virginia's Atlantic coast, Chesapeake Bay, and tidal waters are a source of livelihood and pleasure for commercial and sports fishermen. Small oyster boats dot the docks in Oyster, Virginia, in the state's Eastern Shore region. Courtesy, Virginia Division of Tourism

Below: Boats dock in front of the drawbridge on Chincoteague Island. The island is located off the eastern shore of Virginia and Maryland. Photo by Paul Pavlik

Left: The dock is flooded preparatory to docking vessels at this Newport News shipyard. Courtesy, Virginia State Library

Schools overflowed with students as more and more families moved to the area. A two-shift system was adopted to handle the ever-increasing number of students, which rose from 79,000 in 1940 to 98,000 in 1945. Unfortunately, many teachers had been lured away from the profession by the high salaries of war industries, government jobs, and the armed services, leaving an insufficient number to support the system. In Norfolk, 35 percent of the city's teachers held only emergency certificates. The percentage was even higher in the counties.

Government agencies in the various communities of Hampton Roads also proved insufficient to service their war populations. Most had neither the funds nor the staff to effectively carry out their tasks. In 1943 an estimated 2,800 children needed nursery care, yet Norfolk's three-day nurseries had room for only 150 children. The city's Family Welfare Association had such a poor reputation that even the juvenile court refused to send it referrals. Newport News had no private family agency to provide all-around services in the community, so several different public agencies, with little or no coordination, attempted to administer to family and child problems.

Community recreational facilities, scarcely adequate to meet the needs of the normal popula-

tion, were wholly insufficient to care for the inflated numbers of civilian workers and military personnel. Inevitably servicemen gravitated to bars and disreputable dives. Although the army and the navy attempted to remedy the situation with the construction of movie theaters, gymnasiums, and a large army-navy USO auditorium and recreation arena in Norfolk, sailors and soldiers still swarmed the penny arcades of Norfolk's East Main Street. Consequently, the rates for most crimes in the Hampton Roads communities doubled and, in some areas, even tripled.

While the war boom wreaked its own brand of havoc on the area, the soaring demand for goods and services invigorated the civilian economy. Before the war there were 154,000 persons in the labor force of Hampton Roads. Four years later, with the proliferation of women and children in the work force, that number had increased nearly 50 percent. Unemployment had virtually disappeared, not only among white males but also among women and blacks. As employment rose so did total income. Income payments for the last half of 1942 reached $323 million, $231 million higher than the same period in 1939.

The shipbuilding industry provided the greatest boost to employment during the early war years. By 1942, more than 55,000 people

These enlisted men are bedded down in close quarters before sailing overseas from the Hampton Roads Port of Embarkation in April 1944. Courtesy, U.S. Signal Corps, Hampton Roads Port of Embarkation, Virginia State Library

had been added to the shipyards' payrolls as suppliers raced to meet the demand for war vessels. War supply contracts and project orders awarded to Hampton Roads establishments totaled approximately $1.8 billion through November 1944—more than five times the value of the products of the shipbuilding and repair industry in the entire United States in 1939. Nearly all of this business went to the navy yard and to Newport News Shipbuilding. The navy yard's contribution in World War II exceeded its production in all other wars combined. The private company cut out all other business and built itself into the nation's leading designer and producer of aircraft carriers.

As the area's largest employer continued to pad its payrolls, it fed other commerce. The pressure for goods and services combined with sufficiently high incomes fostered new businesses and bolstered old ones. Shipbuilding employment increased to almost five times its prewar level, while overall business activity expanded threefold during the war years. The additions of new Hampton Roads businesses to the Dun & Bradstreet business reporting service during that period exceeded those of the entire rest of the state.

As residents began buying more, dining out more, and spending more money on higher priced purchases, businesses expanded. By 1943, the number of people employed in all branches of wholesale and retail trade, including eating and drinking establishments, had increased more than 50 percent. Payrolls in these businesses rose from prewar levels of $9.7 million to $21.6 million.

Service industries were likewise affected. The number of hotels, amusements, recreation

This aerial view of the Hampton Roads Port of Embarkation shows the Headquarters Building and Administrative Area, the Chesapeake & Ohio railroad yards, and the Pier Area with ten ships loading. Courtesy, U.S. Signal Corps, Hampton Roads Port of Embarkation, Virginia State Library

Colonna's Shipyard in Norfolk is pictured in 1954. Although the shipyards of Hampton Roads underwent a postwar slump, they maintained a stable economy as they moved into the fifties.

establishments, and personal, domestic, professional, and business services almost doubled by the end of 1943, as did their payrolls. Not surprisingly, more than half the people employed in service industries worked in Norfolk, catering to the navy population. In manufacturing, no industry came close to matching the prosperity of the shipbuilding industry, although makers of clothing, chemicals (mainly fertilizer), and food showed significant expansions. When World War II ended, the boom kept on. The military presence continued to grow as existing military installations were expanded and new ones came to the area. Langley Field underwent considerable expansion under the National Advisory Committee on Aeronautics and the Air Corps. The Army Ground Forces, now the Army Field Forces, moved to Fort Monroe, and the Army Transportation Corps set up headquarters at Fort Eustis. Norfolk's major supply base, the Atlantic Fleet home port, and the new Armed Forces Staff College all contributed to the influx of military personnel.

The civilian population also rose with the return of prewar residents and the immigration of veterans who married Hampton Roads women. Many civilian war workers remained after their jobs ended, further offsetting the postwar outflow of war families and workers. Five years after V-J Day, the population of the Hampton

Roads-Peninsula area exceeded the peak population of the war years.

When shipbuilders were forced to lay off thousands of employees as the navy buildup ceased, unemployment still remained low. Effective buying income in Hampton Roads for 1948 ranged from $4,500 to $4,900 per family, as opposed to a state average of $4,044.

The wholesale, retail, and service industries continued to prosper, fueled by high incomes, low unemployment, and a growing tourist trade. The resort business brought millions of travelers who spent approximately $10 million in the area between May and September.

Spurred by the Peninsula Industrial Committee, the Norfolk Industrial Commission, and the Portsmouth Chamber of Commerce, several businesses established or reestablished operations in the area. U.S. Gypsum Company built a $2 million gypsum plaster and plasterboard plant. Swift and Company established a $700,000 food processing plant. And Ford Motor Company spent $1.5 million reconverting its auto assembly plant to a peacetime operation. Between 1947 and 1948 the value of manufactured goods among Norfolk concerns alone had risen from $250 million to $338 million.

Although momentum inevitably slowed from that of the fevered war pitch, Hampton Roads maintained a stable economy as it moved into the new decade. The world wars had forced the bloating populations of the Hampton Roads cities into a huge, burgeoning metropolis. Construction of the Chesapeake Bay Bridge Tunnel linked the Hampton Roads region with the Eastern Shore, providing more direct motor access to the metropolitan Northeast while bypassing Baltimore and Washington.

Shipbuilding would recover from its postwar slump. By the late sixties, Newport News Shipbuilding and Dry Dock Company was the largest manufacturing employer in the state. Geared up to produce the nuclear aircraft carriers and nuclear attack submarines of a 600-ship navy, the shipyard employed 30,000 workers in 1987.

The shipping industry would be aided by the creation of the Virginia State Ports Authority in 1952. Prior to its inception, outdated facilities at 14 general cargo terminals in the three Hampton Roads port cities were operated by private and government concerns which could not afford to modernize their facilities. Furthermore, civilian business was unevenly distributed among the terminals, clogging piers and slowing operations. Within a decade, the Ports Author-

ity would purchase and improve these piers, then lease them back to their former owners to operate them.

Since the opening of the coal mines in Southwest Virginia, coal has consistently led the exports of Hampton Roads. By the early 1900s, three major railroads were funneling trainloads of coal through Hampton Roads for shipment all over the world. After the United States entered World War I, coal remained the principal export as war-torn Europe looked to America for its fuel supply.

When rails through New York could not support the demand of New England's factories for coal, steamers from Hampton Roads hauled the fuel north. In one year Norfolk's domestic coal shipments jumped from 290,000 tons to 5.5 million tons. Coal shipments took a dive in World War II. To protect against German U-boats, shippers moved coal over all-rail routes, causing coastal trade to sink. Dumpings in 1943 were less than half what they had been just two years before. But as the U-boat menace lessened toward the end of the war, coal shipments began to increase, both to domestic ports and to Europe.

This is the interior of the prefabricated sections that were to form the core of the underwater portions of the Chesapeake Bay Bridge Tunnel. Courtesy, Virginia State Library

Exports picked up again after the war, spurred by a revival of the European economies and a demand for high quality metallurgical coal. By 1952, Hampton Roads exports had risen to 23.1 million tons, 22.4 million tons of which were coal. Prospects for coal exports brightened in the seventies when the energy crisis drove up the price of oil and forced countries the world over to substitute coal for oil as a primary fuel in electric power plants. In 1974 some 38 million tons of coal is estimated to have passed through Hampton Roads. By 1980, the figure would reach 100 million tons.

That year labor unrest disrupted shipments from Poland and Australia, America's greatest competitors for European and Asian consumption. Customers from all over the world flocked to Hampton Roads for coal. As many as 160 colliers crowded into the port on a given day, waiting to be loaded. The armada packed the anchorages at Hampton Roads, eventually spilling into Cape Charles on the Eastern Shore. Midyear marked a 40-ship backlog, and coal exporters worried that the lengthy waits, which cost ships thousands of dollars a day, would discourage coal buyers from returning.

Exports were destined to fall off in any case. With labor problems settled, Poland and Australia reclaimed their market share. South Africa, another coal exporter, expanded its export capacity, while Canada and Colombia crowded into the international market. By the mid-1980s, oil prices collapsed, prompting Europeans to drop plans to switch from oil to coal as a fuel for numerous electric power plants. Despite adversity, Hampton Roads remains the world's largest coal exporting port.

In recent years general cargo shipments have taken up the slack. Launching an aggressive marketing campaign, Hampton Roads began winning business for containerized cargo from other U.S. ports, especially Baltimore. Several major shipping companies have transferred operations to Hampton Roads, distinguishing it as the fastest-growing container-handling port in the U.S. during the mid-1980s. The region's superior ports and railroads also have made it an attractive site for foreign investment.

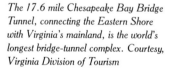

The 17.6 mile Chesapeake Bay Bridge Tunnel, connecting the Eastern Shore with Virginia's mainland, is the world's longest bridge-tunnel complex. Courtesy, Virginia Division of Tourism

Collis P. Huntington

The story goes that Collis P. Huntington was a 16-year-old traveling salesman when he first laid eyes on Hampton Roads in 1837. Even at that time, he would later say, he thought there was no better place in the country for a city to blossom.

Some 40 years later Huntington returned, a railroad baron in search of an eastern terminus for his Chesapeake & Ohio Railway. His Old Dominion Land Company bought up major parcels for the creation of such a town. Huntington, always a man of vision, added coal piers, believing that one day the harbor would be a deepwater port.

In January 1886 Chesapeake Dry Dock & Construction Company was chartered with Huntington as its chairman. Over the next few years the company grew quickly, renowned for its ship repair work. When the surrounding community was insufficient to handle the increasing number of employees, Huntington used his personal funds for the development of a community for his workers, subsidizing the construction of 138 two-story brick houses and a four-room schoolhouse.

In 1890 the company name was changed to Newport News Shipbuilding and Dry Dock Company, and shipbuilding became its emphasis. Although the navy would become the company's primary contractor, that relationship began on shaky ground. As Christmas approached, the news reached Huntington that the Portsmouth Navy Yard had taken in a German steamship for repairs. Huntington protested to U.S. Navy Secretary B.F. Tracy in a telegram:

I was very much surprised and aggrieved to know that the government should have come in and taken this work after the owners of the shipyard at Newport News have been to the great expense they have

incurred in preparing to do just this kind of work.

Collis P. Huntington. From Cirker, Dictionary of American Portraits, Dover, 1967

Within three years the shipyard began a stream of navy work that would keep it afloat for the next century. Huntington died in 1900, but Newport News Shipbuilding and Dry Dock Company kept its lead in the industry as a major supplier through every American war.

After World War II, demand dropped and the shipyard was able to stay in business by converting ships to civilian use. The fifties brought a turnaround when the company entered the nuclear age with the construction of the aircraft carrier *Enterprise*. The shipyard became the only producer capable of constructing all types of navy nuclear vessels.

The company became increasingly dependent on government contract work, as did other yards across the country. In 1968, fearful of a hostile takeover, shipyard officials agreed to merge with the Houston-based Tenneco Corporation, believing that the backing of a major corporation would buffet the company from the fluctuations of the shipbuilding business. At the time of the merger, the shipyard had a backlog of orders totaling nearly $500 million. By 1976 the backlog had grown to nearly $2 billion. Today Newport News Shipbuilding and Dry Dock Company is still the nation's industry leader.

The Dulles Corridor has become one of the country's principal high-tech centers with more than 1,000 businesses, professional firms, and associations. Access to international transportation is just one of the factors which attracts such businesses. As early as 1946, Washington National Airport in Arlington County was serving seven airlines. Courtesy, Richmond Newspapers, Inc.

CHAPTER 10

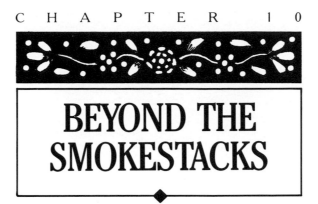

BEYOND THE SMOKESTACKS

In the nearly four centuries since the founding of Jamestown, Virginia has evolved from a fragile agricultural-based colony on the edge of a hostile new world into a community pioneering the frontiers of the post-industrial society. Virginia has one of the most balanced, diversified economies of any state in the nation.

Many generations-old industries maintain their grip on the economy. Railroading, coal mining, forestry, and agriculture remain major contributors to jobs and income. In recent years Virginia has ranked fifth in the nation in tobacco production, sixth in coal production, seventh in apple production, and thirteenth in lumber production.

The smokestacks of old-line industries such as textiles, furniture, transportation equipment, and chemicals still punctuate Virginia's skylines. Among other accomplishments, the state boasts the world's largest privately owned shipyard, the world's largest cigarette-manufacturing plant, the world's largest textile mill under one roof, and the world's largest hot dog production plant. Manufacturing concerns engage a work force of nearly a half-million.

But in the last 20 years new service and high-tech industries have emerged. Northern Virginia has emerged as one of the nation's centers in telecommunications, software programming, and aerospace. Virginia companies are active in biotechnology, robotics, fiber optics, and many other cutting-edge industries.

Between 1970 and 1980 Virginia's nonagricultural work force grew by 3.4 percent each year, compared to the national average of 2.5 percent. By 1987, Virginia was one of the few states to have shown an increase in manufacturing jobs since the brutal recession of 1980-1981. Throughout the past decade Virginia has maintained one of the lowest unemployment rates in the country, and its economy has consistently grown faster than the national average.

The increase in jobs has been matched by rising incomes. In the mid-1980s—some 120 years after the Civil War—the average income per capita for Virginians finally surpassed the national average. Prosperity has concentrated along a swath of extraordinary vitality known as the Golden Crescent. A band of urban-suburban development running from the Northern Virginian suburbs of Washington through Richmond and into Hampton Roads is marked by low unemployment, high incomes, and vigorous industry.

Pockets of deprivation persist in rural Virginia, where many communities staked their livelihood on the fortunes of a handful of manufacturing industries. Under the pressure of foreign imports and changing consumer trends, traditional industries such as textiles and tobacco endured prolonged periods of contraction. Although most companies have survived intact, it has only been through heavy investment in modern equipment and ruthless slashing of jobs. Even

then many of these communities have shown considerable resilience. Aggressive marketing has recruited new manufacturing plants for depressed mill towns.

Lured by moderate taxes, excellent roads and airports, a high quality of life, and modest labor costs, more and more high-tech companies are locating in Virginia. Not only is the state attracting the gold-collar geniuses responsible for high-tech innovations, it is also producing them. Institutions of higher learning across Virginia are offering curricula geared to advanced technology. Three universities—the University of Virginia, Virginia Commonwealth University, and Virginia Polytechnic Institute and State University—are among the nation's top 100 research universities in total research and development expenditures. And in the last two decades, George Mason University has emerged as a leading research center, having a Nobel laureate

in economics on its faculty and a world-class "center of excellence" for software engineering.

High-tech industry has entered every corner of the state. The Roanoke Valley, still the leading manufacturing center of Southwest Virginia, is home to a wide range of high-tech companies: ITT's Electro-Optical Products Division manufactures fiber optic components and systems, as well as night vision devices there. Nord Instruments Company assembles circuit boards, while Keltech produces industrial electronics and computer controls. Almost a dozen medical and commercial laboratories are located in the area. Nearly 20 percent of the area's 21,000 manufacturing employees are involved in the production of electrical and electronic machinery.

Roanoke is an anchor of the emerging I-81 corridor, named for the growth of industry along the interstate highway. The other focal point of development is Blacksburg, home to Virginia Tech. ITT and Virginia Tech have seeded a number of entrepreneurial firms in the fields of fiber optics, bioengineering, robotics, and electric motors.

Hampton Roads also has enormous high-tech potential. Between the National Aeronautics and Space Administration (NASA) research facility at Langley, Newport News Shipbuilding (the only builder of nuclear aircraft carriers in the nation), the Canon copier plant, the Virginia Institute for Marine Science, and a host of software firms supplying services to the naval establishment, Hampton Roads boasts one of the largest concentrations of scientific and engineering talent in the country.

Many of the area's high-tech companies provide support services for NASA. Modern

Machine & Tool, for example, is active in aerospace research and development, while Wyle Laboratories designs and manufactures electronic and electro-mechanical systems. In Hampton and Newport News, Gambro manufactures dialysis filters and bloodlines for artificial kidney machines. In Norfolk, Dow Corning Ophthalmics and Lombart Lenses Division of American Sterilizer Company produce contact lenses. More than two dozen laboratories operate in Hampton Roads today.

Richmond, historically Virginia's industrial leader, also has a number of high-tech firms. Robertshaw Controls, a manufacturer of control systems, is headquartered there, as is A.H. Robins Company, a diversified multinational pharmaceutical company. The AT&T printed wiring board production facility there is one of

Virginia Polytechinic Institute, located in Blacksburg, offers programs which are in step with the growth of high tech industry in the state. Courtesy, Virginia State Library

the most modern in the world. The Richmond area also has more than two dozen medical and commercial testing labs.

Lynchburg and Charlottesville also claim a share of the state's high-tech market. In Lynchburg, International Circuit Technology manufactures printed circuit boards, and Paktron, a division of Illinois Tool Works, produces electronic components. Babcock & Wilcox is a leader in the design and maintenance of nuclear power plants. Some 3,600 people are employed by communications companies in the Lynchburg area, while in Charlottesville, headquarters to Comdial Corporation, more than 2,000 people are employed in the manufacture of communications equipment. Charlottesville also is home to the University of Virginia, with its research-oriented medical and engineering schools, as well as General Electric's factory automation division.

The shift from mills to microchips is most evident in Northern Virginia, where high-technology manufacturing as well as research and development firms play a major role in the local economy. In the last two decades, Northern Virginia has been transformed from a bedroom community into an urban sprawl of high rises and concrete. By the early 1980s, more than 800 high-tech firms and organizations had settled in the region, employing almost 63,000 people. The Dulles corridor, stretching from Tysons Corner to Washington Dulles International Airport, is becoming one of the country's principal high-tech centers, with more than 1,000 businesses, professional firms, and associations. In the software industry alone, the ever-increasing presence of high-tech firms has placed the region in the league with California's Silicon Valley and Boston's Route 128.

Economists attribute Northern Virginia's magnetism to several factors, primarily its proximity to Washington. At the turn of the century, there was little development in the region outside of Alexandria, then a minor river port and commercial center. As the role of the federal government grew, however, so did the size of the federal establishment across the Potomac in Washington. Even so, Arlington and Fairfax counties were little more than bedroom commu-

Completed in 1943, the Pentagon, which houses the U.S. Department of Defense, takes up 34 acres in Arlington, Virginia. Photo by Jay Freis. Courtesy, Image Bank West

nities for years. One of the greatest boons to regional development was the construction of the Pentagon on the Virginia side of the Potomac.

As the defense department expanded in the decades following World War II, it spilled into the tremendous Crystal City complex. The growing Pentagon also contracted jobs to think tanks, research firms, systems management companies, and a host of other so-called "Beltway Bandits."

Defense spending has not been the only driving force in Northern Virginia's rise to prominence. Many government agencies have expanded across the river into Northern Virginia with many private organizations following closely behind. The Washington area has attracted thousands of trade associations whose job it is to monitor and lobby legislation, and many have settled in Fairfax County, Arlington County, and Alexandria.

The federal bureaucracy also is the nation's largest customer for computer hardware and super-sophisticated systems software. To participate in this lucrative market, virtually every major computer and systems-management company in the country has set up operations in the Washington area. Similarly, the telecommunications industry settled in the area in order to keep tabs on the Federal Communications Commission (FCC). For decades telecommunications had been the monopoly of AT&T Communications. With the breakup of Ma Bell, telecommunications firms have proliferated, creating the world's most competitive telephone and data-transmission industry. Most have a major presence in Washington's Virginia suburbs.

Northern Virginia has amassed a critical measure of capital, skilled labor, and entrepreneurial talent in a handful of high-tech fields. The region has one of the largest concentrations of engineers and scientists in the world. George Mason University, a modest branch of the University of Virginia a generation ago, has expanded dramatically. Working closely with the local business community, the university has designed a curriculum to supply the trained work force demanded by high-tech industry. In a short

time, for example, the university has built and staffed an impressive software engineering school.

Access to air transportation is a primary consideration. Arlington is the site of Washington National Airport, and Washington Dulles International Airport straddles the Fairfax and Loudoun county lines. The federal government has now relinquished control of both facilities to a regional airport commission.

Alexandria, Arlington, Fairfax, and Prince William enjoy a superior quality of life, with public school systems among the best in the nation, as well as having excellent recreational facilities. Cooperative local governments have enabled development to proceed rapidly, finding creative ways to meet the region's water, sewer, and transportation needs.

Fairfax County is rapidly becoming the hub of high tech in Virginia. Among the growing concentration of firms are the giants of telecommunications, the sovereigns of software, and tomorrow's wizards of aerospace. Fairfax has all the benefits that Virginia can offer. It is 15 minutes from the seat of federal government, and has one of the most highly educated labor pools in the country, with a greater percentage of college graduates than Boston, Chicago, Dallas, Los Angeles, New York, or San Francisco.

Quality of life is also a major drawing card. Companies on the move are pleased to

Because of its moderate taxes, modest labor costs, excellent road systems and airports, and high quality of life, Virginia has attracted major industries to all areas of the state. Expansion of Byrd Airport, now Richmond International Airport, was one outcome of this economic development. In this 1968 photo, construction of a new taxiway and apron is surveyed by an airport aide from the terminal roof. Courtesy, Richmond Newspapers, Inc.

Right: Governor Charles S. Robb organized a Special Task Force on Science and Technology in 1983, and as a result the Center for Innovative Techonology was established. Its goal was to link the capabilities of major research universities in the state to high tech industries. Courtesy, Virginia State Library

Below: On the historic campus of the University of Virginia, important research is ongoing in the medical and engineering schools. Courtesy, Printing Services, Archives, University of Virginia Library

bring their employees to a county where unemployment is nearly half the state's rate and less than half the nation's rate, and where the mean income level for an average household is more than $50,000, fifth highest among U.S. counties. The Fairfax County Public School System, one of the best in the country, offers another plus. Approximately 50 percent of its teachers hold master's or doctoral degrees. In 1984 more than 37 percent of Virginia's National Merit Scholarship Exam semifinalists came from Fairfax County.

Educational opportunities in the area match stride with the evolution of high technology. Three major universities offer programs in the area which address the growth of high tech: George Mason University, the University of Virginia's Division of Continuing Education at Falls Church, and Virginia Polytechnic Institute and State University's Dulles Graduate Center.

Washington Dulles International Airport has accelerated its pace to meet the growing demand of corporate needs. After Congress turned the airport's operations over to a regional commission, terminal space was added, runway capacity was increased, and more airlines began crowding in. Within three years commercial passenger traffic had doubled.

More and more high-tech companies are cashing in on Fairfax County's available assets. With well over half the state's telecommunications firms, Fairfax had become a repository for industry giants by the mid-1980s. AT&T Communications, GTE Telenet, Comstat General Telesystems, and Dynalectron Corporation were among those who chose Fairfax, with its access to major markets and its gold-collar workers.

The county is also fertile ground for some of the world's leading software technology. Approximately 200 software companies employ one of every seven Fairfax workers. Small firms are numerous, but industry giants take up a lot of turf and hire a multitude of technicians. Both Sperry Corporation in Reston and Systems Development Corporation in Tysons Corner employ 2,000 people, while TRW Federal Systems Group, headquartered in the Fair Lakes area, is staffed by 3,000.

Now recognized as a national center for high-tech excellence, Fairfax County is growing from strength to strength. As a result of Governor Charles S. Robb's Special Task Force on Science and Technology in 1983, the Center for Innovative Technology (CIT) was established in the county to link the capabilities of the state's major research universities to its technically advanced industries. In its first several years, the CIT—funded by state and industry—backed more than 220 projects involved in the development of technology and its applications to industry.

In 1985 the county opened its Thomas Jefferson Science and Technology High School, a four-year program for students with aptitudes in science, mathematics, engineering, and computer science. Local technology-oriented companies such as Atlantic Research Corporation, IBM,

TRW, and Dynalectron Corporation provide funding for specialized, technology-based laboratories for students to actively apply the scientific principles they learn in the classroom. AT&T, for instance, sponsored the school's Telecommunications Laboratory. Satellite Business Systems, Comsat General Telesystems, Sony Corporation, NEC America, and Rolm provided lab equipment, which includes a satellite earth station, a television studio and control room, a weather station, and a radio station. A Life Science and Biotechnology Laboratory for

Adjoining the Blues Armory in the 600 block of E. Marshall Street, at the northern end of Richmond's Sixth Street Marketplace, is the Crystal Palace. This 96-foot high, glass-enclosed pavilion houses specialty shops, market booths, open seating areas, and a stage. A glass-enclosed bridge, spanning Broad Street, brings the city's historic past and revitalized present together. Courtesy, Virginia Division of Tourism

Above: Preston Shannon and members of the CSX Corporation, Hays T. Watkins and Prime F. Osborn, III, signed the $7 million merger of Seaboard Coast Line Industries and the Chessie System, Inc., on November 1, 1980. Like Norfolk Southern, CSX is one of the largest railroad systems in the western hemisphere. Courtesy, Richmond Newspapers, Inc.

Facing page: The city of Richmond has blossomed into a major regional financial center. Photo by Everett C. Johnson. Courtesy, Southern Stock Photo

investigation and experimentation in life sciences was sponsored by Hazleton Laboratories, Meloy Laboratories, and FMC Corporation.

Also in 1985 the county was selected as the site for the Software Productivity Consortium, a research center where 15 of the country's top aerospace corporations share research on state-of-the-art software and software development techniques. The technology developed by the consortium will be used by federal defense and intelligence agencies as well as by private industry. The establishment of the research center in Fairfax is expected to add significantly to the area's prominence as a leader in high technology.

In 1987 Fairfax became a major landmark in the international effort to expand the frontiers of space when NASA chose Reston as the site for its space station headquarters. The research and development of a manned station in space has drawn thousands to the county as high-tech professionals, as well as major contractors, line up to bid for jobs.

As the ongoing revolutions in computers, telecommunications, and biotechnology continue to unfold, Northern Virginia businesses will be in the vanguard. Blessed by access to the nation's capital, two major airports, a superbly skilled labor force, and Virginia's favorable business climate, the region is destined to become a leading force in the world economy of the twenty-first century.

But Hampton Roads, Richmond, Roanoke-Blacksburg, and Charlottesville will be close behind. Medical research centers in Charlottesville, Richmond, and Norfolk, for example, are giving birth to a new biomedical industry. Businesses south of the Occoquan River may not be pushing back the frontiers of science in "Star Wars" research, but they are harnessing technological breakthroughs in the production of goods and services. American consumers still demand a steady supply of durable and nondurable products, and Virginia's manufacturing centers are providing them.

In cities like Danville, Martinsville, and Galax, superautomated textile factories are turning out fabrics for apparel, furniture, automobile interiors, and draperies. Factories of the future can be found in Philip Morris' cigarette-manufacturing plant in Richmond, and in smaller communities like Marion, Stuart's Draft, and Orange. In Waynesboro, Genicom Corporation designs and manufactures top-of-the-line computer printers.

Of course, there's more to economic development than high tech. The city of Richmond has blossomed into a major regional financial center. Two other Richmond firms—Best Products and Circuit City Stores—have revolutionized the retailing industry with bold new concepts in discount selling. In the last 20 years James River Corporation has built a continent-wide empire of pulp and paper plants. CSX Corporation and Norfolk Southern have assembled two of the largest railroad systems in the Western Hemisphere.

By the late 1980s, Virginia was on the move. The shift in economic power to the Commonwealth could be seen in the rapid growth of its largest corporate citizens and in the decisions of several Fortune 500 companies—Mobil Corporation, the multinational oil company, foremost among them—to relocate their headquarters to Virginia locales. As long as state government and the spirit of enterprise work hand in hand, Virginia seems destined to regain the mantle of economic leadership it had 200 years ago.

*A worker performs a delicate balancing
act at a Virginia construction site. Photo
by Robert Llewellyn*

PARTNERS IN PROGRESS

A close working relationship between the state government and the business community is traditional in Virginia. It dates from the founding of England's "First Colony," from an era when the government of the colony and its business interests were one and the same.

European adventurers saw in the new world a whole new range of economic opportunities. Spanish treasure fleets and French fur traders had already demonstrated that there were riches to be wrested from the wilderness. The Virginia Company planned to establish an American colony that would unearth gold and silver by the ton, convert the Indians to Christianity and trade with them, and open new markets for British manufactured goods.

King James I provided the company with a charter; the investors contributed funds to finance provisions and passage for the 120 colonists who sailed from London on December 20, 1606. Stockholders in the venture included laymen and divines, nobles and knights, merchants and mechanics, and the trade guilds of London.

The colonists and their investors quickly learned that no gold, silver, or copper were to be found in Virginia, and that the natives had little interest in the white men's religion. Worse still, colonial relations with the Indians tended to be violent rather than commercial, and saving their own lives proved a more immediate challenge for the whites than saving heathen souls.

Like countless organizations and associations since, the Virginia Company responded to its early failures by reorganizing. The settlers were discouraged, diseased, starving, and preparing to abandon the colony when Lord De La Warr, the replacement governor, arrived in 1609 with fresh provisions and a revised charter.

One suspects that the colonists were more appreciative of the foodstuffs than of the parchment. A third charter was promulgated in 1612 (and annulled in 1624 when Virginia became a royal colony). The new rights and liberties conveyed by the charters were doubtlessly important to the colonists, but more heady attractions were on the way.

Meanwhile John Rolfe imported tobacco seed from the West Indies, crossed it with a locally grown variety, and came up with a smooth-smoking hybrid that captured the English market. By 1618 Virginia was exporting 25 tons of tobacco annually and the colonists had found their gold mine.

Another dramatic change for the better came with the Virginia Company's decision to make settlement more attractive by offering land

Facing page: Virginia coal miners take a rare break from their labor to pose for this group portrait. Photo by Robert Llewellyn

grants to colonists who completed their indentures. Their policy meant that in the new world, any man could become a land-owning aristocrat.

Within 10 years plantations extended 20 miles along the James River, and dreams of owning land were bringing hundreds of new settlers to the colony each year.

Tobacco and real estate thus became the foundation of the Virginia economy. And when demand for tobacco eventually weakened, King Cotton kept the plantation at the center of the Old Dominion's political, economic, and social order. Despite Civil War, Reconstruction, and industrial revolution—through two world wars, the Great Depression, and the beginnings of the space age—the remembered glories of the plantation era have remained deeply embedded in the soul of the Old Dominion.

Virginia did not avidly seek progress. While the Yankee North industrialized, Virginia clung to her plantations. Industrialism held little appeal in the Commonwealth. Richmond's Tredegar Iron Works, a factory run largely with slave labor, was the great exception to the belief that heavy industry had no place in the South.

Virginia cherishes history. Bronze and marble sculptures throughout the state give tangible form to the memories of almost four centuries of heroism, while oral tradition and family chronicles recount the trials and triumphs of tens of thousands more who did not find their way to granite pedestals.

The Civil War and the abolition of slavery left Virginia's financial institutions and cotton fields empty. Her finest farms had become cemeteries. Proud plantations, mortgaged beyond hope of repayment, were vulnerable to the auctioneer's hammer. Virginia again lay at the edge of the abyss, and again she was saved by tobacco and land.

New capital flowed from the North, cash carried in carpetbags by investors who saw not devastation, but opportunity. Land speculation, tobacco, railroads, lumber mills, and

papermills—these were the magnets that attracted investments and rebuilt the Virginia economy.

Virginia values heritage, lineage, and tradition. Yet Virginia has her eyes on the future, too. The Old Dominion and the new Commonwealth have a great deal in common.

Once land ownership was a dream that built a new world; now real estate speculation and development help fuel the economy. Tobacco is still the leading crop, though modern agribusiness operations have replaced the white fences and black faces of the antebellum plantations. And traditional Virginia hospitality has evolved into a sophisticated hotel, restaurant, and tourism industry.

Transportation in Virginia once meant horse-drawn carriages on barely passable roads and boats floating graciously along slow-flowing rivers. Now it means powerful railways and vital airlines like USAir—though some of the highways may still, occasionally, remind tourists and residents alike of the state's laissez-faire traditions.

As for the precious minerals sought by the colonists of the Virginia Company, they have been found: not gold, silver, or copper, but aluminum—and the silicon in the computers of thousands of offices and hundreds of high-technology consultants, designers, publishers, and manufacturers. For though Virginia shunned the smokestacks of the nineteenth century, she has welcomed the advances of the international technologies of the twenty-first century.

The organizations whose stories are told on the following pages have chosen to support this important literary and civic project. They illustrate the variety of ways in which individuals and businesses have contributed to the growth and development of Virginia. They illustrate, too, the extent to which the civic involvement of the Commonwealth's commercial establishments and educational institutions have made Virginia an exceptional state in which to live and work.

VIRGINIA CHAMBER OF COMMERCE

An artist's rendering of the Virginia Chamber of Commerce headquarters at 9 South Fifth Street in Richmond.

In the main entry lobby of the Virginia Chamber of Commerce hangs a cured and framed leaf of tobacco. There are no "thank you for not smoking" signs here. Tobacco has been king in Virginia for more than 350 years. The monarch may be showing a few signs of stress, but tobacco is still the state's leading crop, and the Virginia Chamber of Commerce shows appropriate respect.

The chamber sees as its mission the elimination of intrastate, intercom-munity competition. "We want every-one in Virginia working together for the best interests of the entire state," says Edwin C. Luther, III, executive vice-president of the chamber.

The tools of the Virginia Chamber of Commerce are public information, re-search, public relations, publications, and supporting the consensus of the business community's political interests. "The Virginia Chamber is a catalyst," says Luther. "If there's consensus among our membership on any issue, we can help make things happen."

The Virginia Chamber of Com-merce was born in 1924, created by a public-spirited group of citizens led by Dr. Joseph H. Smith of Petersburg. Smith was elected as the chamber's first president, and Colonel Leroy Hodges was appointed managing director. Hodges served until 1938. Only three other men have served as the cham-ber's leading professional administrator: Verbon E. Kemp (1938-1964), Richard S. Gillis, Jr. (1964-1981), and Win Luther, who has headed the chamber's profes-sional staff since 1981.

Executive authority at the Vir-ginia Chamber of Commerce rests with its 41-member board of directors. Leigh B. Middleditch, Jr., of Charlottes-ville is president.

Throughout its history the cham-ber has been one of the state's most active advocates of excellence in educa-tion. "The business community is the consumer of the product of the education system," says Luther. "Public policies that benefit education also benefit the business community and the entire state."

The chamber has consistently ad-vocated good labor/management rela-tions, public safety issues, international trade, and tourism and industrial devel-opment. Two programs created by the chamber, the overseas trade missions and promotional activities concerning tourism and industrial development, proved so successful that they are now run by the state government. The cham-ber continues to sponsor the Virginia Conference on World Trade, the na-tion's oldest regional conference on in-ternational business.

The chamber's top priorities for the next few years include expanding its legislative program to become a preem-inent legislative force in the state, and improving its educational and informa-tion program to provide more specific programs that directly benefit members.

"Our job," says Luther, "is to help Virginia compete in the new economic climate. In the future we need to attract high-technology and information-systems industries, and improve our ports and our air, sea, and rail facilities."

That's the spirit that has made the Virginia Chamber of Commerce the state's leading Partner in Progress.

MARKEL CORPORATION

The Markel organization was begun by Samuel A. Markel shortly after World War I with the formation of a small mutual insurance company to meet the needs of an emerging public transportation industry—first buses and later trucks. In 1930 Markel Service, Inc., was established to provide the underwriting, safety, and claims services for the insurance company.

As the insurance requirements of the growing transportation industry increased, the capacity of this small insurance company was exceeded. In the early 1950s Markel Service changed its role from manager of a single affiliated insurance firm to a general agency representing several insurance companies.

In 1951 its operations extended into Canada with the creation of Markel Service Canada, Ltd., providing underwriting, safety, and claims services for the Canadian trucking industry. This entity went public in 1972 as Markel Financial Holdings, Ltd., with the capital raised used to form Markel Insurance Company of Canada.

In 1959 National Claims Service was formed as an independent claims adjusting company. Previously an in-house claims department, National Claims had to build and develop its own client base and image in the marketplace.

Significant changes in both the transportation and insurance industries in the early 1970s prompted the decision to diversify. The firm developed products in the excess and surplus markets; municipal liability coverages for law enforcement, public officials, and school boards; animal mortality; and nurses' professional liability. Emphasis was placed on developing marketing techniques and strategies to identify products and distribution systems that represented the maximum potential to the company.

The firm wanted to move into underwriting, and stock was sold to a London-based insurance organization to raise the necessary funds. In 1980 Essex Insurance Company was formed to offer excess and surplus coverages and reinsurance.

In the late 1970s the National

Claims Service was expanded through the creation of North American Claims Management Company, offering claims management and supervision services to other insurers and underwriters.

Markel Corporation was formed in 1980 as a holding company to provide centralized management of financial, marketing, and human resources. Today the firm is a diversified insurance organization. Subsidiaries include Markel Service, Inc., Essex Insurance Company, Markel American Insurance Company, National Claims Service, Inc., Gordon Boyd & Company, Inc., North American Claims Management Company, and Lindsey & Newsom Insur-

Today Markel Corporation is a multifaceted insurance organization that, through its subsidiaries, serves as an insurance broker and underwriting manager, an insurer, and a provider of claims administration service. Pictured is the new Markel corporate headquarters, completed in November 1987.

In 1930 the trucking industry was starting to take off, and Markel Service, Inc., was formed. Since then Markel has been a vital part of the transportation industry, diversifying to meet the changing insurance needs of the American motor carrier.

ance Adjusters, Inc.

Markel also maintains a minority interest in Shand Morahan & Company, Inc., and in Fairfax Financial Holdings, Ltd. (formerly Markel Financial Holdings, Ltd.), a publicly owned Canadian firm with subsidiaries of its own, including Markel Insurance Company of Canada, Morden & Helwig Limited, and Sphere Reinsurance Company of Canada.

Markel Corporation completed its initial public stock offering in December 1986. Alan I. Kirshner is president and chairman of the board. Anthony F. Markel and Steven A. Markel are executive vice-presidents.

SOLITE CORPORATION

John W. Roberts founded Solite Corporation in 1947 to supply the United States from the Atlantic Ocean to the Mississippi River with lightweight aggregate. Today the company serves most of the nation, and Roberts continues to serve as president.

Solite Corporation is an integrated, closely held company operated by its 45 owner-managers. It was formed in 1947 by John W. Roberts, who continues to serve as its president.

When he started Solite, Roberts hoped to create an organization capable of serving the United States from the Atlantic Ocean to the Mississippi River with lightweight aggregate. His venture has grown to fulfill that vision and to vastly exceed it. Both by establishing its own new "building blocks" of businesses and acquiring others, the firm has evolved in a planned progression into a unique company structured of five interlocked and coordinated divisions, each supporting the others.

The central part of the pyramid is the Solite Lightweight Aggregate Division. The balance of the Solite pyramid consists of plants and distribution centers that mine, manufacture, and sell bituminous coal; liquid burnable waste materials; natural aggregates such as sand, gravel, and crushed stone; ready-mix concrete; the masonry units commonly known as Solite blocks; and other building materials. Other corporate activities include the repair, rebuilding, design, and fabrication of machinery and other merchandise.

The Solite Lightweight Aggregate Division was organized in 1947. Its first plant was located in Buckingham County, Virginia. This plant is today called the A.F. Old Plant—after one of Roberts' partners, a man who was in charge of production for the first 25 years. The second Solite plant is on the Virginia-North Carolina line. The other four are in North Carolina, New York, Kentucky, and Florida.

All Solite plants are located near both navigable waterways and railroad lines, enabling the company to ship to customers via rail, road, or water, and giving it ready and reliable access to markets throughout the eastern United States. Reliability, quality, and service are the foundation of Solite's popularity with its customers. Because of its service—and because of the intrinsic qualities of its lightweight aggregate—the product "Solite" has never become a commodity, and the trademark "Solite" has become recognized as the standard of the industry, the lightweight aggregate by which others are measured in value.

After a decade of building lightweight aggregate plants, the corporation diversified through the acquisition of a block plant in Roanoke, Virginia. This was the first of seven plants located there and in Lynchburg, South Boston, and Chesapeake, Virginia; and Eden, Charlotte, and Hickory, North Carolina. These plants all produce Solite masonry units, SolarBlock units for passive solar construction, and other blocks to suit

The Chesapeake Bay Bridge in Annapolis, Maryland, has Solite concrete in its deck. The Solite has proven more durable than the stone concrete also used in the bridge.

custom architectural specifications. They also handle building materials, ground cover, lintels, and related merchandise as a service to the building trade.

The ConAgg Division is composed of the transportation firm that delivers the Block Division's masonry units; the Massy Concrete Company that furnishes the Richmond area with ready-mix concrete; Caroline Stone, which furnishes the Northern Neck and northern Virginia with crushed stone and rip rap; and the Southern Materials Division, which supplies distribution plants in northern Virginia and the Hampton Roads area.

Three of the company's operations are involved with construction of its plants and facilities, design and manufacture of machinery, and overhaul of heavy hauling equipment.

The Coal Division, formed in 1974, has developed surface and deep mines in West Virginia and Kentucky. Its Harlan, Kentucky, mine—located on the infamous site where the name "Bloody" Harlan originated—is now recognized for its safe and highly productive operating practices. It ships coal not only to the Solite plants but also to industries and utilities throughout the Southeast.

The Oldover Division, founded in 1972, is an integrated company that col-

The Solite concrete used in the Crystal City Plaza reduced the dead weight on its foundations.

lects industrial waste and transports it to Solite plants or other industrial furnaces. The firm was formed to destroy flammable industrial waste products by using them as fuels. From the list of chemicals classified as hazardous, it selected certain ones that could be safely used in its rotary kilns.

The process, as well as safely destroying hazardous waste, has contributed pioneering methods and new efficiencies in industrial furnaces. Solite and Oldover became the largest user of these fuels in the United States, thereby providing a service to industry and to the environment.

Such concern for the environment is part of Solite's corporate policy. The organization is dedicated to being a good neighbor and a responsible corporate citizen. It has reclaimed land, conserved topsoil, and planned for the beneficial use of its mining lands even before it was required to do so by law. Recently, the firm has harvested timber from trees that it planted 30 years ago on former mining properties.

Solite's safety record is widely admired. The sand and gravel industry has no other company in the Southeast that can match its 18-year no-lost-time accident record. The Oldover Division has a perfect record for its 14 years of over-the-road tanker transportation of liquid burnable waste fuels. One or more of the lightweight aggregate plants have won the international safety competition each year since the competition has existed. Its Eden machine division has had a perfect 11-year record since it started.

The Solite strategy for the 1980s calls for strengthening its corporate position in each of the markets it serves through further improving its service and quality in order to form a firm foundation for future growth. Long-range planning has always been an important component of management at Solite Corporation, and executive teams are even now working on plans for the year 2000. With a mineral acquisition policy that has resulted in a steady buildup of mineral reserves, the corporation now has holdings with proven reserves that will last well toward the end of the twenty-first century.

Solite concrete, because of its strength to weight ratio, was used on the roof of the Capitol in Washington, D.C.

VIRGINIA MUTUAL INSURANCE COMPANY

Edward N. Hardy, Jr., president from 1955 to 1972 and currently chairman of the board of directors.

C. Benton Evans, CPCU, the current president of Virginia Mutual Insurance Company.

Charles W. Peterson, president from 1972 to 1981.

For more than a half-century Virginia Mutual Insurance Company has been meeting the insurance needs of a wide range of Virginia clients. Many of the businesses that first signed up with Virginia Mutual still work with the company, but that is not surprising. Loyalty is valued at Virginia Mutual, and many of the corporate employees have spent their entire professional lives in its offices.

Virginia Mutual was chartered September 5, 1935, as the Virginia Auto Mutual Insurance Company (it took its current name in 1949, in recognition of its rapidly expanding line of coverages). The firm was founded by a group of leaders in the growing transportation industry—with the aid of their attorneys. The principal organizer was attorney E.N. Hardy, Jr.

Judge Oscar L. Shewmake, a member of the organizing committee, became the first president. He was succeeded in 1946 by S.A. Jessup, another of the venture's organizers. Hardy himself served as president from 1955 to 1972, and is still chairman of the board of directors.

Hardy was a young attorney in the 1930s, when he and his associates first thought of organizing an insurance company. His partners included a congressman and others active in civic affairs. The enterprise specialized in transportation law, representing several bus firms and long-distance trucking operations, as well as the Virginia Highway Users Association. These clients all needed insurance coverage, yet found policies hard to obtain, and, as Hardy recalls, "the premiums were exorbitant."

The need for a mutual insurance company was further emphasized by the situation in which the motor transportation industry in Virginia found itself following the enactment of the Federal Motor Carrier Act of 1935. That law required that common carriers operating under certificates of public convenience and necessity must file policies of insurance or indemnity bonds, and set statutory limits.

In anticipation of the new federal law, the organizers of Virginia Mutual started work back in 1934. Under the state laws then in effect, one could form a mutual insurance firm without paid-in capital. "We had no difficulty obtaining the needed number of applications," recalls Hardy, "but we did have some trouble obtaining paid-up policies."

In order to help with soliciting new policies, Hardy traveled throughout the state, visiting commercial transit operators and telling them about the new company. Finally the organization met the charter requirements, and on November 27, 1935, it obtained its license from the state insurance department.

The business expanded slowly. It stayed exclusively in Virginia for the first two or three years, then extended to neighboring jurisdictions—Maryland, North Carolina, and the District of Columbia—as its clients became interstate carriers. Even after expansion brought the organization into South Carolina, Georgia, and Delaware, it continued to write policies primarily in Virginia and North Carolina; today, with almost 100 employees and 800 agents, the firm continues to write policies in Virginia and North Carolina.

From its earliest days Virginia Mutual has stressed careful selection of risks, prompt investigation and close attention to accidents and claims, and an active safety department. The safety department is structured as a service to its insureds. Its work has frequently received national attention and recognition.

The early days were difficult. "Buses and trucks were target risks," remembers Hardy. "We lost a lot of lawsuits because we had trouble finding sympathetic juries. Business was great for our law firm, but rough on the insurance company." In response, Virginia Mutual broadened its practice, adding workmen's compensation along with fire and casualty policies, making it a full-service operation.

During World War II most of the organization's principals entered mili-

tary service. Judge Shewmake remained president for the duration. Business remained profitable, especially as gas rationing kept automobile traffic to a minimum and lowered the accident rate for the firm's bus and truck clients.

After the war bus and truck operations expanded remarkably; also, the boom in home construction and ownership fueled by returning GIs led to a rapid expansion in the company's home owner business coverage. By 1950 the underwriting of bus and truck operators had dropped to 24 percent of Virginia Mutual's total volume. Today only a small proportion of Virginia Mutual policies cover transportation companies.

Charles Peterson joined Virginia Mutual in 1936 as an auditor. He stayed with the firm for 51 years, serving as president from 1972 to 1981. "Over the course of my 50 years with the company there were some rough days," he recalls, "but it was a wonderful feeling when we achieved our first million dollars in surplus, and great to have the sense of accomplishment when we first moved into our own building." Virginia Mutual moved into its headquarters at 4015 Fitzhugh Avenue in Richmond in 1955.

Safety and Service Pay Dividends is the company motto. "We think first of our insureds," says C. Benton Evans,

the president of Virginia Mutual. "That's the first priority. Next is our agents. That's why we still have several of the policyholders that we started with in 1935. Several of the agents and agencies that have worked with us over the years are still with us. We work on that."

This home office was occupied by Virginia Mutual Insurance Company from 1937 to 1955.

Completed in 1955, this is the current home office of Virginia Mutual Insurance Company.

Evans, the 1976 National Field Man of the Year of the National Association of Professional Insurance Agents, has been with Virginia Mutual Insurance Company since 1949. He became a member of the board of directors in 1973, and has served as president since 1981.

NORFOLK STATE UNIVERSITY

James A. Bowser Memorial Hall, Norfolk State's Industrial Technical Building, was constructed in 1959.

For more than a half-century Norfolk State University has emphasized its mission as a "people's university" with an open-door policy. All students, regardless of socioeconomic status, may benefit from educational opportunities to the fullest extent of their capabilities.

The youngest of Virginia's five predominantly black institutions, NSU has become the largest in the state and third largest in the nation. The student body is about 7,700 and growing.

During the Great Depression educators and civic leaders felt compelled to provide alternatives to unemployed black youths unable to continue their education. Out of this need sprang the Norfolk Unit of Virginia Union University, a private sectarian university in Richmond.

Several prominent businessmen and educators are credited with the foresight to form the college. Dr. Samuel F. Scott was the first director, and Dr. Lyman B. Brooks became the second di-

rector and the first president, serving the college for 37 years. The second and current president, Dr. Harrison B. Wilson, has served for more than 12 years.

Eighty-five students attended the first classes, held in September 1935 on the second floor of what was once the Hunton Branch YMCA Building on Brambleton Avenue. By 1944 the school had become known as the Norfolk Division of Virginia State College, eligible for state funding.

To provide space for needed expansion, the City of Norfolk sold the college its 50-acre Memorial Park Golf Course as a permanent campus site for one dollar. Construction began in 1953 on an administration/classroom building, the start of an ambitious program that has since added more than two dozen buildings and more than 70 additional acres to the campus.

On February 1, 1969, by legislative enactment, Norfolk State College emerged. The school has undergone five name changes, receiving university status in February 1979.

Course offerings also kept pace with community needs, growing from predominantly liberal arts offerings to include vocational and scientific disciplines. Today nine schools offer degrees

G.W.C. Brown Memorial Hall, formerly known as Tidewater Hall, was built in 1955 and was Norfolk State's old administration building.

in more than 70 academic programs, including 15 accredited graduate programs.

The critical shortage of blacks in the sciences nationwide has prompted NSU to play a leading role in educating students in this field through creation of the Ronald I. Dozoretz National Institute for Minorities in Applied Sciences. NSU also boasts outstanding ROTC programs, the oldest being an Army program that is the largest of a nonmilitary school in Virginia, and a female cadet enrollment that is the second largest in the U.S. The naval program is smaller but is experiencing rapid growth.

A favorite self-description is that Norfolk State is "where the student is Number One and the faculty is Special."

Built in 1984, Harrison B. Wilson Hall is Norfolk State's new administration building.

DOUGHTIE'S FOODS, INC.

From a one-family operation that started in its founder's garage in 1952, to a multimillion-dollar corporation that manufactures 35 varieties of barbecue sauce and distributes to customers in 26 states, Portsmouth's Doughtie's Foods, Inc., is ready to expand nationwide. Throughout its years of success the Doughtie family has remained the major shareholder, and personalized service to all customers is still the company's byword.

Though founder Bob Doughtie died in 1982, his stamp is apparent in that personal approach. Doughtie had first tried his hand as a railroad brakeman before going to work for a Port Norfolk barbecue house, Chubby's. As the story goes, he thought the barbecue the establishment was buying was too greasy, so he decided to make his own. He bought pork from Smithfield, cooked it, and pulled it apart by hand. He worked out his own sauce recipe and mixed it by hand in big vats in the wee hours of the morning. Soon everyone in the family was involved. While they were busy packaging the product—400 pounds per week—Doughtie went to his grandmother's to nap on the couch. By mid-morning he was out selling the packaged product, working from a little beige station wagon with a pig painted on it.

Within 10 years Doughtie had purchased Portsmouth Frozen Food Products. He incorporated and got a Small Business Administration loan in 1963 to build a $225,000 plant, where the company continues to grow today. By 1964 Doughtie's was processing hamburger patties for fast-food chains, and its food distribution arm handled several hundred products statewide.

Before long Doughtie's opened a sales distribution center in Tuxedo, Maryland, to serve the Washington-Baltimore market. In 1972, when the firm went public, Doughtie was named Virginia's small businessman of the year. During the 1970s Doughtie's ac-

quired several other organizations in Maryland and Virginia.

Manufacturing division sales have since exceeded 7 million pounds of barbecue and one million pounds of chili per year. Other divisions include distribution, food service (home and institutional), and DFI Acceptance (freezer purchases). A $2.5-million expansion to the headquarters will provide additional warehouse space for produce, fresh meats, and cheese coolers, and will substantially increase the storage capacity for the grocery inventory.

Though sales were once completed by truck vendors, a delivery method reminiscent of selling baked

goods or dry cleaning, today's methods have changed, with salesmen wiring orders in to headquarters via computers. But while contemporary technology may have changed some business procedures, Doughtie's manufacturing division expects future growth by serving traditional customer needs with a new twist. Convenience stores, now adding sit-down areas for eating, are the next targeted growth area for Doughtie's manufactured food products.

Founder Bob Doughtie stands by one of the company's delivery trucks during the early days of the business. Photo circa 1950

Today Doughtie's Foods distributes its products to customers in 26 states and is ready for nationwide expansion.

VIRGINIA PORT AUTHORITY

Dominating the waterfront skyline like giant structures on the *Star Wars* movie set, three bright-orange, state-of-the-art container cranes at Norfolk International Terminals symbolize a dramatic revolution in worldwide port development sparked by the Virginia Port Authority. With high-speed dual-hoist technology designed to increase handling capacity at the terminals from approximately 25 containers per hour to about 50 per hour, the monolithic structures are not only taller than any other

An aerial view of Portsmouth Marine Terminal in 1986. The City of Portsmouth was the first to participate in port unification in 1971. Downtown Norfolk is in the background (left center). Courtesy, Backus Aerial Photography, Inc.

cranes around but faster as well, capable of working the largest ships in the world. The only ones of their kind in the United States, they are dramatic examples of the kind of innovative technology applied by the VPA and its operating arm, Virginia International Terminals, Inc.

As the state's leading agency for international transportation and maritime commerce, the VPA is officially charged with providing and marketing the marine terminal facilities through which the shipping trade takes place. In recent years the VPA has become one of the most aggressive players among the nation's ports.

The Port of Hampton Roads is naturally blessed with long, straight, deep channels. Its harbor, now charac-

A replica of the Godspeed, *the 68-foot ship that brought the first settlers to Jamestown in 1607, is readied for loading at Norfolk International Terminals to sail to Felixstowe, England. From there she attempted to recreate the original voyage.*

terized by modern terminals and protected from changeable currents, is 18 miles from the open sea. Ocean carriers from all over the world, and the nation's foremost truck and rail transporters—including Norfolk Southern and CSX Transportation, both headquartered in Virginia—today provide vital infrastructure links for the future.

How the Virginia Port Authority came to claim such a top distinction

among the world's ports dates back to 1607. Virginia's maritime industry began with the arrival of the *Godspeed,* when the first English colonists settled at Jamestown, on the James River. Created for purposes of trade, this colony laid the foundation for port development in Virginia and the nation. The colonists depended entirely on supplies brought over by sea from England. As forests were cleared and land brought into production, the colony's output was returned by sea to English markets. One of the first exports was tobacco, still a major Virginia export today, with approximately 45 percent of all U.S. tobacco and tobacco products moving annually through the Port of Hampton Roads.

The vessels of the early 1600s were small and could sail into the numerous creeks and rivers of the Tidewater area to deliver their cargoes directly to plantations that used the goods and produced the return loads. As early as 1640 efforts were made to establish ports where the ships could call to deliver and receive cargo, and where—from the government's standpoint—taxes could be readily assessed and collected.

Because of its proximity to the original colony at Jamestown, one of the first major ports was Hampton. In 1682 Norfolk was established, its principal reason for existence being its favorable location for seaborne commerce. Larger ships could then carry greater amounts of cargo to be loaded and unloaded and on their way out to sea in shorter periods of time, thereby saving money. What is today referred to as a "load center" concept began on a much smaller scale years ago. It is now a premier factor in port selection by transportation managers worldwide.

One of the first major port facilities in Norfolk was built on the triangle of land bounded by Main Street, Granby Street, and the Elizabeth River, in Norfolk. In March 1761 the Virginia General Assembly appointed a group of trustees and directors, instructing them to "enlarge the land, secure it (from washing away), and build a wharf and storehouses there on," to replace earlier facilities, that had deteriorated to the

A standard crane easily lifts a truck for loading onto a ship at Norfolk International Terminals, the largest of the facilities owned by the Virginia Port Authority. Courtesy, Backus Aerial Photography, Inc.

point of requiring replacement.

Later, in 1789—concurrent with the ratification of the United States Constitution—the federal government entered its first relationship with the maritime industry, collecting duties on imported goods. This was done primarily to raise revenue to operate the government and later to protect infant U.S. industries from competition with more heavily industrialized nations of the world, primarily Great Britain.

In return for the duties collected on imported goods, the federal government became responsible for marking safe channels in the navigable waters of the nation. The U.S. Army Corps of Engineers was assigned the task of creating and maintaining channels and anchorages.

The Commonwealth of Virginia first took an active role in the maritime industry in 1922, when the general assembly established the Hampton Roads Port Commission, an advisory body.

Thirty years later, in 1952, then-Governor John S. Battle signed legislation creating an independent agency in state government, the Virginia State Ports Authority. From this point forward the port's modern era developed.

In 1965 the City of Norfolk arranged to acquire the local existing terminal, which had been constructed by the federal government in 1918-1919. Known as the "Army Base," this facility had been declared surplus. Built as a conventional breakbulk terminal, it was equipped with two finger piers, warehouses, railroad tracks, cranes, and other amenities needed by a breakbulk terminal. Concurrently, the City of Newport News entered an agreement with the Chesapeake and Ohio Railroad to acquire that line's merchandise terminal.

Norfolk immediately converted part of the terminal to a container berth, one of the first East Coast ports to de-

velop facilities for cargo in containers—large metal boxes of uniform size that could be handled faster and more efficiently than palletized or bundled breakbulk cargo. The first container crane was purchased, and in late 1967 a one-berth container terminal began operation in addition to the existing breakbulk activity that had been acquired with the original purchase. The following year the city purchased the terminal from the U.S. Maritime Administration.

The Virginia Chamber of Commerce formed a task force in 1971 to parallel then-Governor Linwood Holton's Management Study of the Ports, a mission that became known as the "unification" of the ports of Virginia. The general assembly changed the agency's name to the Virginia Port Authority and directed it to operate as a successful business enterprise.

Soon afterward the City of Portsmouth became the first to enter the new program of port unification, conveying

The Chessie System Railroad's Pier 14 was put into commercial operation in the summer of 1949 and is still one of the most modern coal transfer facilities on the East Coast. Though tonnage fluctuates in the world markets, Hampton Roads is still the top coal-exporting port in the country.

all rights, title, and interest in its terminal to the Virginia Port Authority.

However, until a few years ago each major local waterfront community marketed its own terminal facilities. Landmark legislation from the Virginia General Assembly finally consolidated all of the terminals under the one agency

More than 400 General Electric locomotive engines were shipped to the People's Republic of China in 1984 and 1985, making Newport News Marine Terminal the leading facility in the nation for such specialized cargo.

in 1981, with the transfer of operational control placed in Virginia International Terminals, Inc., and completed two years later. That action more than any other has spurred the port's success to the point that it was the most rapidly expanding port in the country for the two-year period 1985-1986. General cargo tonnage virtually doubled, from over 2 million tons to about 4.5 million tons and still growing. Deregulation of the various sectors of the transportation industry has given the port countless additional marketing opportunities.

During that same two-year period, for example, 15 steamship lines inaugurated new service through the port, bringing the total to more than 90. In 1986 the agency opened an office in

A ship departing from the ports of Virginia leaves with cargo on its way to markets all over the world. It will return fully loaded, too, making Hampton Roads distinct among East Coast ports in its balance of import to export shipments.

Hong Kong, supplementing a network of field offices at three domestic and three overseas locations. VEXTRAC, the VPA's export trading company, has enabled many small and medium-size Virginia businesses to enter the international export market. The VPA was also the first port in the United States to create an operational, fully automated cargo clearance program in conjunction with the U.S. Customs Service.

The port was the first to sign an agreement with the U.S. Army Corps of Engineers for a major harbor-deepening project under the Water Resources Act of 1986. After a 15-year wait for legislation to be passed, construction of the first phase of the deeper Thimble Shoals Channel—to be extended from 45 to 50 feet—finally began in March 1987, another national first. The deeper channel means that supercolliers can load to their fullest capacity in Hampton Roads, without having to top off elsewhere or without incurring greater costs by having to delay sailing until high tide. That is expected to keep the port—and the nation—competitive in the world coal market; at 40 to 50 million tons per year, Hampton Roads remains the world's leading coal-exporting port.

The port's traditionally strong and cooperative relationship between management and labor has also contributed to its success. Even as far back as the early post-Civil War days, when gangs were mostly black and managers were mostly white, the port's geography helped. Far enough south to escape the stridency of northeastern labor movements and far enough north to avoid upheavals in the Deep South, Hampton Roads has enjoyed relatively smoother relations than its competitors along the coast. When strikes were called on the national level, for example, they seldom involved local issues.

Thanks to the efforts of several governors, specific actions on behalf of the port have enhanced the agency's structure and position in overseas markets. Efforts to see the harbor-deepening project fulfilled garnered support not only from these leaders but also from congressmen and senators. Beginning with Governor John N. Dalton, each

Hampton Roads was one of the first ports on the East Coast to develop container facilities in 1967.

recent governor has advanced Virginia's interests in international trade during overseas visits. Former Governor Charles S. Robb was influential in developing long-term trade relationships for the Commonwealth in the Far East, resulting in shipment of more than 400 locomotives manufactured by General Electric in Erie, Pennsylvania, to the People's Republic of China.

In 1986 Governor Gerald S. Baliles called a special session of the Virginia General Assembly on transportation issues. Benchmark legislation earmarked 4 percent of all new tax revenues for expansion and a new terminal, or an estimated $200 million, the first time in the agency's history that there has been a steady and dependable revenue stream. The following year Governor Baliles proclaimed the Year of Trade, embarking on three overseas trade trips that netted sizable international commerce projects for the state. Additional trade with both Chinas and the prospect of a dedicated automobile import facility were among the major accomplishments from those visits.

Plans also advanced to create a Virginia Inland Port (VIP), an inland rail and truck terminal in Front Royal, Virginia, designed to facilitate cargo transfer between the port and the Midwest, one of the port's primary markets.

Directing the flow of traffic for an annual foreign trade volume worth $13 billion and creating 120,000 jobs with tax revenues in excess of $300 million annually has required stamina and dedication not only from the VPA but from Virginia's elected officials as well. Their consistent commitment recognizes the vital role the port plays in the Commonwealth's economy, ensuring the Port of Hampton Roads' place as "the natural mid-Atlantic load center" well into the next century.

Natural rubber from Southeast Asia is one of the most important break-bulk commodities to be imported through Hampton Roads. Its volume is the highest of any commodity shipped to the port in both import and export tonnage.

O'SULLIVAN CORPORATION

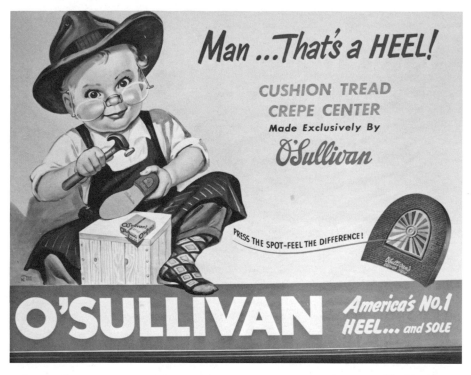

O'Sullivan Corporation traces its roots back to 1896 to a printing press in Lowell, Massachusetts. Humphrey O'Sullivan was a printer who nailed pieces of rubber floor mat to his shoes to relieve the stress of standing on hard ground all day. He patented his idea and promoted his invention as "America's No. 1 Heel." Pictured here are some of the company's early advertisements.

The O'Sullivan Corporation of Winchester, Virginia, is one of America's largest manufacturers of vinyl and of injection-molded plastic products. As a company that provides products vital to the modern life-style, it should typically have been created in the late 1950s or early 1960s—just soon enough to have provided the context for the classic scene in *The Graduate* where Dustin Hoffman is told that the future of America and his own best interests lay with that growing industry.

But the O'Sullivan Corporation instead traces its roots to a printing press in Lowell, Massachusetts, and as far back as 1896. Humphrey O'Sullivan was a printer. Long days standing in front of his press brought aching legs and sore feet. To relieve the stress, he nailed pieces of rubber floor mat to his shoes.

O'Sullivan patented the idea, and his O'Sullivan Rubber Company promoted his invention as "America's No. 1 Heel." At first the heels were manufactured for O'Sullivan by the Boston Belting Company. As demand expanded, the Goodrich Rubber Company of Akron, Ohio, became the supplier. In 1908 O'Sullivan sold his interest in the patents for a substantial sum—an impressive return on his initial $7,000 investment and moment of genius.

Corporate historians tell us that the immediate success of O'Sullivan was due at least as much to his promotion and marketing skills as it was to the need for his product. Company cars all carried highly visible advertising, and the "Little Cobbler" Kid O'Sullivan trademark quickly became widely recognized. In 1932 the O'Sullivan Rubber Company moved to Winchester, Virginia, its present home.

World War II accelerated the development of synthetic rubber. Not only was natural rubber suddenly unavailable, but synthetic products developed for the war effort proved attractive and cost effective in civilian applications as well. O'Sullivan saw the writing on the wall, and in 1949 completed a vinyl sheeting plant. Four years later, in 1953, the firm developed a plastic metal laminate process and built another factory.

These early O'Sullivan plants and processes supplied their products primarily to luggage and business machine manufacturers. The growing American automobile industry firms also became early customers for O'Sullivan plastics. In 1956 the firm began manufacturing vinyl for padded automobile dashboards, a product that continues to be among the company's most important.

In 1962 O'Sullivan expanded from

vinyl and rubber products to injection molding by purchasing a Hialeah, Florida, concern that manufactured plastic components by this new and promising process. Injection molding is a technologically sophisticated process requiring elaborate and expensive machinery but producing a high-quality product. It was the beginning of O'Sullivan's move to make itself a national leader in the process.

In 1968 O'Sullivan moved this division from Hialeah to a new building at the O'Sullivan complex in Winchester. Now known as the Gulfstream Division, it continues to be a major supplier of injection-molded parts for the automobile industry. Two years later, recognizing that rubber products no longer constituted its main business, the firm changed its name to O'Sullivan Corporation.

O'Sullivan acquired a new plant in the Winchester Industrial Park in 1976. The new plant completed the transition from the old era, manufacturing injection-molded thermoplastic unit soles for the footwear industry, as well as some small injection-molded parts for the Gulfstream Division. In 1978 O'Sullivan added a vinyl sheeting plant in Lebanon, Pennsylvania, and sharply increased the capacity of the Plastics Division.

In 1982 the Plastics Division product line was expanded by acquisition of a plant in Newton Upper Falls, Massachusetts. The plant produces roller-polished clear vinyl film and press polished sheeting—a top-quality product that remains in high demand. The company later purchased another sheet vinyl plant in Yerington, Nevada. The newest product is a laminated vinyl sheet that is used for pond and canal lining and water-treatment facilities.

Today O'Sullivan Corporation is composed of two major divisions: Plastics and Gulfstream. (The business sold the last of its rubber products interests in 1986.) Both are supported by research and development, new product engineering and development, plant engineering and maintenance, materials management, industrial relations, industrial engineering, management in-

formation, accounting, and marketing. O'Sullivan Corporation today encompasses more than one million square feet of manufacturing and office space, and employs more than 2,000 people, 1,700 in Virginia alone. The chairman of the board and chief executive officer of O'Sullivan is Arthur H. Bryant II. An Alexandria native, Bryant had previously worked with Herbert Bryant, Inc., his family corporation. He came to O'Sullivan in 1975 as executive vice-president. The following year he became president and chief operating officer. In 1984 he became chairman and president.

"We stress two things at O'Sullivan," says Bryant. "Customer service and quality. We don't sell price. We do sell quality. That philosophy is paying off."

James T. Holland is president and chief operating officer of O'Sullivan Corporation. Holland was elected president in 1986, and had been executive vice-

Today O'Sullivan Corporation is composed of two divisions, Plastics and Gulfstream—a manufacturer of injection-molded parts for the automobile industry. Stressing customer service and quality, the firm has been given numerous awards, some of which are pictured here.

president since 1984. Holland joined the company in 1976. He served as vice-president, treasurer, and chief financial officer prior to 1984.

The growth of O'Sullivan Corporation has been spectacular in recent years. Between 1975 and 1987 the value of outstanding stock increased from $6.4 million to $187 million. Despite the extraordinary capital investment required by the injection-molding process, the firm maintains a conservative financial policy and carries little debt. The stock is traded on the American Exchange, but much of it remains concentrated in relatively few hands.

DYNCORP

With a new-era high-technology name to match its long record of distinguished accomplishments, the former Dynalectron Corporation of Reston, Virginia, is ready to greet the next episode of its dynamic history as DynCorp. Long a fixture in northern Virginia and a leader of the Old Dominion's technological community, DynCorp provides diverse services worldwide to private industry and government.

With the end of World War II, soldiers returned to their civilian pursuits, and industry resumed production of automobiles and vacuum cleaners instead of tanks and guns. The reviving economy brought many new companies, each seeking a unique place in the new era. Among them was California Eastern Airways, Inc., a Delaware Corporation formed, in part, by returning aviators. Within six months of its 1946 launch, California Eastern was providing commercial flights between Oakland, California, and New York.

In 1951 and 1952 California Eastern acquired Land-Air, Inc., and the Air Carrier Service Corporation, two other creations of returning veteran pilots. By coming together the three found a new

strength and began to build a worldwide technology-based service company. The firm's flight operations ended in 1957, and four years later it adopted the name of Dynalectron Corporation.

Dynalectron grew rapidly through the 1960s and 1970s, expanding both by acquisitions and through internal developments. By the end of the 1970s Dynalectron was a leader in the development of sophisticated petroleum and petrochemical processes, one of the leaders among commercial aviation service companies, and, by the mid-1980s, one of the nation's 100 largest defense con-

This FIA-18 Hornet being worked on by DynCorp people exemplifies the nearly 20,000 aircraft maintained, modified, repaired, or serviced by approximately 3,500 DynCorp employees at military installations worldwide.

tractors. By then Dynalectron was also one of America's 100 largest diversified service companies, and, with operations in both the United States and Canada, the fourth-largest electrical contractor in North America.

Since 1946 DynCorp has built an organization that produces more than $800 million in revenues, a company that ranks as one of the nation's top 100 diversified services firms.

The Technical Services Group remains the flagship of DynCorp. Technical Services has been providing quality services to agencies of the U.S. government for more than 35 years.

Technical Services' Aerospace Operations, headquartered at Fort Worth, Texas, provides a wide range of services to defense installations worldwide. In the Washington, D.C., metropolitan area, Aerospace Operations provides technical and engineering support services at the Naval Air Test Center at Pautuxent, Maryland.

Another division of Technical Services, Applied Technology Operations, manages and maintains test ranges and

DynCorp's Commercial Aviation Group, DynAir, is one of the largest independent providers of ground-support services in the United States.

instrumentation installations pertaining to the development, performance, and analysis of tests on weapons systems and other military and aerospace equipment. Applied Technology provides services to all three branches of the armed forces.

Support Services operations of the Technical Services Group specializes in operating and maintaining government and military facilities. Locally the group provides base engineering and maintenance services at the U.S. Army Engineering Center, Fort Belvoir, Virginia. Other Technical Services units repair and overhaul naval shipboard combat weapons systems, conduct ship operations, and provide logistic support.

System Services, also based in McLean, supplies industrial and government clients with complete security services worldwide and provides sophisticated telecommunications services.

The DynAir Group supplies a wide range of ground support services to international and domestic commercial and cargo carriers at major airports throughout the country. DynAir specializes in supporting passenger and commercial airlines by providing "total ground support." That includes aircraft maintenance, passenger and security services, fueling, ground transportation, fuel handling, facility and equipment maintenance and repair, cargo services, and electronic and avionic support. DynAir serves more than 130 clients at more than 80 U.S. airports from New York and Miami to Anchorage and Honolulu.

DynAir Services, Inc., based in McLean, Virginia, provides ground support services to more than 90 international and domestic air carriers at major gateway airports throughout the United States. CFE Services, Inc., headquartered in Norfolk, Virginia, provides personnel and equipment at almost 60 airports in more than 30 states to handle freight for cargo aircraft. DynAir Fueling, Inc., provides aviation fuel storage, handling, and into-place delivery at 15 airports in the United States and its territories.

The Specialty Contracting Group's operations include electrical contracting

for commercial and industrial customers in the United States, and electrical and mechanical contracting and installation services in Canada. The group is especially active as a subcontractor in the construction of large hotels, office buildings, and shopping malls. More recently it has developed unique capabilities in automated industrial systems, including automobile assembly and food processing.

With more than 16,000 employees stationed around the world, this Virginia corporation has a substantial impact. The firm continues its restructuring efforts, and at year-end 1987 was implementing a leveraged buyout of the company in conjunction with an employee stock ownership plan.

Jorge Carnicero, one of the founders of DynCorp, is chairman of the board of directors. Dan R. Bannister is president and chief executive officer. James H. Duggan is executive vice-president and chief operating officer. T. Eugene Blanchard is senior vice-president and chief financial officer.

Today's DynCorp is a very different organization than that of a few years ago. It will continue to change as new

The newest operating group at DynCorp is the DynService Network, a specialist in depot-level repair and overhaul of electronic and electromechanical components of computers, peripherals, and telecommunication systems.

In recent years DynCorp's Specialty Contracting Group has specialized in industrial construction such as this sophisticated automobile assembly plant.

personnel, refocused energies, and new priorities all have visible impact on the shape and future of the company.

THE EVANS COMPANY

The Evans Company is one of the largest commercial real estate development and management companies in the Washington metropolitan area. The Randolph Building in McLean, Virginia, has 180,000 square feet and houses the firm's headquarters.

construction. All properties will be developed within the next 10 to 15 years.

In the beginning Evans developed a small shopping mall in northwest Washington, D.C. Later he began to develop in the Tysons Corner area, located in northern Virginia. Tysons Corner is now one of the nation's fastest-growing urban areas.

"We have been fortunate to have the foresight and luck, with respect to the right place and time, to acquire and assemble properties," says Juliana BJE Greenleaf, vice-president / marketing and design, and one of Evans' first employees.

Greenleaf joined The Evans Company in 1978, along with David's youngest brother, James. James currently serves as executive vice-president/development and construction. The three worked together to develop the company's first project, the John Marshall Building, in McLean, Virginia. When the firm moved there in 1980, it expanded its personnel to eight. Stephen J.

The SAIC (Science Application International Corporation) Tysons campus in Tysons Corner is managed by The Evans Company. Building I has 312,000 square feet and Buildings II and III on which construction started in August 1987, have 300,000 square feet.

Hunters Branch (Phase I and II), above, on I-66 in Vienna, Virginia, is a 57-acre high-rise office project with 350 residential units and a total of 1.2 million square feet of office space.

David W. Evans, founder of The Evans Company, based in McLean, Virginia, started his commercial real estate development and management firm in 1972 in a small office in Washington, D.C.

His company is now one of the largest developers in the Washington metropolitan area, with approximately 70 employees and 30 million square feet of property in some stage of development, either existing, planned, or under

One Fair Oaks in Fairfax, Virginia, contains 215,000 square feet of office space.

Washington Park Office Building, with 105,000 square feet in Washington, D.C., is one of three structures the firm has built in the Washington, D.C., area.

Garchik, who joined the firm in 1981, is the company's president.

The Evans Company moved in 1985 to its present location in the Randolph Building at 8251 Greensboro Drive—a structure also developed by The Evans Company. The business occupies one floor of the building. Some of the other tenants include Primark, Arthur Anderson, and Dean-Witter.

In other buildings, Evans manages such full-building tenants as MCI, SAIC, Mobil, and ICF. In fact, several of its tenants are *Fortune* 500 companies.

In 1987 The Evans Company developed a half-million square feet of office space and was in the process of constructing an additional one million square feet. It had completed four of nine planned buildings for McLean, three buildings in the District of Columbia, one in Fairfax, and one of six buildings planned for Vienna, Virginia.

The company attributes its focus on northern Virginia to the area's growth potential. "It's an area where large companies can still consolidate," explains Greenleaf. She points out that northern Virginia's access to the airports and the capital make it a good place in which to expand. In addition, northern Virginia offers excellent educational benefits and life-styles.

The firm's involvement contrib-

utes to the area's overall growth, in addition to its increased number of office parks. The Evans Company has been active in industry-related projects, such as contributing funds for road work and traffic improvements. Its executives are also active on the boards of major industry-related organizations.

"We do care," says Greenleaf. "We want to produce financially successful projects for the owners, some-

Plaza America is an Evans Company 27-acre project with a total of 1.2 million square feet of office space to be built in Reston, Virginia.

thing that *Fortune* 500 and *Fortune* 100 tenants feel proud to be a part of."

The Evans Company owes much of its success to its professional relationships. Greenleaf says, "We work very well together as a team. There's no sense of competition within our company or with whom we work." David Evans adds, "It's our company. We all have contributed."

THE MASON HIRST COMPANIES

T. Mason Hirst (left), founder of the firm and grandfather of the current president, with his Rio truck in 1916.

From a cattle dealership in the early 1900s to providing offices for designing the U.S. Space Station in the 1980s—the history of The Mason Hirst Companies is a study in responding to customers' needs.

T. Mason Hirst, the founder, began his career in 1911 as a cattle broker. As northern Virginia grew, people asked him for farms, and Hirst found himself in the real estate business. Selling farms was profitable, and in 1921 he established Mason Hirst as a real estate firm.

Today The Mason Hirst Companies is an affiliation of real estate development and investment businesses. The major product lines of The Mason Hirst Companies include commercial development, responding especially to the demand for large-scale office environments for aerospace, defense, and computer-intensive firms having ultra-sophisticated security and communication requirements. The company also acquires and renovates existing income-producing properties. In addition, Mason Hirst does residential development and commercial brokerage. One affiliate, the Jefferson Management Company, is a commercial property management firm.

T. Mason Hirst ran his cattle and

Owners Tom and Joanna Hirst meet with their partner, David Fitch.

farm business out of his home in Annandale. His son, Omer L. Hirst, who became a president of the company, was born there. The Hirst family lived and worked in the house until 1952, when it was converted entirely to business purposes. Mason Hirst operated there until 1985, when the firm moved to larger quarters in Reston.

In addition to running the real estate firm, Omer Hirst served for 22 years in the Virginia State Legislature. Always a champion of better transportation, Senator Hirst conceived the idea of the Dulles parallel lanes, a major tollway that links Dulles International Airport to Tysons Corner. He was also the chief patron of the bill to create the George Mason Law School.

Thomson M. Hirst, the current president, began working for the family business when he was six years old, helping out as an office boy. He obtained his realtor's license at the age of 19 and worked his way through college and graduate school selling property. He assumed the presidency in 1972 after receiving a master's degree in urban planning from Harvard. He earned his bachelor's degree in urban history from Princeton in 1964.

Tom's wife, Joanna, is vice-president and chief financial officer. After earning her bachelor's degree in economics from Harvard, she secured a master's degree from MIT in urban

Mason Hirst was selected to provide the headquarters for the U.S. Space Station, PSC Division.

planning with a minor in finance. Like Omer and Tom, Joanna graduated from college with Magna Cum Laude and Phi Beta Kappa honors.

Mason Hirst's organizational and technological creativity has always kept it on the cutting edge of the new technology. In 1913 Hirst was the first cattle dealer in northern Virginia to acquire a truck. Years later the company became the first local land development operation to use computers. The firm is con-

This building in the Lake Fairfax Business Center contains 277,000 square feet of space and houses such companies as Grumman Aerospace, Booz Allan Hamilton, Wyle Labs, Ford Aerospace, and Barrios technology.

stantly developing new software and analytical techniques.

The company is devoted to completing complex tasks with speed and quality. It follows rigorous scheduling techniques and an aggressive bonus/penalty system to expedite the development of property. The goal is to service customers with highly tailored needs and early move-in dates. For Mason Hirst, the period from initial design concept to the move-in of a tenant often has an elapsed time of less than 12 months.

Mason Hirst has benefited greatly from the leadership and capability of women. Edna Hirst, wife of the founder, was a co-owner and co-worker with her husband. Just as he was the first cattle dealer to own a truck, she was the first

woman to drive a car down Alexandria's King Street. Today Joanna Hirst is a co-owner of the company, and 50 percent of the current executive staff is made up of women.

To service customer demand, Mason Hirst is now experiencing its greatest growth rate ever. Its staff has been growing 25 percent per annum, and its commercial portfolio is growing at a much higher rate as new projects and new product lines are added. It now has more than 2.5 million square feet of space in planning and development, and it will be adding eight to 10 new projects in the near future. Among its successes are the international headquarters of Freddie Mac, an ultrasecure facility for the largest electronics defense contractor in the United States, and a major complex from which Grumman Aerospace will design the U.S. Space Station.

Along with the desire for continued growth, the firm's owners feel a concern for the land, the local government, and community affairs. "Enlightened self-interest demands that we take part of each day to help solve problems for the community at large," state the principals. "Public service creates a prosperous and successful community in which everybody benefits. We are committed to setting high standards in our business as well as our community activities."

USAIR

The mail must go through! With its unique air-mail pickup service, USAir (then All American Aviation) delivered the mail to remote locations in Pennsylvania, West Virginia, Delaware, and Ohio.

USAir's newest aircraft—the Boeing 737-700—is the most advanced, quiet, and fuel-efficient aircraft of its size and range.

USAir has become the leading airline serving Virginia. Long a leader in the Northeast, USAir recently acquired California-based Pacific Southwest Airlines (PSA) and North Carolina-based Piedmont Aviation, becoming one of America's most popular, prominent, and profitable airlines.

USAir and PSA operations were integrated in the spring of 1988, while Piedmont operations will be merged into USAir in early 1989. After that merger, USAir will rank as the nation's second-largest airline company in terms of passenger boardings.

USAir's current connecting hubs are at Pittsburgh and Philadelphia. Over the next several years, as USAir expands to include the routes previously operated by PSA and Piedmont, its network of hubs will expand to include Baltimore, Charlotte, Dayton, and Syracuse as well.

The national headquarters of USAir is at National Airport in Washington, D.C. Washington and northern Virginia were among the first communities served by USAir when, under the name of All American Aviation, it began carrying passengers in 1949. Already a leading air carrier in Virginia, USAir—due to its acquisition of Piedmont Airlines and its commuter system—is now the leading airline serving the Commonwealth.

USAir first took to the skies carrying mail to small towns in the Allegheny Mountain region of western Pennsylvania, making use of a technological breakthrough created by Dr. Lytle S. Adams, a Chicago dentist. Adams developed a device that would enable an airplane to pick up and deliver mail sacks without having to land. He demonstrated his ingenious system at the Chicago World's Fair, where he met champion glider pilot and businessman Richard C. du Pont.

Du Pont was fascinated. He decided to start a company that would provide air-mail pickup and delivery service to isolated locations using Adams' device. First he chartered All American Aviation, Inc. as a Delaware corporation. Then he filed bids on two experimental air-mail pickup routes advertised by the United States Post Office. The routes covered a mountainous, remote, challenging area.

All American Aviation won both routes without contest. The bids established Air Mail Routes 1001 and 1002 connecting cities in Pennsylvania, West Virginia, Delaware, and Ohio.

The largest sections of each route lay in the Allegheny Mountains and required flying over difficult terrain known for some of the worst-possible weather and conditions. More exacting conditions for testing air-mail pickup would be hard to find, but All American Aviation went ahead.

The first air-mail pickup flight was on May 12, 1939. Norm Rintoul piloted the small plane that snatched a mail sack suspended between two steel masts in Latrobe, Pennsylvania. Flight mechanic Victor Yesulaites operated the winch that reeled in the bag.

All American Aviation carried the mail for 10 years with a team of pilots, flight mechanics, and ground employees who returned romance and adventure to aviation. The stories of those who flew

All set for an on-time departure on USAir's (then All American Airways) first scheduled passenger flight on March 7, 1949.

the scarlet Stinson Reliants may remind listeners of the barnstorming days of the 1920s, but records show that it was also a serious and profitable business.

During the early years of air-mail pickup flights, du Pont headed the company. One of America's leading experts in gliders, du Pont left All American Aviation during World War II to help the U.S. Army Air Corps establish its glider program. All American Aviation engineers working under his direction redesigned pickup devices for gliders used to transport troops. Major Halsey R. Bazley succeeded du Pont as president in 1942.

With the introduction of the local-service airline era following World War II, All American Aviation decided that its best future lay with carrying passengers as well as the mail. It applied to become a local-service airline, part of the federally subsidized system of short-haul carriers.

All American Aviation received government approval to carry passengers early in 1949. To support its new activities, the airline moved its headquarters from Wilmington to Washington, D.C., and changed its name to All American Airways. All American Airways initiated its passenger service on March 7, 1949, with a fleet of 11 DC-3s. The first major cities on the All American system were Washington, Baltimore, Philadelphia, New York, Pittsburgh, Buffalo, and Cincinnati—with service to many of the smaller cities in between.

Robert M. Love guided All American through the transition from air-mail pickup to scheduled passenger service. Love remained active with the airline until 1975, when he was named director emeritus after serving as president, chairman, and as a member of the board of directors.

By 1953, when the company changed its name to Allegheny Airlines, Inc., the fleet consisted of 13 DC-3s, and the route network had expanded to Erie, Pennsylvania; Cleveland, Ohio; and Parkersburg and Huntington, West Virginia.

Based in the populous East with its many important short-haul markets, Allegheny grew rapidly, developing new ticketing, reservations, and baggage-handling systems to meet the increasing demands of short-haul air transport.

In 1953 Leslie O. Barnes was named president and Henry A. Satterwhite joined the board of directors. Satterwhite served as chairman of the board from 1956 to 1978. He and Barnes piloted Allegheny through the "feeder-line" era, through mergers with Mohawk and Lake Central airlines, and into the jet age.

In 1959 Allegheny expanded to several New England cities and became the first airline to put the Convair 540 turboprops into service. By 1963 the airline that had started with 11 DC-3s had a fleet of 38 aircraft—23 Convair 440 jet-props and 15 Martin Executives. The growing fleet required increasingly specialized facilities so Allegheny moved its maintenance, engineering, flight operations, and flight control personnel from Washington to a new, multimillion-dollar facility at Greater Pittsburgh International Airport.

One of the nation's largest passenger-carrying airlines, USAir operates more than 1,600 flight departures per day and carries more than 30 million passengers per year.

In 1966 Allegheny introduced its first pure jet, the DC-9. The company's last piston-engine aircraft, a Convair, was phased out of service in September 1977, although newer piston-engined aircraft are now used by all of the airlines that are part of the Allegheny Commuter System.

The Allegheny Commuter System, USAir's innovative network of independent airlines that provides efficient, convenient service to smaller localities, first took wing as a commuter airline assuming Allegheny's service between Hagerstown and Baltimore with four daily round-trip flights.

This Allegheny Commuter program enabled Allegheny to serve smaller markets without requiring federal subsidy payments. At the same time, the communities gained by receiving more frequent service and the same benefits—joint fares, reservations, baggage checking—they had received from Allegheny itself.

The first Allegheny Commuter flight took off on November 15, 1967. Today a full network of Allegheny Commuter airlines contract with USAir to carry more than 2 million passengers per year between local and connecting hub airports. One of the Allegheny Commuters, Pennsylvania Airlines, is a wholly owned subsidiary of USAir Group, Inc.

Allegheny was ready for more, but in the era of federal regulation of air transportation, airlines could only grow through acquisition. By merging with Indianapolis-based Lake Central Airlines (effective July 1, 1968), the Allegheny system expanded to 77 airports serving an area in which more than 50 percent of the nation's population lived.

Allegheny stretched its regulated wings even farther in 1972, when it merged with Mohawk Airlines based in Utica, New York. That merger made Allegheny the nation's sixth-largest passenger-carrying airline.

With its expanded route system, its strong Allegheny Commuter network, and a fleet of 37 DC-9s, 31 BAC 1-11s, and 40 Convair 580s, Allegheny was positioned for continued growth. In 1974 Allegheny became the first local-service airline to make itself totally self-sufficient, allowing it to be removed from the federal subsidy program.

Barnes retired as president in 1975 and the board of directors elected Edwin I. Colodny to succeed him. Colodny had joined Allegheny in 1957 as assistant to the president; he held several other executive positions before being named chief executive officer. Colodny is now chairman of the board, president, and chief executive officer of the airline.

The modern age of American aviation began in 1978 with the passage of the Airline Deregulation Act, a law that radically altered the nature of the indus-

try. It brought with it a rapid growth in passenger volume on all scheduled airlines in the United States. Allegheny was no exception. With both the business and vacation travel markets expanding rapidly, each month brought new records for numbers of passengers carried.

To meet new public demands, the airline modernized its equipment, phased out the last of the Convair 580s, and became an all-jet fleet. With both public interest and value growing, the firm's stock was listed on the New York Exchange.

Responding to the new competitive atmosphere, Allegheny adopted innovative pricing practices offering travelers a variety of discount fare plans. It also started service to Houston—followed by new service to Orlando, Tampa, and West Palm Beach. The following year Allegheny added flights to Birmingham, Phoenix, Tucson, New Orleans, and Raleigh-Durham.

Allegheny had become a major airline and was planning to expand its route network across the country. But market research revealed that much of the public still, incorrectly, perceived the company as a small, local-service carrier. Consultants suggested that Allegheny would not shake the "small and local" image without changing its name. Corporate executives sought a name that would reflect the airline's new size and scope. On October 28, 1979, Allegheny Airlines became USAir.

In December 1986 USAir Group (the holding company for USAir), announced that it had agreed to purchase PSA. With the approval of the Department of Transportation, that purchase became final in late May 1987, and the operations were merged in 1988. With this acquisition USAir is now a major carrier in the California market, one of the nation's busiest air travel corridors.

On March 6, 1987, USAir Group announced that it had agreed to purchase Piedmont Aviation, a North Carolina-based airline with a history

and tradition remarkably similar to that of USAir. The Department of Transportation's approval was received on October 30, 1987, and the acquisition was completed on November 5.

The acquisition and eventual integration of Piedmont and PSA into USAir creates a comprehensive network providing convenient service to more than 100 cities throughout the nation and international service to Canada, Mexico, and Great Britain.

With its modern fleet of comfortable, quiet, and efficient aircraft; its flexible operations hubs; and its strong balance sheet, USAir is one of the nation's most successful airlines. The firm has flown through the storms of deregulation, emerging stronger than ever with both continuous profits and outstanding customer loyalty. According to Colodny, USAir's net and operating margins continue to be among the best in the industry. "The company has reported a profit

in every year since 1976," he says.

"Our number-one objective is to remain financially strong," says Colodny. "Over the years we have followed a policy of controlled growth. We will stay strong by continuing prudent financial planning, and by continuing to serve our markets well. Our scheduling philosophy has been geared to serving the business traveler, and we will continue this emphasis."

In 1984 USAir introduced America to the latest aviation technology with a new aircraft type—the Boeing 737-300. This 138-seat twin-engine jet, which USAir helped design, is the most advanced, fuel-efficient, and quiet jet of its size and range. Its large on-board storage compartments brought new convenience to business travel. In late 1988 USAir will introduce an even newer aircraft, the 105-passenger Fokker 100.

USAir and Virginia have flown a long way together.

Edwin I. Colodny, chairman of the board and president of USAir Group, Inc., and USAir, Inc.

MARTHA WASHINGTON INN

A National Historic Landmark, the Martha Washington Inn combines its age and country identity with luxury to come up with a highly unique experience. All of the 61 rooms are decorated with antiques or period reproductions, and no two are the same. The hotel offers four-diamond dining and accommodations, roaring fires and afternoon tea, travel and gift shops, banquet facilities for up to 500 people, and an exclusive social club.

The inn's recent climb from quaintness to excellence is largely due to its current owners, The United Company. The privately owned holding company purchased the inn in April 1984. Construction began the following November and was completed in about a year. In all, The United Company spent approximately $7.5 million to add new wiring, plumbing, fire escapes, an elevator, cable television, a new telephone system, new heating, air conditioning, furnishings, three kitchens, and a full-service bakery.

"We essentially gutted the building and rebuilt the interior," says David Hoyt, president of the leisure and manufacturing group of The United Company. Builders left the brick walls intact so the hotel could maintain its historic-landmark status, but they reinforced them with concrete and steel. "A consultant said the roof was practically holding up the building," relates Hoyt.

Amazingly, the inn was kept open throughout the renovation. The main structure—now the mansion wing—was built from 1830 to 1832 by General Francis Preston for himself and his wife, Sara Buchanan Campbell Preston, who was a niece of Patrick Henry. Preston died in 1836. His family kept the home until 1858, when it was sold to the Holston Conference of the United Methodist Church for $21,000.

The conference altered the building to suit the needs of a girls' finishing school. Martha Washington College opened on March 15, 1860. College officials added several buildings and wings to the Preston home and altered the floor plan of the original wing.

The college survived the Civil War, while serving as a training

The Martha Washington Inn is a restored National Historic Landmark that combines the charm and hospitality of a bygone era with all the most modern amenities of today. Pictured here is the President's Club room before (above) and after (right) its renovation.

barracks and as a hospital for wounded Confederate and Union soldiers. Current Martha Washington Inn employees tell ghost stories of ruined loves between soldiers and the "Martha girls" who served as their nurses. The war took its toll on the college. Debt and declining enrollment ate away at the endowment until 1919, when Emory and Henry College assumed its debt and continued to operate it as a girls' school. In 1923 Martha Washington College lost its full accreditation, resulting in a further decline in enrollment.

The college closed in 1932. The property remained idle until 1935, when George G. Barnhill reopened it as the Martha Washington Inn. Its mountain surroundings and across-the-street proximity to the renowned Barter Theatre have accounted for several of its prestigious guests, including Tennessee Williams, Eleanor Roosevelt, Harry S. Truman, Elizabeth Taylor, and Paul Newman.

The inn has operated as a hotel since Barnhill's purchase, but steadily grew outdated and decrepit until its purchase by The United Company. Now the Martha Washington Inn possesses the charm of a bygone era yet includes ev-

ery modern convenience.

Located in the far southwestern corner of Virginia on Daniel Boone's Wilderness Trail is Abingdon's own country inn. Elegant parlors, guest rooms individually furnished with classic antiques, delightful afternoon tea, and delicious southern fare are only a sampling of the graceful refinement that characterizes the Martha Washington Inn.

HOTEL ROANOKE

Built in 1882 in the style of English Tudor, Hotel Roanoke overlooks downtown Roanoke and the surrounding Blue Ridge Mountains. This is how it looked in 1895.

$1.2-million investment in 1955 added 56 guest rooms for a total of more than 400 rooms, each with a television and other improvements.

Today Hotel Roanoke continues its tradition and reputation as one of the finest hotels in the state. It currently boasts 400 guest rooms, 11 meeting rooms, a grand ballroom with space for 650 people at seated banquets and 1,200 for receptions, cocktail lounges such as The Whistle Stop and the new Lobby Bar, and The Regency Room, an excellent gourmet restaurant serving only the

Since 1882 Hotel Roanoke, the award-winning hotel and restaurant, has been overlooking downtown Roanoke and the surrounding Blue Ridge Mountains of southwest Virginia. Throughout its history this grand old hotel has combined southern charm, comfort, and elegance with frequent restoration in order to maintain its tradition and originality.

When the Shenandoah Valley Railroad moved its headquarters from Hagerstown, Maryland, to Big Lick in 1882 in order to form Norfolk and Western Railroad, railroad officials decided that a good, large hotel would be needed. And so, with an investment of $45,000 by N&W, construction was begun in the late spring of 1882 on a 10-acre knoll overlooking the city of Roanoke. The hotel officially opened on December 25, 1882. Looking much the same then as it does today, it was constructed of wood in the English Tudor style, with an interior appointed with carved oak, hand-rubbed English walnut, cherry and ash woods, polished hardwood floors, and gaslight chandeliers. There were three or more elevators, a spacious lobby with an elegant stairway, a steam laundry, a bakery, an ice plant, barrooms and restaurants, and a kitchen equipped with the finest culinary appliances.

On July 1, 1898, disaster beset Hotel Roanoke when the third floor caught fire and caused extensive damage. Since its reopening in January 1899, the hotel

Hotel Roanoke today combines nostalgic elegance and charm with the most modern amenities for a complete hotel experience.

has been renovated and rebuilt several times. The $225,000 addition in December 1931 was proof that Hotel Roanoke was in keeping with the arrival of the technological age. The new guest rooms included such then-modern amenities as electric fans, telephones, combination bathtub and shower, and running ice water—luxuries not normally found in the average home at the time. A real luxury came along in 1937, when the hotel became totally air-conditioned, enabling visitors to seek relief from hot weather and allergies. Then, in 1948, an ice machine was installed that, still today, produces more than five tons of cracked or shaved ice every 24 hours. A

best in full-course breakfasts, lunches, and dinners. A European-trained chef heads up a staff of 23 in the kitchen, maintaining a consistently superlative menu from day to day. There is a full-size Olympic pool for use in both winter and summer, and tennis and golf privileges at nearby facilities.

Doreen M. Hamilton, general manager of Hotel Roanoke, sums up the present restoration of the hotel best by saying "the assignment is to restore rather than modernize, so that the hotel maintains the flavor of its original design and preserves its historical significance." The hotel has definitely succeeded in maintaining its flavor and originality, and the professionalism and warm friendliness of the Hotel Roanoke staff ensure the return of visitors year after year.

CSX CORPORATION

A Chespeake and Ohio Railway steam locomotive (left) in the 1940s. The Chesapeake and Ohio is now part of CSX Corporation.

A CSX freight train in Kentucky.

CSX Corporation is a high-technology, contemporary name for a modern organization. But while CSX is both as new as electronic data transmission, the company is also as traditional as southern hospitality.

Historically CSX traces its roots to the earliest days of American railroading and the Baltimore and Ohio line, one of the first great American railroads.

The B&O was a Maryland corporation formed in 1828. Originally chartered to run from Baltimore to the Ohio River, the B&O eventually stretched its tracks north to Philadelphia and New York, and west to Chicago and St. Louis. During its long history, it acquired many smaller northeastern and midwestern railroads, eventually sharing domination of regional transportation with such other giants as the New York Central and the Pennsylvania Railroad.

The B&O later came under the control of The Chesapeake and Ohio Railway Company, a railroad with a long and distinguished history of its own. Incorporated in Virginia in 1878, the C&O's principal operations ran from the coal fields of West Virginia, eastern Kentucky, and southern Ohio eastward to Washington, west to Louisville, Cincinnati, and Chicago, and north to Canada.

Like the B&O, The Chesapeake and Ohio Railway expanded by acquiring other lines. Over almost a century the C&O grew to become one of the most powerful and important railroad systems in the East. In 1963 it gained control of the Baltimore & Ohio.

Chessie System, Inc., was reorganized in 1973 as a Virginia Corporation formed to hold the assets of not only the C&O and B&O, but also the Chicago South Shore and South Bend Railroad; Western Maryland Railway Company; and several other railroads and related industries. Chessie System, Inc., in turn, became one of the two great companies whose merger created CSX.

The other component of the merger that created CSX, Seaboard Coast Line Industries, Inc., boasted a similar and equally complex history of its own. A Delaware corporation created in 1967, SCLI subsidiaries and related companies included Seaboard Coast Line Railroad Company; the Louisville and Nashville Railroad Company; The Carolina, Clinchfield and Ohio Railway; and Georgia Railroad.

The November 1, 1980, merger of Chessie System, Inc., and Seaboard Coast Line Industries, Inc., that created CSX generated extensive excitement in corporate America, especially in the transportation industry. Prime F. Osborn III, chairman and chief executive officer of Seaboard, and Hays T. Watkins, chairman and president of Chessie, became chairman and president, respectively, of CSX. Observers questioned whether the new company would be too big and complex for successful management, or whether it would prove to be the forerunner of industrial reorganization.

A CSX freight train speeds goods across the high iron network of railroad tracks.

CSX is a totally integrated transportation company.

CSX moved carefully and deliberately in integrating the two systems, achieving the goal of full, single-system service by the end of 1985. But the CSX Corporation that is emerging today has clearly moved well beyond that simple definition of activities. Instead, today we are witnessing the creation of a new-era corporation designed for global competition.

The new CSX is organized into discrete, semiautonomous units, each responsible for its own contribution to the corporate structure.

CSX Transportation combines rail, truck, barge, and warehouse services to meet the distribution needs of the global marketplace. With the recent acquisition of Sea-Land Corporation, the CSX's transportation enterprises have moved closer to becoming an integrated, international, one-stop transportation service.

CSX Energy is responsible for sales and transmission of natural gas, and natural gas liquids processing, production, and marketing. It includes Texas Gas Transmission Corporation, which operates a 6,000-mile natural gas pipeline system.

CSX Technology specializes in electronic data transmission and system development. CSX Technology supports the other CSX units with state-of-the-art information and communications systems, and develops information systems for external markets. In addition, the group includes LIGHTNET, a 5,000-mile fiber-optic network being developed in part by CSX Technology.

CSX Properties manages the corporation's hotel, resort, and real estate development interests, including the exotic chain of Rockresorts, with properties in the United States and the Caribbean; CSX Hotels, which owns the legendary Greenbrier Resort Hotel; and CSX Realty, which manages the company's real estate development activities.

The natural gas transmission interests were acquired by CSX in mid-1983 as part of Texas Gas Resources Corporation. The same acquisition brought Texas Gas Resources' barging subsidiary, American Commercial Lines, Inc., under CSX control in late 1984.

The most recent development at CSX is its 1987 merger with Sea-Land Corporation. The combination of the largest rail system east of the Mississippi and the extensive inland barge system with Sea-Land's vast international liner services has made CSX one of the largest transportation complexes in the world.

"We will have more emphasis on worldwide transportation needs rather than just regional needs," predicts Watkins. "The addition of Sea-Land is a good step in that direction."

The beloved sleeping cat logo of the Chessie System has been retired at CSX, but history and tradition are still active parts of this dynamic corporation. Fast freights and Amtrak passenger trains still highball over CSX Transportation tracks, where steam engines once pulled Pullman cars and luxurious first-class diners. And the same tradition of pride, skill, and innovation that once tied the nation together with steel rails and wooden ties is now dedicated to making CSX Corporation a major international marketing and service organization.

CSX piggyback trains keep thousands of truck trailers off our nation's highways, and provide door-to-door service to customers.

NEWPORT NEWS SHIPBUILDING

Sometimes a city's reputation is so strongly entwined with a local product or industry that you can't think of one without the other. Indeed Newport News, Virginia, means shipbuilding, reflecting the world-renowned ships craftsmen have built at Newport News Shipbuilding since 1886.

The company's output includes famous military vessels, such as the great aircraft carriers that turned the tide of battle in World War II and today's impressive Nimitz-class carriers that maintain a necessary national presence when world tensions reach the danger point. The lead design yard for the Navy's new Seawolf-class attack submarine, Newport News designed and continues to build the Los Angeles-class attack submarines.

In addition, it enjoys an enviable reputation for commercial shipbuilding, with nearly 500 of its 725 ships of that variety. A few, such as the transoceanic luxury liner S.S. *United States,* have shared the glory of their Navy counter-

Dry Dock One, shown here under construction, was a 600-foot dock hailed as "a wonder of the age" by the maritime press in 1889.

Hull number one, the tugboat Dorothy, *at the outfitting wharf in 1891. The Dry Dock Pump House is in the immediate background, with the first shipway trestle further back.*

parts, though most provide a less heralded efficiency appreciated only within the shipping industry.

For years the yard has been Virginia's largest private employer and the country's largest privately owned shipyard. It has successfully adapted to constantly varying industry conditions, anticipating and acting upon the need for improved facilities and technology. Today computer technology is fundamental to virtually every operation, and shipyard personnel have developed

much of the required software.

The most striking example of this technology is modular ship construction. Newport News applies computer know-how to design and build huge, more completed sections of ships separately and then assemble the sections into one structure. Such techniques permit faster and more efficient construction, keeping the yard a strong competitor for contracts.

Most work takes place at its Virginia headquarters, with satellite engineering offices in Honolulu, Hawaii; San Diego, California; Milwaukee, Wisconsin; Philadelphia, Pennsylvania; Washington, D.C.; and Asheville, North Carolina. The yard also has production plants at Asheville and at Greeneville, Tennessee.

Two major subsidiaries are Newport News Industrial Corporation, providing repair and maintenance services to the commercial power-generation industry, and Charlottesville-based Sperry Marine, designing and building advanced marine electronic instrumentation and communication systems.

Newport News boasts one of the richest histories in American industry. Founded by Collis P. Huntington, it was incorporated in 1886 as the Chesapeake Dry Dock and Construction Company. The fledgling yard began by repairing sailing schooners. Its first dry dock, hailed as "a wonder of the age," opened three years later with the docking of the

Special trains brought tens of thousands to watch the launching of the battleship Virginia *in 1904. Gay Montague, 12-year-old daughter of the governor, christened the ship.*

naval monitor *Puritan.* In 1890 the company name was changed to Newport News Shipbuilding and Dry Dock Company.

The yard soon received a contract for its first hull, a 90-foot tugboat named *Dorothy.* The tug remained in active service more than 60 years until it was damaged in a collision. In 1976 the yard retrieved and restored *Dorothy,* now permanently on display as a tribute to the company's five generations of shipbuilders.

Newport News' first U.S. Navy ship, the 234-foot gunboat *Nashville,* was launched in 1895 and fired the first shot in the Spanish-American War. The shipyard pioneered submarine construction in 1905 by building five of the earliest successfully operated submersibles. In 1907 seven of the 16 battleships in President Teddy Roosevelt's Great White Fleet were built at Newport News Shipbuilding. By World War I some 20 percent of the total Navy tonnage had been built there. And, since building the first ship designed as an aircraft carrier, *Ranger,* in 1930, the yard has designed and built virtually every class of aircraft carrier.

With no ships constructed during the recession of the early 1920s, the company diversified, manufacturing railroad cars, traffic signal lights, and various types of industrial equipment. The firm also entered the power-generation field, the only nonshipbuilding activity it continued beyond the Depression. Newport News has built hydroturbines for more than 130 hydroelectric projects, from Grand Coulee in Washington State to Dnieperstroi in the Soviet Union.

A highlight of the 1950s was delivery of the 990-foot passenger liner *United States.* The largest passenger ship ever built in this country, she still holds the record for the fastest crossing of the Atlantic in both directions, averaging almost 42 land miles per hour on a full day's run.

Early 1961 saw completion of USS *Enterprise,* the world's first nuclear-powered aircraft carrier. In 1968 Newport News was purchased by Houston-based Tenneco, a diversified interna-

The United States *in 1952, during sea trials— the largest and fastest passenger ship ever built in the United States.*

tional company. Four years later began the largest physical change in the firm's history, construction of a new North Yard on 150 acres of landfill.

Originally built for commercial ship construction, this yard is now the construction site for the nation's Nimitz-class aircraft carriers. This portion of the shipyard features a 900-ton-capacity gantry crane towering 23 stories over the largest dry dock in the Western Hemisphere, and an 11-acre all-enclosed steel production facility. Many operations in the complex are automated, from steel handling and fabrication to the erection and transportation of huge subassemblies.

In recent years the shipyard has made extensive capital investments, often in computer technology, to improve its capability further. A fully integrated

system blends computer-aided design and computer-aided manufacturing techniques with a computer-based information source. Two- and three-dimensional drafting equipment and computer-aided engineering facilities support computation powers at micro speeds.

Management functions in production planning, purchasing, inventory control, production control, finance, and personnel are tied into computer systems with the latest hardware and software available.

High-technology has become a reality at Newport News Shipbuilding, reaffirming the shipyard's traditional commitment to a leadership role within the industry.

The launching of the USS Albany *in 1987 represented the end of an era of sliding submarine launches. In the future submarines at Newport News will be constructed and launched on level land.*

FRANKLIN FEDERAL SAVINGS AND LOAN ASSOCIATION

Thousands of financial institutions across the nation had failed; unemployment was rampant; and the stock market recorded the worst slump in its history. By March 1933 the Great Depression had also prompted an unprecedented week-long banking holiday—a week when people could not cash checks or withdraw savings.

The economic climate was bleak. Precious little money was available for capital investment, and James B. Bourne, a 42-year-old Sandston bookkeeper, recognized that desperate situations required bold action. Something had to be done to help area home owners satisfy notes held on the property.

On October 24, 1933, Bourne brought together a small group of Sandston residents to discuss organization of a building and loan association that, he suggested, could raise funds through federal agencies and private investment. They agreed to apply for a federal charter and set out to acquire the necessary $2,500.

Despite a multitude of uncertainties, the requirement was over-subscribed by $209.50, and on November 24 Federal Charter No. 30 was issued to the Federal Savings and Loan Association of Sandston, Virginia. There were 15 directors, 64 depositors (shareholders), and 3 elected officers—H.H. Fricke, president; C.B. Robinson, vicepresident; and Bourne, who became secretary/treasurer and managing officer.

The Federal Savings & Loan Association of Sandston, Virginia (pictured here), was chartered November 24, 1933. Despite the hard times in which it started, the institution grew and became what is today known as Franklin Federal Savings & Loan Association.

The Franklin Street office of Franklin Federal Savings & Loan, circa 1941.

Cost of a full share was $100, and for those with less to invest (some of those first 64 depositors put in as little as 50 cents), installment thrift shares were available. Under this plan, monthly payments were made until the $100 was satisfied.

For every $100 in deposits the association received, the U.S. Treasury would purchase two preferred shares, which enabled the new federal savings and loan to expedite capital funding. These shares later were repurchased by the association.

Initial loan applications were received in February 1934, and on October 8 the association was issued Certificate No. 7 by the Federal Savings and Loan Insurance Corporation. The tiny Sandston group had become one of the first such organizations in the nation to gain federal coverage.

In February 1937 the name was changed to the First Federal Savings and Loan Association of Sandston, and two years later Bourne became president. Original projections—that maximum capital probably would not exceed $250,000 and that customers would come mainly from the immediate Sandston area—proved somewhat conservative. By 1941 First Federal of Sandston had grown to more than $3 million, and its customer base included much of the surrounding area. Business expansion soon dictated the need for new quarters, and that same year the firm moved to 616 East Franklin Street, where it was renamed Franklin Federal Savings and Loan Association.

Franklin Federal's Seventh and Broad Street building today.

Good news and bad came in the early 1940s. The good news was that savings increased dramatically, the bad, that insufficient demand for mortgage loans meant a decline in interest rates on savings accounts to 2 percent.

Growth continued, and by the end of 1945 assets topped $7.8 million. Once more space became a consideration, and in 1952 property was purchased at Seventh and Broad streets for a new home office. A branch was opened at Three Chopt Road and Patterson Avenue in Richmond's west end two years later.

Assets climbed to more than $21 million in 1955, there were 28 employees, and it was time to dedicate the new building. It proudly featured both savings and loan departments in the main lobby, which boasted "soft music, carpeted floors, and quiet surroundings" and a vault was "conveniently located on the first floor with no steps to climb."

James B. Bourne, Jr., succeeded his father at the helm in 1959, and, at age 29, became the youngest savings and loan president in Virginia. He proved a highly capable leader despite his youth and relative inexperience (he had been with the firm only five years).

In six years assets doubled from $38.1 million to $75.6 million, and four additional branches were opened. In 1963 Franklin Federal was the first savings and loan in the area to pay interest on savings accounts from day of deposit to day of withdrawal. Under the younger Bourne's direction the company moved into the electronic age with installation of a punched card data system (1961), random access computer (1965), and an IBM System 370 (1975), all to provide more efficient customer service.

During 1973-1974 the main office was treated to a complete face-lift. Today the firm maintains this location, as well as its five branches spread geographically to the west, east, north, and south of Richmond, with one in nearby Mechanicsville.

More than 50 people are employed by Franklin Federal, and assets have reached a little more than $310 million. This represents approximately 1,000 times the original expectation and 100,000 times the initial capitalization.

Size, of course, is critical—an important yardstick for measuring success. And so is philosophy. Franklin Federal's objectives are "to promote thrift by providing a convenient and safe method for people to save and invest money . . . and to provide for the sound and economic financing of homes."

KLANN INCORPORATED

"A manufacturer of components for organs has to be a master of many trades," says Paul Klann, owner of Klann Incorporated. "We're experts at coil winding, woodworking, injection molding, electromechanical devices, solid-state products, and more, so our facilities and skills of our employees have to be tops."

Klann company expertise, acquired in manufacturing parts for pipe and electronic organs for more than 75 years, is now being applied in new directions. Klann Incorporated, Waynesboro, has become one of Virginia's leading full-service manufacturers of custom, injection-molded plastic components.

The founder of Klann Incorporated, August A. Klann, was born in Prussia in 1872. He apprenticed as a cabinetmaker and in 1898, after working briefly in Vienna, Munich, and Paris, sailed to San Francisco—with an overland crossing through Panama.

"He wanted to go as far as he could," says Paul Klann. "He just missed a boat for Tanzania, which was then a German colony. He then made a dockside decision and changed his destination to San Francisco."

Within a day of his arrival, an organ builder hired Klann to build consoles. That career ended when he cut off the fingers of his left hand with a saw. He stopped the bleeding by plunging his hand into a pot of hot glue. The quick action saved his life.

Klann studied drafting in Germany after the accident, and later returned to San Francisco. A brief career taking photographs with a balloon-mounted, remote-controlled camera ended when the balloon crashed shortly after takeoff. He left immediately after the earthquake of 1906, moving to Alliance, Ohio.

In 1902 Klann patented an electric valve used to control air entering organ pipes, and eight years later started manufacturing his invention. In 1916 he moved his company to Waynesboro, to be near Barckhuff Organs, his best customer.

By the late 1920s August Klann had 60 employees and was selling organ parts throughout the United States and Europe. His facilities included a ma-chine shop where he designed and made his own tools, dies, and, quite often, complete machinery.

August Klann married Frances Wetzel, the sister of a friend; they had two children, Bertha and Paul. Paul and

August Klann, founder of Klann Incorporated, pictured here at age 70. Photo taken in 1942.

Frances Klann, wife and supporter of August Klann and mother of Paul—the current chief executive officer of Klann Incorporated. Photo taken in 1942.

his wife, Virginia, have two sons, Phillip and Curtis. Curtis Klann, a computer analyst, recently joined the family business.

Paul Klann, born in 1922, started working for his father immediately after returning from World War II service in the Navy, and took over the firm in 1952, when his father died. Under Paul Klann's leadership, the company completed its transition from manufacturing organ parts to more general applications of injection molding and related technologies.

Klann Incorporated, while still the recognized leader in organ parts and custom-finished consoles, is better known today as the only firm in Virginia with capabilities in both temporary and long-term molding needs. That allows Klann to take a product from concept through design, prototype, testing, and into full production.

Klann Incorporated specializes in working with engineering materials demanded by today's high-tech industries, such as American Safety Razor, Coburn Optical, Du Pont, General Electric, Genicom, Log Etronics, and many others.

TAYLOR & SLEDD

The diversified food-service and transportation firm known today as Taylor & Sledd traces its roots to 1875, when James H. Capers first set up shop as a food broker in Richmond. In 1907 his grandson, Hunter C. Sledd, moved from Powhattan, Virginia, to take over the business—then a one-man operation in an office shared by H.P. Taylor, Jr., another food broker. In 1918 they decided to join forces, and also added a new service: warehousing products for clients.

It was a humble local product, salt herring, that brought Taylor & Sledd major recognition. Under their Tidewater label, salt herring and herring roe became staple products of the Richmond region. The brand name was shared by many producers, all of whom supplied the fledgling company. With its widespread recognition the Tidewater label brought success, growth, and expansion to new activities.

The salt herring was hand packed until 1946; then a new concern for hygiene and the return of Hunter Sledd, Jr., from the Navy, brought a transition to mechanized packaging. The change came none too soon for the young veteran, whose earliest memories of working in the family firm included the inability to rid his hands of the smell of herring. Hunter Sledd, Jr., became president of the company in 1955. Today he is chairman of the board.

The firm has changed over the years in many remarkable ways. In 1932 it acquired the Pocahontas label, a brand that has become familiar throughout the nation—especially in institutional kitchens. Long a favorite of homemakers in the Southeast, Pocahontas products have acquired an enviable reputation among professional nutritionists. Pocahontas Foods USA became an autonomous division of Taylor & Sledd.

The warehousing activities started in 1918 now constitute a separate corporate division: Ranco Warehouse Company, Inc. The truck fleet, which began in the early years with a local delivery van, became T&S Transportation, Inc., when trucking was deregulated. Canners Warehouse Corporation handles real estate investments for the

Taylor & Sledd is a diversified food-service and transportation firm. It now handles 15,000 products covering the entire food-service industry.

organization, which operates through a holding company, Taylor & Sledd Industries.

The original food brokerage operation still continues under the name of Taylor & Sledd, Inc. The firm now handles 15,000 products covering the entire food-service industry. Among them are such Virginia products as canned apples and apple products, tomatoes and tomato products, sweet potatoes, and Irish potatoes. An outstanding testing and quality-control laboratory with a full-time food technologist provides institutional dieticians with full nutritional data on all products.

Taylor & Sledd moved to its current Ranco Road location in Henrico County in 1968. The organization has expanded its facilities several times since then—most recently in 1980, when it added almost 100,000 square feet of plant and office space. The president of the company is Robert C. Sledd, the fourth generation of his family to head the firm.

LLOYD ELECTRIC COMPANY, INC.

Barnett-Brewbaker Electric Company, Inc., was founded in 1920, with A. Buford Barnett as president and Jess W. Brewbaker as secretary. The following year they hired J. Lewis Lloyd as manager of the shop. In those days their firm specialized in automobile starter and generator armature rewinding, and small electric motor repairing. The first location was at 125 West Salem Avenue, Roanoke, Virginia.

During his first year of employment Lloyd began buying company stock from the shareholders, and by 1925 owned all 40 shares issued. He kept the original name until 1945, then changed it to Lloyd Electric Company, a proprietorship. Sometime in the year 1930 the business was moved to 334-338 West Salem Avenue, where it remained until 1951, the year a new building was constructed at 521 West Salem Avenue.

In 1955 Lloyd's son, Dean, joined the operation. A graduate electrical engineer from Virginia Tech, Dean helped guide the company toward an earnest effort of sales promotion and area expansion. Upon the senior Lloyd's death in 1959, Dean and his mother operated the business as a partnership. In 1962 Lloyd Electric was again incorporated.

The third Lloyd generation came into the business in 1978, when Richard, Dean's son, joined the company. Today Richard Lloyd holds the position of vice-president/sales.

Advances in technology have brought changes to rotating electrical apparatus manufacturing, which, in turn, brought new importance to the repair and servicing of electrical equipment. Lloyd Electric has prospered and grown through its efforts to keep up with new processes. Today a large part of Lloyd's business comes from customizing electric motors to suit customers' industrial needs. "If a customer has changes in the power requirements for a motor," Dean Lloyd says, "we'll design a winding for the motor to meet those needs."

In addition, the sale of new equip-

ment is now a large portion of the firm's revenue, bringing a steadily growing customer base. Lloyd's specialties include AC/DC drives and industrial controls, which are sold both to contractors and industries. Fueled by new service-related business in the agricultural and poultry industries, Dean Lloyd has watched his business spread to serve markets in Harrisonburg, Winchester, and Danville. The company has established a satellite plant in Harrisonburg to meet demand.

In December 1978 the organization relocated to its current headquarters, a 16,000-square-foot service center

Dean S. Lloyd is president and treasurer of Lloyd Electric Company, Inc., carrying on a family tradition of leadership.

at 605 Third Street, Southeast. A year later Lloyd Electric passed the milestone of one million dollars in annual sales; by 1986 annual sales had grown to $2.6 million. Today the company has 35 employees.

"You've got to respond quickly to the customer's needs," Lloyd said when asked about the key to the future of the electrical business. "We stress the quality of our work, not in image but in substance."

Richard D. Lloyd, vice-president/sales, stands in front of Lloyd Electric Company's current location at 605 Third Street.

MARSTELLER CORPORATION

Every Monday morning Marsteller Corporation specialists report to projects in Virginia, North Carolina, Tennessee, West Virginia, or the District of Columbia. Throughout this Middle Atlantic area they install gymnasium floors; sanitary base and floors for pharmaceutical, food processing, or hospital rooms; and abrasion resistant heavy duty floors for the textile, rubber, tobacco, and chemical industry.

Marsteller construction specialists also install corrosion resistant coatings; build chemical resistant, potable water approved liners for tanks or lagoons; and construct sun decks, "the roofs that you can walk on," or liquid applied roofs. The firm also supplies custom cut limestone, granite, and marble.

The company has not forgotten its origin in 1887, building monuments and mausoleums. Recently the first large private mausoleum constructed in Roanoke in 50 years was built by Marsteller in Evergreen Cemetery. Marsteller is working on a significant monument to the former governor, J. Lindsey Almond, Jr.

Inspired by its founder, J.H. Marsteller, the corporation continues to evolve, but always holds craftsmanship and efficiency foremost, designing each product and service for the individual project.

J.H. Marsteller was a Pennsylvania Dutchman from Bucks County, Pennsylvania. Not wanting to become a farmer on his family's farm, he apprenticed at the age of 17 in stone carving and lettering, and in 1887 came to the Roanoke Valley, having heard there was good business opportunity opening up in the Magic City.

Marsteller's first business was in Salem with a partner. After the partnership dissolved and he became sole owner, he opened a business in Roanoke, known as City Marble Works, at 503 South Jefferson Street. Marsteller used one of the first high-wheeled bicycles in the area, which he would take with him on trains for riding into the countryside on sales calls. A horse and buggy supplanted the bicycle, and still later he used automobiles and became one of the

pioneer automobile dealers in Virginia with the Model Garage. As the business continued to grow and prosper, the firm moved to another location on Campbell Avenue and then to Church Avenue. In 1925 it built a large plant and office just below Memorial Bridge, which is the present Richardson-Wayland Electrical Corporation. Today the main office is at 1809 Franklin Road, Southwest.

When J.H. Marsteller died on May 7, 1929, he was succeeded by his son, Dudley L. Marsteller. Since 1967 Dudley L. Marsteller, Jr., has been president, with Elmer D. Holdway, vice-president; F.W. Danahy, secretary; Peter G. Shick, controller; and Edward A. Zini, assistant vice-president and general superintendent.

More than 100 years and three generations later, the Marsteller Corporation is a major operation serving the Middle Atlantic states, specializing in thin terrazzo and industrial flooring, athletic surfaces, corrosion coatings, sun decks, building stone, monuments, and mausoleums.

ETHYL CORPORATION

Ethyl Corporation's corporate headquarters in Richmond, Virginia.

Floyd Dewey Gottwald served as president of Albemarle Paper for more than two decades and led the company into expansion and diversification.

"I'll take the ethyl."

Back in the days when every gas station routinely provided full service to all customers, an entire generation of Americans grew up knowing that "ethyl" was another name for "high-test," or premium, gasoline. "Ethyl" was a synonym for high performance. Things may have changed at the gas pump, but for the petroleum, chemicals, plastics, and other industries, Ethyl Corporation still means high performance and high technology.

The original Ethyl Gasoline Corporation was chartered in 1924, a joint creation of General Motors and Standard Oil Corporation of New Jersey. At the time General Motors held the basic patents on the introduction of tetraethyl lead into gasoline as an antiknock additive, and Standard Oil, under the leadership of John D. Rockefeller, controlled the American oil industry. It was a natural combination.

On November 30, 1962, a more modern style of corporate relationship, a friendly takeover, was consummated when the Albemarle Paper Manufacturing Company of Richmond acquired Ethyl Corporation (Delaware), creating Ethyl Corporation of Virginia.

Founded in 1887, Albemarle Paper was a highly respected but relatively small corporation with less than $50 million in assets. It paid $200 million for Ethyl, a case of "Jonah swallowing the whale," as it was described by several commentators at the time. To Albemarle president Floyd D. Gottwald, it was simply a case of Albemarle "enlarging and diversifying" the company's business.

Gottwald joined Albemarle in 1918 as an office clerk. He later served as export manager, production manager, assistant secretary, and executive vice-president before becoming president in 1941. When Gottwald took over Albemarle, annual sales hovered around the $4-million level, and corporate net worth was approximately $2 million.

The start of Gottwald's administration coincided with the start of World War II, a period that saw company sales drop sharply. Worse still, on April 20, 1943, a large boiler-type piece of equipment at one of the firm's Richmond paper mills exploded, killing nine people, injuring a dozen more, and seriously damaging the plant. Gottwald shut down the facility and considered liquidating the operation.

Instead, he took a deep breath, rolled up his sleeves, and went back to work. Gradually he consolidated his control of Albemarle Paper, resolved internal conflicts, repaired and reopened the shattered paper plant, and undertook an extensive refinancing and expansion program.

By the mid-1950s, with many of its early problems resolved, Albemarle began acquiring other paper and paper-product manufacturers. It took over Raymond Bag Company of Middletown, Ohio, in 1955 and Interstate Bag Company of Walden, New York, two years later. In 1959 Albemarle purchased Randolph Paper Box Corporation of Richmond, and Richmond Container Corporation. That program, including the 1960 purchase of the Armstrong Corporation of Baltimore, was designed to make Albemarle Paper a dominant force in the folding-box manufacturing industry.

In 1957 Albemarle expanded its land holdings along the James River and purchased the property of the nineteenth-century Tredegar Ironworks Gun Foundry. Tredegar was one of the few outstanding industrial plants of the antebellum South, and served as the arsenal of the Confederacy. (In 1972 Ethyl began rebuilding the historic gun foundry, and restoration work continues today.)

Just before the Ethyl acquisition, Albemarle's sales had climbed to more than $44 million, and its net worth had reached $25 million. The new Ethyl continued to operate Albemarle as a subsidiary and briefly considered expanding its paper operations. Ethyl even ventured into the fine printing paper business and acquired Oxford Paper Company of Rumford, Maine, in 1967.

Almost as quickly, Ethyl began divesting its other paper-manufacturing and -processing operations. In 1969 Ethyl sold its Richmond-based paper facilities to the newly formed James River Corporation. In 1976 it sold the Oxford Paper Company to Boise Cascade, ending Albemarle's 89-year history as a papermaker and ushering in a new era for Ethyl.

Today's Ethyl Corporation is a diversified producer of performance chemicals for the petroleum industry, high-technology chemicals, plastics, and aluminum products, and has interests in oil, gas, and coal. Ethyl also owns First Colony Life Insurance Company.

Ethyl purchased VisQueen Film and formed its Plastics Group in 1963, formed its Aluminum Group in 1966, and initiated European chemical operations in 1967. Acquisitions led Ethyl into coal-leasing and -processing in 1974, lubricant additives in 1975, and agricultural chemicals in 1978; Ethyl acquired First Colony Life Insurance Company in 1982.

Floyd Gottwald died in 1982, almost two decades after he had passed the company's top two offices on to his sons. Floyd Gottwald, Jr., became chairman of the board in 1968 and chief executive officer two years later. Bruce Gottwald became president and chief operating officer of Ethyl in 1970. Both retain those positions.

Ethyl Corporation had 1987 sales and insurance revenues in excess of $2.58 billion, and a work force of more than 10,000 employees. The corporate headquarters is in Richmond, with executive offices in Baton Rouge, Louisiana, and facilities throughout the United States and in Canada, England, and Belgium.

Ethyl's divisions make products ranging from detergent intermediates such as alkyl dimethyl amines, to petroleum additives such as viscosity index improvers. In between are molded plastic parts for automobiles and business machines, polyethylene film products, aluminum and vinyl extrusions, windows and doors, and innovative life insurance products. Now entering its second century, Ethyl Corporation is changing to serve a changing world.

The Tredegar Ironworks, a nineteenth-century gun foundry, was an industrial plant of the antebellum South and served as the arsenal of the Confederacy. In 1957 it was purchased by Ethyl and restoration work continues today.

REYNOLDS METALS COMPANY

As a pioneer in both the production and recycling of aluminum products, and as the manufacturer of Reynolds Wrap—perhaps the most familiar kitchen product in the country—Reynolds Metals Company has made a distinguished contribution to modern life. From beer and soft drink cans to automobile parts, home siding, and aircraft components, it is difficult to imagine modern life without the products of this outstanding Richmond-based corporation.

The enterprise was started by Richard S. Reynolds when he left the family tobacco business headed by his uncle. The new Reynolds Corporation involved itself in the manufacture of several different products with varying degrees of success. The most productive

Reynolds pioneered consumer aluminum recycling by making it convenient. For the past six years the company has recycled more aluminum beverage cans than its can division manufactures.

Each of these 30,000-pound coils yields nearly 130,000 rolls of Reynolds Wrap, America's first commercially successful and still most popular household aluminum foil.

of Richard Reynolds' efforts proved to be his United States Foil Company, which manufactured foil wrappers for cigarette packages. In 1928 he reorganized United States Foil into Reynolds Metals Company.

Reynolds Metals Company soon grew to become a major American corporation and a critical component of the national economy and defense. In 1939, as German supplies of aluminum disappeared from the open market, Richard Reynolds decided to become a producer of aluminum as well as a processor. He mortgaged the firm, built a production plant in Alabama, and began mining bauxite—the ore from which aluminum is produced—in Arkansas. Throughout World War II Reynolds was a major supplier of this commodity, which proved vital to aircraft manufacture and the war effort.

Demand for aluminum dropped sharply after the war, but Reynolds proved more than prepared to meet the challenge. New products including Reynolds Wrap brought aluminum into the consumer market. And as consumers learned more about light, attractive, durable aluminum, they wanted more of it. Reynolds Metals Company was happy to meet the demand.

Today's Reynolds Metals Com-

pany is a major integrated manufacturer of a wide variety of aluminum and plastic products; is involved in the development of gold and other precious metals, mineral, and real estate properties; and is a leader in aluminum recycling. From its Richmond headquarters the firm operates 53 plants in the United States (along with plants or interests in operations in 18 other countries) and employs 26,000 people.

Aluminum continues to be the company's core business, but other activities include plastic building products, packaging, and consumer lines. Reynolds also recently acquired Cut-Rite-brand products and has substantial interests in Richmond-based Eskimo Pie. In 1987 net sales exceeded $4 billion for the first time. William O. Bourke is president and chief executive officer of the firm.

Reynolds Metals Company remains proudest of its work in recycling, a program that began in 1968 and now recovers more than one million pounds of this precious national resource every day. "By recycling aluminum for the service of society," says David P. Reynolds, a son of the founder and chairman of the board, "we bring new life to quality and new quality to life."

Reynolds Wrap continues to be the flagship brand of Reynolds Metals Company's consumer products, which today include plastic and wax-paper wraps and a growing variety of other household management products.

INFILCO DEGREMONT, INC.

You may never have heard of Richmond-based Infilco Degremont, and the names of its best-selling equipment—the Accelator Clarifier, Superpulsator Clarifier, Vortair, Climber Screen® mechanical bar screens, and Greenleaf Filters—are not household words. But everyone has probably seen its installations at work. The company's customers include municipal governments, public utilities, and industry, but the ultimate beneficiaries of Infilco Degremont technology are people and the environment.

"Infilco" comes from the original firm, International Filter Company. "Degremont" is a French company that merged Infilco with its own operations. Together they formed Infilco Degremont, a water- and wastewater-treatment company.

International Filter was formed in 1894 in Chicago. Its first products, simple disc filters, attached to water faucets and filtered the drinking water, which then came directly from Lake Michigan. Infilco expanded into filtration and chemical-treatment facilities, becoming the worldwide leader in water- and wastewater-treatment systems and equipment.

P.N. Engel, the founder of Infilco, died in 1952. His family sold the firm in 1960 to General American Transportation, which sold it 10 years later to Westinghouse. Westinghouse brought Infilco to Richmond; then, in 1974, sold it to Degremont, Inc., the American subsidiary of Degremont, S.A. The two companies had worked together for a brief period following World War II. This second relationship proved much more enduring.

Infilco Degremont has undergone several transfers of ownership within the Degremont corporate structure. In 1987, 80 percent of the shares of Infilco Degremont were transferred to GWC Corp., a holding company ultimately owned by Lyonnaise des Eaux, the parent company of Degremont, S.A.

As part of the Lyonnaise and Degremont worldwide network, Infilco Degremont, Inc., has access to extraordinary operational, research, and applied development proficiency. From research in Degremont's central laboratory in Paris, to installations anywhere on

This sculpture of a dove sipping pure water proudly symbolizes the work of Infilco Degremont and stands in the lobby of the company's Richmond headquarters.

earth, Degremont, S.A., is the giant of its field. Degremont, S.A., has offices and subsidiaries in 86 countries.

Most industries sell a tool, or a machine, or a product. At Infilco Degremont, the primary unit is a plant, a complete system capable of providing pure water and of purifying wastewater for an entire industrial installation or a city. Richmond and Henrico County rely on Infilco Degremont plants. So do Newport News and several Virginia Power Co. installations.

The 130 employees of Infilco Degremont are primarily engineers. They analyze water samples, design plants to meet specific requirements, supervise

fabrication (the company works with fabricators near the job site) and installation, initiate operations, and train the operators.

Since the 1940s Infilco Degremont has completed almost 4,000 installations. The company now generates $30 to $35 million in annual sales, typically providing more than 100 new plants each year and installing expansion equipment in existing facilities.

C&P TELEPHONE OF VIRGINIA

Home and office equipment such as personal computers, facsimile machines, and other standard data devices can be linked together through the Integrated Services Digital Network (ISDN). ISDN allows customers to access any kind of voice data or video service over existing telephone lines.

The telephone came to the South in 1878, brought to Richmond by a group of Yankee entrepreneurs. The telephone was still a strange invention of yet-to-be-demonstrated usefulness, but J.M. Ormes and his Boston syndicate had great expectations. They also had a license from the National Bell Telephone Company that conveyed authority to use Bell Company patents in Virginia, West Virginia (south of the B&O Railroad), North and South Carolina, Georgia, Florida, and Alabama.

Bell executives expected Ormes and his syndicate to have difficulty—Western Union's competing telephone system was already advancing in the city of Richmond, and the rest of Ormes' territory appeared to be too sparsely populated to hold much potential. But Ormes launched a zealous and imaginative marketing and promotion campaign, and over the next three years he established Bell telephone exchanges in Richmond, Petersburg, Norfolk, Lynchburg, and Danville.

The Richmond exchange—the first in the old Confederacy—opened for service on April 1, 1879. It served 38 subscribers, including the Exchange and Ballard hotels, First National Bank, Pullman Palace Car Company, and the Chesapeake and Ohio Railway Company. National Bell executives were impressed. In 1880 the Ormes syndicate sold its Richmond exchange along with the rest of the franchise to a newly organized Bell subsidiary, Southern Bell Telephone and Telegraph.

The first Richmond switchboard was installed on the top floor of a building at 1219 East Main Street. It was 16 feet long and operated by a group of four young boys. A single bell strike alerted the operator that a call was coming in—and to the number of the caller. A clock-like device was used to complete the

connection between caller and operator, and then between operator and recipient.

The competition between Western Union and Bell ended soon after Bell's victory in patent litigation. A negotiated settlement in Virginia left Southern Bell in possession of the exclusive right to provide telephone service throughout its region—along with the existing exchanges originally constructed by Western Union. If the Southern Bell executives were anticipating smooth sailing in the wake of that victory, they were soon disillusioned.

With the end of competition, new problems emerged in the relationships between telephone company, government agencies, and customers of the telephone company. In 1894 the Richmond Chamber of Commerce complained about Southern Bell's rates and service, and two independent telephone companies were formed. Southern Bell applied to the courts, but the ruling favored the plans of the newly formed companies.

In 1902 Virginia created its State

With the transition from male to female operators during the early 1880s, the umbrella type switchboard was eventually introduced. This is what the interior of the Richmond Central Office looked like in the early 1900s.

Corporation Commission, a three-member board that was given extraordinary authority and charged (along with other responsibilities) with regulating the activities of telephone service providers.

In 1903 the rival companies consolidated (again over Bell's litigated objections), and then, one month later, went out of business. Southern Bell was again Richmond's sole telephone company.

Richmond was not alone in pioneering telephone developments for the South. The Alexandria exchange opened in 1881. A young Alexandria woman, Betty Keyes, signed on with the exchange in May 1882. One of the first women employed as a telephone operator in Virginia, she claimed another bit of history when, in August 1882, she completed the first telephone call from Alexandria to Washington, D.C.

Southern Bell changed its name to Chesapeake and Potomac Telephone Company of Virginia in 1912.

The history of C&P Virginia is filled with countless episodes of heroic actions by individual employees and by the company, all in the service of the nation, and state and local communities. C&P and its employees have overcome tornados, major fires, blizzards, numerous floods, and devastating hurricanes. Crews routinely have been called upon to work around the clock, under adverse circumstances in the wake of these disasters.

Much of the technological history of C&P is already well known (or remembered) by everyone. With reliable telephone communications so much a part of our daily lives, the technological history of C&P is the history of part of many households and businesses. That history includes such marvels as the conversion from operators to dial telephones and the introduction of international service, electronic switchboards, direct distance dialing, and sophisticated high-speed digital switching equipment.

C&P Telephone of Virginia is one of four C&P companies. The others are C&P of Maryland, West Virginia, and Washington, D.C. The C&P companies comprise a division of Bell Atlantic, one of the regional operating companies that were created under the federally mandated 1984 reorganization of the American Telephone and Telegraph

Optical fibers, these hair-thin strands of glass, carry voices, data, and television signals on beams of light across millions of miles. Just one of these fibers can carry over 12,000 telephone conversations. Pictured here are (in the foreground) one fiber, and (in the background) a copper cable.

Company. C&P Telephone of Virginia has more than 100,000 employees and generates $1.5 billion in annual revenues.

The latest chapter in the technological history of C&P Telephone is the introduction of advanced technology digital switching systems and fiber-optic cabling, systems that provide clearer, faster, quieter communications and do so with greatly improved efficiency.

C&P has recently installed enhanced 911 service in all of the major communities it serves. The new system not only facilitates emergency communication, but also provides computerized data to emergency personnel and helps to speed the response.

The new C&P Telephone of Virginia faces competition from other suppliers of many of its services. Its response has been to provide its traditional outstanding quality, and to combine quality service with aggressive marketing. There is nothing new about that technique at C&P. It is exactly the same combination that enabled J.M. Ormes to beat the competition and carve a place in Virginia for his telephone company more than a century ago.

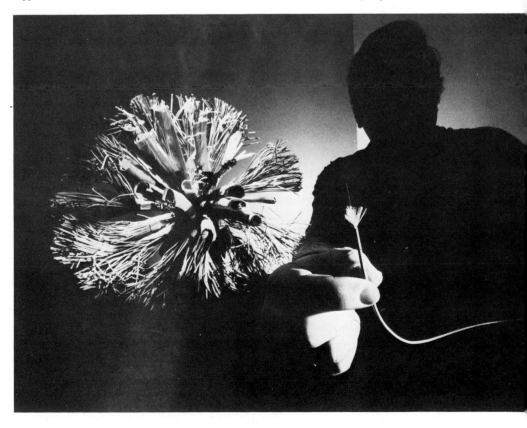

NORFOLK SOUTHERN CORPORATION

Arnold B. McKinnon, chairman, president, and chief executive officer of Norfolk Southern.

Leadership and a pioneering spirit have been part of Norfolk Southern Corporation's history since before the company achieved its present organizational structure. From Southern Railway's beginnings in 1827, followed by the first link in what was to become Norfolk and Western a decade later in Central Virginia, the two predecessor systems laid the foundation for a company that constantly demonstrates its commitment to developing the geographic areas and customers that the corporation serves today.

Chartered in 1982, Norfolk Southern's roots have long been in Virginia, both of its railroads having been incorporated there. The decision to locate the merged administrative offices in Norfolk recognized that the city's image and its downtown had changed dramatically since World War II, making it an attractive site for a corporate headquarters. Company executives making the decision credited concerned city officials who were sensitive to the needs of business and industry, as well as the city's broad new base of cultural assets and first-class medical facilities.

Under the banner of "thoroughbred pride," the modern company has expanded far beyond its rail origins into a growing transportation, industrial, and marketing service network. The only *Fortune* 500 service corporation headquartered in Hampton Roads, NS serves a 20-state region in the North, South, and Midwest. NS is also a major motor carrier since acquiring North American Van Lines Inc. Its Pocahontas Land Group, a major natural resource company formed in 1901, holds roughly 650,000 acres of high-quality metallurgical and low-sulfur utility coals, as well as smaller natural gas and timber holdings. NS also has substantial real estate developments in Washington, D.C., and Charlotte, North Carolina. And it is a money manager with substantial short- and long-term investment portfolios.

In terms of miles of road and railway operating revenue, NS ranks fifth in the industry. Its assets are in the $10-billion range, with net income in the range of a half-billion dollars. *Business Week* has ranked NS 86th among America's top 1,000 most valuable companies, with a market value of $6.2 billion. In the same ranking, NS placed second in the railroad industry group. *Fortune*'s annual survey of America's most admired corporations placed it the top-rated company in the railroad industry.

The group of companies that comprise the corporation satisfies goals of quality and excellence in service. Many of the nation's top corporations are long-term customers. North American Van Lines provides many of the trucking services NS routinely needs, including moving company materials, equipment, and office furniture. The real estate group is moving beyond its traditional industrial development role with an expanding commercial development program. And NS intends that future growth and investment opportunities will also be carefully and deliberately selected.

During the first half of the nineteenth century, a few plucky individuals made career choices that determined

The Roanoke railroad works in 1896.

the survival of the industries and companies at their command. One such person was William Mahone, who got his start as chief engineer of the Norfolk and Petersburg at the age of 26. Under his direction a track was laid prior to the Civil War—the world's first railroad war—from Norfolk to Petersburg across the Great Dismal Swamp. The logs were felled and placed across the right-of-way to form a floating roadbed, also known as a corduroy road, upon which the roadbed was built. Mahone became Norfolk and Western's first president at age 33. His Dismal Swamp track still exists today as part of NS's main line carrying millions of tons of coal to piers in Norfolk. After the Civil War, from which he emerged as a major general, Mahone combined three railroads into the Atlantic, Mississippi & Ohio Railroad, which became the immediate predecessor of the Norfolk and Western.

NW workers designed and built, in its Roanoke shops, and operated some of the finest steam engines in the world at that time. Among them were the Class I steam passenger locomotive and a whole series of heavy-duty freight locomotives as well. The steam locomotives were replaced by diesels in the 1960s.

In 1827 the South Carolina Canal & Rail Road Co. became the first to carry passengers in regular scheduled service. The earliest of the more than

The Norfolk and Western Class J steam passenger locomotive was one of the finest during its time; today Number 611 has been restored for excursion service.

125 railroads that combined and recombined to form Southern Railway, its first passenger trip was made Christmas Day 1830 on *The Best Friend of Charleston.* One passenger described an early trip as travel "on the wings of the wind at the speed of 15 to 25 miles an hour, anni-

hilating time and space and leaving all the world behind."

The Southern Railway was incorporated in 1894. It has been involved in transportation to and from the Tidewater area when it acquired the Atlantic & Danville Railway, now part of the NW system and renamed the Norfolk, Franklin & Danville. Southern once even had its own navy, which floated freight by barge across the Elizabeth River from Pinners Point to Norfolk.

Prior to 1959 the Virginian Railway, a major hauler of coal to its own pier in Norfolk, had its corporate headquarters in Norfolk at the Terminal Building on old East Main Street. But in the first major rail merger of modern times, the Virginian was absorbed by the NW in a deal struck with representatives of Eastern Gas & Fuel Company, which owned a controlling interest in the old Virginian. As a result, the latter's headquarters were closed, and the staff moved to Roanoke in 1959. The Virginian-NW merger started the trend that resulted in Norfolk Southern's returning to Norfolk in 1982 as the most

Pictured here is one of Norfolk Southern's new RoadRailer® highway-rail trailer units.

A view of Norfolk Southern's lines today.

profitable rail system in the United States.

Today NW's lines run an average of 450 road freight trains daily, primarily east-west between Norfolk and Kansas City, Missouri, serving communities and shippers in 14 states. The old Southern operates more than 10,000 miles of railroad in 13 states, serving most major cities south of the Potomac and Ohio rivers and east of the Mississippi.

Technological advances are an integral part of NS' history, originating with Southern's Cincinnati-Chattanooga line, which had the first automatic

block signals in U.S. railroading. In 1941 the line bought and placed in service the world's first diesel-electric road freight locomotive. In recent years railroads have been among the first computer users for traffic control, and current developments revolve around the design of energy-efficient locomotives, lighter-weight freight cars, and advanced data transmission.

The corporation's diversified business base reflects a strong accent on marketing and commitment to the industrial and agricultural development of areas the railway serves. Its industrial development department works with state and local development groups and

with commercial developers to encourage location of new industry and expansion of existing industry.

One of the most important of these existing industries is coal, a commodity that has been moving from railroad cars to ships over the docks at Lamberts Point in Norfolk since 1885. Norfolk Southern's involvement with coal dates from the 1830s, when the Chesterfield Railroad, a Southern predecessor, ran downhill from the coal fields in Midlothian, Virginia, to the banks of the James River opposite Richmond. With mules loaded on one farm wagon and coal on others, the group of wagons coasted over iron-capped rail to the river. Then the mules pulled the empty wagons back uphill to the coal pits.

In 1883 N&W's New River division began handling coal from southwest Virginia's Pocahontas region. That same year the railroad completed construction of Pier 1 at Lamberts Point in Norfolk. Then-Mayor William Lamb, upon arrival of the first car of coal, said, "This car is a precursor of a trade which is destined to make our port the most important station on the Atlantic Coast."

That first pier, accommodating ships with a 26-foot draft, could dump 3,000 tons of coal daily. Today Pier 6, a descendant of Pier 1, can dispose of that tonnage in 12 minutes. Its yard holds 7,500 cars. The largest and fastest such facility in the world, Pier 6 was completed in 1962 at a cost of $28 million. Coal and coke are the principal commodities NS handles, serving more than 200 mines, moving coal for use by domestic steel and electric utility companies and plants in foreign countries using high-quality metallurgical steel. Shipments are made over the piers to 24 foreign countries, primarily Italy, Brazil, France, Spain, Belgium, Holland, and Turkey.

Lamberts Point has become the finest facility in the world for the transshipment of metallurgical coal. In a year's time the facility has shipped more than 42 million tons. With nearly 55,000 open-top hopper cars to its name, each with a replacement cost of approximately $40,000, NS has an ongoing commitment to coal. Its fleet of 2,200 locomotives is 50-percent dedicated to hauling coal.

Pier 6 is constantly upgraded. Recent years have seen the addition of an automatic coal sampler, a computer to manage car inventory, a device to handle frozen coal, and a new loop track to accommodate inbound trains with up to 220 cars. NS has also invested $15 million of its own funds to dredge the pier in conjunction with the deepening of the Hampton Roads channel to a 50-foot depth. Two modern ship loaders feed a steady stream of coal into the vast maws of a vessel's cargo compartment.

Though coal provides more volume and revenue than any other commodity, it accounts for a substantially greater proportion of tonnage than it does of revenue. Much of NS' coal traffic is quality-conforming low-sulfur steam coal for electric utility generating plants, as well as metallurgical coal for making steel. For the future, acceleration of the worldwide trend toward use of coal rather than oil should help domestic and export coal traffic levels. If federal environmental standards for clean air are elevated, there should be a major jump in demand.

Motor vehicles, motor vehicle parts, food and similar products, chemicals, and steel and metal products comprise the bulk of N&W's merchandise traffic. Cocoa beans and natural rubber are primary breakbulk commodities handled at Lambert's Point Docks in Norfolk.

As Norfolk Southern faces tomorrow's challenges, it continues to form liaisons with other Virginia entities crucial to its success. It is working closely with the Virginia Port Authority in the development of the port's new inland terminal at Front Royal, and it maintains a vibrant presence in communities where its employees live and work, especially Hampton Roads and Roanoke. The Norfolk Southern Foundation actively supports welfare, educational, arts, and cultural activities and endowments all over its 20-state system.

Norfolk Southern has been moving coal from railroad cars to ships, over the docks at Lamberts Point, since 1885. Pier 6 is the largest and fastest facility of its kind in the world. Serving more than 200 mines, Norfolk Southern handles and transports coal and coke for shipment to 24 foreign countries.

ANDERSON & STRUDWICK

Edward Clifford Anderson, co-founder of Anderson & Strudwick.

In 1948 Edward Clifford Anderson decided to leave his family's investment services firm and set up his own shop. The company he left was one of the most successful in Virginia, but Anderson did not hesitate—even though setting up his own office meant using orange crates as temporary desks.

His new partner, Edmund Strudwick, Jr., had also been working at the same firm. Strudwick's background was in life insurance work; his father was president of Atlantic Life. However, Strudwick wanted to make his own company a place where he could help ordinary people, not just wealthy clients, on an effective financial security program.

Anderson & Strudwick soon became a successful component of the Richmond financial scene. The best way to grow themselves, the partners decided, was to help new businesses. Among their early clients were Commonwealth Natural Gas, Strother Drug, Atlantic Industries of Miami, and Doughtie's Foods

of Norfolk. As the firm grew, it acquired established companies as clients. Ethyl Corporation and Albemarle Paper both came to Anderson & Strudwick for assistance with new stock issues.

George W. Anderson joined the firm in 1950. A direct descendant of both Thomas Jefferson and Wilson Cary Nicholas, a former Virginia governor, George Anderson is an accomplished yachtsman, pilot, skier, duck hunter, and pianist. He has led the organization since the early 1960s, now serving as chairman of Anderson & Strudwick Group and as president of all of its subsidiaries. "One thing my father taught us was to be well rounded and participate in a broad range of activities."

Edward Anderson also taught that the customer is the first priority, that the corporation's first emphasis should always be on offering quality investment advice and on raising money for growing, deserving companies in the mid-Atlantic region—dictates still followed by the firm.

The orange-crate desks are long gone; Anderson & Strudwick and its subsidiaries have 115 people on staff. The original offices were at 807 East Main Street. Some might say that the firm has not gone far at all—its current offices are at 1108 East Main—but it now occupies the top floors of that building, with the executive offices in the penthouse. The firm also has offices in Charlottesville, Fredericksburg, Lynchburg, and Washington.

The Anderson & Strudwick Group includes not only the brokerage house, Anderson & Strudwick, Inc. (licensed in 23 states and the District of Columbia), but Financial Advisors, Inc. (specializing in "jumbo" certificates of deposit); Anderson & Strudwick Real Estate Corporation (commercial real estate); Virginia Business Exchange (brokerage for small and medium-size businesses); and Capital Management of Virginia (investment adviser).

Established as a partnership, Anderson & Strudwick Group is now a closely held private corporation. Charles A. Mills III is vice-chairman of the holding company and executive vice-president of the brokerage firm.

COFFEE BUTLER SERVICE, INC.

The folks at Coffee Butler Service, Inc., have been into coffee breaks for more than 20 years. Thomas E. Williams, president of Coffee Butler, could not be more pleased. He and his people have made providing a full range of employee break products and services a $25-million-per-year business.

From its plant and corporate headquarters in Alexandria and a service center in South Carolina, Coffee Butler provides full coffee break services to employees of companies throughout Pennsylvania, Maryland, the District of Columbia, Virginia, North and South Carolina, and Georgia.

The firm not only sells a full line of commercial coffee brands, but imports, blends, and roasts its own coffee as well. And, it also provides everything else needed for coffee breaks—from beverages and cups, to coffee brewers and microwave ovens, to inventory and ordering services.

Williams was a successful insurance sales executive in 1967 when he decided to make a career change. A friend offered to put up the initial capital, and the two went into the coffee service business, a new commercial activity that looked promising for the Washington

area. The two entrepreneurs started the business in an old house that they rented for $80 per month.

Their first taste proved bitter, however, when the coffee brewers they purchased turned out to be unreliable. "We went through our initial capital quickly," recalls Williams, "without much income to show for it."

Then things turned around. Williams added to the capital investment and purchased 25 new brewers. The new service proved popular with Washington-area businesses and staffs. Word spread, and soon Coffee Butler's growing fleet of distinctive trucks was delivering a widening range of products and services. In 1972 the firm moved to a warehouse and plant in Fairfax County and five years later started roasting its own coffee.

Steve Swink, executive vice-president, joined the company in 1977. He and Williams proved to be a well-brewed team. "This is a people business, a service business," says Williams. "It's highly labor intensive. Steve takes care of our people while I concentrate on long-range growth concepts, finance, and industry affairs." Williams is past president of the National Coffee Service

Headquartered in Alexandria, Coffee Butler Service, Inc., provides full coffee break services to employees of companies throughout Pennsylvania, Maryland, the District of Columbia, Virginia, North and South Carolina, and Georgia. And in addition to selling a full line of commercial coffee brands, Coffee Butler Service, Inc., also imports, blends, and roasts its own coffee as well.

Association.

Coffee Butler moved to its Alexandria warehouse, roasting plant, and corporate headquarters complex in 1984. The company now has a fleet of 65 trucks and serves an average of 7.5 million cups of coffee every month. Coffee sales account for only 65 percent of the firm's business, however. The rest is in soups, cocoa, canned soft drinks, snack foods, service contracts, institutional sales, and related activities.

"Our success formula is simple," says Williams. "We provide customized and personalized service. We tailor the selection of brewing equipment, the product, the service frequency, and other ingredients to our customers' needs. Then we follow through."

Coffee Butler Service, Inc., also brews a great cup of coffee.

VIRGINIA POWER

Virginia Power—like the state it serves—is deeply rooted in American history. The principal subsidiary of Dominion Resources Inc., it has built on its heritage to become one of today's most progressive electric utilities.

Virginia Power ranks high among utilities in operations, safety, and financial performance. Its rates are below the national average and it remains in the forefront of new technology. Also, its community service programs are nationally recognized.

Virginia Power serves nearly 4 million people in a 30,000-square-mile area covering most of two states. From the mountains of western Virginia to the Atlantic beaches, from the high-rise buildings of suburban Washington, D.C., to the farmlands of northeastern

Consumers Ice Company in Richmond was one of more than 200 diverse operations to share in Virginia Power's corporate history. Photo circa 1890

North Carolina, the company serves a healthy, growing economy.

The firm's roots reach back to 1787—just six years after the surrender of Lord Cornwallis at Yorktown and the end of the American Revolution. That year the Virginia General Assembly authorized establishment of the Appomattox Trustees, a firm whose original purpose was to improve the navigability of the Appomattox River.

Since then 235 businesses as diverse as water power, real estate, horseshoe manufacturing, ice making, coal mining, laundry, railway, ferry service, and street lighting have become part of Virginia Power's corporate ancestry. One of them, the Richmond Union Passenger Railway Company, built an electric streetcar system in 1888—making Richmond the first city in the nation with a successful electric trolley system.

In 1891 the Virginia Passenger and Power Company was franchised in Richmond to establish and operate elec-

tric railways and power plants. Like many streetcar companies of the time, it opened attractive amusement parks at the end of its trolley lines to encourage riders.

The parks created by Virginia Power's ancestors included Forest Hill Park in Richmond, Frye Springs in Charlottesville, and Ferndale Park in Petersburg. Most parks had dance pavilions, bowling alleys, fun houses, and roller coasters. Some even had houses showing primitive moving pictures. The parks succeeded beautifully, and rail lines to them became a backbone for urban growth.

The Virginia Railway and Power Company was incorporated to acquire three of the largest railway firms in Richmond on June 29, 1909—the real corporate birthday of Virginia Power as a utility.

Two years later the growing organization merged with several railway companies in the Hampton Roads area. The primary business of this new, larger organization remained street railways. The sale of surplus electricity was almost incidental.

A major milestone occurred in 1925. Stone & Webster, Inc., a New York engineering and consulting firm, and four investment companies formed a syndicate to buy Virginia Railway and Power. A holding company—Engineers Public Service—was established to own and manage this property and others.

The still-growing operation soon merged with several smaller utilities and acquired a service area in North Carolina. And there were other changes. The corporation began to deemphasize transportation and stress power. Its name became Virginia Electric and Power Company. Customers shortened it to "Vepco," and that name stuck for nearly 60 years.

Vepco began to promote the real benefits of electricity actively. It sold appliances and even offered five-dollar rebates on used equipment, such as old

The Richmond Union Passenger Railway Co., another Virginia Power ancestor, built the nation's first successful electric streetcar system in Richmond in 1888.

Built in 1909, the Virginia Railway and Power Company building at Seventh and Franklin streets in Richmond served as Virginia Power's headquarters until 1978. The building is still the largest nonreinforced concrete structure in the world.

water heaters, to encourage purchases of new appliances.

A Home Service Department was created and offered cooking classes to teach customers how to use the new electric kitchen equipment, and to explain the latest developments in lighting and electricity.

Rural families were targeted in company promotions on the advantages and uses of electricity. Company representatives toured farming communities in demonstration trucks packed with the latest electrical machinery and appliances to make farm life easier. City residents saw the newest appliances in the utility's business offices or on touring demonstration buses.

Electric Living centers were built in district offices to demonstrate the latest in electric laborsaving devices for the home.

Growth was dramatic. Then, in 1940, change came from outside. The Securities and Exchange Commission brought proceedings against Engineers Public Service under the Public Utilities Holding Company Act. After a long le-

gal battle Engineers reluctantly chose to liquidate and dissolve. Thus, in July 1947 Vepco became an independent, publicly owned utility with 11,000 shareholders and 450,000 customers.

The firm had grown dramatically even during the legal proceedings. It had merged with Virginia Public Ser-

vice Company, a firm serving northern and western Virginia, more than doubling the size of its service area and becoming one of the nation's largest electric utilities.

In 1965 the organization, now known as Virginia Power, built the first commercial 500,000-volt transmission system in the free world.

In the late 1960s, with the cost of coal rising and with growing concerns over environmental pollution, most of the company's power stations were switched from coal to oil, then an inexpensive, clean, and readily available fuel.

But conditions soon changed.

The Arab oil embargo of the early 1970s drove up the price of oil. In response, Virginia Power began the nation's largest program of converting oil-burning generating units to the more

Virginia Public Service Company line crews and service trucks in Alexandria, Virginia, circa 1930. Virginia Public Service merged with Vepco in 1944, resulting in one of the nation's largest electric utilities.

economical coal. Twelve units were converted before the program was completed.

To expand its fuel options, Virginia Power became a pioneer in the use of nuclear power. Working with other utilities during the 1950s and 1960s, the firm designed, built, operated, and decommissioned an experimental nuclear station in South Carolina.

Between 1970 and 1980 Virginia Power constructed four economical nuclear units that now generate some of the least expensive electricity in the country. The company is the nation's third-largest private producer of nuclear electricity.

Virginia Power was one of the first utilities in the nation to build a simulated control room for intensive nuclear operator training. Such simulators are now standard at U.S. nuclear stations.

The firm's Surry station recently became the first nuclear plant in the United States licensed to store spent nuclear fuel above ground. The spent fuel is kept in large casks mounted on a concrete pad. The casks will provide the station with sufficient storage space until a permanent federal facility is in operation.

A major restructuring took place in 1983 resulting in the formation of a holding company, Dominion Resources Inc. Virginia Power remained DRI's principal subsidiary, and is responsible for 95 percent of its business. The restructuring eventually resulted in Virginia Power's gas division, Virginia Natural Gas, becoming an independent subsidiary of Dominion Resources.

In 1984 the electric utility—then still named Vepco—began to conduct business as Virginia Power in Virginia and as North Carolina Power in North Carolina, reflecting the states it served.

Today Virginia Power generates electricity with 4 nuclear, 17 coal-fired, 2 oil-fired, and 13 hydroelectric units, and six pumped storage units owned jointly with a neighboring utility. Most of the power is generated by economical nuclear and coal units.

During off-peak periods energy from these coal and nuclear units is stored in the company's huge Bath

In the 1920s and 1930s Vepco representatives toured farming communities in demonstration trucks loaded with the latest in electrical machinery and appliances.

County pumped storage station—the largest facility of its kind in the world. The station regenerates electricity when demand for power is heavy.

Virginia Power's generating units are among the most productive in the industry. Their efficiency has helped the utility to hold rate increases far below inflation since 1980.

Faced with uncertain growth in demand for electricity and changing conditions in the electric-utility industry, Virginia Power is committed to maintaining a flexible strategy to meet its customers' future electricity needs. The emphasis on flexibility allows the firm to maximize its options among available energy sources, and yet minimize the costs and risks faced by customers if demand growth is different than expected.

Additional generating capacity will be needed during the coming years to supply the power needs of the service area's growing population and its healthy industrial and commercial expansion. To reduce and delay the need for expensive construction projects, the organization has a comprehensive, coordinated program to encourage customers to conserve energy.

Ultimately, however, the firm must depend on its own system. Making the most of existing generating units is an important part of this effort, and Virginia Power has programs under way aimed at existing stations, "uprating" them to higher power levels where possible and extending their lives.

The company is a leader in explor-

Vepco promoted the many uses of electricity to its customers through window displays in its district offices. The firm also sold appliances and offered cooking classes to teach the public how to use the new electric kitchen equipment.

ing potential new technologies for generating power—such as photovoltaic panels to convert sunlight directly into electricity and turbines that make electricity by tapping the wind power.

In addition, the utility is participating in the development of advanced coal technologies that offer the potential for clean, efficient use of abundant coal supplies.

Virginia Power strongly believes that its business responsibilities include corporate citizenship, and it is eager to be a good corporate neighbor in the communities it serves. The company and individual employees support many charities, such as the United Way and Energy Share, the firm's own program to provide heating assistance for those in need. Every year Virginia Power ranks among the top firms in the nation in numbers of employees and family members in the March of Dimes teamwalk.

The corporation also sponsors employee participation efforts such as the Speakers' Bureau and has a nationally recognized employee volunteer pro-

gram that supports a variety of community service activities.

Virginia Power employees are outstanding. Its service area is economically healthy and growing. It is a low-cost producer with a good match between generating capacity and demand, and a strong transmission and distribution system.

Proud of its heritage but not bound to the past, Virginia Power re-

mains confident of its ability to shape the future in ways that will benefit its customers and the communities it serves.

A pioneer in the use of nuclear power, Virginia Power is currently the nation's third-largest producer of nuclear energy. The company's Surry power station (pictured) is located near Williamsburg, Virginia, in Surry County.

FLOW GENERAL INC.

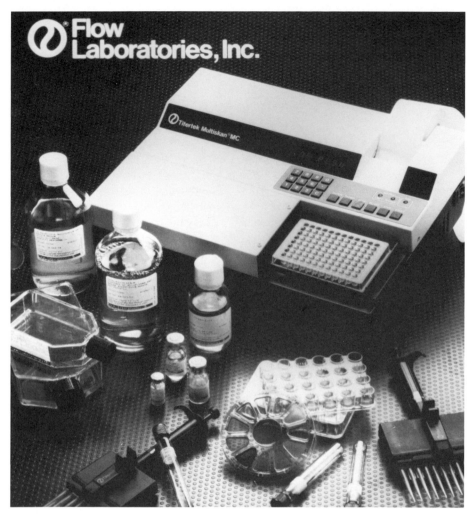

Flow Laboratories is an international supplier of products to biomedical and biotechnology organizations. Product lines include cellular biology, enzyme immunoassay, clean air, and laboratory disposables.

Flow General Inc. is an international, technology-based services and products company. Its corporate headquarters as well as several major operating units are located in McLean, Virginia, a small community just inside the Capital Beltway. Flow General engages in three segments of business activity: research and analysis services, biomedical products, and electronics and software products.

The firm is well known in the markets it serves. It has annual sales of more than $200 million, and its stock is listed on the New York Stock Exchange. Yet this major northern Virginia company maintains a low profile, perhaps reflecting both the technological sophistication of its ventures as well as recent events

At Flow General, research and analysis services are performed primarily for the Department of Defense.

at the corporation.

The history of today's Flow General is one of intertwined events, reflecting both the emergence of Virginia as a desirable home for technical enterprise and the evolution of trends in technology-driven competition—both in

domestic and international markets.

Flow Laboratories was founded in Rosslyn, Virginia, in 1961. Its founders were three engineers and a business consultant; the firm started in a basement garage with equipment that included a microscope purchased from a pawnshop. Within a few months the laboratory staff was supplying medical researchers with tissue culture products, and the company began to grow.

That same year, but a continent away, General Research Corporation (originally called Defense Research Corporation) was founded in Santa Barbara, California. The Santa Barbara group consisted of six scientists in a small office complex located over a bowling alley. The group had cause to celebrate early in their careers when, after several weeks of intense work, they won an Air Force contract to study advanced concepts for ballistic missile defense. The founders' concept of providing high-quality independent research on important matters of national security was becoming a reality.

By 1966 General Research had obtained several contracts from the Department of Defense and opened a branch office in Rosslyn. To provide financing for continued growth, General Research went public in 1967. By then

Flow Laboratories had operations in Maryland, Virginia, California, and Scotland. Discussions between the founders of both organizations led to the acquisition of Flow Laboratories by General Research in 1969.

Both companies continued gaining customer acceptance, and continued to grow both internally and through acquisitions. In 1976 the two merged, forming Flow General Inc.

The early 1980s produced rapid growth and heightened investor enthusiasm for Flow General as the firm continued to acquire new corporate components. Some of Flow General's biological research activity and capability received much public attention as the first wave of enthusiasm for the emerging biotechnology industry moved through the financial community. At one point Flow General stock sold for in excess of 40 times earnings.

The forward momentum broke under a series of legal, financial, and organizational problems—all corollaries of the organization's rapid and uncontrolled growth. In 1983, to the shock of principals and observers alike, Flow General appeared to be near bankruptcy.

A three-year retrenchment moved the company from large losses to break-even operations as it cut costs, refocused its priorities, reduced its work force, implemented new methods of operation, adopted strict standards of ethical conduct, and made changes of directors, officers, and managers.

During this period Grant C. Ehrlich (one of the founders of General Research) was elected chairman of the board, and Robert E. Wengler, president and chief executive officer of General Research, was elected president and chief executive officer of Flow General. Richard Hozik was elected president of Flow Laboratories.

The new leadership team developed a strategic plan calling for controlled growth while staying within business areas traceable to the firm's origins in biomedicine and defense. Internal growth has become vigorous, and the company's future is once again expected to evolve in ways that rely on its substantial base in technology and existing market positions. The firm has reorganized into three groups of semi-autonomous operations, each with its own expertise, accountability, and area of responsibility. As a result of harmonious management, the whole is stronger than the sum of its parts.

At Flow General, research and analysis services are performed primarily for the Department of Defense. General Research Corporation has a reputation for innovation and technical excellence in blending skills in systems analysis, physical sciences, computer sciences, and economics to perform professional studies on a wide range of programs beneficial to the national security of the United States.

SWL, Inc., is a highly regarded studies and support organization in naval electronic warfare activities.

Flow Laboratories is an international supplier of products to biomedical and biotechnology organizations. Product lines include cellular biology, enzyme immunoassay, clean air, laboratory disposables, and more.

Moseley Associates, Inc., is a leading supplier of electronic products to the radio and television broadcast industry.

Semifab, Inc., provides automated materials-processing products to semiconductor device manufacturers.

Its recent losses now a part of its history, Flow General Inc. is ready to continue the pattern of increasing its recently reestablished business activities. Excellence in the attractive technologies and markets it knows best should serve the company well as it moves into the 1990s.

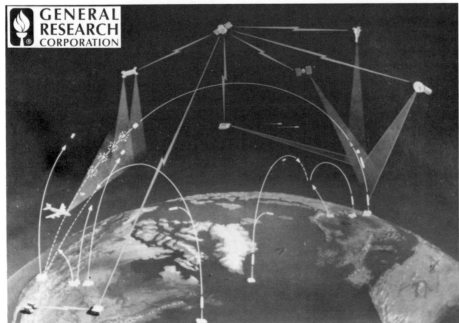

General Research Corporation has a reputation for innovation and technical excellence in blending skills in systems analysis, physical sciences, computer sciences, and economics in performing sophisticated research and analysis.

HUNGERFORD MECHANICAL CORPORATION

One of the greatest works of art at the new West Wing of the Virginia Museum of Fine Arts will never be seen by gallery visitors. Behind the scenes, in the walls, floors, and ceilings, in the basement and crawl spaces, is a complex network of 17 tons of stainless-steel ducts for the museum's environmental control system. To protect the museum's priceless collection, the heating, ventilating, and air conditioning (HVAC in construction trades jargon) system had to be the best.

To build it the museum and its general contractor selected the Hungerford Mechanical Corporation of Richmond. That came as no surprise to observers. Hungerford has been helping to build Virginia since 1947, when its parent firm, Hungerford, Inc., was founded by Arthur M. Hungerford, Jr. (His father, Arthur M. Hungerford, Sr., is still fondly remembered in Richmond as the founder of Hungerford Coal and Oil Corporation.)

A Richmond-based mechanical contractor, Hungerford, Inc., has evolved from a residential plumbing and heating contractor and has become a diversified multistate construction firm. In 1977 Hungerford, Inc., created Hungerford Mechanical Corporation as a wholly owned subsidiary.

Hungerford specializes in complex assignments. Many of its commercial contracts have been hospitals where medical gas transmission lines and other unique requirements demand the highest-quality design, materials, fabrication, and installation. The MCV-North Hospital, VCU-MCV Cancer Center, Richmond Community Hospital, Henrico Doctors Hospital, Chippenham Hospital, Petersburg Hospital Addition, Johnston-Willis Hospital, and Tidewater Memorial Hospital are among the numerous recent projects executed by Hungerford.

Other corporate projects include the Visitors Center at Colonial Williamsburg, the Best Products corporate headquarters north of Richmond, the Medical Education Building at the University of Virginia, the Martha Jefferson Hospital in Charlottesville, the Brunswick County Correctional Institute, and the Renaissance Apartments, renovated Jefferson Sheraton, and Commonwealth Park hotels in Richmond.

Hungerford's residential department installs the electrical, HVAC, and plumbing systems in more than 400 single-family houses each year. The sheet-metal shop fabricates in excess of one million pounds of metal annually. The commercial department works on plans and specification projects ranging from $200,000 to $10-million contracts, including hotels, schools, shopping centers, hospitals, and office buildings. The electrical and service departments both provide support to Hungerford projects and work independently on an individual job basis as well.

"The strengths of our company lie in its office and field experience, quality personnel and workmanship, and progressive attitudes," says Arthur M. Hungerford, Jr., chairman of the board of Hungerford Mechanical Corporation.

Charles Dedian is president and general manager. Arthur M. Hungerford III, PE, vice-president, heads the company's design/build activities. William C. Hungerford, his brother, is vice-president in the finance department.

Hungerford Mechanical Corporation's leadership consists of Charles Dedian, president and general manager (left), and Arthur M. Hungerford, Jr., chairman of the board (right).

RANDOLPH-MACON COLLEGE

Washington-Franklin Hall, built in 1871 and renovated in 1987, is the oldest brick building in Ashland. It now houses the college's Department of History and is listed on the National Register of Historic Places.

Since its founding by Methodists in 1830, Randolph-Macon College has maintained a tradition of excellence in liberal arts education.

With an enrollment of approximately 1,000 students and a student-faculty ratio of 11 to one, Randolph-Macon offers each student the benefits of intensive interaction with faculty and the individual attention necessary to foster academic achievement and personal growth. Graduates of the college have achieved distinction in a wide range of professions, and more than 60 percent eventually pursue formal study beyond the bachelor's level.

Randolph-Macon's sustained commitment to academic excellence has been acknowledged with the establishment of a Phi Beta Kappa chapter on campus. Only 10 percent of the colleges in the nation have been granted a charter by this prestigious academic honorary society. Furthermore, since 1920 a higher percentage of Randolph-Macon graduates has gone on to earn Ph.D. degrees than that of any other private college in Virginia.

Students may select a major field of study from among 21 academic disciplines, with courses available in nine additional areas. While maintaining an emphasis on the traditional liberal arts curriculum, Randolph-Macon also requires students to acquire basic computer proficiency and understand the effects of technological innovation on society. The institution's computer system, to which each student has access, is located in the Copley Science Center—a multimillion-dollar complex housing specialized laboratories, scientific

The multimillion-dollar Copley Science Center contains specialized laboratories, scientific equipment, and areas for individual student research.

Mary Branch Dormitory sits amidst a grove of oaks and maples.

equipment, and individual areas for student research.

The McGraw-Page Library contains more than 130,000 volumes and 720 periodicals, and a recently completed addition provides space for another 100,000 volumes. Other facilities include an observatory with a 12-inch reflecting telescope, a modern language laboratory, a 700-seat auditorium, and the spacious, two-story Estes Dining Hall.

There have been many changes at Randolph-Macon since 1830, when the original campus was opened in Boydton, near the Virginia-North Carolina border. That site became inaccessible with the destruction of railways during the Civil War, and in 1868 the institution moved to its present location in Ashland, a small town 15 miles north of Richmond. Washington-Franklin Hall, the first permanent brick building constructed on the Ashland campus (in 1871), was recently renovated and reopened for academic use. Of the 40 buildings located on the 100-acre Ashland campus, Washington-Franklin Hall and five other structures are listed on the National Register of Historic Places.

As Randolph-Macon College has grown and expanded its modern education facilities, it has retained its original purpose, serving as an institution dedicated to the search for truth. This guiding vision and commitment to academic excellence remain the cornerstones of Randolph-Macon's tradition of quality.

RICHMOND, FREDERICKSBURG AND POTOMAC RAILROAD COMPANY

Let your imagination roam free and hear that lonesome whistle blow. Listen to the sound of freight cars banging in the night as switch engines move them through the yards, making up the long trains that tomorrow will carry wheat and tobacco, and new automobiles, and coal and steel to a waiting nation.

Let your imagination roam free, if you will, but today's Richmond, Fredericksburg and Potomac Railroad is a lot more than a railroad. "We're not just working on the railroad anymore," says the company's 1986 annual report, and with good reason. Corporate real estate interests include a mixture of high-rise office and residential buildings, hotels, and office/warehouse developments in various strategic locations such as Crystal City in Arlington, Interstate Center in Richmond, Dabney Center in Henrico City, and the proposed Potomac Greens complex in Alexandria.

The Richmond, Fredericksburg and Potomac Railroad Company still runs more than a few trains and maintains a lot of track and right-of-way. Transportation continues to be a mainstay of this great Virginia company. With its increasingly modern tracks and yards and its new, computerized marketing and car inventory control system,

A passenger train departs from the Broad Street Station in 1949 behind one of the Richmond, Fredericksburg and Potomac Railroad Company's (RF&P) Governor class steam locomotives. Today the station serves as the Virginia Science Museum.

the firm is highballing toward the twenty-first century.

However, memories of steam whistles and luxurious passenger cars are part of this railroad, which was chartered by the Virginia General Assembly in 1834. Just as railroads helped to develop the natural resources and potential of the nation, the RF&P played a critical role in the development of the Commonwealth of Virginia.

The founders of the RF&P envisioned a line from Richmond through Fredericksburg, to some point on the Potomac River where connection could be made with steamboats for Washington. By 1837 the tracks had reached Fredericksburg, but delays, distractions, and the Civil War would all intervene before the original plan was realized.

Along the way the railroad made a lot of history. Land purchased in 1836 for use as a source of timber was subdivided and put up for sale in 1854. The area, originally known as Slash Cottage, became the town of Ashland. When Randolph-Macon College moved to the community in 1868, RF&P donated more than 19 acres to the institution.

The first engine, the Augusta, was built in England and purchased in 1835. Early RF&P rolling stock included 5 passenger cars, 2 baggage cars, one horsecar, 20 boxcars, and 3 coal cars. In 1849 the railroad purchased two flatcars, each equipped with 12 crates to accommodate freight—so containerization is not such a new idea, after all.

Early track consisted of wooden strips or "stringers," atop which was placed flat, English-made strap iron rail. The firm switched to the then-radical new "T" rail in 1854. The new all-steel rail was more durable, stronger, smoother, and less expensive. It was also a homegrown product, manufactured at Richmond's Tredegar Iron Works.

There was no "right way" to build

The Orange Blossom Special, *shown here southbound on the RF&P, is the fastest freight train operating in North America.*

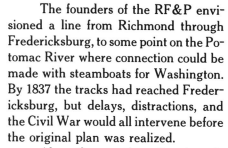

a railroad. In many cases tools, techniques, and machinery were created by the people who performed the work—the Gandy Dancers who would build, sing, and drive their way into American history, legend, and folk traditions. Today special computer-assisted machinery is used to lay track, but even the most sophisticated devices still rely on strong railroaders who swing heavy sledgehammers.

The Civil War halted expansion and improvements. During most of the war only that portion of the railroad between Richmond and Hamilton's Crossing (about four miles south of Fredericksburg) was controlled by friendly forces. The remainder was in Union hands. (The railroad later purchased the house where General Stonewall Jackson died, restored it, opened it to the public, and in 1936 donated it to the federal government.)

When the war ended the company discovered that most of the bridges were down, much of the track torn up, and all of its engines and cars were worn out or destroyed. However, by 1866 the RF&P was placing new sleeping cars in service and by 1872 was installing new air brakes on locomotives and passenger cars.

On July 2, 1872, the RF&P connected with the Alexandria and Fredericksburg Railway, thus establishing for the first time an all-rail route to Washington from Richmond and points south, and, for the first time, linking North and South with a chain of steel rails.

As the technology of railroading changed, so did the RF&P. Hooks for flying pickups of mailbags were installed in 1874; locomotives were converted from wood-burners to coal-fired steam engines by 1883; fast freight service was instituted in 1888; and by 1890 the wooden bridges had been replaced by more durable structures. Double-tracking to Washington was completed in 1905, and the following year the Potomac Yard at Alexandria—now one of the largest freight classification yards on the East Coast—was opened.

The Crystal City complex in Arlington is the highlight of the RF&P's real estate activity.

During two world wars the RF&P played critical roles, moving people and material and supplying the war effort. The marine base at Quantico and the Army post at Fort Belvoir near Alexandria were both particularly dependent on the railroad. In 1943 more than 8.5 million passengers and 14 million tons of freight, most of it war related, traveled on RF&P trains.

The 1950s saw the transition to diesel-powered locomotives. One by one, the great engines named for generals, governors, and statesmen were retired from service; the last regularly scheduled steam engine ended its run in 1953. The diesels that replaced them were powerful and efficient, but they carried numbers instead of names.

The 1950s also witnessed the first welded rail and piggyback (trailer-on-flatcar) service. The 1960s witnessed the

purchase of the defunct Dahlgren Railroad and the beginning of RF&P real estate development activities. The 1970s saw cooperation with other railroads on such projects as Tropicana Products' "Orange Juice Train" for citrus products and the Auto Train carrying cars and tourists to Florida.

Today such beloved passenger trains as the *Old Dominion* and the *Blue and Gray Clipper* run no more, but Amtrak's *Silver Star* still carries passengers over the RF&P while the *Orange Blossom Special* and *Juice Train* still carry the freight with the style, efficiency, and pride of great railroaders.

Interstate Center, a five-building office complex in Richmond, was recently developed by the RF&P Development Corporation.

SOUTHERN STATES COOPERATIVE, INC.

W.G. Wysor, the founder of Virginia Seed Service (later Southern States Cooperative) and the company's first general manager from 1923-1948.

Gene A. James, president and chief executive officer of Southern States Cooperative.

The guiding principle for Southern States Cooperative, Inc., is "helping the man on the land." It has been that way since the cooperative was formed. Adhering to that principle has made the organization one of the nation's largest and most successful farmer cooperatives.

Southern States began operations as the Virginia Seed Service (VSS), organized by a group of Virginia farmers who had learned some hard lessons about the agricultural establishment. First, they knew that much of the seed sold to them was not adapted to local climate and soil conditions. Second, they knew that the state crop improvement association was producing certified local seed, but could find no channels to distribute it.

For the 150 farmers who met in Richmond that April night in 1923, the lesson was clear. If they wanted a supplier that would be run for the farmers, it would have to be run by the farmers.

VSS knew its product, and—unlike many other suppliers of the day—it was willing to share that knowledge. Customers of VSS were told of the seed's origin, variety, germination, and weed content. Despite such problems as a lack of credit or capital, and the opposition of most retail farm suppliers, the com-

pany survived and grew.

Each of the services provided by Southern States has been offered in response to the needs of its individual member/owners. Feed service was added in 1925, and fertilizer the following year. In both cases the new services were able to provide quality products at a reasonable price by cutting profit margins. The fertilizer manufacturing plant purchased by Southern States' directors in 1936 is still among the largest farmer-owned fertilizer mixing plants in the nation.

Growth occurred along logical

The early warehouse and offices of Virginia Seed Service, the predecessor organization of Southern States Cooperative, were located in Richmond.

lines as needs were identified and solutions found. After binder twine was successfully added to the cooperative's offerings in 1928, the organization rapidly expanded the range of commodities offered to members. By the 1950s regional warehouses maintained inventories of more than 3,000 farm supplies. In 1967 the cooperative launched a catalog service, which was able to offer an additional 3,000 items to members. Petroleum service was added in 1938, and 10 years later Southern States joined with two other cooperatives to purchase an oil refinery in Texas.

Much of Southern States' growth occurred during the crisis-ridden Depression era of the 1930s. During the drought of 1930 the organization helped farmers pool and distribute vitally needed hay on a cooperative basis. VSS obtained supplies from the Midwest, some from as far away as the Platte River Valley in Nebraska. Later the organization initiated a self-insurance program for the cooperative and its local affiliates, and pioneered projects in the development and delivery of feed, fertilizer, petroleum, and farm supplies.

In 1933 the group changed its name from Virginia Seed Service to Southern States Cooperative. The following year the directors extended their marketing region from Virginia to Maryland and Delaware.

The home office, since 1978, of Southern States Cooperative at 6606 West Broad Street in Richmond.

During World War II the cooperative turned its attention to an all-out food production effort, taking the position that its obligation to members and to the nation took precedence, even at the risk of some operating losses. Facilities construction was impossible; equipment replacement was out of the question. Despite temptations brought on by scarcities, the cooperative maintained its fair-price schedule. Long before the end of the war, supplies and services were being rationed, even to long-term members.

West Virginia joined the Southern States family in 1941, following a merger with Cooperative Farm Services, a West Virginia Farm Bureau-sponsored association. The Kentucky Farm Bureau invited Southern States to the land of the bluegrass in 1944.

In addition to purchasing supplies for members, Southern States also has served as a marketer of farm commodities, helping members deal with volatile markets and economic instabilities. Grain marketing offers a year-round service to farmers—who can sell their grain for immediate cash, contract for future sales, and receive information on local, national, and international grain markets.

In 1945 the organization began the publication and distribution of *Cooperative Farmer,* a magazine that provides members with the latest information on many matters of professional concern.

Through the years Southern States has established working relationships with other regional cooperatives to increase buying power and expand services to its members. The organization is also active on a national level, representing the interests of farmers through participating in such organizations as the National Council of Farmer Cooperatives.

The growth of Southern States has been reflected in the size and location of the offices that house its administrative activities. From the Virginia Seed Service's rented office on the third floor

of an old warehouse in 1923, the cooperative moved to its first purchased office building at Seventh and Main streets in 1947.

After outgrowing that facility, the cooperative erected an eight-story structure in the Brookfield Office Park on West Broad Street in Henrico County. In this modern building the management and staff of Southern States Cooperative, Inc., conduct the business of one of the nation's most respected self-help organizations.

Today Southern States is active throughout Virginia, Maryland, Delaware, Kentucky, West Virginia, and (since 1986) North Carolina. It distributes supplies at fair prices through ap-

Southern States' grain elevator and feed mill in Richmond. The grain elevator is one of 15 owned by the cooperative, and the feed mill is one of 11 in Southern States' system.

proximately 550 cooperative dealers, and markets small grains, corn, and soybeans for its members in some areas.

As from its inception Southern States Cooperative, Inc., is owned by its farmer members—individuals and local farm cooperatives. The president and chief executive officer is Gene A. James, who first went to work for the cooperative as a manager trainee in 1953. With more than 132,000 members, the cooperative's annual volume now exceeds $660 million.

HAUNI RICHMOND, INC.

Dr. Kurt A. Körber started his company in a battered Hamburg railway station in July 1946. World War II had ended in Germany barely a year before, but Körber's eyes were on the future, not the past. He had an idea for the design of high-speed tobacco processing machinery, and other ideas about new ways to martial the forces of international business toward solving sociopolitical problems.

The name Hauni is derived from two sources: "HA" for the old Hanseatic League, a medieval international trading association, and "UNI" for Universelle, the name of Dr. Körber's former employer in Dresden. To Körber, the name symbolized the goals and values of his new organization. It was a big dream for a company that started with seven people working in the basement of a bombed-out factory.

By 1950 Körber had developed a machine that could produce cigarettes in high volume, and was working on another that would also attach filters. His new machine was a technology in search of an application. Filter cigarettes had no following in Europe, and it was not until 1954 that American manufacturers recognized their marketing potential and ordered some of Hauni's new machines. Today's versions of these machines are capable of making filter-tipped cigarettes at the incredible rate of 8,000 per minute.

Körber immediately recognized that the American tobacco industry was his real market, and that a Virginia base would be needed to sell, install, and service his cigarette-making machines. He came to Richmond, set up an office in the Jefferson Hotel, and bought a vacant storage building on Rhoadmiller Street.

The building was renovated and refitted under the direction of staff brought in from Germany. For the first three years all machine parts were made in Hamburg. Only sales, assembly, and service were part of the American operation. Gradually, Hauni Richmond expanded to include manufacturing, and the firm soon outgrew its original facilities.

Dr. Körber did not believe in debt. All Hauni expansion and capital investment was paid in cash, and in 1971, when the company bought land near Richmond International Airport and built its new plant and headquarters, it, too, was paid for without borrowing. So were the first heat treating furnaces, which were installed in 1962.

The new complex replaced the original 13,000-square-foot converted warehouse with an ultramodern 100,000-square-foot plant devoted to both the development and the manufacture of new products. The payroll jumped from six to 85, and a whole new technology was introduced with numerically controlled machine tools. In-house computers produced the tapes that were fed into the automated machines.

Körber did not confine his efforts to Hauni Richmond. He continued building his Hamburg-based group as an international organization capable of supplying top-grade production units and control systems to various branches of industry, including paper processing, tobacco and food machinery, and machine tools. Körber AG is headquartered in Hamburg; it has plants throughout West Germany, as well as in France, Switzerland, and the United States. American divisions include the Pemco Company in Sheboygan, Wisconsin, and Hauni Richmond, Inc.

Dr. Körber's impatience with traditional corporate structures is reflected at Hauni Richmond. Relationships between employees and management are close and cordial. Most matters are handled with as little paperwork as possible. The administrative apparatus is held to a minimum. The result is a highly prized flexibility, high employee understanding and appreciation of company goals, and close ties between individuals and the company.

Dr. Körber, founder and chairman of the supervisory board of Körber, AG, and a group of vocational exchange students in Washington, D.C.

Protos, Hauni's high-speed cigarette-making machine.

Hauni Richmond's main divisions—Engineering, Sales and Service, Manufacturing, Finance, Employee Relations, and the commercial Heat Treating Shop—are staffed by more than 180 employees. In addition to working in such traditional areas as cigarette makers and tippers, Hauni Richmond continues to develop other product lines.

"We are machine builders," says Dr. Hans Oppe, president of Hauni Richmond. "The cigarette industry is going through a new phase. That gives us the opportunity to apply our wealth of engineering and machinery design know-how in new directions. In the future, we will be applying the technology that allowed us to revolutionize cigarette making in nontobacco fields."

Heat treating, brazing, and metallurgical consultation continue to be a significant part of the Hauni program. The Richmond facility has a wide selection of specialized heat treating machinery that attracts customers from throughout the eastern states. It also offers the unique services of a metallurgical consulting team. "We are a small and flexible plant," says Oppe. "We have a short response time and the

ability to adapt to highly specialized applications."

"We don't follow the standard," was Dr. Körber's motto. "We set the standard." Hauni Richmond follows that motto.

Körber's vision is fulfilled at Hauni in other ways as well. The Cultural Rela-

tion Fellowship Program, initiated in 1980, offers three-month working visits of American vocational students to the Federal Republic of Germany, and return working trips of German students to the United States.

Dr. Körber holds a strong belief that the "fostering of cultural relations among nations is a responsibility, as well as an opportunity, that cannot be left solely to governmental and religious institutions. Its importance to better understanding among all people of the world requires the participation of the business community and its leaders."

The Cultural Relation Fellowship Program is operated by the Körber Foundation, the majority stockholder of Körber AG. The foundation devotes all its assets to the operation of extensive programs for the advancement of education, scientific research, cultural institutions, health care, and international understanding.

Heat treating and brazing equipment at Hauni Richmond, Inc.

CHESAPEAKE CORPORATION

These trees, harvested at a Chesapeake logging site, are sent to various locations. Logs are graded and used for their highest economic value, from lumber and plywood to pulpwood.

The history of Chesapeake Corporation, a pioneer papermaking firm, is also the history of West Point, Virginia. This town on the York River, 38 miles from Richmond, dates from 1861 when railroads from Richmond connected with steamship traffic on the York. It was an auspicious occasion, but even residents of the tiny community were distracted by talk of secession and the coming storm. Civil War and economic dislocations throughout the South long kept progress far from the struggling community.

In 1913 the Fox Paper Company of Cincinnati decided that the combination of "cordial local citizens," plentiful water, good transportation, and the vast expanse of southern pine forests made West Point the ideal location for a new pulp mill. Harry Nichols, the president of Fox Paper, knew that his company needed a reliable source of pulp for its own manufacturing processes. Building his own pulp mill, he thought, would assure that supply and generate substantial profits on its own.

Nichols' project attracted support from several of the most sophisticated business leaders and investors in the Midwest. Among its sponsors were William Cooper Proctor (of Proctor & Gamble); William S. Rowe, president of the First National Bank of Cincinnati; and Richard P. Ernst, later a United

States Senator from Kentucky. To build the mill, Nichols formed a corporation, the Chesapeake Pulp and Paper Company. Chartered on January 11, 1913, it was capitalized at $300,000.

The corporation's West Point mill produced pulp by the Kraft process, the German word meaning strong. Kraft products are made from a sulphate process of pulping wood. The pulp itself is cellulose fiber, the wood fiber, separated and processed from its natural state in trees. Kraft pulp becomes the raw material for Kraft products—either paper, paperboard, or containerboard.

The site for the mill was a gift from the Southern Railway, which ran a spur from its main line to the mill, but the company decided to run its own river transport system to bring the wood to the mill. Chesapeake opened its West Point mill on May 16, 1914. By 1916 the mill had more than 200 people on the payroll. In the summer of 1917 the company completed its first plant expansion.

Growing wartime shortages, especially wastepaper and labor, caused major problems for the new firm. Then Harry Nichols, the president of Chesa-

Chesapeake maintains an inventory of treated lumber at its Fredericksburg, Virginia, plant to promptly fill customer orders. Chesapeake now has plants covering the northeast United States.

peake, was drafted by Bernard Baruch to administer the pulp and paper division of the War Industries Board. To avoid conflict of interest, Nichols sought to lease his own company to another operator. The wartime emergency ended in 1918, but Nichols had already concluded a lease with a group of New York and Canadian interests.

The firm that took over the mill was incorporated on October 18, 1918, as the Chesapeake Corporation. Its first president was Christoffer Hannevig, heir to a Norwegian shipping family and a Wall Street investor whose companies included such stars as North Atlantic Insurance, Liberty Marine, and the Pusey & Jones Shipbuilding Company. The future appeared rosy, but postwar depression, financial reverses for Han-

Steam plumes streak the winter evening sky as logs are placed into the water flume in the wood yard at the West Point, Virginia, mill.

nevig, and a lingering legal dispute over wartime claims by Hannevig and the Norwegian government against the United States threw the corporation into bankruptcy in 1921.

Complex refinancing and reorganization maneuvers brought Chesapeake first under the control of the Norwegian Atlas Insurance Company, Ltd., and then of Wat Ellerson, president of the Albemarle Paper Manufacturing Company of Richmond. Ellerson and his associates successfully forced the New York and Cincinnati interests off the Chesapeake board, and transformed it into a Virginia-based and -controlled corporation.

For the first five years of its administration, the new board of directors reinvested all Chesapeake profits in plant improvements. That internally generated capital purchased new technology, much of it requiring machinery imported from Europe, that brought lower production and shipping costs. When the price of pulp rose sharply in 1925, the Chesapeake Corporation was well positioned to take full advantage of the opportunity.

In 1926 the Chesapeake Corporation paid its first dividend, the start of a tradition of profitability unbroken except for the Depression years of 1931 and 1932.

As Chesapeake expanded, its number of customers and products grew. Pulp remained the primary source of sales revenue. Even under Chesapeake's new management, Fox Paper Company remained a customer of the West Point mill. In 1921 Ellerson made his Albemarle Paper Manufacturing Company a Chesapeake client. By 1927 Chesapeake listed 27 customers representing mills throughout the South, Middle Atlantic area, and the Midwest.

In addition to its pulp, used primarily in the manufacture of heavy-duty brown kraft paper and Albemarle's blotting papers, the West Point mill also produced a crude turpentine and "test jute paperboard," or "box board," and other products. By 1926 the West Point plant was producing an average of 85 tons of pulp and paper products every day.

In 1928 Chesapeake and Albemarle jointly created the Albemarle-Chesapeake Company to build a new paper mill at West Point. The firm would combine Albemarle technology

A wood-treating tube is being installed here in the latest Chesapeake treating plant. Chesapeake produces both CCA and fire-retardant products.

OXY-BRITE® bleached market pulp is being loaded at the West Point mill. This oceangoing port allows direct shipments to European and other markets.

The Tri-King, Chesapeake's $73-million paper machine, makes TRI-KRAFT®, a unique three-ply linerboard that is stronger, smoother, and cleaner than competitive products, and TRI-LITE®, a unique and improved mottle white linerboard.

with the excess pulp capacity of the Chesapeake mill. For the still small town of West Point, the creation of the new company and new mill was the best news since the arrival of the railroad.

The Albemarle-Chesapeake Four drinier machine that would be the heart of the new mill was the largest kraft paper machine in the nation. Built by Pusey and Jones, the machine was 286 feet, six inches long. Transporting it to West Point required 100 freight cars. Housing it and its support equipment required a mill 434 feet long by 76 feet wide. The total cost of plant and machinery exceeded one million dollars.

After an extended series of start-up difficulties, Chesapeake abandoned efforts to produce kraft paper and converted the new machine to the production of kraft board. The product, more than 100 tons of it per day, became widely popular as the facing and backing material for corrugated boxes.

As Chesapeake and Albemarle-Chesapeake prospered, so did West Point, Virginia. The town increased in population and spawned a new community, Port Richmond. In 1924 the communities built a new high school and, with the help of a gift from the Chesapeake Corporation, established the King

William County Public Library and Community Center.

By 1930 talking motion pictures had arrived at the Wonderland Theatre. West Point was linked to Richmond by gravel roadways as well as the railroad, and motor freight operators were forcing steamship lines out of business. The local business community was expanding rapidly, fueled by the pulp and paper mill payrolls. Then the stock market crashed, and took the national economy with it.

Chesapeake and Albemarle-Chesapeake both recovered quickly from the onset of the Great Depression. As orders fell off the mills cut salaries and wages, 20 percent for officers and 10 percent for laborers, and Chesapeake canceled its dividend. In 1932 mills elsewhere in the country closed, but both West Point operations continued.

By 1934 employment was back to pre-Depression levels, Chesapeake resumed paying dividends to stockholders, and company earnings reached the million-dollar milestone. In response, the firm even began issuing Christmas bonus checks, an unannounced corporate gift reflecting the year's profitability.

The continuing success also provided Albemarle Paper with cash needed to purchase a pulp mill of its own. Another round of complex negotiations and dealings followed, leaving Albemarle as a minority owner of Ches-

apeake Corporation, and Chesapeake as the owner of Albemarle-Chesapeake and its kraft board mill. In 1940 the two West Point mills were formally united under a single corporate mantle.

Production soared to meet defense demands during World War II, but that same combination produced a drastic labor shortage at West Point. Several women took jobs in the mill, and a few others cut pulp wood in the forests. For a while German and Italian prisoners of war worked for Chesapeake. Despite its labor shortages, the company was never forced to curtail production, and in 1944 Chesapeake stock was offered for sale on the New York Stock Exchange.

Manuel Crocker McDonald became president of Chesapeake in 1945, and Elis Olsson became chairman of the corporation. McDonald resigned in 1951, and was succeeded by Sture Olsson, son of the chairman. Carl Olsson, Sture's brother, became vice-president and general woodlands manager. A cousin, Erik Zimmerman, became vice-president and general superintendent.

The 1960s brought integration to the West Point school system, and a new paper milling machine to Chesapeake.

The control room of the number three paper machine at Wisconsin Tissue in Menasha, Wisconsin, monitors all functions of the machine as it produces 208-inch-wide rolls of high-quality tissue and toweling stock. This machine is among the fastest of its kind in the world and has held the world production record.

Costs of design, construction, and installation of the new machine, including the new power plant needed to operate it, comprised a substantial portion of the $21-million expansion program of 1962-1964.

Chesapeake devoted the second part of the decade to modernizing and improving its box-manufacturing subsidiaries: David Weber Company, Miller Container Corporation, and Baltimore Box Company. In 1965 Chesapeake also entered into a joint venture with U.S. Plywood, the Chesapeake Bay Plywood Corporation, with a plant at Pocomoke City, Maryland. Chesapeake acquired sole ownership of the plant in 1980.

In 1968 Sture Olsson resigned from the presidency of the corporation and accepted an appointment as chairman of the board. Lawrence H. Camp

A flexo-folder-gluer and high-speed conveyor system at Chesapeake Corporation in Richmond. Chesapeake has 11 container/display plants covering the central, eastern, and southeastern markets.

was elected president and chief executive officer of the Chesapeake Corporation. Camp faced many challenges, but chief among them was growing environmental awareness and increasing federal and state regulation. Between 1973 and 1984 the West Point Industrial Development Authority issued $58.5 million in revenue bonds to finance pollution control and solid-waste-disposal facilities at Chesapeake.

J. Carter Fox was elected president of Chesapeake Corporation in 1980. He started his administration with a comprehensive reorganization of the firm's executive structure, and initiated a diversification program with the acquisition of Homecraft Corporation, a manufacturer of panelized homes.

In 1984 Chesapeake acquired Color-Box, Inc., of Richmond, Indiana, a corrugated-container plant specializing in point-of-purchase packaging. It was the 10th container plant acquired by Chesapeake. To enhance its identification with the parent company, "Chesapeake Corporation" became the name of nine of them, and Southern Corrugated changed its name to Chesa-

peake Display & Packaging Company. The firm's wood product subsidiaries also took the corporate name.

In 1985 Chesapeake acquired Wisconsin Tissue Mills Inc., of Menasha, Wisconsin, and Plainwell Paper Co., Inc., of Plainwell, Michigan, from the Philip Morris Corporation. Chesapeake also added a third giant papermaking machine to the West Point mill in 1985. This newest machine produces a three-ply paperboard sold under the name TRI-KRAFT®. That same year the company set up Delmarva Properties as an "unconsolidated real estate subsidiary."

Today's Chesapeake Corporation is an integrated paper and forest products company. Its major products are unbleached kraft paperboard and paper, bleached hardwood pulp, commercial and industrial tissue products, technical specialty papers, and premium coated and uncoated printing papers.

The operation also converts paperboard and other materials into corrugated containers, displays, and other packaging products; converts timber into lumber and plywood products; and manufactures panelized house packages. Chesapeake operates through 23 company-owned locations in nine states.

In 1986 sales totaled $599.8 million, and the corporation appeared on the Fortune magazine list of the 500 largest companies in the United States.

REAL TITLE COMPANY, INC.

In real estate circles they still talk about the developer who built a high-rise on land that he did not really own. It seems that when he bought the land, the woman who signed the deed as the wife of the seller wasn't. When the man's real wife filed suit several years later, the title to a multimillion-dollar structure was at issue. That, concludes the story, is why smart buyers and all financial institutions insist on the purchase of title insurance.

Title insurance is elimination of risk insurance, whereby the insurer guarantees that the title to a piece of property is clear, and assumes all risks stemming from any challenges to it. Associated with title insurance is title search, the process of checking real estate records to make sure that all transactions have been properly recorded, and that ownership of the land and land rights conveys as agreed in deeds, contracts, and covenants.

Northern Virginia's Real Title dominates the full-service title business in its region. Residential, commercial, and industrial developers such as Charles E. Smith Company, Artery, International Developers, Inc., the Henry A. Long Company, and the Evan Companies—organizations that have developed many of the shopping malls and high-rise complexes in northern Virginia—all rely on Real Title as the single source of real estate title, escrow, title insurance, and settlement services.

Real Title is the agent for Lawyers Title Insurance Corporation, a Richmond-based organization that has been providing title insurance throughout the Commonwealth since 1925.

The company was founded in 1927 by Charles T. Jesse, Walter T. McCarthy, and Henry J. Klinge. The original subscribers sold their firm to Herbert N. Morgan in 1972.

Morgan was a country boy from Jackson, Tennessee. A graduate of Jackson High School, he ran a Texaco service station for a year before joining first the local police force and then starting a brief career as a professional boxer. In 1951 he joined the United States Air Force, which made him a special agent with the Office of Special Investigations (OSI), and posted him at bases in West Germany. The Air Force also provided the opportunity for him to take the college-level courses that later allowed him to enter the Washington College of Law at American University.

Herbert N. Morgan, president of Real Title Company, Inc.

Fresh from law school in 1960 Morgan joined Lawyers Title Insurance Corporation, where he prepared for a position with Real Title. He spent the next 12 years helping to build the local title service business, becoming involved in local politics and carefully studying the nature of the title service business throughout the nation.

In 1971 he was elected from the 23rd District to the Virginia House of Delegates, where he served on the Finance, Labor, and Nominations and Confirmations committees.

Morgan purchased Real Title from its founding partners in 1972, immediately dissolving the existing corporation and reorganizing it as a sole proprietorship.

Over the next 15 years he adopted many of the more advanced real estate title service techniques, modifying them to fit Virginia's conservative legal structure and streamlining them to meet the demands of the fast-paced real estate environment of northern Virginia. He decided to follow suit with principal creditors in searching titles and delivering papers for attorneys. Instead, he added his own settlement services, making Real Title the region's first full-service real estate title company.

In the process he acquired the Southern Abstract Company in 1976, adopting its charter and corporate structure, and reorganizing it as Real Title Company, Inc. With the new structure in place, Morgan's organization was able to offer the complete mix of title search, title insurance agency, and settlement.

From its base of 15 employees in 1972, Real Title now has more than 100 lawyers, title examiners, underwriters, settlement specialists, and paralegal personnel. Its clients include major developers, law firms, and corporations. Most recently Real Title handled much of the title work for Mobil Oil Corporation when it moved its headquarters from New York City to northern Virginia.

The company has five operating locations, with the principal office in Fairfax, Virginia. Other Virginia locations are Arlington, Lake Ridge, and Alexandria. The fifth office is in Washington, D.C. In 1987 Real Title processed approximately $3 billion in escrow accounts and investments.

Morgan and his wife, Joyce Wallace Morgan, remain the sole owners of Real Title. The Morgans also have extensive additional real estate interests throughout the region. He is chairman of the Sequoia Building Corporation and a partner in International Developers, Incorporated.

Morgan is a director and member of the advisory board of the Arlington Corps of the Salvation Army, a director and past president of the Virginia Land Title Association, a past president of the Arlington County Chamber of Commerce, and a past director of the Virginia Chamber of Commerce. He is also a former trustee of Virginia Commonwealth University.

On his wall hang numerous citations and certificates, and pictures of him in the company of local, state, and national luminaries such as J. Edgar Hoover and President and Mrs. Ronald Reagan. This is one good ol' boy who has come a long way from that filling station in Jackson, Tennessee.

BURKE & HERBERT BANK & TRUST CO.

The eagle may be the bird that most Americans associate with money, but in Alexandria, Virginia, the reigning bank bird is C.S. Taylor Burke, Jr.'s, parrot, Runyon. Burke is president and chief executive officer of the Burke & Herbert Bank & Trust Co. Runyon is the bank's chief parrot. David M. Burke, a cousin of Taylor Burke, is executive vice-president of the bank. The assistant parrot is named Harvey.

The parrot thing started some 25 years ago when Taylor Burke bought Runyon as a pet. His wife refused to allow the bird in the house, so it came to live at the bank. Customers loved it. So did the press.

So did Taylor Burke, who has outstanding instincts for public relations

Burke & Herbert Bank & Trust Co.'s main office is located here at 100 South Fairfax Street in Alexandria.

and a statewide reputation as an unconventional but exceptionally good banker. In the past five years alone, his bank's assets have risen from $96 million to more than $250 million.

"We're a small bank," says Taylor Burke. "That lets us give our customers individual attention. The pipeline to management is always open to handle any problem. It also means we can work quickly and usually make our decisions on loans within a week.

"In our neighborhoods, we have a reputation as a service-oriented bank. We don't have to worry about an elaborate marketing program because our customers do our selling for us."

Burke & Herbert attracts a wide range of customers. The cars in the parking lot range from exotic imports to battered Chevy trucks, and the customers wear everything from riding habits to old work clothes. Descendants of the first families of Virginia bank here, as

did John L. Lewis until his United Mine Workers bought their own bank in Washington.

Tradition and history are important parts of the Burke & Herbert style. The headquarters building of the bank is at King and Fairfax streets in the heart of Old Town Alexandria. It is protected by ornamental, skillfully crafted, wrought-iron grillwork. Dark paneling, marble counters, and brass partitions dominate the interior, along with the old-fashioned but impressively massive steel vault. This is a banking house, not a shopping-center convenience store for money.

Not that Burke & Herbert has anything against conveniently located branch banking. It has seven branches in northern Virginia, and a network of automated teller machines. The new technology was reluctantly adopted at the bank—which only recently started using numbers for the accounts. Until a

Colonel Arthur Herbert, founder.

few years ago the records were filed under customers' names. Now all banking operations are fully automated.

Burke & Herbert has no intention of following other modern trends and becoming part of some regional megabank. "We expect to remain independent," insists Taylor Burke. "Our earnings are good, our growth is good, and the book value of our stock is going up faster than if we joined one of the chains."

The bank traces its origins to John Woolfolk Burke and Arthur Herbert, who opened their general banking business in 1852. Both came from distinguished Virginia families. Burke was a native of Caroline County; Herbert was a great-grandson of Colonel John Carlyle, one of the founders of Alexandria.

Throughout most of its history, the bank has operated as an unincorporated, unregulated partnership, relying solely on the judgment of its management for conducting its affairs. Services offered until 1933 by the bank included acting as a dealer, broker, and agent for stock, real estate (including western land and land warrants), international and domestic bank notes and currencies, and collections of rents and other debts.

The business affairs of the Burke and Herbert bank were interrupted when Union troops occupied Alexandria. Burke stayed in Alexandria with his wife, a granddaughter of Thomas Jefferson; Arthur Herbert led the Old Virginia Rifles, fighting with the 17th Virginia Regiment from First Manassas to Appomattox Court House, rising to the rank of full colonel.

The bank closed during the war, but assured its continued reputation by not allowing any of its depositors to suffer losses. At the outbreak of hostilities, Burke & Herbert was the depository for moneys paid by the Mount Vernon Ladies Association to John A. Washington, Jr., for the purchase of Mount Vernon. Washington served with General Robert E. Lee, and Burke personally hid the money from Union authorities before smuggling it to George W. Riggs of the Corcoran and Riggs Banking House in Washington. Burke was later arrested on unspecified charges and spent 10 weeks in the Old Capitol Prison.

The bank reopened after the war, first as the Banking House of J.W. Burke, and then as Burke, Herbert & Co., with a new partner, Jourdon W. Maury. Maury left the bank in 1869 and the firm's name was changed to Burke & Herbert. The bank moved to its present location, on the northwest corner of King and Fairfax streets, in 1871, and started construction of its current headquarters building in 1904.

Since then Burke & Herbert has continued doing business without interruption. Colonel Herbert retired from the bank in 1899 and sold his interest to his partner's three sons, Nicholas Philip Trist Burke, Henry Randolph Burke, and Julian T. Burke.

Nicholas predeceased his father, but Henry and Julian took over the bank in 1907. Julian's sons, C.S. Taylor Burke and Julian T. Burke, Jr., became part-

John Woolfolk Burke, founder.

ners in the bank shortly after the death of their grandfather.

C.S. Taylor Burke was president of Burke & Herbert in 1933, when Franklin D. Roosevelt closed the banks throughout the nation. Burke & Herbert was among the first banks permitted to reopen, unconditionally, by the federal inspectors. In accord with requirements of the Banking Act of 1933, the institution incorporated in Virginia as the Burke & Herbert Bank & Trust Co.

C.S. Taylor Burke, Jr., joined the bank after serving in World War II. He became president in 1963. The last member of the Herbert family to serve on the bank's board was Mark Alexander Herbert Smith. Two of Taylor Burke's sons are active in the bank. C.S. Taylor Burke III is a vice-president; Edmund Hunt Burke is an assistant vice-president.

Charles K. Collum is senior vice-president and cashier.

INTERNATIONAL DEVELOPERS, INC.

International Developers, Inc. (IDI), has been responsible for some of the most dramatic real estate developments in northern Virginia and the entire National Capital Area. IDI is headed by Giuseppe Cecchi, who, because of his achievements, is one of the most talked about real estate developers in northern Virginia.

Cecchi and a group of European investors formed IDI in 1975. Since then

International Developers, Inc. (IDI), is well known throughout northern Virginia as well as in Montgomery County, Maryland, and the District of Columbia. Company projects include both new condominium communities and condominium conversions, hotels, and mixed-use commercial and office centers. Pictured here is a rendering of IDI's Ballston Metro Center, the centerpiece of Ballston in Arlington.

he has changed the skyline of the region. IDI projects are located throughout northern Virginia, including Alexandria, and Arlington and Fairfax counties, as well as in Montgomery County, Maryland, and the District of Columbia. Projects include both new condominium communities and condominium conversions, hotels, mixed-use commercial and office centers, and several complete planned communities.

In all, IDI is responsible for more than 20 major real estate developments, all award-winning success stories, and each an architectural contribution to the National Capital Area.

Cecchi, born in Milan, Italy, was the child of middle-class parents. Both his father and grandfather were professional engineers. As soon as he was graduated as a professional engineer

from the University of Milan, Cecchi joined Societa Generale Immobilaire (SGI), a large development com pany based in Italy. He came to the United States in 1959 to open a New York City office for SGI. Four years later the organization made him project manager of a large mixed-use project on the Potomac River in Washington. The firm called its project Watergate.

To most of the world, "Watergate" has come to mean the bungled burglary that eventually brought an end to the Nixon administration. In Washington, however, "Watergate" is the prime residential/hotel/office/shopping development along the Potomac River, next to the Kennedy Center, that is still the supreme symbol of the fashionable life.

Watergate became Cecchi's trademark. Its distinctive architecture, its financial success, and its glamour all attached themselves to the young Italian executive. By the time it was finished, Cecchi was president of SGI's Washington subsidiaries.

In 1975 Gianni Trotta, an Italian developer and former SGI director, asked Cecchi to join a group of international investors who wanted to organize a new real estate firm in the United States and, after 20 years of service, Cecchi resigned from SGI. In June 1975 International Developers, Inc., was created with Trotta as chairman of the board and Cecchi as president.

From its executive offices in Arlington, IDI began to change the skyline. Its first construction project was The Rotonda, a five-building, 1,168-unit condominium community in the McLean area of Fairfax County. The Rotonda became one of the hottest properties on the Washington area market. Almost all the units were sold before completion, making it the first of many successful IDI condominium projects.

As the Metrorail system expanded throughout the region, so did IDI. Company projects include mixed-use developments at the Rosslyn and Ballston Metro stations, and a residential development, the four-building, 1,016-unit Montebello condominiums, near the Huntington Metro station.

The Rosslyn Center includes IDI's

own corporate offices, as well as space leased to Boeing, Magnavox, and other major corporations, and the elegant Tivoli Restaurant. The 26-story Ballston Center will tower more than 30 feet over its neighbors. It will include a 210-room hotel, 277 condominium units, and 193,000 square feet of office space, plus retail shops, a health club, and restaurants.

IDI's most recent project is Techworld—The World Technology Trade Center—currently under development on a four-acre site halfway between the Capitol and the White House, and immediately adjacent to the Washington Convention Center.

Techworld will include an 800-room Ramada Renaissance convention hotel, approximately one million square feet of showroom and office space, and approximately 90,000 square feet of retail and service establishments. It will

house a 150,000-square-foot Conference Center and training and education facilities. It will offer underground parking for 2,000 vehicles. That all adds up to the largest single private real estate development in the District of Columbia.

Construction of Techworld was long delayed by extended administrative procedures, debates, and a complex lawsuit. Many developers, faced with the opposition of diverse interest groups and several federal agencies, might have abandoned the project. Not Giuseppe Cecchi.

Excavation for Phase I of the project began in December 1986. The first phase of the trade center and the hotel are scheduled to be ready for occupancy in mid-1989. The entire project is scheduled for completion by the end of 1990.

In 1986 Cecchi formed a new partnership with a group of prominent northern Virginia businessmen to ac-

Pictured here is The Rotonda, a five-building, 1,168-unit condominium community in the McLean area of Fairfax County that was the first IDI construction project.

quire IDI and its sister company, Intercontinental Realty, Inc., from the original European investors, and consolidated the two firms into a single company. Giuseppe Cecchi is now president and chief executive officer of the newly reorganized IDI. The directors are Duane Beckhorn, Myron Erkiletian, John T. Hazel, Jr., Herbert N. Morgan, Milton V. Peterson, and William G. Thomas.

IDI has 100 employees. The firm's completed and under-construction projects through 1987 are valued at more than $1.3 billion, with several additional multimillion-dollar projects just coming off the drawing boards.

GUIFFRÉ DISTRIBUTING COMPANY

Two major American historical events, the Great Depression and the end of Prohibition, combined to help create the Guiffré (pronounce it Ja-Fray, with the accent on the second syllable) Distributing Company. The third element was a dynamic, hard-punching ex-boxer, ex-shoemaker, and ex-real estate developer named Tony Guiffré.

Sicilian by birth, Tony Guiffré came to the United States as a child in approximately 1885. In Washington, Tony sold newspapers when he was seven years old, and war bonds during World War I. The family moved to the Alexandria area in roughly 1925. A shoemaker by trade, he built a business making orthopedic shoes. When the government condemned his store in 1926, he took the settlement and purchased land in Potomac, Virginia, a suburb of Alexandria, later known as Del Ray.

There are many family legends about Tony Guiffré. They tell how, for a while, he boxed professionally under an assumed name in order to earn money for his family. That training stood him in good stead when the Ku Klux Klan sent three thugs to warn him to get out of town. He beat them up, then called the police to report an "assault and battery." According to the story still told by his grandson, he told the police

Current president Joseph M. "Joe" Guiffré.

that "They assaulted, and I battered."

At the Del Ray property, Tony Guiffré and his wife, Theresa, built what may well have been the area's first multiuse residential commercial complex. That is the modern terminology, at least, for the frame building that housed several retail operations, a three-car garage out back, and two apartments upstairs, plus the Guiffré family living quarters.

Then came the Great Depression. Land values dropped, and Guiffré found himself unable to lease the stores. Undaunted, he decided to use them himself. He opened a hardware store in one, a pool hall in the second, and a shoe repair shop in the third. His wife operated a delicatessen in the fourth. And there are several different versions about the nature of the business conducted in the garages.

The official version is that Tony stocked 25 cases of "near beer," the low-alcohol version that was legal during Prohibition. Tony stored the beer in his garages, and used his family car to make deliveries. Orders were taken one day, and delivered the next.

With the end of Prohibition came a new style of business, and the real birth of Guiffré Distributing. While Virginia debated over its post-Prohibition alcohol laws and the legislators talked, Tony acted. He would drive to the District of Columbia to buy stock, and deliver it directly to his customers.

The company still consisted of the family car, with Tony Guiffré as delivery man, stock boy, salesman, order taker, and accountant. The firm sold Old German, Arrow beer, and Senate beer made by the Old Heurich Brewery in Washington.

In May 1934 the business was fully licensed, and justified the purchase of a delivery truck. Tony also increased the stock to 50 cases, and built a small office in the garage warehouse. Two years later the firm added a second truck, and, in 1936, the addition of a new premium beer. Tony made arrangements with Anheuser-Busch to be the direct representative for Budweiser, the "King of Beers." It marked the beginning of a business relationship continued even today.

At the time Budweiser was a relatively unknown, high-priced product. It was an import to the area, and had a hard time competing with the local products, but as the popularity increased, so did the volume of business conducted by Guiffré Distributing. Tony knew from the beginning that he needed a premium product whose quality he could rely on for long-term growth.

When Tony Guiffré died in 1943, he left a profitable, thriving company to Theresa. Earlier his oldest son, Guy A. Guiffré, Sr., had sold the Central Liquor Store in Washington, D.C., and had be-

Tony Guiffré, founder of Guiffré Distributing Company.

The executive committee of Guiffré Distributing Company are (left to right) Ann Guiffré, secretary/treasurer; R.W. "Bill" Anholt, general manager; Joseph M. "Joe" Guiffré, president; J. Michael "Mike" Guiffré, vice-president; and Julie Guiffré Misko, vice-president.

come a company driver-salesman. Guy continued to operate his route. Theresa took over the office work.

At the end of World War II Guy's brother, Joseph, joined the business, and their mother slowed down. In 1947 Guiffré Distributing moved to a new warehouse at 1018 North Henry Street in Alexandria. With railway delivery services at the front and back doors, and a fleet of four delivery trucks, the Guiffré brothers and Budweiser beer became a major factor in the northern Virginia beer market.

Theresa Guiffré died in 1953, leaving the business to Guy and Joseph. Joseph purchased his brother's interest in the company in 1956, and Guy retired.

At the time Joseph's son, Joseph M., was a recent graduate of Georgetown and a Latin and English teacher at a Silver Spring high school. It took little persuasion for his father to convince him to leave teaching and take over as a driver-salesman on the Old Town, Alexandria, route. (The route paid $85 per week as compared to $60 a week for teaching.) Joseph A. Guiffré died suddenly and unexpectedly at a civic dinner

The Guiffré Distributing Company office and warehouse, located in Springfield, Virginia.

in 1963.

Joseph M. Guiffré is now the president and chief executive officer of Guiffré Distributing. His wife, Ann, works for the company as do two of his children. They represent the fourth generation of the family working in the business.

The firm moved to its Industrial Road, Springfield, location in 1983. With 75 employees and a fleet of 16 trucks, the company now delivers 2 million cases of beer per year.

Guiffré now stores its draft beer in a refrigerator that is larger than the entire Henry Street facility. The packaged goods are stored in an environmentally controlled room almost an acre in size. The firm is continually adding new products to the line, which now includes

wine coolers, bottled water, soft drinks, snack foods, and related products. Annual gross sales exceed $20 million.

Joseph M. Guiffré is a member of the board of the Virginia Department of Transportation. He also served on the board of Washington and Lee Savings and Loan Association, and on the board of the Alexandria National Bank, the same bank that originally lent his grandfather the money needed to develop the Del Ray property.

The fourth generation, represented by Julie and Mike Guiffré, looks forward to many more years representing the Guiffré Distributing Company in the northern Virginia community.

ERKILETIAN CONSTRUCTION CORPORATION

An artist's rendering of Erkiletian Construction Corporation's Park Center, which is still in the building process. It will be a 41-acre development with more than 10 acres of lawns, terraces, plazas, and woods; in excess of 1.3 million square feet of office space; 1,574 apartments; more than 7,000 parking spaces; and featuring restaurants, shops, and banking and financial services.

Since 1967 Erkiletian Construction Corporation of Alexandria has made its name stand for first-quality construction throughout the northern Virginia area and beyond.

The list of Erkiletian Construction Corporation projects is short but impressive. It includes Woodburn Village Apartments (Sections I and II) in Fairfax, Virginia; Quince Orchard Clusters Apartments (Sections I and II) in Gaithersburg, Maryland; the award-winning TOR Apartments in Columbia, Maryland; Peachtree Apartments in McLean, Virginia; and Park Center Apartments in Alexandria, Virginia. Erkiletian Construction's office buildings include 8200 Greensboro Drive in Tysons Corner;

Park Center I, II, and Kiosk in Alexandria; and Park Center IV.

Erkiletian projects typically have distinctive and unique features that set them apart. Close attention to detailing and constant concern over tenant requirements are routine elements of all of them. And each makes a strong architectural comment, a bold statement that is a reflection of the hard-driving, cigar-smoking executive who runs this Virginia corporation.

His accomplishments have not gone unnoticed by the construction industry. Myron "Mike" Erkiletian was the 1972 Builder of the Year of the State of Virginia Home Builders Association. In 1977 he was designated Man of the Year by the Northern Virginia Builders Association.

The Magazine Brothers Construction Company of Washington gave Erkiletian his start in the construction business in 1960. He worked in that firm's construction purchasing department, becoming involved with planning, sequencing, and buying. He was only 24 years old, fresh from four years at Pur-

due University, and carrying a brand-new master's degree in business administration from Columbia University. In 1962 he joined Societa Generale Immobiliare to become an assistant to his friend Guiseppe Cecchi, the project manager, to develop the unique Watergate complex in Washington, D.C. "I didn't mind doing everybody's staff work as long as I learned something," he remembers of those years.

In 1963 Erkiletian, with the help of Sheldon and Sam Magazine, with Barry Rosenberg built the Hampton East Apartments in the District of Columbia. The next year a friend from college, Jerry Kaplan, joined Erkiletian in a venture they called Hallmark Construction. Hallmark completed three jobs—Stanton Hill Apartments in the Anacostia section of the District of Columbia; Glen Willow Apartments in Seat Pleasant, Maryland; and a town house development in Leesburg, Virginia.

The partners dissolved Hallmark in 1967, and Erkiletian, on his own, formed Franklin Construction, which in early 1971 became Erkiletian Construction with a group of investors led by his good friend Jeff Glosser. Erkiletian Construction became a major part of the local industry, building Woodburn Village, Quince Orchard, TOR, and Peach Tree.

Real estate construction is a cyclical business, perilously strewn with good and bad times. Erkiletian remembers 1974-1975 as particularly difficult. "We really had to stretch," he says. "But that's when we started Park Center."

Reflecting his pride in the Park Center project, he changed the name of his firm from Franklin to Erkiletian Construction. The massive Alexandria complex offers views of the U.S. Capitol and the Pentagon. Still in process (building IV became available for leasing in 1987), Park Center has become Erkiletian's proudest contribution to the community.

"You try to build a product that will always be a little ahead of its time. You put time and energy into design and efficiency. You solve problems and never try to escape from them. Of course, it all has to be economically productive, or it just doesn't work."

Erkiletian's corporate offices are in Park Center. Most of the people who work there have worked with Erkiletian for many years. They include vice-presidents Jack Moran, Bill Wade, Joe Schmidt, and John Hall, as well as field superintendents Jack Jackson, Roger Proctor, Bill Denton, and Pat Dolan. Erkiletian is as proud of his people as he is of his buildings.

Other long-term relationships include the Gates Hudson Company, which has been managing Erkiletian's properties since 1981, and International Development Incorporated, of which Erkiletian is a part owner. "My people do all the work and leave me free. I'm doing exactly what I wanted to do, and I'm still enjoying doing it. That's the deal."

The "deal" at the 41-acre Park Center site includes more than 10 acres of lawns, terraces, plazas, and woods; in excess of 1.3 million square feet of office space; 1,574 apartments; more than 7,000 parking spaces; restaurants, shops, and banking and financial services; and a new fitness center, The Center Club.

The Center Club is typical of Erkiletian projects. The $8-million award-winning Center Club is a 47,000-square-foot, two-level, complete health club facility, lavishly designed and elegantly appointed. Despite its efficient underground location, it makes dramatic use of light and open spaces. Following the Erkiletian philosophy, it is designed to be slightly ahead of its time, offering complete facilities, with a six-lane 25-meter swimming pool, computerized exercise equipment, electronically paced indoor jogging track, luxurious locker rooms, whirlpools, saunas, and massage rooms, along with the traditional basketball, volleyball, badminton, nautilus center, racquetball courts, and sun rooms. The Center Club also offers a fully staffed nursery, and a delightful restaurant is next door.

"I don't want to build monuments," says Erkiletian. "I want my buildings to be active, living places filled with lively people. Everything has to work."

Erkiletian works as hard at community service as he does at construction. He is a member of the Governor's Advisory Board for Virginia Industrial Development, the Board of Visitors of George Mason University, the George Mason Institute Board, the Washington Airports Task Force Board, and the board of directors of International Development, Inc. He is also the Virginia governor's appointee to four-state Chesapeake Bay Pact, secretary/treasurer of the Mount Vernon Society, a trustee of the endowment fund of the Diocese of

The $8-million award-winning Center Club, an Erkiletian Construction Corporation project, is a 47,000-square-foot, two-level, complete health club facility located in Park Center. Pictured here is the reception area.

the Armenian Church of North America, and a past treasurer and lifetime director of the Northern Virginia Builders Association.

"This is Virginia," he says. "This is where we live. We want to be involved."

361

WAYNE INSULATION CO., INC.

As founder and president of Wayne Insulation Co., Inc., Wayne M. Whitlow is a living example of the traditional Old Dominion entrepreneurial spirit. With a personal touch, he strives to maintain a company that produces good service and quality work.

In the late 1940s Wayne Whitlow of Danieltown, Virginia, began his insulation career working for another contractor in the Washington, D.C., area. Upon realizing his ability to handle the work, Whitlow decided to start his own firm. In 1950 he founded W.M. Whitlow Insulation Contractor. He hired one employee and started work in the Washington, D.C., metropolitan area.

In the early years the firm offered only pipe, boiler, and duct insulation services. The District Heights Apartments in District Heights, Maryland, gave Whitlow Insulation its first contract. After that, prior contacts and job bidding brought the two-man team plenty of work.

In 1956 Whitlow incorporated the firm and changed the name to Wayne Insulation Co., Inc., as it is still known today. Over the years the business expanded to include a wide variety of insulation services for both commercial and residential clients. This included services such as covering underground pipe; installation of rock wool, fiberglass, and urethane foam; asbestos removal; and the installation of ceiling tiles, which the firm has since discontinued. Currently about 90 percent of Wayne Insulation's commercial work is pipe covering jobs received from mechanical contractors; bidding jobs directly brings in the rest of the commercial work.

Although the only office is located in Alexandria, Virginia, Wayne Insulation has now completed projects throughout Virginia, as well as in Connecticut, Pennsylvania, North Carolina, West Virginia, Tennessee, Kentucky, and Florida. For out-of-town contracts, the firm sends only a base group from Alexandria to run the job and then hires local labor.

Wayne Insulation receives many of its large contracts from government agencies. Some of these projects include renovation jobs at the Naval Operating Base in Norfolk, Virginia; the Naval Yard in Philadelphia, Pennsylvania; the Submarine Base in Groton, Connecticut; the Veterans' Hospital in Pikeville, Kentucky; and the St. Elizabeth's Hospital, the Federal Bureau of Investigation, the Central Intelligence Agency, and the Andrews Air Force Base Hospital, all in the Washington, D.C., metropolitan area.

Over the past 37 years Wayne Whitlow has managed to take his company from a two-man team to a large corporation averaging 70 employees. He attributes part of his success to the family-type network that he has created around him. Over the years many of his own relatives have worked for him, and many of his employees have shared the work arena with their own family members.

Perhaps it is this sense of unity that explains why so many employees have worked for Wayne Insulation for 10 years or more. In fact, Daniel Lee Gray, Whitlow's first employee, continues to work there today. Whitlow also boasts that his two sons have chosen to work with him to ensure the successful continuance of the company.

The desire for good service and quality work continues to direct the efforts of Wayne Whitlow. He demands that careful attention be given to all jobs. Recently one satisfied customer wrote, "Thanks so much for your help! Your insulation of 'this old house' has kept me from freezing."

"You all must be the only Virginia Gentlemen in the state—before you all, I was convinced it was only distilled and in a bottle!"

THE CARDWELL MACHINE COMPANY

Charles A. Hotchkiss, president of The Cardwell Machine Company.

Richmond's Cardwell Machine Company traces its roots to 1829, when Hiram M. Smith began manufacturing farm implements on Main Street in Richmond. John W. Cardwell started a similar business on Cary Street in 1849.

Each grew and expanded, and during the Civil War both switched from manufacturing farm implements to producing war materials—gun carriages, shovels, munitions cases, and even hay presses for Jeb Stuart's cavalry.

After the war Cardwell acquired

The Cardwell Machine Company office and plant complex in Richmond.

a partner, Samuel Freedley of Philadelphia. The new firm, J.W. Cardwell & Co., began manufacturing hydraulic presses and pumps, and tobacco factory machinery, as well as agricultural implements. With Freedley's capital, the firm was able to resume its activities, discovering a new prosperity in the reunited country.

John Cardwell died in 1888, and Freedley purchased his share of the business. In February 1890 the company secured the second charter of incorporation issued by the Commonwealth of Virginia, and became The Cardwell Machine Company. In 1891 Cardwell purchased the H.M. Smith Company.

Cardwell grew along with the tobacco industry. The firm's line of tobacco-processing equipment sold worldwide. The company also introduced many new uses of hydraulically operated presses for wool, for oil extraction from cotton and other seeds, as well as for tobacco applications.

From 1926 through the Great Depression years the company experienced hard times, and was forced to sell the large factory it built in 1895 and move to more modest quarters.

World War II saw the introduction of the American blended cigarette to the world by U.S. servicemen. By war's end Cardwell had recovered from the reverses suffered the previous decade, and in 1949 was reorganized under new ownership.

In 1954 Cardwell formed a British subsidiary, now known as The Cardwell Machine Company (UK) Ltd. This firm, with its access to the European Common Market, has become a market leader in Europe, Africa, and the Indian subcontinent.

In the early 1970s Cardwell introduced a new line of tobacco machinery that established the firm as the world's leader of tobacco-leaf-processing equipment.

The Swedish Match Group of Stockholm purchased the Cardwell companies in 1974; they were sold to a group of Cardwell employees eight years later. Diversification began immediately, and today Cardwell is a supplier of significance to the food-processing industry, as well as to the tobacco industry.

John Cardwell provided strong leadership as chief executive in the early days, as did Walter W. Craigie, 1949 to 1974, and Henry S. Holland III, 1974 to 1983. The current president, Charles A. Hotchkiss, who began his career at The Cardwell Machine Company in 1954, believes the firm is well positioned to enter the decade of the 1990s in a strong financial condition and with new and diversified product lines.

WEST*GROUP, INC.

A low-profile firm that has developed some of the highest profile real estate in northern Virginia, WEST*GROUP, Inc., is a real estate development and management organization that provides a full range of professional services to affiliated real estate investment organizations.

The individual executives of WEST*GROUP may not be household names throughout Virginia, but their buildings and developments are among the most important in the region:

—WEST*PARK and WEST*GATE, the core developments of Tysons Corner, are located at the intersection of the Capital Beltway and I-66, midway between Dulles International Airport and downtown Washington.

—The Parkway Building is in Alexandria's historic district, minutes from National Airport.

—Springfield Corporate Center and Springfield Tower Shopping Center occupy the southwest intersection of the Beltway and I-395.

—Other developments occupy prime locations in Maryland's Montgomery County, including Executive Plaza, Research West, and WEST*FARM.

The founders of WEST*GROUP are G.T. Halpin, Thomas F. Nicholson, Colonel Rudolph G. Seeley, and Charles B. Ewing, Jr. They have been sponsoring and developing real estate for more than 30 years. In 1960 Halpin

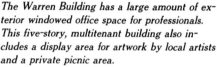

and Nicholson formed a private real estate investment company, Commonwealth Capital, Inc., that participated in the development of the Landmark Regional Shopping Center in northern Virginia. Commonwealth Capital later bought the 136-acre Storm Farm and joined it with the neighboring 138-acre Ulfelder Farm. (The Ulfelders bought the property in 1928; their heirs are still partners. The two properties now anchor the section of Fairfax County known as Tysons Corner.

Seeley joined Halpin and Nicholson in 1962, when they formed the Westgate Corporation; Ewing joined them in 1963.

The development of WEST*GATE was the first major office and residential development in the area. It offered a mix of technology, business, government, nearby housing, convenient shopping, and neighboring educational institutions. WEST*GATE consists of 26 office buildings with more

The Warren Building has a large amount of exterior windowed office space for professionals. This five-story, multitenant building also includes a display area for artwork by local artists and a private picnic area.

than 2.5 million square feet, 600 apartments and rental town houses, and a shopping center.

WEST*PARK was conceived in 1970, when the WEST*GROUP principals acquired a 313-acre parcel in the Tysons Corner Quadrangle. Today WEST*PARK contains approximately 3 million square feet of office space in 17 buildings.

"The WEST*GROUP philosophy is pride," says Kathryn MacLane, a vice-president and the corporate secretary. "We're all residents and citizens of Virginia. We do things we can be proud of, and have fun doing, and make money. But pride in out product is first.

"WEST*GROUP is keyed to accomplishment, not to personal publicity. We've been here a long time, and we'll be around for a long time."

The largest landowner in Tysons Corner, WEST*GROUP also has more than 8 million square feet of real estate in the Washington area under its management. It also developed and either owns or manages another 1,400 residential units.

WEST*GROUP itself is a closely held private corporation. Halpin is chairman and president. The other three

*WEST*PARK, the premier office park community in northern Virginia, is proud to be the home for many corporate headquarters. The buildings are placed in a well-landscaped, campus-like setting.*

principals are executive vice-presidents. The firm or its principals are participants in more than 60 individual partnerships and 23 related corporations, all doing business through contracts with WEST*GROUP.

WEST*GROUP provides its contracting affiliates with all phases of development services, including land acquisition, planning, zoning, financing, general contracting, property management, and leasing. The firm is proud of the numerous awards won by its developments, and is especially proud of its two "Subbies," the 1978 and 1985 awards for construction from the Virginia Association of Subcontractors to the state's "Outstanding Owner Developer."

WEST*GROUP is also proud of its tenants—both for their achievements and their contributions to the community. Tenants of WEST*GATE include MITRE Corporation, United Airlines, TRW, and GTE. Tenants of WEST*PARK include BDM, Unisys, Data General, and CONTEL-ASC.

Projects now in progress will provide headquarters space for the Federal Home Loan Mortgage Corporation, "Freddie Mac," which has become a joint venture partner in the development of its new 1.5-million-square-foot headquarters complex in WEST*PARK, and a 440,000-square-foot headquarters complex for BDM.

And the organization is not done yet. More than 150 acres of zoned property remain to be developed for a variety of high-density uses, including a retail commercial center and approximately 3.5 million square feet of office and hotel space.

The principals of WEST*GROUP are all active leaders in local, regional, and national affairs.

Halpin is a director of the Science Museum of Virginia and a member of the boards of directors of Bell Atlantic Corporation, Crestar, and Syracuse Uni-

Construction is under way for the first phase of the international headquarters for BDM. This two-building complex will be completed in the summer of 1988.

versity. He has also worked closely with Wolf Trap Farm Park in northern Virginia, George Mason University, Marymount College, and the Virginia Foundation of Independent Colleges.

Nicholson is a founder and director of Innisfree, a center in a rural, agricultural setting that provides physical care and support for retarded adults. He is also a member of the board of directors of Crestar.

Ewing is a director of the Fairfax Hospital Association Corporation and a trustee of the Association of Graduates, United States Military Academy, West Point. He is a director of Sorran Bank.

Seeley, who died in January 1988, was a past president of the Fairfax City Chamber of Commerce and of the Salvation Army. He was a director of the

*The Hayes Building is a 310,000-square-foot office structure located on a ridge that offers extraordinary views of the wooded campus area of WEST*GATE Office Park. Its high ratio of exterior windowed offices to interior space offers employees a vista of the Tysons Corner scene as well as the National Cathedral towers in the distance.*

Fairfax Symphony, the George Mason Foundation, and the Virginia Museum. He also served as a director for Dominion Bankshares in Roanoke, and still serves on the board of Dominion Bank of Northern Virginia in Vienna.

WEST*GROUP itself is active in community affairs, providing substantial support to people-oriented programs involving education, health care, and the arts.

BRENCO, INC.

George H. Whitfield founded Brenco to fulfill a lifelong dream, and led the company through the transition from a bronze foundry to an international manufacturer of precision-tapered roller bearings for railroad and industrial uses.

The "clickety clack" of railroad wheels is part of American folk culture. At Brenco, Inc., it is also part of the sweet sound of success. Brenco manufactures bearings, the device that sits between the wheel and the railroad car and allows the wheel to turn freely while holding it firmly in place. American railroad cars have been running on Brenco bearings since 1949.

The firm's blue-and-white sign is highly visible on the drive along Interstate 95 just south of Petersburg, the stylized "B" composed of roller bearings and the name Brenco Bearings. It marks the plant and corporate headquarters complex of a company that had net sales in 1987 exceeding $33 million. But when George H. Whitfield founded the business, he had trouble selling his initial stock issue and raising the $100,000 he needed to start Brenco.

Whitfield was managing Ameri-

can Brake Shoe's southeastern district sales office in Richmond when he decided to go into business for himself. Most of the area's professional investors rejected his requests for underwriting. Those who participated in the venture included Mrs. Harry T. McIntyre, a family friend of the Whitfields, and Charles L. Reed, the lawyer who helped organize the company. One sales representative took his commissions in Brenco stock.

The new company was molded as a brass foundry, a production facility for bronze journal bearings for railroad cars. Fortunately, the business required relatively little capitalization. Customers shipped worn-out bearings to Brenco, which melted down the scrap, poured fresh castings, machined and lined them, and shipped them back to the railroads.

Because almost no raw materials inventory was required, working capital needs were modest. Better still, the bronze journal bearing required replacement every three or four years.

Whitfield constructed his first foundry and machine shop in Peters-

burg, Virginia, at a site where three major railroads—the Norfolk and Western, Atlantic Coast Line, and Seaboard—converged. The product's weight and low selling price limited the sale of bronze journal bearings to regions around plant sites, and Brenco found ready markets.

Brenco began manufacturing bronze journal bearings in 1950. A few months later the Korean War broke out, and material flowed from plants throughout America to the ports. It flowed in railroad cars that rode on bearings, assuring Brenco's prosperity through the difficult start-up years.

The future appeared to be outstanding, but Whitfield recognized a need to anticipate change. During a visit to Europe he learned that European railroads were using a whole new

Harley Sorenson, a longtime Brenco employee, and a railroad inspector make a general inspection of Brenco bearings for railcar application in 1953.

Chairman Bryan Whitfield (right) and president Craig Rice (left) believe that the future of Brenco lies with the talent of its people.

technology—frictionless roller bearings. Whitfield realized that roller bearings were safer, more reliable, required little service, and lasted the life of the railroad car. Eventually he knew that despite the high initial cost of the new components, tapered roller bearings would replace the older system.

Whitfield persuaded his board of directors to begin research immediately on the production of tapered roller bearings. Again his timing was impeccable. American railcar manufacturers began adopting the new technology in 1960, and in the early 1970s the Association of American Railroads mandated the use of roller bearings on all new railcars. Owing to Whitfield's foresight, Brenco was perfectly positioned to provide the industry with a high-quality product.

The tapered roller bearing is a precision component requiring sophisticated manufacturing technology. Brenco built a new plant in 1962, designed specifically to produce tapered roller bearings. The plant was equipped with the most up-to-date grinding equipment and heat-treating furnaces available at the time.

In 1964 Brenco added its own plant to manufacture bearing parts out of rolled ring steel forgings. In 1972 the firm began the manufacture of its own seals. Today Brenco manufactures more of its own components than any other railroad bearing manufacturer, a capability that allows it to maintain the highest quality-control standards in the industry. By 1979 Brenco was producing almost half of the tapered roller bearings sold in the United States.

When Whitfield originally capitalized his company, he offered common stock in lots of 100 shares at $62.50 per share. On Brenco's 25th anniversary in 1974, the stock represented by one lot of those initial shares had a market value of more than $750,000, and the $600,000 quarterly dividend represented six times the initial $100,000 capital investment.

A new generation of Brenco executives assumed control of the firm in 1986, when Needham B. Whitfield, the son of the founder of Brenco (George Whitfield died in 1971), became chairman of the board and chief executive officer. He credits Brenco's success to the company's commitment to quality. "The purpose of Brenco is to provide superior products and excellent service to our customers," says Whitfield. "We compete on the basis of the quality of our products and the excellence of our service."

"Over the years," says J. Craig Rice, current president of Brenco, "many larger competitors have taken a run at us. Brenco has always found a way to win out. We have a lot of big-name competitors now, and intense foreign competition, but our people have

Brenco employees proudly stand behind their product.

always kept us in the fight and given us the edge."

As railroads have moved away from labor-intensive activities, such as servicing their own rolling stock, Brenco has moved in. The company is also rapidly building its international sales, and now provides tapered roller bearings to railroads in Canada, Europe, Mexico, India, South America, and Australia. The organization is diversifying into manufacturing automotive parts, including ring gears and drive gears for automatic transmissions.

But then, as its 40-year history readily indicates, adjusting to new markets and new technologies is standard operating procedure at Brenco, Inc.

SCOPE INCORPORATED, A LEXICON COMPANY

With military aircraft flying at incredible speeds and weapons routinely fired far from sight of their targets, target classification, learning to distinguish friend from foe (and from neutrals), has become a critical challenge of the electronic age. One pioneer and leading contributor in the development of target classification devices is SCOPE Incorporated, of Reston, Virginia.

SCOPE is a full-service electronics

company specializing in the application of advanced computer, signal-processing, electro-optical, and manufacturing technology.

Industrial customers know SCOPE primarily for the company's bar-code readers and other optical scanning systems. Defense contractors know SCOPE not only for target classification devices, but for its TEMPEST equipment. TEMPEST is a federal standard for data-processing equipment that has been specially modified to prevent electronic eavesdropping. SCOPE's Defense Data Network (DDN) Microgateway System is another family of products that has brought the firm international recognition.

The roots of SCOPE go back more than 30 years. The company was founded in 1957 (long before there was a Washington Beltway) by R.E. Williams and a small team of engineers and scientists. By the early 1960s the firm had made its mark as a defense department con-

Michael Levy is chairman of the board and chief executive officer of SCOPE Incorporated, a Lexicon Company.

tractor. SCOPE moved to Reston in 1962.

Among its unique capabilities is SCOPE's capacity to take concepts through the entire acquisition cycle: exploratory development, advanced development, engineering development, manufacturing, and field support. Control of the full acquisition cycle has allowed SCOPE to maintain its extraordinary "QA," its widely admired quality aspects control system.

SCOPE was acquired in a widely publicized takeover by the Lexicon Corporation of Fort Lauderdale, Florida, in 1985. Michael Levy, president and chief executive officer of Lexicon, became chairman of the board and chief executive officer of SCOPE. Lexicon was recently listed by *INC.* magazine as one of America's 100 fastest-growing small public companies.

Levy is the inventor of the world's first hand-held electronic language translator, an innovative consumer product marketed by Lexicon in the late 1970s. In September 1985 he brought Edward R. Olson in as president and chief operating officer of SCOPE. Under their leadership, SCOPE and Lexicon divested several product lines and consolidated operations into three SCOPE divisions: Signal Technology, Defense Systems, and Industrial Systems.

As part of Lexicon, SCOPE has once again become a major component of northern Virginia's high-technology community. From revenues of $8.5 million in 1985, when Lexicon purchased a controlling interest, the firm generated revenues of $17 million in fiscal year 1987 and anticipates revenues exceeding $25 million in 1988.

SCOPE Incorporated employs more than 250 people. In addition to its plant and corporate headquarters unit in Reston, the company operates two facilities in Herndon, close to Dulles International Airport.

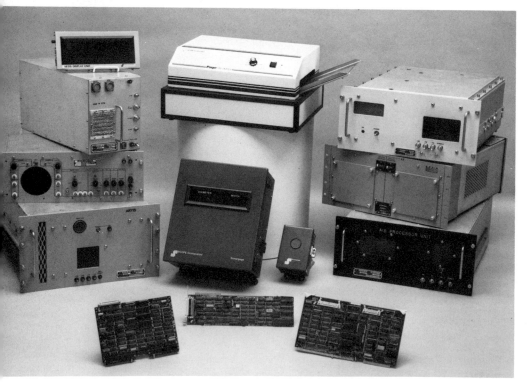

SCOPE Incorporated produces a diverse line of modern high-technology products at its plants in Reston and Herndon, Virginia.

SOUTH ATLANTIC COAL COMPANY, INC.

R.E. Perkinson, president of South Atlantic Coal Company.

Coal mining, the economic backbone of southwestern Virginia, historically has been run by several different companies. On February 14, 1974, Jno. McCall Coal Company, Inc., and R.E.P. Sales, Inc., incorporated South Atlantic Coal Company, Inc., to consolidate the many individually owned and operated mining companies in western Virginia and eastern Kentucky. Since then the firm has run efficiently and union-free to reduce fuel costs for its customers.

From 1974 to 1982 South Atlantic Coal Company acquired minority interests in several mining companies and consolidated them to create a new organizational structure for the mining industry in that region. The firm obtains mineral leases and provides permitting, environmental upkeep, mine engineering projections, and advisory services to contractors, who mine and deliver the coal to South Atlantic's preparation facilities. Race Fork Coal Corporation and Permac, Inc., are two of the firm's Virginia coal preparation plants.

South Atlantic Coal Company, Inc., has an exclusive sales agreement with Jno. McCall Company, Inc., to sell it all the coal produced at its mine locations. South Atlantic is an independent organization.

The president of South Atlantic, R.E. Perkinson, worked for C.A.

Clyborne, an agent for Jno. McCall Coal Company, until Clyborne's death in 1972. At that time the sales operations were consolidated under one corporation, and South Atlantic was formed. Perkinson also serves as the executive vice-president of Jno. McCall's southern division.

J.M. McCall, Jr., joined the family business, Jno. McCall Coal Company, in 1946 after serving as a pilot in World War II. He became president five years later. In 1972 he assumed the vice-presidency of South Atlantic Coal Company.

Jno. McCall Coal Company, Inc., is one of America's oldest independent coal suppliers and one of the largest coal exporters in the eastern United States. Established in the 1920s in Baltimore, Maryland, the firm has since opened branch sales offices in Bluefield, West Virginia; Richmond, Virginia; Cincinnati, Ohio; and Detroit, Michigan. McCall provides metallurgical and steam grades of coal to customers in Europe, Asia, South and Central America, as well as the United States.

Pictured here are preparation plants, located in Buchanan County, owned by subsidiaries of South Atlantic Coal Company.

BILL'S BARBECUE, INC.

W.S. Richardson, Sr., purchased Bill's Barbecue in 1943 from his sister, Ethel Richardson Batts. A past president of the Virginia Restaurant Association, Richardson was also named Restaurateur of the Year on two different occasions in recognition for his many years of devoted and significant service to the restaurant industry in Virginia. Courtesy, Arthur Clarke Studio

Don't call Bill's Barbecue fast food because it takes more than 14 hours to prepare. However, you can call it fast service, which is what you will find at any of the eight locations. Bill's Barbecue is a local chain of drive-ins, called stores, never restaurants, by its owner and many longtime customers. It has be-

come a Richmond tradition. From Bill's Famous Barbecue Sandwiches to the limeade and Peak-Of-Flavor® pies (the icebox pies are made with real whipped cream), there is no place anywhere quite like Bill's Barbecue.

The very first Bill's opened in 1930 in Norfolk, and the first Bill's in Richmond opened at 3216 North Boulevard in 1931. Ethel Richardson Batts and her brother, W.S. "Steve" Richardson, Sr., kept the Richmond store going through the Great Depression by sheer force of will and hard work, and by providing good food at reasonable prices. That store was moved to 927 Myers Street in 1942, and the following year Steve Richardson, Sr., became the sole owner of Bill's Barbecue.

"Aunt Ethel and Dad ran the business during the Depression when nobody could afford to eat out," recalls Steve Jr., "and Dad bought it during

World War II, when the meat and sugar we needed to cook was rationed, as was the gasoline our customers needed to get to us." Bill's not only survived, it grew. The second Bill's in Richmond, 5805 West Broad Street, opened in November 1947.

Bill's Barbecue was incorporated in 1949, and Steve Jr. came to work for his father full time 10 years later. The chain continued to expand with a commissary opening in 1961, acquisition of Bill's Virginia Barbecue in 1971, and stores at 700 East Main and 8820 West Broad Street opening in 1975 and 1976, respectively. The newest stores are at 20 North Providence Road and 11230 Midlothian Turnpike, and they are the first Bill's to have drive-thru window service. Today the eight Bill's stores have a combined seating capacity exceeding 500, do extensive carry-out business, and cater many Richmond affairs. It all adds up to annual sales in excess of $5 million.

Ethel Richardson Batts (at far left, in the white beret) began Bill's Barbecue in 1930 in Norfolk, Virginia. She is standing in front of what is believed to be the first Bill's Barbecue Drive-In Restaurant. The 200-square-foot building was located at 21st Street and Monticello Avenue in Norfolk.

Drive-thru windows are replacing curb service at some of today's Bill's Barbecue Drive-In restaurants. Standing beside one of the new drive-thru windows are company president W.S. Richardson, Jr., and Rhoda Richardson Long, orientation and training coordinator for the company.

However, Bill's retains the atmosphere that made it famous, and some stores still offer curb service. Just park in the right slot, wait a minute, and someone will be out to take your order and hang the tray on the car window just like you remember.

The Richardson family not only built Bill's Barbecue, they have also played a major role in the restaurant industry in Virginia. Steve Sr. was one of the organizers of the Virginia Restaurant Association (VRA) in 1946, and served as a director for many years beginning in 1949. He was president of the VRA in 1954, and in 1956 and 1960 received the Sidney J. Weilman Award in recognition of his efforts and accomplishments in the advancement of the restaurant industry in the Commonwealth of Virginia. This award later became known as the Restaurateur of the Year Award, and Steve Jr., who served as president of the VRA in 1980, received it in 1981.

Today Bill's Barbecue is owned by the same family corporation started in 1949 by Steve Richardson, Sr., who died in 1980. His oldest son, Steve Jr., is president, and Rhoda, Steve Sr.'s only daughter, trains new employees and helps supervise the operations of all the stores. Other family members with interest in Bill's Barbecue include Lorraine Richardson, Steve Sr.'s widow, who

serves on the board of directors; Steve Sr.'s other sons, William Samuel, William Christopher, and William Robert, all of whom worked at Bill's while growing up, but now pursue other careers; and numerous grandchildren.

The real stars of Bill's Barbecue are its employees and customers. They are extremely loyal. Many Richmond residents have been eating regularly at Bill's all their lives, and many families now have three generations of Bill's Barbecue customers. Many employees have been with the company all their working lives, and management strives to make a career at Bill's something to be proud

of. Bill's Barbecue, Inc., continues to grow and remains committed to the quality food and service that made it a Richmond tradition.

Grouped in front of the sign in front of the oldest continuously operated Bill's Barbecue in Richmond, Virginia, are nine members of the Bill's Barbecue family with 21 to 40 years of service. They are (from left) W.S. Richardson, Jr., 30 years; Kathleen Hockfelder, 30 years; James Hill, 39 years; Lou Marsh, 21 years; Annie Hall, 21 years; W. Michael Gooding, 22 years; Marjorie A. Wall, 36 years; Richard Henderson, 40 years; and Madeline Jackson, 21 years.

OLD DOMINION UNIVERSITY

The Batten Arts and Letters Building, with the Education Building in the foreground, on the Old Dominion University campus.

Old Dominion University is located in Norfolk, Virginia, the center of a metropolitan area with a population of approximately 1.3 million. Norfolk is the hub of the world's largest natural harbor and is regarded as a national leader in business and industry. A major recreational area known for its beaches and historic landmarks, Norfolk also profits from its relationship with the Navy and its proximity to Washington, D.C., and the Outer Banks of North Carolina.

The creation of Old Dominion filled an important need in the Norfolk community. In the 1920s this area had the dubious distinction of being the largest English-speaking community in the world without an institution of higher education. Several leading citizens of the community were active in an effort to encourage the development or the relocation of a college in Norfolk.

Led by Robert Morton Hughes and A.H. Foreman, this small and tenacious group convinced the College of William and Mary's president, J.A.C. Chandler, to consider establishing a branch in Norfolk. The idea of using the old Larchmont School for a college was put forward, and the Norfolk City Council, led by Mayor S. Heth Tyler, proposed to William and Mary that it be the location for the new branch.

In March 1930 the Board of Visitors of William and Mary convened in a special meeting and accepted the old Larchmont School from the City of Norfolk. In June the first students were enrolled, and by September 125 men and 81 women were registered for classes. The total cost of acquiring and renovating the school was $51,415.

Expansion and recognition for its accomplishments occurred in rapid succession. The 1960s brought significant change with the severance of ties with

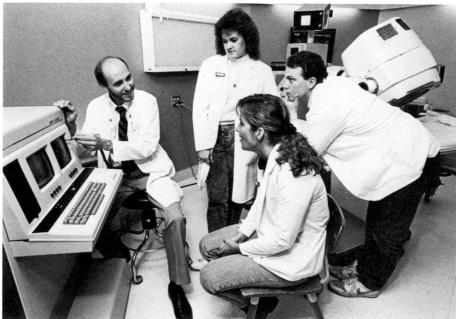

Students in the College of Health Sciences receive instruction on a nuclear medicine computer that is fed data from a mobile gamma camera (upper right-hand corner).

the College of William and Mary in 1962. The Norfolk Division became Old Dominion College, a separate institution with its own Board of Visitors. As early as 1965 a legislative study commission on higher education in Virginia recommended that Old Dominion College be designated a university. The Board of Visitors studied the matter carefully and, on June 13, 1968, voted to change the name of the college to Old Dominion University.

Enrollment increased from approximately 9,000 to 12,000 during the 1970s. The operating budget nearly doubled, the physical plant expanded, and faculty salaries increased. The quality of the faculty also improved as the university sought persons who would contribute to the fulfillment of the institution's mission.

The number of doctoral programs increased from two to 11. In addition, the emphasis on research and private fund raising produced significant results.

From a small, two-year division located in the old Larchmont School, Old Dominion University has grown to more than 3,000 faculty and staff serving 15,000 students. Among the changes the university has witnessed since 1985 with the presidency of Joseph M. Marchello are: the introduction of a college structure with six separately constituted colleges, including Arts and Letters, Business and Public Administration, Darden College of Education, Engineering and Technology, Health Sciences, and Sciences; reorganization of student services; adoption of a new visual identity program; and an aggressive review of the university's master plan.

Considerable progress has been made toward a Fine Arts Center, and expansion of the Child Study Center is under way. The Virginia Center for World Trade was established and is operating at a high level of quality in cooperation with the governor and other state agencies.

New York Times columnist Tom Wicker, one of several prominent visitors who regularly come to Old Dominion University as part of its Literary Festival and the Glennan and Waldo Family Lecture Series.

Research has grown to more than $10 million per year. The university has established a Peninsula Graduate Engineering Center and the General Assembly has approved the establishment of a graduate center in Virginia Beach. Centers for Ergonomics, Artificial Intelligence, Coastal Engineering, Biotechnology, Real Estate, and Reading and Literacy have been established.

The university is shifting in character from a commuter campus to one in which more students are living on and around campus. This has led to the reintroduction of a yearbook, a resurgence in its Greek life, and an enriched undergraduate experience in and out of the classroom.

The heart of a university and its strength is its faculty. Old Dominion fac-

An impromptu game of touch football on the academic campus outside the Kaufman/ Duckworth Engineering Hall.

ulty continue to provide outstanding teaching, research, and service. A considerable number receive honors and awards and make the institution strong and vibrant.

In 1985, at his inauguration ceremony, president Marchello quoted Benjamin Disraeli and defined a university as "a place of light, liberty, learning, and intellectual encounter. It is a place where people prepare for the future, fulfill their present, and grow through experimentation." Within this definition, Old Dominion is fast becoming a great university.

J. KENNON PERRIN CONSTRUCTION COMPANY, INC.

John Kennon Perrin, founder of J. Kennon Perrin Construction Company. Photo circa 1945

J. Kennon Perrin followed his father and two older brothers when he went into the construction industry upon completion of high school in 1933. His first job was with J. Binford Walford, a prominent Richmond architect. Within a year he joined the general contracting firm of Doyle and Russell, where his father was employed as an estimator.

Perrin continued his education by taking construction courses at the Vir-

ginia Mechanics Institute. In his spare time he began a quantity survey business, providing estimating services for subcontractors. Over the next several years Perrin worked for several general contractors as a superintendent on projects in Virginia and Maryland.

Perrin started J. Kennon Perrin Construction Company in June 1938, when he acted as a general contractor, securing bids and supervising the construction of a small, one-story duplex house in Richmond. Perrin's client was the late Morton G. Thalhimer, founder of the Richmond real estate firm that bears his name. That job was followed by an assignment as superintendent for the Harry B. Graham Company's construction of a high school in Mineral, Virginia.

Perrin returned to Richmond in the fall of 1939 and reactivated his quantity survey business. In December of that year he secured a contract to build four more houses for Thalhimer.

Despite wartime shortages of construction materials, the firm grew rapidly during the 1940s. Perrin's major client, Uncle Sam, had no trouble obtaining supplies. Company projects included mess halls, U.S.O. buildings,

barracks, and training facilities at Fort Lee, Camp Picket, and Camp A.P. Hill.

One of the organization's most unusual military projects was the construction of a full-scale replica of Richmond's Byrd Airport. Located several miles from the real airport, it was built as a decoy in the event of a German bombing raid. Fortunately, enemy bombers never arrived to test the concept.

Two notable J. Kennon Perrin Construction Company projects during the 1940s were the Thalhimer Brothers Department Store in Richmond and Eastern State Hospital in Williamsburg. The Eastern State Hospital project consisted of a large complex of hospital buildings, employee residences, and a central heating plant.

The company entered the heavy construction field in the 1940s, building and repairing bridges. In the 1950s Perrin began work for the electrical utility industry. To date the firm has completed hundreds of miles of electrical transmission line foundations, substation foundations, underground electrical utilities, district headquarters, and numerous support facilities at nuclear and fossil fuel power plants.

J. Kennon Perrin has become noted for the many different types of construction projects it has built throughout Virginia, North Carolina, Maryland, and West Virginia. The company's project list includes office buildings, factories, industrial plants, warehouses, hospitals, laboratories, shopping centers, parking decks, airport hangars, radio and television stations, schools, dormitories, libraries, theaters and arenas, restaurants, museums, apartments, motels and hotels, clubhouses, trucking and bus terminals, funeral homes, jails, and churches.

The company has also been noted for its restoration work on historic buildings, including the dismantling and reconstruction of the Cecil House for the Valentine Museum, and the restoration

An extension of a Richmond landmark, Thalhimer Brothers Department Store is among the best known Perrin projects. Courtesy, Dementi-Foster Studios

The Universal Corporation corporate headquarters in Richmond, Virginia. This building represents four major Perrin projects spanning 42 years, consisting of 100,000 square feet of new construction and more than 50,000 square feet of renovation.

and adaptive reuse of the Chesterman at 100 West Franklin Street in Richmond. Colonial Williamsburg has called on J. Kennon Perrin for several jobs, including the restoration of the interior of the John Greenhow Store.

The firm has seen several of its projects go through many stages. It completed the original building at West Broad and Hamilton streets in Richmond in 1947 as a new facility for Standard Oil of New Jersey. Twenty years later Perrin renovated and expanded the building as the new headquarters for Universal Leaf. Other additions were completed in 1974 and 1988.

Among Perrin's most difficult and visible projects was the dismantling of Richmond's Marshall Street Viaduct, a half-mile-long, 28-bay truss steel bridge that crossed the main north- and southbound lanes and two exit ramps of Interstate 95, and the main line of both the Seaboard and CSX railroads. Numerous buildings and streets were directly below the viaduct. The conditions of the job were unusual. The structure had to be dismantled without disrupting rail or highway traffic and without deenergizing a 12,500-volt power line. The workers involved with the viaduct project still swap stories about how they pulled it off.

J. Kennon Perrin Company was incorporated in Virginia in October 1965. Five years later it acquired Wise Contracting Company, the organization that, in a joint venture with two other construction companies, built the Pentagon during World War II. Wise Contracting operated as an independent subsidiary of J. Kennon Perrin until 1980, when it was fully merged into the parent firm.

Kennon Perrin died in February 1984, and his oldest son, John Kennon Perrin, Jr., became president of the company. A graduate of Hampden Sydney College, and with an M.B.A. from the University of Virginia's Graduate School of Business Administration, John had worked for Albemarle Paper in Richmond and the Interstate Bag Company in New York, both subsidiaries of the Ethyl Corporation. In 1969 he returned to Richmond as business manager of Hankins and Anderson Consulting Engineers. He joined the family construction business in July 1970.

In recent years the firm has concentrated its efforts in the private sector, moving heavily into the design-build construction market. The company represents a line of pre-engineered metal buildings and recently completed a nine-building complex that houses a new group of rides in the Italian section of the Busch Gardens theme park in Williamsburg.

In 1988, with the completion of Summerhill at Stony Point at a cost of $7.5 million, Perrin has made a significant move into the multifamily housing market. Summerhill is a 90-unit cluster home retirement community with a central lodge/activities center and extensive landscaping. Many of the clusters consist of one-story, two-unit structures that are similar to Perrin's first project, the house built back in 1938.

J. Kennon Perrin Construction Company, Inc., holds Virginia Contractors registration number one. With thousands of completed projects representing hundreds of millions of dollars behind it, the firm is on the threshold of its second half-century as "the sign of construction in the Commonwealth."

John K. Perrin, chairman of the board and president. Courtesy, Dementi-Foster Studios

A. SMITH BOWMAN DISTILLERY

An aerial view of the A. Smith Bowman Distill-ery in Sunset Hills, Virginia, in the 1960s.

A. Smith Bowman Distillery, located in Fairfax County, is the oldest family-owned distillery in the United States and the only legal bourbon still in the state of Virginia. For more than 50 years this company has maintained the satisfaction and appreciation of its followers with its smooth bourbon, Virginia Gentleman, and, more recently, Bowman's Virginia Vodka and Virginia Gentleman Gin.

Bowman moved to Virginia in 1927 and bought 4,000 acres of farmland in Sunset Hills for $44 an acre, shortly thereafter buying 3,000 additional acres. He had previously made his fortune as owner of an Indianapolis motor coach company and in Canadian wheat. After Prohibition was repealed in 1935, Bowman started his distillery and two years later sold his first batch of whiskey. Today Virginia Gentleman Bourbon is aged about four years, and is famous up and down the East Coast and enjoyed nationwide.

Over the years Bowman and his sons, A. Smith, Jr., and E. DeLong, made small amounts of their product and sold it by word of mouth. The sons sold most of the land in the early 1960s, but maintained about 35 acres for their business. A new bottling house was built in 1966 along with some plant modernization, and two years later a new warehouse was added. Bowman Distillery had its best year ever in 1970, selling its total production of 178,000 cases of whiskey with almost no advertising or marketing expenses. The following year the popularity of bourbon (and dark liquor as a whole) bottomed out, and tastes changed to white liquors such as vodka, gin, and rum. Competition with industry giants was unavoidable. However, the Bowmans believed they could remain a small business and still be successsful.

The Bowman brothers continued

to run the family business, but added on to their operation by hiring executives who would certainly increase the sales and marketing savvy of the company. Yet at the same time, the Bowmans managed to keep things in the family. Robert E. Lee IV, brother-in-law of Smith Bowman, Jr., is vice-president/marketing and sales, while DeLong's son-in-law, John Buchanan Adams, is vice-president/productions. These men, along with each of the 52 employees involved in every other facet of distilling, have helped the firm bounce back from whiskey's fall in popularity and, in fact, have helped the company continue to grow.

The distillery was located in Sunset Hills, one of Fairfax County's oldest communities, until September 1987, when it moved to a rehabilitated manufacturing plant in Spotsylvania County. The move was prompted primarily by the change in the area surrounding the old plant. Once sweeping farmland, Sunset Hills became part of the planned community of Reston in the segmented

suburbs of Washington, D.C., several years ago.

Bowman distills its bourbon much the way it did at its start in 1935. A cooked corn, malt, and rye mash is cooled with nearby pond water, and is then fermented in cypress tubs for three days. The mash is then piped through a copper still and stored for four to five years in charred oak wood barrels. "Everything we do is small," says Bob Lee. "We still use copper stills, cypress fermenting tubs, and a lot of personal care . . . [our products] are geared to the Virginia constituency in taste, price, and package."

The company conducts more than 60 percent of its business in Virginia, where liquor sales are state controlled. In addition to Virginia, most of the sales are concentrated in Maryland, North Carolina, West Virginia, Pennsylvania, and Washington, D.C.

In 1983 Bowman Distillery expanded its traditional product line to include Bowman's Virginia Vodka, which has become quite popular. It was the

number-one-selling alcoholic beverage in Virginia in 1986. In November 1986 Bowman introduced Virginia Gentleman Gin. Although it is still too early to evaluate the success of the gin in terms of sales, the firm is hoping the success of its new gin will mirror that of its fine vodka.

Because of the company's small size, it has always made high-quality products suitable for discriminating tastes. Since its inception, Bowman's Virginia Gentleman Bourbon has been imbibed by Virginians with a sense of pride and an instinct for good, smooth taste. The drinkability of the firm's vodka and gin will most certainly continue to be discovered, much as its bourbon was, and Virginia's number-one distillery will be sure to make it happen.

The entrance to the relocated A. Smith Bowman Distillery in Spotsylvania County, Virginia.

377

MARYMOUNT UNIVERSITY

The growth of Marymount University from an enrollment of 13 students in 1950, the year of its founding, to 3,000 students in 1988 is emblematic of the dramatic growth of northern Virginia as a business and cultural population center.

Marymount University is an independent coeducational institution enrolling 1,700 students in undergraduate programs and 1,300 students in graduate programs. The main campus is located on a hillside in residential Arlington, Virginia. Visible from residence halls are the Potomac River, the Washington Monument, the Lincoln Memorial, and other landmarks of Washington, D.C.

The university owns a nearby satellite campus at the intersection of Lee Highway and Spout Run Parkway with continuous shuttle bus service connecting it to the main campus on Glebe Road. Other off-campus educational

Marymount University was founded in 1950 by a Roman Catholic religious order, Religious of the Sacred Heart of Mary, as a women's college. Today a 3,000-student, coeducational institution, it offers degree programs in four schools: Arts and Sciences, Business Administration, Education and Human Services, and Nursing.

centers are maintained at the Pentagon and at several high-technology firms in McLean and Reston.

Marymount University was founded as a women's college in 1950 at the suggestion of Bishop Peter L. Ireton of Richmond. A Roman Catholic religious order long associated with women's education purchased the Arlington property that is now the main campus. The order, the Religious of the Sacred Heart of Mary, was led by an energetic educator, Mother Gerard Phelan, in its efforts to make a college out of an old Arlington estate formerly the home of Admiral Presley Rixey, surgeon general to President Theodore Roosevelt. The same order had already founded Marymount College in Tarrytown, New York, and several elementary and secondary schools throughout the country.

The first challenge was to erect a physical facility. The principal structure on the estate was a gracious colonial mansion with a columned portico. This was maintained as a focal entrance structure and is now known as Main House. Soon other buildings followed, and a modern academic/residential complex rose from the rolling hillside where Admiral Rixey and "Teddy" Roosevelt had once rode to the hounds.

From 1950 to 1972 the college offered only the associate degree. In 1973 it became a senior college offering the bachelor's degree in more than 20 fields. In 1979 graduate programs leading to the master's degree were added.

The first male students were admitted in 1972 in a nursing program sponsored by the National Institutes of Health in Bethesda, Maryland. The institution continued to focus on the education of women at the undergraduate level, but beginning in 1979, with the addition of coeducational graduate programs, male students began to matriculate in increasing numbers. In 1986 the institution responded to its changing student profile by becoming coeducational at all levels and changing its name to Marymount University.

Marymount University is accredited at the master's and bachelor's level by the Commission on Colleges of the Southern Association of Colleges and Schools. Specialized accreditation has been granted to the education programs by the National Council for the Accreditation of Teacher Education, to the interior design programs by the Foundation for Interior Design Education Research, and to the nursing programs by the National League for Nursing and the Com-

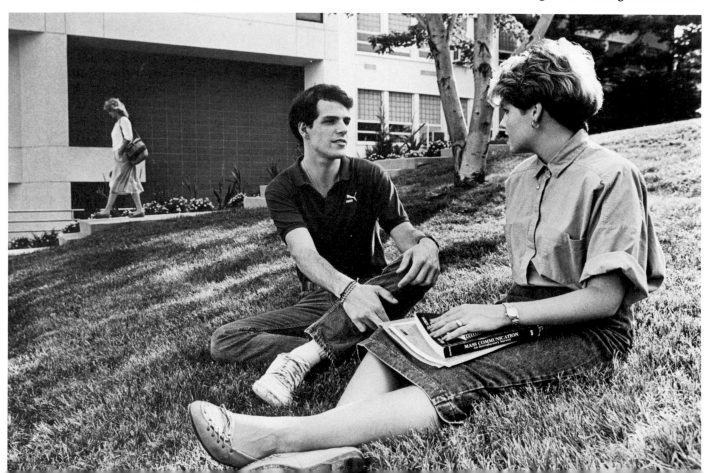

The college was built on and around an old Arlington estate, formerly the home of Admiral Presley Rixey, surgeon general to President Theodore Roosevelt. From the main campus residence halls such national landmarks as the Washington Monument, the Lincoln Memorial, and the Potomac River can be seen.

monwealth of Virginia State Board of Nursing.

The institution is a member of the Consortium of Universities of the Washington Metropolitan Area and of the Consortium for Continuing Higher Education in Northern Virginia.

The university enrolls approximately 3,000 students, more than 2,000 of whom are Virginia residents. More than 30 states and 20 foreign countries are represented in the total student population. Maryland, New York, the District of Columbia, New Jersey, Pennsylvania, and Connecticut are states providing the next-largest student enrollments. Approximately 600 students live in campus residence halls.

Faculty are recruited nationally. There are 90 full-time faculty members supplemented by approximately 100 part-time faculty, more than 60 percent of whom hold the doctorate degree.

Degree programs are offered in four schools: Arts and Sciences, Business Administration, Education and Human Services, and Nursing. Each school offers both undergraduate and graduate degrees. The most popular programs include the Master of Business Administration; the Bachelor of Arts programs in Communication Arts, Education, Interior Design, Nursing, and Psychology; and the Master of Arts in Human Resource Development.

The institution is governed by an autonomous board of trustees consisting of more than 30 men and women from all walks of life and including several alumni. The president and chief executive officer is Sister Marie Majella Berg, RSHM, who has held that post since 1960. Other officers include Dr. Alice S. Mandanis, provost and chief operating officer; Dr. Linda R. McMahon, vice-president/student services; and Sister M. Michelle Murphy, vice-president/financial affairs.

Main House is the central focal point of the Marymount University campus. It was at one time the colonial mansion of Admiral Presley Rixey.

PRIMARK CORPORATION

Robert W. Stewart, chairman and chief executive officer of Primark Corporation.

Primark was established at year-end 1981, when it was spun off from American Natural Resources. Although Primark has grown to own several other entities, Michigan Consolidated Gas Company (MichCon) was Primark's first wholly owned subsidiary. MichCon is one of the largest gas distributors in the country, servicing the metropolitan areas of Detroit, Grand Rapids, Ann Arbor, Muskegon, and the upper peninsular region of Michigan. While service has been the cornerstone of MichCon's philosophy, effective management and innovative marketing have been the keys to the company's success. MichCon is a major supporter of free competition in the natural gas business and in 1986 effectively reduced its average cost of gas 38 percent.

In 1983 Primark began its first diversification effort with the formation of Primark Financial Services. Today Primark Financial Services is the umbrella for Primark's financial related subsidiaries, including Telerent Leasing, Primark Leasing Corporation, and Westmark Financial Group. Telerent Leasing is the largest independent leasing company for the U.S. lodging industry. Telerent sells and leases state-of-the-art televisions along with antennae and satellite earth stations to hotel/motel chains such as Holiday Inn, Sheraton, Hilton, and Best Western. Primark Leasing Corporation leases natural gas storage facilities in Michigan. Westmark Financial Group provides mortgage and insurance services.

Primark's telecommunications subsidiary is Hospital Satellite Network, Inc. (HSN). Acquired in 1983 as a venture capital investment, HSN has developed into a national television network for health care professionals that broadcasts programming 24 hours a day directly to hospitals, via satellite. Since it began broadcasting on December 1, 1983, HSN has been a pioneer in providing innovative, high-quality video education programming and communi-

Primark is a diversified corporation with interests in natural gas, aviation, medical information, and finance. More important, Primark subsidiaries provide services to people: More than one million families depend on natural gas to heat their homes and cook their food, physicians and nurses depend on the latest health information to help care for their patients, business executives depend on overnight delivery services to expedite important information, and thousands of homeowners depend on mortgage loans and insurance policies to support and protect their real estate investments. Primark employs more than 5,000 people in its operations throughout the United States.

cations services to health care facilities nationwide. HSN serves two distinct markets: health care professionals and their patients through HSN's base subscription service, and organizations and companies seeking to reach these health care professionals through HSN's access network. The growth in HSN's base subscription hospitals has been dramatic, from 10 hospitals in 1983 to 503 hospitals at the end of September 1987. Through its subscription and access services, HSN can access more than 1,300 hospitals.

The Aviation Group (TAG), Primark's latest major acquisition, was acquired in late 1985. TAG currently provides flight and maintenance services for 67 freight aircraft, making it the largest contract operator of its kind in the world. A majority of these aircraft are customer owned by companies that TAG services such as Emery, Purolator Courier, CF Air, and Flying Tigers.

As Primark became more diversified, company officials saw the need to physically relocate the headquarters. In January 1984 Primark began a study of the Washington, D.C., suburbs for relocation from Detroit, Michigan.

Primark moved its corporate offices to the northern Virginia area for a variety of reasons: It is a good place to work and live, it provides an opportunity to interact with federal regulators on the various business segments of Primark, and it has close proximity and solid transportation links to the capitol.

As a relative newcomer to the Washington, D.C., area, Primark is still in the process of developing a relationship with the community. The firm has contributed to various charitable organizations in the northern Virginia and Washington, D.C., area. Primark is also actively involved in the Washington Board of Trade and the Fairfax Chamber of Commerce.

Robert W. Stewart, Primark's chairman and chief executive officer since its inception, has guided Primark from a utility holding company to a highly diversified corporation. To further assist in Primark's diversification program, Joseph E. Kasputys became president and chief operating officer

on June 25, 1987. Kasputys was previously the executive vice-president of McGraw-Hill, and former president and chief executive officer at Data Resources, Inc.

Primark Corporation plans to continue growing. Management continues to evaluate various industries that would complement the organization's existing

Joseph E. Kasputys, president and chief operating officer of Primark Corporation.

companies. Primark has a solid asset base in high-growth companies and stable utility operations. Its future diversification efforts will be designed to preserve and enhance this base.

LYNCHBURG COLLEGE

From an outside glimpse, the 2,300-student Lynchburg College, set on a grassy hill sheltered with trees and brick walls, appears to be a small liberal arts school in a medium-size city, with a proportionate scope of influence and interest. But a chat with president George Rainsford quickly dispels first impressions.

"From this hillside we have an extensive outreach," he says. "We like to think of ourselves as a college with university choices." Rainsford preaches international outreach and looking beyond one's local borders as an essential for higher education. "Skills, interests, values" and "education for public life, for private life, and for service" are phrases frequently used as he talks about the mission of Lynchburg College.

The college, historically related to the Christian Church (Disciples of Christ), was founded in 1903 as Virginia Christian College by Dr. Josephus Hopwood, who had previously founded Milligan College in Tennessee. Seventy-five young men and women, most of them from Milligan, enrolled in the first session. Many teachers also followed Hopwood from Milligan. Westover Hall, formerly a hotel, housed the entire college its first six years. Hopwood and his associates purchased the Westover Hotel in Lynchburg with a down payment of $500.

Virginia Christian College changed its name to Lynchburg College

in 1919. Its enrollment soon grew to 200, and in 1927 it was admitted to the Southern Association of Colleges and Secondary Schools with full accreditation.

Educational provisions of the G.I. Bill of Rights did a lot to boost the college's enrollment throughout the 1940s. Dr. Riley B. Montgomery served as president in one of the college's biggest growth periods, when enrollment tripled to 750 students by 1948.

From 1936 to 1948 the college fought to keep up with the incredible influx of students. The faculty grew from 28 to 69. As educators were in demand all over the country, Lynchburg improved its appeal by adding pension plan and tenure and retirement policies.

Westover Hall, formerly a hotel, housed the entire college for its first six years—from 1903 to 1909.

Student guidance, counseling, and government were broadened and strengthened to meet the needs of a more mature student body, and the library almost doubled its number of volumes.

A summer program, which began in 1936 with 52 students, topped 400 by 1948. During those years the college also established a health and physical education program.

In the mid-1950s a grant from the Ford Foundation helped the college keep up with faculty salary demands and improve the curriculum. Enrollment was on the rise to 849 by the 1960-1961 session.

The school continued to grow from 1964 to 1978, during Dr. M. Carey Brewer's tenure as president. Ten major buildings were added to the campus, including Burton Student Center, Turner Gymnasium, Wake Field House, Knight-Capron Library, Dillard Fine Arts Center, and several dormitories.

Rainsford came to the college in

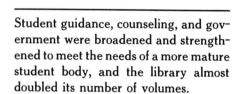

Hopwood Hall, built in 1909 as one of the first academic buildings, still occupies a central position among the 20 structures serving the college campus located on 214 acres within the city limits.

August 1983 from Kalamazoo College in Michigan, where he served as president and professor of history. His academic life and credentials are extensive, enriched wih academic degrees from the University of Colorado, University of Denver, Stanford, and Yale.

As Rainsford says, Lynchburg is "in the human development business with a commitment to the education of the whole person." He believes that many of today's students are trained to be technically competent without being taught the difference between right and wrong. Rainsford emphasizes that education must be a matter of attitudes and values in addition to subject matter.

Potential is the key requirement for Lynchburg College students. "We

The Lynchburg College soccer team has completed 31 consecutive nonlosing seasons and is a perennial power in Division III Soccer.

recognize that students come to us with different skills and interests. Through the teaching-learning process we encourage them to reach their full potential. Outcome is important," says Rainsford. For this reason freshmen are taught by full professors and the student/faculty ratio is 15 to one.

One of Rainsford's goals is to recruit more minority students, faculty, and staff. Consistent with his international outlook for the college, he points out that the world population is increasingly nonwhite, and Lynchburg has a responsibility to reflect the makeup of that population in its student body and to educate its students for world citizenship.

In this decade Lynchburg College has added a school of business, department of nursing, gerontology center, and department of communications, as well as programs in international studies, computer science, and international business. Its ACCESS program is instrumental in helping area students, ages 25 and over, pursue undergraduate degrees.

Lynchburg College maintains close working relations with businesses

Lynchburg College students, during a month-long tour of Asia, join Han Nam University students for a group shot in front of the Hall of Great Prayer in Sognisan Mountains in Korea.

and colleges in the area, including Randolph-Macon College, Sweet Briar College, and Central Virginia Community College. A special grant in international business is designed to assist area businesses with international outreach. Students studying toward B.S. degrees in nursing work in 14 area health care facilities. The college, in cooperation with the chamber of commerce, funds the campus Center for Economic Education to assist public schools in the area. In addition, Lynchburg College is the regional down link for the statewide microwave network that broadcasts graduate courses in engineering.

Under the direction of Norris Houghton, co-founder of the Phoenix Theatre, Lynchburg College presented a precedent-breaking production of Romeo and Juliet *using the modernized Shakespearean dialogue of Elizabethan historian A.L. Rowse, a frequent guest on the Lynchburg campus.*

THE LANE COMPANY, INC.

John Edward Lane purchased a bankrupt packing-box plant for $500 at an auction in 1912. He sent his son, Edward Hudson, to the small town in Virginia where the plant was located with instructions to start manufacturing cedar chests. Edward recalls, "I was nearly 21 years old at the time. I had no manufacturing experience, and I had never before heard of a cedar chest."

Edward invited his former woodworking instructor, Mr. Loop, to come along and take a look at the factory. One look was all they needed; agreeing that "you couldn't make toothpicks" with the rusty and obsolete machinery in the small plant, they sat down to decide what to do. The next day Edward placed an order for $50,000 worth of new machinery. That sunny day in Altavista, Virginia, saw the birth of a multimillion-dollar industry.

The company was incorporated as The Standard Red Cedar Chest Company—the senior Lane, skeptical about its prospects, unwilling to commit the family name. Edward became the vice-president. In a 40- by 90-foot corrugated iron building, with a "staff" of three woodworkers, the firm began manufacturing cedar chests.

It was touch and go for The Standard Red Cedar Chest Company in

The Lane Company has 16 plants in four states. This is the main office and plant in Altavista.

those first years. Edward had to be personnel director, purchasing agent (they were savvy enough to acquire their own source of the finest Tennessee-grown cedar wood), bookkeeper, salesman, and promotion and advertising manager. His marriage to Myrtle Clyde Bell in 1914 inspired a goal for the enterprise—maker of the world's finest cedar chests for people in love.

America's entry into World War I presented the company with a dilemma: close or convert to the manufacture of pine ammunition boxes. It converted. The ammunition box process evolved into a moving conveyor system, and the firm became one of the first furniture manufacturers to develop an assembly line.

The Standard Red Cedar Chest Company began its second decade by hiring an advertising agency. The agency immediately convinced the owners to shed their cumbersome title. The first advertising spread that appeared in the *Saturday Evening Post* featured "Lane Cedar Chests." Lane ads featured a number of glamorous young movie starlets, among them Bonita Granville, Mary Brian, and Shirley Temple. "In My Little Hope Chest," sung by Nancy Carroll, was the theme song of the Paramount picture, *Honey*. A later success-

A Lane cedar chest, one of more than 100 styles the company offers today.

ful promotional program offered the world's first moth insurance policies, free, with every Lane Cedar Chest.

Arthur D. Little Associates of Cambridge, Massachusetts, was hired to research ways of improving both product and production. The company's first exclusively Lane sales force was recruited, and the firm built its marketing plan around gift-giving events.

With the Girl Graduate Program the company acquires lists of young women graduating from high school and sends them gift certificates for free miniature cedar chests, to be picked up at their local furniture stores. Today Lane dealers distribute more than 400,000 miniature cedar chests every year.

On its 75th anniversary The Lane Company, Inc., has not only become a synonym for the cedar chest, but has become one of the industry's most diversified makers of nearly every type of fine furniture, with 16 factories in four states. There are now more than 100 styles of Lane Cedar Chests in a wide variety of woods and finishes. The romantic tradition, originating so many years ago with dowry chests and perpetuated so effectively by Lane, sets the chest apart from all other merchandise bought in furniture stores as the perfect gift, for women of all ages.

FIGGIE INTERNATIONAL INC.

They call it Virginia Center, a dignified name for a simple concept that is, nonetheless, breathtaking in the scope of its imagination. North of Richmond, near the intersections of I-295 with I-95 and U.S. 1, Virginia Center is a 1,500-acre mixed-use complex now under development by Figgie International Inc.

Virginia Center will include an inn, offices, recreation facilities, a shopping center, and sites for the full range of business support services. It is already the home of The Crossings Golf Course, the first buildings in the Virginia Center Technology Park, and the headquarters of Figgie International.

Figgie International is a diversified operating company with more than 40 divisions. Rawlings Sporting Goods, Fred Perry Sportswear (U.K.), Ltd., "Automatic" Sprinkler Corporation, and Interstate Electronics are among its best known business companies. Other Figgie International companies offer a staggering range of goods and services, including fire trucks, investigative and security services, industrial mobile platforms, aviation support services, and insurance, among many others. The company has operations in Australia, Europe, Latin America, the Caribbean Basin, and the Far East.

The man behind Figgie International is Harry E. Figgie, Jr., a native of Cleveland, Ohio. In 1963 Figgie purchased "Automatic" Sprinkler Corporation of America, a distressed company with annual sales of $22 million. Within a year the firm was again profitable. By 1969 Figgie had built his company

through a series of acquisitions into an integrated producer of fire protection equipment and industrial and consumer products, and a diversified holding company with more than 53 operating divisions.

In 1970 Figgie International shifted from an acquisition phase to consolidation and began an extended period of internal growth. That same period was marked by increasing recognition of the new importance of the service economy. Figgie devoted attention in the 1970s to developing its services group by building its internal service divisions into autonomous profit centers working with outside clients. The result has been the growth of insurance, financial, real estate development, and other service operations.

The success of the new strategy is reflected in record sales and income over the past few years. Sales, income, and other barometers of corporate perfor-

Virginia Center is a mixed-use complex now under development by Figgie International Inc., where it is already the home of Figgie's international headquarters (top) and The Crossings Golf Course (above).

mance have all moved up sharply in recent years. Figgie International is a member of the select *Fortune* 500 group of America's largest corporations.

The company adopted its current name, Figgie International Inc. in 1981. It relocated from Willoughby, Ohio, to Richmond, Virginia, in the early 1980s. With that move came the birth of Virginia Center. A high-quality environment, Virginia Center's development plan and covenants protect the beautiful natural setting and control the design of landscaping and architecture. The plan blends the proposed uses into a functional and aesthetically successful integrated community.

ELECTROPLATE-RITE CORPORATION

Off Interstate 81 in southwestern Virginia, Johnny W. Dickerson and his family—wife and vice-president/secretary Louise, son and first vice-president Keith, daughter and treasurer Regina, and one son, Johnny Jr., a junior in high school, who helps when needed—run a little business. The "little" business, Electroplate-Rite Corporation, located in Dublin, employs 50 people, completes 600 jobs per month, and serves a 300-mile radius with the help of two delivery trucks.

Dickerson began his career in electroplating in Chicago in 1953, when he worked as an apprentice plating operator for the Plate-Rite Company. After five years he moved up to foreman, and in 1961 he moved to Virginia to supervise the plating department of Inland Motor Corporation.

Six years later Dickerson left Inland Motor to begin his own business. He and Louise set up shop in a 700-square-foot building behind the Dublin Animal Hospital. For six weeks Dickerson ran his business, whose name comes from its founder's Chicago employment, on a part-time basis while winding up his work at Inland Motor. "Back then I had a lot of energy," he laughs.

In the beginning the couple worked many long hours, with Johnny running the equipment and Louise handling the paperwork and packing. The

With its headquarters still located in Dublin, Electroplate-Rite Corporation today has expanded facilities, employs 50 people, completes 600 jobs per month, and serves a 300-mile radius with the help of two delivery trucks.

Johnny W. Dickerson set up his own business, Electroplate-Rite Corporation, in 1966 in this 700-square-foot building behind the Dublin Animal Hospital.

company grew to eight employees after the first year. In January 1970 the 15-person firm moved to a new plant, which offered approximately 12,000 square feet. By August of that year 30 people worked for Electroplate-Rite.

Since 1975 the employee count has remained about the same, 50, but production and sales have both climbed, largely due to the company's low turnover rate. According to Keith Dickerson, at least eight people have worked for the firm more than 10 years.

In 1978 the company installed a

wastewater-treatment facility, which was not required by law until the early 1980s. According to community guidelines Electroplate-Rite meets drinking water standards. The Dickersons estimate 10 to 20 percent of the annual budget goes toward conservation, which over the past decade totals nearly a half-million dollars.

Also in 1978 the company improved production by installing a semi-automatic rack zinc line. Zinc is its most popular plating material, followed by copper, nickel, and chrome. The firm also has in-house capabilities for tin, brass, phosphate, and silver, as well as anodizing and chromating on aluminum. Although it can plate amounts and items as small as a handful of screws, Electroplate-Rite services such large businesses as AT&T, Reynolds Metal, and Volvo White Truck.

In 1985 Electroplate-Rite Corporation added 3,000 square feet of office space and 10,000 square feet to the plant facility. Future plans for the firm include adding a fully automatic zinc plater, computerizing the office, and adding a full-time sales force.

"We're steadily adding on to the corporation for the benefit of the customer," Johnny Dickerson says. "Trends change every day so we have to change lines to keep up with the customer."

LILLIAN VERNON CORPORATION

Local development officials spent thousands of hours hammering out a carefully crafted plan before Lillian Katz consented to move a major part of her business from New York to Virginia Beach. Competition for her firm's new warehouse and distribution center was intense—20 cities in seven states wooed her business. Negotiations were so secret that not even the city council knew this corporate plum might come to town until early 1987.

Lillian Katz is the energetic president of one of the largest mail-order specialty gift catalogs in the United States. Lillian Vernon is named for its founder and the city where it began, Mt. Vernon, New York.

Lillian herself had been awed by the huge expanses of land throughout Virginia Beach, quite unlike the concrete ribbons she was accustomed to in the North. The region's large labor pool, a large tract of land available at the right price, and an efficient port were all influential factors. A videotape stressing the resort city's low employment turnover and high quality of life finally clinched the deal, and in the spring of 1987 construction began on a 454,156-square-foot facility on a 52-acre site. A retail store in Virginia is also contemplated.

Founded in 1951, the company

Lillian Katz, founder and president.

grew as a classic American success story. Born in Leipzig, Germany, in 1927, Lillian Menasche had fled with her family to Holland to escape the Nazis, arriving in New York in 1937. At age 24, married and expecting her first child, she started her mail-order business with

The new Lillian Vernon warehouse and distribution center, on 52 acres in Virginia Beach.

$2,000 of wedding gift money. Her offer consisted of a leather handbag and belt, purchased from her father's business, monogrammed at no extra charge. The first ad, a small black-and-white layout in *Seventeen* magazine, brought in $16,000 in orders in just six weeks. Lillian filled them at her kitchen table.

Today she has become one of the most successful and well-known businesswomen in America. The firm has grown to more than $125 million annually in sales—with both of Lillian's sons now company executives, and as many as 1,300 employees during the peak Christmas season. A pioneer in a field once dominated by men, she is known as an innovator, one of the first Americans to import from China after diplomatic relations were established. The business is global, with merchandise from more than 33 nations, and offices in Florence, Italy, and Hong Kong.

Lillian Vernon has thrived and found a major market niche among 6,500 competitors. Its corporate headquarters, state-of-the-art customer communications center, and retail store will remain in New York. The company went public in August 1987, listing on the American Stock Exchange. It is anticipating more growth as a result of its new home in Virginia.

THE LITTLE OIL COMPANY, INC.

Charles Malcolm Little, founder of the Little Oil Company.

"The Little Guardian," a stylized, saluting toy-soldier figure in a red, white, and black uniform, has long been recognized throughout central Virginia as the symbol of The Little Oil Company, Incorporated, a Richmond-based firm that has been providing the region with petro-

leum products and service since 1921.

Charles Malcolm Little, the founder of Little Oil, was born August 25, 1883, at Parkton, Maryland, a son of John C. and Clara Bacon Little. His family had been Maryland residents for many generations, since James Calder, a great-great-grandfather of Charles Malcolm Little, first came from the family estate in Scotland to settle in Maryland. Sir Robert Walter Calder, a younger brother of James, was captain of the British fleet at Cape St. Vincent in 1797, and later served as first sea lord of the British Admiralty.

A student at The Boys Latin School in Baltimore, Charles Malcolm Little later took courses at a business college before beginning his career in 1902 with a Baltimore steamship line. A growing interest in the rapidly evolving new technology soon took him to Pittsburgh, where he worked with the Westinghouse Electric Company. Two years in the smoke and noise of turn-of-the-century Pittsburgh proved more than sufficient, and Little returned to Baltimore. At this time he accepted a job with the famous Old Bay Line, which operated scheduled service between Baltimore and Norfolk, Virginia.

In 1909 a move was made to Rich-

mond and a position was obtained with a company that was then starting out in the oil business. At this time the primary petroleum products were kerosene for domestic lighting, and lubricants for machinery and horse-drawn conveyances. The automobile had not yet become a leading consumer of petroleum products, but the new era was rapidly dawning on both the highways and in the perceptions of businessmen. Charles Malcolm Little looked ahead and dreamed of what was to come.

In 1921 Little started his own oil business, opening The Little Oil Company at Ninth and Dinwiddie streets. The first major step consisted of a two-room metal building with cold running water for hand washing and an "outside privy." His office force consisted of a bookkeeper and two young brothers as drivers, who served him well through the growing years, up to the time of their retirement. Little Oil first delivered kerosene from door to door in horse-drawn tank carriages, later graduating to two Mack tank trucks. This was only the beginning of a fleet of modern trucks that was to develop in the years that followed. The company provided ESSO products, produced and distributed by Standard Oil of New Jersey. Standard,

In the early days of Little Oil, the firm delivered kerosene in horse-drawn wagons as portrayed in this picture by Lucy Keel.

The "Little Guardian," symbol of the Little Oil Company, stands on guard outside company headquarters.

created by John D. Rockefeller, had a virtual monopoly on the oil business during these early times.

Memories of those early days are quite vivid to the children of Charles Malcolm Little, and they fondly recall various incidents from the sharing of his love to the "firmness" of being a boss.

During the mid-1930s fuel oil for domestic heating became a major product. Homes were large and not insulated, using a large volume of fuel in order to keep everyone comfortable. Little Oil prospered and found that additional storage facilities were needed. Thus came the first major sign of expansion, and these needed facilities were built. Included in the construction were two rooms to be used as office space. This growth included two new trucks, with drivers hired for each.

Little Oil terminated its distributorship program with ESSO and became the area distributor for Mobil Oil. At this time it was once again found to be in need of additional facilities and space. The decision was made to relocate, and a site at Commerce Road (formerly known as Ninth Street Road) and Riverside was chosen. In addition to the necessary loading facilities, the new construction included a combination office and warehouse building. Little Oil looked ahead and saw a prosperous future with great potential. At the time Commerce Road was little more than a two-rut country road. Now it is a major thoroughfare paralleling Interstate 95, and Little's distinctively decorated stor-

This station at Belvedere and Cary streets in Richmond was one of the first opened by Little Oil.

age tanks are clearly visible from this major highway.

Charles Malcolm Little died in 1950, the victim of a freak accident while a spectator at stock car races at the Atlantic Rural Exposition grounds in Richmond. A sportsman and fox hunter as well as a businessman, he remained active with the Country Club of Virginia, the Virginia Fox Hunters' Association, and the Richmond and Virginia chambers of commerce throughout his life.

Upon the death of Charles Malcolm Little, leadership was assumed by his son, Charles Malcolm Little, Jr., under whose direction and guidance the company expanded and grew into one of the leading petroleum distributorships in the area. Branch locations were opened in Petersburg, Powhatan, and Louisa.

In July 1958 the greatly increased number of office personnel moved into a new office building directly across Commerce Road from the former combination office and warehouse. All administrative aspects of the business are

handled from this location, while the distribution of petroleum products now occupies the entirety of the original site.

Additional expansions under the leadership of Charles Malcolm Little, Jr., were the 1975 acquisition of State Oil Company, located in Ashland, and the 1982 acquisition of Dod Oil Company, located in Staunton.

Charles Malcolm Little, Jr., remained president until his retirement in October 1985. He was succeeded by his sister, Anne Little Ward, under whose leadership the firm continues to grow and prosper.

Today's Little Oil Company has more than 100 employees, 45 service and tank trucks, and 14 million gallons of storage capacity along the riverfront. In addition to the company's service stations, Little Oil has been in the convenience store business for approximately 15 years. The four most recent openings have been in Fairfield, Staunton, Waynesboro, and Buena Vista.

Since 1954 Little Oil has been affiliated with the Phillips 66 Company (except for the Staunton facility, which sells EXXON). The organization finds that its real estate activities—buying, selling, and leasing of stations and stores—is an increasing portion of the business. Another important facet of the daily operations is the sale and service of furnaces and air conditioning systems to both commercial and residential customers.

The year 1987 marked the 66th anniversary of The Little Oil Company, Incorporated, and its continuous service in the central Virginia area—all the fulfilled dreams of a young Charles Malcolm Little as he looked ahead to the future back in the early 1900s.

A growing tank storage capacity and fleet of delivery trucks gave evidence of the post-World War II boom for Little Oil.

VULCAN MATERIALS COMPANY MIDEAST DIVISION

It was 1912, near Mount Ulla in the farms and forests of Rowan County, North Carolina. William Ellison Graham had left the farm three years earlier. He bought a pair of mules and hauled logs for a sawmill; then he bought a wheeler—a mule-drawn scoop for grading roads—and worked for a road contractor. Now, at the age of 25, he was going into business for himself.

Automobiles were becoming popular—more than one million were sold that year—and cities and counties could

Two views of a Vulcan Materials Company project—Interstate 95 in Springfield, Virginia, looking north toward Washington, D.C.

hardly keep pace with the demand for new roads. Graham recognized the opportunity and had bid on and won his first county road contract. But to do the job he needed more mules, so he went to an uncle and asked him to underwrite a loan to buy the animals.

The uncle, Graham told his children years later, wanted two days to think about it, and when Graham returned for the verdict, he was told: "Ellison, I'm going to let you have the money, but first I want you to answer one question for me. What are you going to do with those mules when you get all the roads built?"

W.E. Graham never ran out of roads to build; the mules gave way to

steam engines and diesels, and some 70 years later the business Graham started with two mules had grown into the Mideast Division of Vulcan Materials Company, the nation's leading commercial producer of crushed stone.

By 1920 Graham's growing operations required 175 mules. His three oldest sons were beginning to learn the business as water boys and load checkers when the stock market crash of 1929 struck. Graham moved his family and the few pieces of equipment he was able to salvage from Mount Ulla to Cleveland and started over.

Times were hard. Graham put together a crew and contracted for parts of the few road-building jobs that were available. In 1933 he formed a partnership, but by 1941 business was up and the Grahams formed a family partnership, W.E. Graham & Sons, General Contractors.

The new venture's first job was the Roanoke, Virginia, airport. America had entered World War II by the time the project was finished, and the war effort became part of the Grahams' work. Jobs included the airport at Norfolk, Virginia, and the roads at the Radford, Virginia, munitions plant.

After the war highway construction resumed, and the Grahams continued their expansion, with sons John, William, and Lewis "Luke" in the field, and Page in charge of the purchasing for various operations. Projects included sections of the Blue Ridge Parkway and the West Virginia Turnpike, but it was the Old Fort Ridgecrest Highway, built in western North Carolina in the early 1950s, that won the Grahams acclaim within the industry. The six-mile road, climbing 1,100 feet up the eastern flank of the Appalachians, crosses some of the steepest gorges in the East and required more than 3 million yards of fill, a record at the time.

Stone for those highways either came from the road site and was crushed with portable equipment or was purchased crushed from nearby quarries. Then, in 1946, some unexpected events put W.E. Graham & Sons in the crushed rock business for the first time. The firm underwrote the establishment of a new

quarry from which it planned to buy stone. But before any stone was delivered, the operators abandoned the business and turned the equipment over to the Grahams, who assigned Luke to run it.

At approximately the same time the company began work on U.S. Highway 52 at the northern edge of Winston-Salem and crews were assigned to "walk the hollows" along the route to look for stone. An outcrop of metamorphosed granite roughly the size of an office desk was found some 100 yards from the new route. After some test drilling and a look at the market in the area, Luke decided the outcrop marked an opportunity to establish a permanent quarry. Now named North Quarry, the 115-acre site has produced more than 35 million tons of stone and is expected to last into the middle of the next century.

In 1956 Birmingham Slag of Alabama, run by Charles W. Ireland and his family, merged with Vulcan Detinning Company, a metals processor. The group became the Vulcan Materials Company. On October 1, 1959, W.E. Graham & Sons and its 450 employees became the Graham Division of Vulcan

Materials Company. John Graham became president of the division, and at the time of his death approximately three years later was succeeded by Luke.

Over the next two decades Vulcan became a major supplier of construction material, industrial chemicals, and basic metals—recycled aluminum, steel, and tin. This product mix, though not deliberate, proved beneficial for the company, as did the mix of old-line entrepreneurs and university-trained managers.

The Graham Division decided in the mid-1960s to leave the construction business, and the group's sole product became crushed stone. The division name was changed to Mideast in 1966.

The Mideast Division opened a new quarry in Manassas in 1962. This quarry was combined with the already operating Occoquan Quarry to give Vulcan a prominent position in the growing northern Virginia market. The quarries' sales and credit offices continued to grow, and in 1980 they were transferred to their own location in Springfield, Virginia, and later still to a regional sales office in Manassas, Virginia. The Ma-

Vulcan Materials Company supplies fill for roads and highways through its various quarries, like this one in Occoquan, Virginia.

nassas Quarry, along with Occoquan and Stafford, were well positioned to respond to the phenomenal growth northern Virginia experienced during the 1970s and 1980s.

Graham was a leader in the National Stone Association by helping to create an awards program to recognize accomplishments by operators for beautification and community relations. Vulcan has won more Showplace Awards than any other company, and Mideast has won half of those. North has maintained Showplace status for 10 years, and Mideast plans to have won Showplace status for all 19 of its quarries by 1990.

Improvements in efficiency accompany the firm's concern for the environment, and, according to Grayson, the Mideast Division of Vulcan Materials Company is expected to expand to meet the requirements of a growing number of people and their need for roads, shelter, and work places as economically as possible.

NETWORK SOLUTIONS

Network Solutions was founded in 1979, with the belief that the greatest assets of a business are its human assets. Guided by this founding principle, Network Solutions has become a professional communications systems engineering firm offering extensive custom services in computer network design, implementation, and management.

Emmit J. McHenry is one of the four co-founders of Network Solutions. "We wanted to create an environment for self-expression, a human environment where work would be a celebration instead of drudgery," he recalls. That may not be a typical approach to business, but it works, and so does Network Solutions.

The Network Solutions client list includes some of the largest companies and federal agencies in the northern Virginia/National Capital Area. The company has already won the Certificate of Excellence awarded by the Small Business Administration. But to McHenry, winning that award, like winning a major contract from the National Aeronautics and Space Administration (NASA), was important "because of what it said to our people about themselves."

Gary Desler (president/products group), Ed Peters (senior vice-president/quality), and Tyrone Grigsby (board member) are the other co-founders of Network Solutions.

McHenry was a senior executive with Allstate Insurance before starting his own firm. Desler and Peters both came from intensive computer backgrounds: Peters with the Defense Communications Agency and Desler as a consultant to Bell Labs, Amdahl, and several other commercial and government clients. Grigsby was executive vice-president of Raven Systems and Research of Washington, D.C.

Like the philosophy behind Network Solutions, the mix of talents and experience among the firm's four senior executives is unusual. And like the philosophy, the blend of talents seems to function remarkably well. "We strive for a consistency of quality, people, and systems," says Peters. "Our management principles are more important than

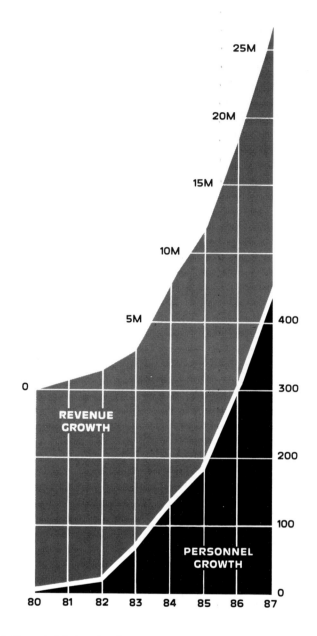

Founded in 1979, Network Solutions has demonstrated aggressive revenue growth and corresponding personnel growth.

any individual, but our people, as individuals, are each extremely important to us."

Network Solutions has more than 400 employees, and, in some ways, the company functions like a small town. Employee Town Meetings are a crucial part of the management style. Town Meetings are held quarterly, and senior management responds directly to questions "with hard answers rather than

soft rhetoric."

The meetings are not held on company time, but the level of participation by employees is high. The active involvement of the firm's people in corporate affairs is a continual gratification to the executive committee, says Peters.

"Our management style emphasizes the human side of the interface," says one company manual. "Machines may be the reason we're invited in, but people are the reason Network Solutions is the company that's invited. And invited back."

In its first few years the firm focused on systems programming services, primarily in the IBM environment. Sensing a demand for quality facility management services, it added operations and training capabilities. The early 1980s brought steady growth, primarily in the nondefense agencies of the federal government.

In 1983 a major contract from the U.S. Army Belvoir Research, Development, and Engineering Center helped to launch the company in a new direction. The system Network Solutions designed and installed became one of the first operational subnetworks of the Defense Data Network (DDN).

In 1985 Network Solutions was named major subcontractor to IBM at the Johnson Space Flight Center in Houston to provide systems programming, configuration, and capacity planning for all institutional mainframes. Later that year it was chosen by the Naval Sea Systems Command (NAVSEA) to design, construct, install, and operate a major data center.

A third 1985 contract, one with the Defense Communications Agency (DCA), called for the corporation to produce a software communications package permitting the agency's IBM/MVS mainframes to interface with DDN. Work begun under that contract eventually resulted in the firm's production of a new product, OPEN-Link®/MVS, which has won widespread popularity among defense contractors, Department of Defense agencies, and commercial entities.

The corporate headquarters of Network Solutions is in Vienna, Virginia. The Space Systems Division is in Houston, Texas. Other offices are in Crystal City, Virginia; Baltimore, Maryland; Washington, D.C.; Dayton, Ohio; Oklahoma City, Oklahoma; and San Diego, Irvine, and San Bernardino, California.

"To strike a target you cannot see except in your mind suggests the importance of creating and maintaining a consistent vision of one's goals. The challenges, the screens that stand between us and the achievement of our goals, cannot be permitted to obscure our vision of the future, a vision so strong that it becomes concrete." Emmit J. McHenry, chairman and chief executive officer of Network Solutions.

GTE SOUTH

Bluefield Telephone Corporation, the predecessor of GTE South, was organized by Judge David E. Johnson and five associates in June 1893. It cost $1,600 to start the company. Offices were located on Bland Street in Bluefield, West Virginia.

By 1896 it had 42 local subscribers, plus one telephone each in Pocahontas and Graham (Bluefield), Virginia, and in Princeton, Athens, and Bramwell, West Virginia. As the coal industry grew, so did telephone service, and in 1898 telephone lines extended into the Flat Top coalfields.

Six years later, in 1904, a joint agreement between Bluefield Telephone and Southern Bell made it possible for residents of the Virginias to communicate over a much broader calling area. Records show a Princeton resident, A.R. Kyle, received the first transAtlantic call when a relative from London phoned on February 21, 1927. The cost of the call, which lasted approxi-

Built-in computerized diagnostics are an important element of central office digital switching systems. Here a GTE employee retrieves a magnetic tape.

mately 23 minutes, has been estimated at $600.

Federal Public Service Corporation of Chicago bought Bluefield Telephone Corporation for $2.5 million on July 24, 1929. The name of the company was not changed.

In 1936 construction began on a 40-mile, $75,000 toll cable project to provide Grundy and other parts of Buchanan County with telephone service. Telephone crew members, working around the clock in order to have service by Christmas Day, were arrested for working on Sunday in violation of the Blue Law.

By 1947 the Bluefield Corporation had come of age and was incorporated under the statutes of Virginia. The following January, by a majority vote of shareholders, the name Bluefield Telephone Corporation was changed to Bluefield Telephone Company.

In July 1954 General Telephone System acquired the firm, which had 25,300 customers at the time, and officially changed the name to General Telephone Company of the Southeast. Company headquarters were established in Bluefield.

During the next five years other telephone companies throughout the southeastern part of the United States were acquired, resulting in an organization that spread across seven states. In 1959 corporate headquarters were moved from Bluefield to Durham, North Carolina.

In 1979 Bluefield became the eighth site in the country and the first in the company's seven-state Southeast Company to place into service GTE No. 3 Electronic Automatic Exchange switching equipment. The $8-million project made it possible to process long-distance calls faster and more efficiently in the two Virginias.

An aggressive work schedule is in progress to install state-of-the-art electronic digital switches in various Virginia locations. The projects, which represent an investment of more than $20 million, are set for Grundy, Big Rock, Rock Gap, and Bluefield, Virginia and Bluefield, West Virginia.

The West Virginia/Virginia Division has 535 employees and serves 90,000 customers. As of January 1, 1988, the corporate name officially became GTE South.

OMEGA WORLD TRAVEL

When Gloria Bohan got into the travel business in 1972, it was a lot different than it is now. Computers were still a luxury reserved for more high-technology industries. Fares were listed in books. And the airlines were still regulated by the government.

"The old way didn't allow for much creativity," says Bohan, president of Omega World Travel. "Now it's more challenging and tougher to run a successful business. In looking back, however, I do, every so often, miss the simplicity of the old days . . . but not for long. Now it's more exciting, and we have a chance to really do innovative things."

The former English teacher heads the 17th-largest travel agency in the country, a business that annually grosses more than $120 million, employs 360 people, and operates more than 65 branches in seven states and Washington, D.C. In 1985 the firm made *INC.* magazine's 500 Fastest Growing Companies in America list, and continues to expand at a rate of at least 30 percent each year.

Bohan was bitten by the travel bug on a honeymoon cruise. When she returned with her husband on their first anniversary, she noticed that a group of travel agents got the royal treatment. Following the "if you can't beat 'em" adage, she opened her first office in Fredericksburg, Virginia.

Gloria Bohan is president and chief executive officer of Omega World Travel. Courtesy, Spring Photography, Inc.

In September 1974 Bohan opened a second office in Woodbridge, and expanded to a third office at Skyline Mall in Falls Church in 1978. The office has served as company headquarters since 1984. Bohan quickly established herself as an innovator in the travel field.

Omega World was one of the first agencies in the area to offer free ticket delivery. Bohan also established a 24-hour, toll-free hot line and a data sheet on each customer that lists their travel preferences.

Bohan's marketing strategy is to open offices in well-populated areas. She is not interested in simple representation; her goal is to dominate the market in a given area. Her offices always have high visibility on the outside and well-planned space on the inside. They even have a uniform look: gray carpets, white countertops, red seats and trim.

Omega became the nation's largest broker of flight coupons in the late 1970s and early 1980s by purchasing 50-percent savings coupons from Eastern Airlines passengers. In an amazing promotion, Bohan's company sponsored a day-long excursion to New York City, including air fare and a bus tour, for $25 in exchange for the tourists' coupons. Seven hundred people took Omega up on the offer. Omega was also one of the first travel agencies to seek government travel contracts when they became available to commercial businesses in 1982.

Today 20 percent of Omega's overall business comes from government travel. In 1986 the firm published its own travel directory, covering discounts on hotels, airlines, and car rentals, for use by government agencies and contractors. The book has been hailed by the industry and users as a real breakthrough in its consolidation of price advantages for those traveling on official government business.

"One of the personally gratifying things is that I've done a lot of good for people," says Bohan. "I can give them the opportunity to grow or to get back in the work force." As head of perhaps the largest female-owned travel agency in the country, Bohan claims the flexibility of the field makes it an excellent career choice for women.

As good as things might be now, Bohan never allows herself to be satisfied. "You can't bank on today," she says. "We're always looking forward to tomorrow." Included in the future are plans to increase the Omega World Travel network with more affiliates and to expand her new travel agent school.

A typical Omega office, seen here, reflects the company's uniform design and motif. This office is located at the Fair Oaks Mall in Fairfax, Virginia.

INTERSTATE ELECTRIC SUPPLY CO., INC.

The original offices and warehouse of Interstate Electric Supply Company, pictured here in 1963.

In 1963 five enterprising individuals gave up their job security and started Interstate Electric Supply. The firm got its start in a renovated bread store in Merrifield, an area in Fairfax, Virginia, near Washington, D.C.

Seven other individuals also accompanied the five owners from another electrical wholesaler and, with the help of their respective spouses, the challenge of day-to-day operations began. The organization's new corporate headquarters in Chantilly, Virginia, 20 miles west of the original Fairfax location, would have been an overnight trip from the madding crowds of Washington 25 years ago.

Interstate Electric Supply started expanding with fast-growing northern Virginia. In 1972 the company opened a branch service center in Frederick, Maryland. Now the Virginia wholesaler was established in a neighboring state. Later another service center was opened in Hagerstown, Maryland. The sole facility in Virginia was joined with a service center in Charlottesville, Virginia. Over the years service centers were opened in Lynchburg, Manassas, Woodbridge, Fredericksburg, Chantilly, and Roanoke, Virginia.

Not to be outdone, Lighting Concepts, a lighting laboratory, was opened in Washington, D.C., completing a circle around the original Fairfax facility. All service centers are full-service operations, staffed to handle the contractor, as well as all phases of commercial, institu-

tional, municipal, and retail sales. Many locations have residential lighting display showrooms.

F. James Carr, president of Interstate Electric Supply, says the company owes much of its success to its aggressive approach to experimenting. "We have not been afraid to try a lot of different ventures," he claims.

The modernization of Interstate began in 1970 with the introduction of computers, which all service centers have, and employees are user competent so they work in the total computer network. Interstate, under the name of Ceiling Fans by Interstate, reintroduced the paddle fan to the market. Also established was a 24-hour hotline for emergency information and customer service.

The lighting laboratory in three

locations can be used for educational purposes for designers, builders, and architects, as well as for seminars for George Washington University, American University, James Madison University, and Howard University. Interstate is involved in sponsoring community projects, as well as a member of various trade organizations. One of the activities Interstate sponsors is a Golf Outing each year that is popular with manufacturers and Interstate customers. It is an all-day affair with dinner and awards.

As a sales/service-oriented company, Interstate emphasizes the training of its employees. "We spend a lot of time and money training our people," says Carr. "All we have to sell is ourselves," adds Michael C. Vincent, vice-president/sales and marketing. "'Our

people make the difference' is the company slogan."

Their commitment seems to be paying off. The firm's largest growth period occurred in the past five to seven years, and *Electrical Wholesale* magazine, a leading trade publication, ranked it as the 41st largest of approximately 7,000 electrical distributors in the nation in 1986. The company anticipates more than $50 million in sales in 1988, and plans are to continue to expand. It currently employs more than 200 people and represents more than 500 manufacturers.

In November 1987 Interstate led the way again by conducting a customer advisory council, the first in its industry. Since 1988 represents Interstate's 25th year in business, the council believed it

should ask customers how they perceive Interstate and their feelings about the firm's sales organization, policies, and service.

Noel W. Baker, vice-president/operations, said Interstate's rating was far above average, and, with the information derived from the council, the next 25 years will bring even more improvement.

Four of Interstate Electric Supply Co., Inc.'s, original 12 principals remain with the firm: Carr, Vincent, Baker, and James Jordan, lighting consultant.

The administration office and master distribution center for Interstate Electric Supply Company today.

SYSTEMS MANAGEMENT AMERICAN CORPORATION

President Ronald Reagan awarded Herman E. Valentine, founder, president, and chairman of Systems Management American Corporation, the 1984 Minority Entrepreneur of the Year Award at a Rose Garden ceremony in October 1984.

According to Herman E. Valentine, chairman and president of Norfolk-based Systems Management American Corporation, the company he started in 1970 was reborn 11 years later.

In 1981 SMA was a successful data-processing firm working major contracts for several government agencies. It had grown in meteoric strides since its founding and was beginning to explore areas with greater long-term growth potential.

Valentine targeted computer systems integration. Through his vision and drive, SMA won the U.S. Navy's Shipboard Non-Tactical ADP Program II (SNAP II) contract in 1981. Under this contract, SMA has designed and engineered integrated computer systems that it is manufacturing, installing, and maintaining on board 600 surface ships and submarines. SNAP II catapulted SMA into the arena of computer systems integration; the company was

reborn.

Since then SMA has been a leader in testing and evaluating off-the-shelf computer equipment to design the best and lowest-cost integrated systems to meet specific, often unusual, requirements. The SNAP II contract is an example of special environmental requirements that SMA successfully engineered into the system. Customizing systems to neutralize the effects of motion, dust, and temperature is called ruggedization, an SMA specialty.

Today SMA carries its integration expertise further into the forefront of computer systems technology—image processing. Among the newest of technologies, image processing converts information on the printed page into an electronically stored form that is easy to manage, instantaneously accessible, and cost effective.

SMA has also applied its expertise to the telecommunications and aerospace industries. Under contract to the Federal Aviation Administration, SMA is designing, integrating, testing, and installing a complete back-up command and communications network and is performing a total upgrade of air traffic

monitor and control systems nationwide. In the aerospace industry, SMA is part of the Rockwell Shuttle Operations Company team at NASA's Johnson Space Center in Houston. There it supports the operations of Rockwell's integrated logistics facility and data requirements within the Mission Control Center during simulated and actual shuttle missions.

Known early for his leadership, Valentine launched his business with $500, a one-room office, one employee, and an answering service. Today, with more than 600 employees in five locations nationwide and average annual sales for 1986 and 1987 of $60 million, SMA is one of the U.S. Navy's top 100 suppliers. It ranks 46th among Virginia's privately held companies and seventh among *Black Enterprise* magazine's top 100 list of black-owned businesses in the country.

At home, Systems Management American Corporation is an important part of the Hampton Roads community. Valentine has advanced the career opportunities of the underprivileged, contributed generously to educational funds, and spearheaded dozens of community drives. To Valentine, all of it is good business.

The Systems Management American (SMA) Corporation facility, in the foreground, a part of the Norfolk skyline, has been a key element in the revitalization of the city's downtown. Courtesy, Jack Will Photography

ECK ENTERPRISES, INC., AND ECK SUPPLY CO.

Take a walk along Main Street in Richmond. As you head west, away from downtown, you'll notice that the buildings are smaller, the neighborhood decidedly less wealthy. Then you pass Belvidere Street and the campus of Virginia Commonwealth University (VCU). Suddenly you're in a land of brass door knockers and remodeled facades. Welcome to the neighborhood that E.C. Eck, Jr., calls "Uptown Richmond."

Uptown Richmond is Eck's creation, the child of his investment and development company, Eck Enterprises. The neighborhood is still in transition. Older buildings, not yet remodeled, are mixed among the freshly reshaped structures that house professional offices, rapidly appreciating residences, trendy boutiques, and the upscale eateries that attract college students and professionals to the area.

It is Eck's dream, first conceived when VCU moved into the run-down neighborhood, that by 1990 the entire Uptown district, encompassing Main and Cary streets from VCU to the Boulevard, will have become a showcase community. He was alone when he started renovating the community. Now other investors and developers have joined the quest.

The business that has become Eck Enterprises and Eck Supply was started by Eck's father, E.C. Eck, as Southeast-

The owners of Eck Enterprises, Inc., F.T. Eck (left) and his brother, E.C. Eck, Jr.

ern Electric Supply Corporation (Sesco). E.C. Eck started working when he graduated from grade school, working his way up to become district manager of Westinghouse Electric Supply. He started Sesco in 1956.

As the business expanded, it purchased additional properties. To manage them, the firm created a real estate subsidiary, EBB Investment Corp. Its owners included E.C. Eck, Walter E. Blackburn, and George W. Broach. EBB Investment later reorganized into Eck Enterprises. It is now owned by Ed Eck, Jr., and his brother, Francis T. Eck,

an attorney who practices law in Richmond.

The electric supply company has also expanded under the management of Ed Eck, Jr. It now has 11 branches—nine in Virginia, one in Charleston, South Carolina, and one in the District of Columbia—and has annual sales of $50 million. The expansion came largely through acquisitions by Eck Enterprises, with distribution managed by Eck Supply. Eck Supply is now a wholly owned subsidiary of the development company.

The Richmond branch of Eck Supply will soon be leaving the original Harvie Street location and moving to Chesterfield County. The Harvie Street complex will retain the executive offices of Eck Enterprises and Eck Supply.

Meanwhile, Uptown Richmond continues to experience changes. Some observers call the restoration of the street to a Victorian elegance, that historically never existed, "Eckatecture." One architectural historian calls Eck's mixture of restored Victorian buildings with the transformation of bland 1950s office buildings into Georgian cottages, "an architectural fantasy."

"Maybe the historians cringe when they see my buildings," says Eck, "but I can't worry about history. I'm the guy taking the risk."

That's what progress is all about.

Uptown Richmond and its newly renovated Victorian, "Eckatecture" look.

SMITHFIELD FOODS, INC.

Taking an important regional pork foods processor in Smithfield, Virginia, and transforming it into a major *Fortune* 500 company with a dominant market position is no small accomplishment. Joseph W. Luter III, whose father and grandfather founded Smithfield Packing Company in 1936, was the head of the firm when it was purchased in 1969 by Smithfield Foods. Though he pursued other business matters for a time, he returned in 1975 as chief executive officer for the entire corporation. The op-

Gwaltney's high visibility in packaged food products made it an asset for Smithfield Packing Company. The product line includes hams, sausage, bacon, and other pork items.

portunity he perceived was to advance the way the company's products—hams, hot dogs, luncheon meats, sausage, and bacon—were manufactured, distributed, and marketed.

The decade following his return was one of the most significant, not only in the company's history but also in the packaged foods industry. High inflation, a harsh recession in the early 1970s, a decline in food consumption, rising prices, changes in warehousing and distribution patterns, and a proliferation of new brands for supermarket sales were among the forces pressuring Smithfield's development. Like other smaller and older family-run regional packers that faced overcapacity and competition

from larger, more automated concerns, the firm saw less than an exciting future from its 1975 perspective.

But in 10 years' time sales exploded from $127 million on tonnage of 167 million pounds to $864 million, topping the one-billion-pound sales figure. The hog slaughtering operation likewise jumped from 890,000 to more than 5.6 million.

Strategic planning brought about this success—and concurrently, Smithfield Foods' rise to a *Fortune* 500 company of national significance—emphasizing increased use of automation, cost cutting, geographical expansion, acquisition, and, most important, listening to the marketplace.

Dollars spent on capital improvements were devoted to making internal operations among the most efficient in the country. Increased mechanization led to more than doubling the efficiency of the kill and cut operations to 950 hogs per hour. Management tiers were streamlined, avoiding costly layers of bureaucracy. Efforts to reduce waste have led to transforming inedible parts of the hog for production of soap, lipstick, and fertilizer.

Where Smithfield Packing's market once stretched from Atlanta to Boston, the benefits of reinvesting earnings into plant operations enabled further market penetration south to Florida and out to New Orleans, the Midwest, and Upstate New York. Beyond the economic advantages it could offer, the company found that retailers also enjoyed offering products that conjured up the images of colonial craftsmanship personified by the brand name.

During the 1980s Smithfield followed a path of expansion and acquisition, adding to its position as a highly successful and efficient producer. In 1982 the firm purchased Gwaltney of Smithfield, Ltd., from ITT, a controversial move in the eyes of the small community that by tradition had been divided into supporters of either Luter or Gwaltney. But Smithfield Packing's increasing efficiency and talent for gaining new market entrance combined well with Gwaltney's high visibility in packaged goods. The purchase of two other

companies brought Smithfield into the ranks of the *Fortune* 500. In 1984 the firm acquired Wisconsin-based Patrick Cudahy Inc., a packer with a national and international sales network for its dry sausage products. In 1985 it purchased Baltimore-based Schluderberg-Kurdle Co., Inc. (Esskay), a specialist in bacon and hot dog products.

The cornerstone of the business remains production. The company is best known for its hams—especially the Genuine Smithfield Ham, which has the longest and most romantic heritage. Its Portsmouth plant for processing hot dogs is one of the largest continuous frankfurter operations in the country, a state-of-the-art facility that turns out some 1.5 million pounds of franks per week.

Another factor contributing to Smithfield's success was placing more emphasis on the consumer. Price consciousness gained importance, and the ability to offer products with a lower salt content became a well-chosen adaptation. Also, as Americans continue their trend of eating more meals away from home, the companies of Smithfield Foods are devoting more resources to food-service divisions.

For future growth, Smithfield Foods, Inc., and Carroll's Foods, Inc., have entered into a joint-venture partnership to raise hogs for processing at the former's two hog processing plants in Smithfield. Since hog production in the Southeast has not kept pace with Smithfield's needs, this step will reduce the large volume of hogs purchased from

Smithfield Packing Company purchased Gwaltney of Smithfield, Ltd., from ITT in 1982.

the Midwest, saving additional dollars in freight costs. The initial phase involves a 10-farm complex that currently houses 5,000 sows, capable of producing 100,000 hogs annually. Its first facility, known as the Gwaltney Complex, is on the site of a 480-acre farm once owned by an ancestor of the Gwaltneys who founded Smithfield's first hog slaughter operation. The master plan calls for additional complexes that, by 1993, will support 100,000 sows, yielding close to 2 million hogs annually. The resulting vertical integration of hog production and processing is expected to enhance Smithfield's leadership in the industry well into the next decade.

WARD/HALL ASSOCIATES

The Center for Innovative Technology, in its first phase, is presently under construction in Fairfax and Loudoun counties, Virginia.

Ward/Hall Associates, a member of the American Institute of Architects, is located in Fairfax, Virginia, and is one of the largest architectural firms in the northern Virginia, District of Columbia, and Maryland areas. Since 1964 the company has grown immensely, from its original partnership of G.T. Ward, Charles Hall, and a staff of five, to 45 individuals who make up the highest degree of professionalism obtainable in the architecture industry.

When George Truman Ward and Charles E. Hall, Jr., decided to go into partnership in Springfield in 1964, both men had excellent backgrounds in architectural education and professionalism. Each obtained a bachelor of science degree in building design and a master of science degree in architecture from Virginia Polytechnic Institute and State University in Blacksburg. The backgrounds of these two men speak for themselves, and reflect, with the support of the rest of the organization, how the firm has achieved a distinguished reputation in the architecture profession as well as a wide variety of projects.

G.T. Ward is a corporate member in the Virginia Society of the American Institute of Architects; a member of the Interfaith Forum on Religion, Art, and Architecture; a member of the honorary leadership fraternity of Omicron Delta Kappa and architectural fraternity of Tau Sigma Delta; recipient of the American Institute of Architects School Medal for Excellence in the Study of Architecture; the current chairman of the Advisory Council for the College of Architecture and Urban Studies at Virginia Polytechnic Institute and State University; a registered architect in Virginia, Maryland, and the District of Columbia and 10 other states; and is involved in many other organizations. He has been a strong supporter of architectural education through the Virginia

Tech Foundation and The Virginia Foundation for Architecture.

He has been a partner-in-charge of numerous federal and local governmental projects, corporate and association headquarters buildings, master planning and land-use projects, church and educational buildings, and projects for the C&P Telephone Company of Virginia and Virginia Power.

In addition, he has had considerable experience in real estate analysis and development as part owner, with Charles Hall and other investors, in Montclair Community in Prince William County and Springfield Tower Office Building, as well as other land-planning and development projects.

Charles Hall began his list of honors at Virginia Polytechnic Institute and State University, where he was a member of the leadership fraternity of Omicron Delta Kappa and president of the honorary architectural fraternity of Tau Sigma Delta. He has received an American Institute of Architecture Award for Excellence in Architecture, and is currently a registered architect in Maryland, the District of Columbia, and Virginia. From 1964 to 1969 he was involved in the master plan of the 1,500-acre Montclair community in Prince William County, Virginia, and since then has worked primarily with highrise office buildings along with local government projects in the counties of Fairfax, Arlington, and Montgomery, and

The Fair Oaks Office Building in Fairfax County, Virginia, was a Ward/Hall Associates project and contains the firm's corporate offices.

The Bethesda Gateway Office Building in Bethesda, Maryland.

the City of Rockville. Finally, he has been a partner-in-charge in various phases of more than 50 office building projects.

Robert J. Burns, Jr., AIA, became an associate in the firm in 1973, and Eric Taylor, AIA, was made an associate in 1984. Recently four other longtime members of the firm became associates: Geoffrey G. Kimmel, AIA; Patrick J. Higgins, AIA; Joseph Saunders, Jr., AIA, and Brian Robertson, AIA. These highly qualified and experienced new associates, together with the firm's acquisition of a Computervision V-X computer-assisted design system early in 1986 greatly strengthen the total capabilities of the organization.

The firm currently employs 45 people, including 13 licensed architects and 12 others with degrees in architecture. Ward/Hall goes to great effort to ensure that its employees develop in every possible aspect of professional architecture. Employees are encouraged to pursue licensing procedures and obtain their American Institute of Architecture memberships, as well as to participate in continuing education, in-house management programs, courses, and seminars.

Each project is headed by a principal or senior associate of the organization, along with a design team. Once the project gets under way, a project architect and associates are responsible for design and technical quality control. Economics for a project are always taken into consideration, with assurance that there is efficient energy and economical first costs, as well as reasonably inexpensive continuing maintenance and operation. The firm also takes care to put together the various elements of aesthetic beauty, functional space planning, sound engineering, and cost-effective construction.

Within the past five years the firm has been involved in many significant projects around the Washington, D.C., northern Virginia, and Maryland areas. One such major project is the Center for

Innovative Technology, assigned by the Commonwealth of Virginia and under authorization by the state legislature. Brought about by former Virginia Governor Charles Robb during his administration and continued under Governor Gerald Baliles' administration, its purpose is to attract high-technology industry, research, and employment to Virginia, and it is closely aligned with several major Virginia universities and colleges that undertake technical research. The $20-million development is located on the line between Fairfax and Loudoun counties, and will include 160,000 square feet of office and exhibit space, with an additional 240,000 square feet used for parking space. A major tenant of the complex that will occupy its own building is the Software Productivity Consortium, a group of U.S. aerospace contractors that produce advanced software. Arquitectonica, an architecture firm from the Coral Gables-Miami, Florida, area, has joined Ward/Hall in this venture, which is to be finished by autumn of 1988.

Ward/Hall has just completed the Virginia Power Northern Division Headquarters, a 78,000-square-foot, two-story office building located in Fairfax County, and is currently completing two large Fairfax County elementary schools with 42 classrooms each, as well as several U.S. Navy Projects in Yorktown and Dam Neck, Virginia, and Bethesda, Maryland.

There are several other projects currently under way, such as Hyde Park, a 1.4-million-square-foot mixed-use project in Rockville, Maryland, that includes a regional shopping center, residential condominiums, and office buildings. A 300-acre office park in Prince Georges, Maryland, and the Presidential Corporate Center, an 8-million-square-foot project, are in the process of completion.

The firm is also constantly involved in many other office buildings, churches, shopping centers, and apartment complexes, mostly in Maryland, the District of Columbia, and northern Virginia areas.

Ward/Hall Associates continues to strive to improve the quality of its staff and to diversify its projects. The firm is constantly aware of the need to dedicate the time and attention to completely understand schedule parameters, to prepare proper proposals, to ensure technical strength of assigned staff, to provide complete documents, and to achieve the most cost-effective pricing of all projects. It also has a reputation for providing excellence in master planning, land planning and rezoning, development and land-use feasibility studies, project programming, architectural design, architectural interiors, space planning, coordination of the total development team, construction administration, and project inspections.

The Virginia Power Northern Division Headquarters in Fairfax County.

VIRGINIA POLYTECHNIC INSTITUTE AND STATE UNIVERSITY

Virginia Tech students walk to classes in front of The R.B. Pamplin College of Business. The university is the largest in the Commonwealth, with more than 22,000 undergraduate and graduate students, and about 2,000 faculty members.

Initially students were housed and classes were conducted within the single building acquired from the Preston and Olin Institute. By the end of the first academic year, however, part of the growing student body had to live in town. In 1873 a dining hall was opened, and two academic buildings and a president's home were completed three years later. The Preston and Olin building burned down in 1913.

In 1896 the general assembly changed the name of the college to Virginia Agricultural and Mechanical College and Polytechnic Institute. In popular use, the names became Virginia Polytechnic Institute, VPI, or Virginia Tech. The phrase "Agricultural and Mechanical College" was dropped in 1944, and in 1970 the school's name was finally changed to Virginia Polytechnic Institute and State University.

The 11th and youngest president of the college, Dr. T. Marshall Hahn, Jr., who served from 1962 to 1974, guided VPI into a new era and built the base for its current status as the largest university in the state and as a nationally recognized center for academic and research excellence.

Virginia Agricultural & Mechanical College, now known as Virginia Polytechnic Institute and State University, opened its doors on October 1, 1872, as the result of the Morrill Act, which encouraged the founding of a land-grant university in each state. The college was established on the grounds of the Preston and Olin Institute at Blacksburg.

The new school represented a novel concept in admissions, recruiting students on the basis of individual abilities and desires, rather than familial wealth and influence. Early officials established 200 scholarships and set the tuition at $40 per year. Today about 54 percent of the student population receives some form of financial aid, and many are still the first members of their families to attend college.

Classes opened with 43 students, two faculty members, a librarian, and the president, Charles Minor. By the end of the year the student body had grown

to 132 and two more teachers had joined the faculty.

VAMC graduated its first class on August 11, 1875. The 12 students received graduation certificates—six as Associates of Agriculture, three as Associates in Mechanics, and three as Associates in Agriculture and Mechanics. William A. Caldwell of Craig County, VAMC's first student, graduated in agriculture and became a traveling salesman for a molasses importing company based in North Carolina.

Doctoral students work in a lab at Virginia Tech's veterinary college, which also has a satellite campus in College Park, Maryland. The university seeks to maintain a balance between arts and sciences in its comprehensive academic program.

Before the 1960s Virginia Tech was largely male and military oriented, and was known primarily as an agricultural school. One of Hahn's first suggestions was that the school be referred to as a university rather than a college. He also ended the school's official association with Radford College, a nearby women's school, thus making Virginia Tech a truly coeducational institution. That same year, 1964, the board of visitors voted to make participation in the Corps of Cadets optional for the first time in the school's history. Today Virginia Tech's student body numbers more than 22,000, of which some 4,000 are graduate students and 9,000 are women. Roughly 75 percent of the undergraduate enrollment is from Virginia, with the remainder representing all other states and more than 80 other countries. About 700 students are in the coeducational Corps of Cadets. The university has nearly 2,000 faculty members and is run by a staff of about 4,000.

Students can choose from almost 200 degree programs on the undergraduate or graduate level. The school's original three departments—literary, scientific, and technical—have given way to seven undergraduate academic colleges—Agriculture and Life Sciences, Architecture and Urban Studies, Arts and Sciences, Business, Education, Engineering, and Human Resources.

In addition to its widely recognized strength in agriculture, engineering, business, and sciences, Tech also receives acclaim from peer institutions and professional groups in theater arts management, hotel and restaurant management, forestry, and marketing education. Other noted departments include accounting, public administration, exercise science, and architecture.

Tech's first professional degree program was inaugurated in 1980, when the first class entered the Virginia-

Tech's rural setting encourages outdoor activities. The 2,400-acre campus is located in the beautiful Blue Ridge Mountains near the Appalachian Trail, a hiking trail that follows the mountain ridges from Maine to Georgia.

Maryland Regional College of Veterinary Medicine.

As a university with a tradition in technical education, Virginia Tech has a long-standing interest in technical advancements and research. Tech's college of engineering and computer science department were among the first academic organizations in the country to require its entering freshmen to own personal computers. Tech now has more than 10,000 PCs on campus, in addition to an IBM 3090 supercomputer.

About 4,500 active research projects are being conducted by Tech. In 1985 the university took on a substantial research mission with northern Virginia's Center for Innovative Technology in Loudoun County.

In recent years universities have seen the importance and potential gains in complementing academic research with the needs of corporations. Tech is no exception—in fact, it is the first university in the state to build a facility for such a purpose. The Virginia Tech Corporate Research Center, Inc., which began construction in 1987, will use university resources to conduct research in

information technology, power electronics, fiber optics, and other areas of corporate concern.

Virginia Tech's research programs are supported by about $75 million in state, federal, corporate, and other external funds. Tech perennially ranks in the top 10 among the nation's universities in the percentage of sponsored research funding from industrial sources. In the 1985-1986 fiscal year, some 17 percent of Tech's total sponsored research expenses came from nongovernment sources, compared with a national average of roughly 5 percent.

In accordance with its founding purpose to educate Virginians, Tech also sponsors the Virginia Cooperative Extension Service, with offices in all counties and most cities of Virginia, to provide information and assistance to citizens of the Commonwealth.

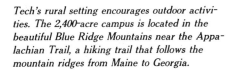

One of the many students who get experience at a computer terminal while attending Virginia Tech. About 10,000 personal computers are in use at Tech—more than any other university in the nation. Freshman engineering and computer science majors are required to own personal computers.

INTA-ROTO

Take a close look at the upholstery and dashboard covering in your car, and notice the intricately grained pattern embossed in the vinyl or other fabric. Now look around at the wood grain patterns of your office wallboard, the elaborately printed wall coverings in your home, or the textured flooring materials under your feet. Such decorative products all result from Inta-Roto technology.

Packaging and other products are also created with the help of Inta-Roto, products that range from textured and printed materials to coated or laminated substrates for use in high-tech industries.

These are all products of the "converting" industry, whose manufacturers process papers, plastics, films, or metals and coat, print, engrave, emboss, and laminate them—convert them—into some other form. And the premier builder of machinery and embossing and gravure rolls and plates for the converting industry is Richmond, Virginia's, Inta-Roto.

The name Inta-Roto comes from "intaglio," an Italian word for gravure printing, and "rotogravure," the high-speed printing by rotary presses. Printing cylinders are engraved by computer-assisted machinery, but the embossing rolls are still created by hand, engraved by craftsmen who hand-craft their own tools and who undergo a lengthy apprenticeship to become masters of the art.

The founders of Inta-Roto were Albert Merz and Otto Rich. In 1947 they left Reynolds Metals to start their own business. They began manufacturing rotogravure presses in an old log cabin.

Today the multibuilding complex fills an extensive site near Richmond International Airport. Despite a 1951 fire that destroyed the company's offices and most of its equipment, Inta-Roto has grown to assume a unique position. The firm introduced its gravure cylinder engraving operations in 1953 and inaugurated its embossing products operations in 1964. Today, as a manufacturer of

A Machine with a Future is a Machine with a Past.

presses, coaters, slitters, laminators, and related machinery, and as an engraver, Inta-Roto is the only single-source manufacturer serving the converting industry.

In addition to its Richmond operations, Inta-Roto has two sister companies, Dornbusch GMBH in Krefeld, West Germany, and Dornbusch & Cia, Ltd., in Sao Paulo, Brazil. Together the group offers the world's largest library of embossing designs, with more than 35,000 embossing tools available to its customers.

Willi Fenske and W.B. Carper, Jr., purchased Inta-Roto from Universal Leaf Tobacco Co., Inc., in 1977. Fenske, with 30 years in the engraving field, is now president. Carper, a long-term employee of the financial and administrative sector of Inta-Roto, is executive vice-president.

JAMES RIVER CORPORATION

Brenton S. Halsey, chairman (left), and Robert C. Williams, president (right), stand in front of the original Albemarle Paper Mill, the forerunner of the James River Corporation.

In 1969, when Richmond's Ethyl Corporation divested itself of most of its paper-manufacturing companies, two ambitious, farsighted executives, Brenton S. Halsey and Robert C. Williams, seized the opportunity and purchased the original Albemarle Paper Mill located on the north shore of the James River.

The specialty paper mill employed 100 people and operated one paper machine. Its major product lines were automotive air and oil filter papers. Halsey and Williams determined that they could turn the mill around, make it profitable, and use it as the base for future expansion and acquisitions. Their "James River Strategy" would emphasize superior product and service performance.

Between 1970 and 1979 James River made nine acquisitions, which brought additional specialty paper product lines, as well as experienced paper-making expertise and management. In 1980 James River purchased the Brown Company from Gulf & Western, not only doubling the firm in size, but also establishing James River in three new businesses: sanitary paper products, disposable food and beverage service products, and paperboard packaging.

In 1982 James River acquired the paper-related assets of American Can.

An artist's rendering of the James River corporate headquarters in Richmond.

This again doubled the company in size and, more important, marked its entry into the consumer products business with the popular Dixie® and Northern® name brands. The 1986 acquisition of Crown Zellerbach brought the business nationwide manufacturing and marketing capabilities, and once again doubled its sales and assets.

Over the course of its brief 18-year history, James River Corporation has grown through a total of 25 domestic acquisitions from a 100-employee enterprise with annual sales of $4 million to a position as a world leader in the pulp and paper industry. The firm employs more than 36,000 people, and its manufacturing facilities are positioned in 29 locations throughout the United States, Canada, and the United Kingdom. James River operates 16 pulp mills, 37 paper mills, and 84 converting plants. Its 112 paper machines produce 3.5 million tons of paper and converted paper products annually. Net sales in 1988 were approximately $5 billion.

In August 1987 James River agreed to purchase a half-interest in Kaysersberg, S.A. Kaysersberg is the leading French producer of sanitary paper products, with consolidated annual sales of $648 million. This recent acquisition has made James River a major player in the international paper industry.

James River Corporation is managed with a corporate staff of only 400 people. A highly decentralized organization gives maximum autonomy to the managers of each operating unit. Most evident is a companywide commitment to "finding a better way" of solving traditional business problems. Employees share in the corporate belief that success is a product of the highest ethical standards, superior value and service to customers, safe and productive jobs, involvement in job-related decision making, profit orientation, and ownership in the firm. Currently more than 75 percent of James River employees are company shareholders. *Fortune, Forbes, Dun's Business Month,* and other authorities continue to rate James River among America's best-managed publicly owned corporations.

GTE SPACENET CORPORATION

GTE SPACENET CORPORATION

For much of America, the first awareness of satellites was of the Russian Sputnik I scientific exploration satellite launched in 1957. We were amazed that a machine placed so high in the sky could communicate with earth. Since that time, we have become much more nonchalant about satellite technology.

GTE Spacenet Corporation's customers use satellite technology in data, video, and voice applications in business every day. The company's system of communications satellites allows data networks that circumvent traditional land lines, real-time video broadcasts for merchandise selection or training sessions, and "live via satellite" coverage of news events.

From its McLean, Virginia, headquarters, GTE Spacenet Corporation operates a multi-satellite system that, as this is written, consists of five satellites offering a variety of coverage options to all 50 states, Puerto Rico, and the U.S. Virgin Islands. Two additional satellites are under construction, and by the time this book is printed, one of these will probably be in geosynchronous orbit, 22,300 miles above the equator.

The May 22, 1984, launch of the *SPACENET I* satellite marked the takeoff of GTE Spacenet as a provider of communication services. Since then, major corporate milestones have included:

—Placing the *SPACENET II, GSTAR I, GSTAR II,* and *SPACENET III* satellites in orbit.

—Establishing itself as a full-service provider of business communication networks and systems for domestic and international data, video, and voice applications.

—Becoming the leading provider of satellite news gathering services, supporting contracts with ABC, CBS, CNN, and Gannett.

—Establishing a 14-site video conferencing network within GTE Corporation.

GTE Spacenet has four primary business areas, including Satellite Services, Network Services, Government Services, and International Systems.

Satellite Services—GTE Spacenet is the leader when it comes to satellite news gathering. Four of the major television broadcast groups—ABC, CBS, CNN, and Gannett—along with numerous affiliate stations have selected GTE Spacenet to support their satellite news gathering initiatives.

Full, partial, and occasional use transponder capability appeals to a variety of customers in business, education, health care, entertainment, and more.

Network services—GTE Spacenet's Skystar® data and video network services are at work improving customer service in the areas of retail, banking, hotel, transportation, and financial services. K mart shoppers are already benefiting from one of the world's largest private data and video communications networks, a system employing the latest in satellite technology. Its applications include accelerated credit card verification at points-of-sale, inventory management, video broadcast merchandise selection, payroll accounting, and other financial management control functions. The network will ultimately enable K mart international headquarters in Troy, Michigan, to communicate quickly and efficiently with the more than 2,100 K mart stores nationwide.

Other GTE Spacenet network services customers include Days Inns, First Union National Bank of North Carolina, Prudential Bache, and Publishers Phototype International (PPI).

Government Services—The United States Secret Service is using a combination of Telenet Communications Corp. and GTE Spacenet to design and install a secured nationwide telecommunications network. The system employs satellite, packet switching, and electronic messaging technologies. GTE Spacenet is implementing an earth sta-

tion network, including flyaway and transportable terminals, and providing network services.

International Systems—GTE Spacenet's International Systems Division, based in Waltham, Massachusetts, has been a world leader in the design and implementation of satellite communications earth stations for nearly 20 years. Earth station facilities have been installed in the Bahamas, Brazil, Burkina Faso, Chile, Costa Rica, the Dominican Republic, Korea, Mali, Nigeria, the Philippines, People's Republic of China, Poland, Thailand, and Venezuela.

Over the past 20 years the International Systems Division has achieved a number of industry "firsts":

—In 1968, in Chile, the installation of the first commercial earth station in Latin America.

—In 1976, the installation of the first Algerian interior service network utilizing an INTELSAT satellite, consisting of 15 stations.

—In 1977, the installation of one of the first Standard "B" earth stations in the world.

—In 1985, the installation of the world's first INTELSAT Vista station in Madagascar.

—In 1987, the installation of the first down-sized Standard "A" INTELSAT earth station in the Bahamas.

GTE Spacenet's advertising tag line, "The New Standard," underscores the company's commitment to continue to redefine "state-of-the-art" in business communications services as it continues to set new standards of innovation in applications for satellite technology.

On May 22, 1984, the launching of the SPACENET 1 satellite marked the real takeoff of GTE Spacenet as a modern corporation.

THE CALVERT COMPANIES, INC.

In a little more than a decade, Robert Calvert Wilcox has built his construction, property management, and real estate development company into an organization comfortably ensconced among *Washington Business Journal*'s top private companies in the greater Washington area.

The Calvert Company was incorporated in 1974, when Wilcox left his job as a mortgage broker and went into business as a general contractor. He only built two homes that year, but he also started building a reputation for the quality construction of skillfully designed, energy-efficient houses. From custom homes the firm expanded into town house development. The company built 24 single-family units in 1981.

"Even in the beginning, business was pretty good," recalls Wilcox, "but I just thought that there had to be a way to do better. I guess you could say ambition was the force that drove us to change."

In the late 1970s and early 1980s Wilcox and his Calvert Company diversified into commercial construction. The organization built hotels in Dumfries, Manassas, and Springfield—all as part

The Calvert Companies' Nashville Days Inn.

of the Econo Lodge chain. Today Calvert properties extend from Connecticut to the Florida Keys, and west to Tennessee.

The Calvert Property Company fulfills the organization's strategic planning and marketing development role, working with both residential and commercial projects. Calvert Property locates development sites, undertakes feasibility and engineering studies, and completes all necessary arrangements leading to construction. Then either Calvert Homes or Calvert Construction takes over.

Residents of northern Virginia are most familiar with the work of Calvert Homes, the original operating unit of The Calvert Companies, Inc., and the subsidiary now responsible for all residential construction. Calvert Homes delivered approximately 160 homes in 1987. Company projects range from exclusive custom homes on multiacre lots to town houses, but most are what Wilcox calls "traditional executive homes."

"We're not aesthetic pioneers," says Wilcox. "We want to please a large percentage of the home buyers in a small sector of the market. Most of our homes sell in the $200,000 to $350,000

range. We offer top-quality construction and materials, and classic design."

Calvert Homes can be found in the subdivisions of Montclair (Prince William County), Copper Crossing (Herndon), Shaker Woods (near Reston), Little Rocky Run (Fairfax County), The Cedars and Peabody Square (Lake Ridge), Oakton Vale and Berrywood Farms (Oakton), Calvert at Lynnwood

Robert C. Wilcox, president and sole owner of The Calvert Companies, Inc.

The Woodbridge Comfort Inn, another Calvert Companies, Inc., property.

(Lake Ridge), Calvert's Glen (Loudoun County), Wetherlea (Warrenton), and Taristock Farms (Leesburg). In 1986 Calvert Construction built 160 units.

Calvert Construction is the builder of all commercial and hotel projects of The Calvert Companies, Inc., and operates as a general contractor for other clients. The construction company has been responsible for the renovation that transformed Baltimore's 85-year-old YMCA building into the new 200-room Baltimore Comfort Inn. More recently, Calvert Construction completed work on Prosperity Woods, Calvert's Leesburg apartment complex. In between the firm has built many of Calvert's hotels, including the Days Inns in South Plainfield, New Jersey, and in Absecon, located near Atlantic City.

Calvert Management, the property management arm of The Calvert Companies, Inc., has more than 2,600 hotel rooms under its care. Calvert-owned hotels include Quality Inns, Comfort Inns, and Days Inns, as well as a Holiday Inn and several Econo Lodges. Calvert Management also oversees the firm's other commercial properties, including the Lee Funeral Home in Manassas (which Calvert Construction transformed from a former automobile service station), and the company's apartment units.

Including those properties under development, Calvert now owns 24 hotels, 13 exclusive residential communities, and an apartment complex. With 700 employees, the company produced more than $60 million in gross sales in 1987. Calvert Enterprises, headquartered in the firm's own Lake Ridge Executive Park in Woodbridge, is the administrative unit of The Calvert Companies, Inc.

"I've taken an essentially entrepreneurial business and institutionalized it," says Wilcox. "We have thorough research, careful planning, and detailed managerial accounting. We have a pool of very talented people.

"My job is to blend the talents and

The Lake Ridge Executive Park serves as the corporate headquarters for The Calvert Companies, Inc.

set the direction. I don't make any decisions unilaterally any more. I rely heavily on our executive committee. They're all good people. I couldn't have begun to do all this by myself. Good people, good luck, and a supportive family. That's what did it."

The next few years at The Calvert Companies, Inc., will feature continued diversification. "We're in an expansion mode," says Wilcox. "Additional hotel construction, expansion of our office complex and apartment building activities, and a shopping center are all in process."

Wilcox is immediate past president of the Northern Virginia Building Industry Association and president of the national Econo Lodges of America Franchisee Association. He is also a former member of the board of directors of the Prince William Symphony Orchestra and of the Washington Bank at Tysons Corner. He serves in several advisory positions, including a recent congressional task force on transportation.

A traditional, executive home—the Cambridge Model—which Calvert Homes builds in northern Virginia.

411

THE HOMESTEAD

A step inside is a step back in time to a place very few ever knew, a place for the wealthy who really knew how to spend their money. Now it has every modern convenience one can imagine—plus a few that do not immediately come to mind—but to step off the veranda into the expansive front lobby, to walk down the lush hallways to the elaborate dining room or the naturally heated springs, brings to mind the linen clothes, the horses and carriages, the grand life-style and gracious hospitality of another time.

The Homestead, located in Hot Springs, Virginia, on a plateau within the Alleghenies, is one of 12 Mobil Five-Star resorts in the United States, an honor it has held for more than 27 years. Porters prevent guests from carrying anything themselves, an entourage of servers wait on every dining table, and throughout the property employees are always eager to answer any question or complete any task.

According to American Indian legend, the allegedly healing waters of Hot Springs were first discovered in the sixteenth century by a traveling brave. Whites recorded their first visit to the valley in the late 1600s, although no visit to the 104-degree-Fahrenheit, mineral-rich springs were recorded until the early 1700s.

Probably the first hotel on the property was built by Thomas Bullitt, who is said to have built it in defense of his own home, which was frequently imposed upon by visitors. He obtained a deed in 1764 and built a lodge called The Homestead two years later.

The refuge for the rich and the aching remained rustic until 1832, when it was purchased by Dr. Thomas Goode. By claiming different pools would cure different ailments, he attracted many guests. Only the wealthiest could afford a two-day stagecoach trip up the mountainside.

In 1891 the hotel and surrounding land were bought by a syndicate headed by a man named M.E. Ingalls. He and his family bought the controlling interest of The Homestead in 1914. Although the ownership was reorganized in 1938 and renamed Virginia Hot Springs, Inc., the Ingalls family still operates the

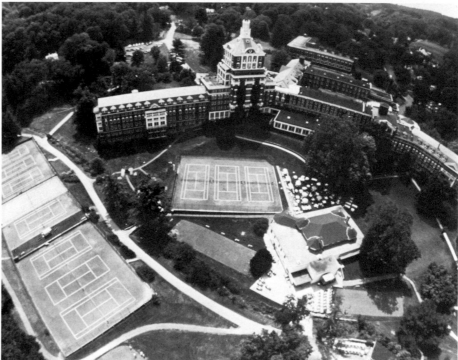

country's oldest hotel owned by a single family.

The hotel continued to grow until 1901, when a fire in the bakery burned the resort to the ground, except for the spa and 11 cottages, built in 1892, and a casino, built the following year. The cottages have served as novelty shops since 1984.

The owners began to rebuild the destroyed resort immediately, and by 1902 the main section was completed. The west wing soon followed, and the east wing was completed in 1914. The tower on the main wing that gives The Homestead its distinctive profile was completed in the spring of 1929.

Today The Homestead proudly

The Homestead, located in Hot Springs, Virginia, has roots dating back to 1766, when Thomas Bullitt built a lodge and called it The Homestead. Today it is a luxurious hotel steeped in the tradition upon which it was built.

meshes tradition with modern amenities in a winning combination. The spa offers sauna, massage, and exercise, in addition to the five springs on the property. Guests can choose from a wide variety of recreational activities, from volleyball to lawn bowling, golf to skiing. Dining ranges from formal gourmet to American grill, and services include in-house doctor and dentist, travel agency, photographer, and dry cleaning.

POTOMAC EDISON COMPANY

Potomac Edison Company serves an area of 7,266 square miles, in all or portions of 28 counties in Virginia, Maryland, and West Virginia. The population of that service area exceeds 660,000; it takes 17,603 miles of power lines to deliver electricity to those customers.

In all, more than 160 individual local companies comprise the family tree that branches from Potomac Edison. These include electric, gas, railway, water, bus, and other organizations. Two of the earliest companies in the United States to hold original incandescent lamp patents issued by Thomas Edison were among them: Edison Electric Illuminated Company of Cumberland (1884) and the Edison Electric Company of Martinsburg (1889). These patents give Potomac Edison the right to use "Edison" as part of the corporate name.

The firm's direct line of descent traces to the Isabella Gas Works founded in Frederick, Maryland, in 1853. By 1922 that organization was op-

erating in Maryland, West Virginia, Pennsylvania, and Virginia under the name Hagerstown and Frederick Railway. In 1922 the railroad was purchased by American Water Works and Electric Company, and renamed Potomac Public Service. In 1923 Potomac Public Service bought the Cumberland Edison Electric Illuminating Company and changed its name to Potomac Edison.

In western Virginia electrical power pioneers included Shirley Carter, S.H. Hansborough, General Charles Thurman, S.L. Hoover, and the Honorable A. Moore, Jr. In 1904 the group organized an electric railway company to build a railway from Winchester to Washington, D.C. The group built a hydroelectric generating plant at an old gristmill near Millville, West Virginia. It later purchased an existing electric light plant owned by the Winchester Gas and Electric Light Company.

The electrical power offshoot proved so successful that they never built their railway. Instead the associa-

Some of the Virginia employees of the Potomac Edison Company stand outside the Kernstown office.

tion extended the transmission network and, in 1913, changed the corporate name to the Northern Virginia Power Company. The new charter dropped all reference to railway construction.

Potomac Edison today is a subsidiary of Allegheny Power System, Inc. Other Allegheny Power subsidiaries are the Monongahela Power Company and the West Penn Power Company. Potomac Edison annually sells more than 13 billion kilowatt-hours of power. Most of that comes from coal-powered generating stations, including several that are owned jointly by all three Allegheny Power subsidiaries.

Potomac Edison Company has offices in northern Virginia, the eastern panhandle of West Virginia, and western Maryland. The firm has more than 1,000 employees.

THE BYRD NEWSPAPERS

Throughout the Shenandoah Valley, "The Newspaper" means either *The Winchester Star* (evenings, 21,000 circulation), or the Harrisonburg *Daily News-Record* (mornings, 31,000 circulation), or one of the weekly newspapers in the Byrd group: *The Shenandoah Valley-Herald* (Woodstock, Shenandoah County); *Page News and Courier* (Luray, Page County); *Front Royal-Warren Sentinel* (Front Royal, Warren County); *The Valley Banner* (Elkton, Rockingham County); and farther to the southeast, *Nelson County Times* (Lovingston, Nelson County); and *Amherst New Era-Progress* (Amherst, Amherst County).

The Shenandoah Valley starts at the northern border of the state, 70 miles west of Washington, D.C., and runs south deep into the heart of Virginia. This is apple country in the north around Winchester and Frederick County, and poultry country around Harrisonburg and Rockingham County, the latter being the nation's turkey capital.

The valley is a region deeply rooted in Virginia history and agriculture. It also is an area with much appeal for small and light industry. During the past several decades both the Winchester area and the Harrisonburg area have attracted many new plants; each has become highly diversified.

Senator Harry F. Byrd, Jr., an employee and executive of Byrd Newspapers since 1935, now serves as chairman.

Winchester is an important medical center with a $100-million complex nearing completion. Harrisonburg is the home of the 10,000-student James Madison University; in nearby Rockingham County, the Coors Brewery is establishing its first eastern facility, eventually investing nearly one billion dollars in Rockingham County.

While the concerns of the Byrd Newspapers remain as fundamental as apple pie and Thanksgiving turkey, the technology of the Byrd Newspapers may be as advanced as any in the state. In 1964 *The Star* was the first daily newspaper in Virginia to go to offset printing, a method now used by nearly all newspapers except the largest. The Byrd Newspapers' traditional philosophy is to keep the newspapers as modern in both design and equipment as advanced technology will permit. Editorially, the newspapers are conservative and independent politically, having supported both Democrats and Republicans.

The Winchester Star was established in 1896 and was purchased two years later by its editorial writer, Richard Evelyn Byrd, who was editor and publisher until 1908. His son, Harry Flood Byrd, later governor of Virginia and United States senator, was publisher from 1908 to 1945. He was succeeded by Harry F. Byrd, Jr., former United States senator and the current chairman, whose son, Thomas T. Byrd, is now the publisher.

The Daily News-Record of Harrisonburg traces its antecedents to the *Rockingham Register,* a weekly founded in 1822 that merged with *The Record,* another weekly, in 1903. The newspaper, now a daily, took its current form in 1913. Harry F. Byrd, Jr., became publisher in 1938 and continues as publisher and chief executive officer. Richard R. J. Morin is editor and general manager.

Thomas T. Byrd, a fifth-generation publisher whose father, grandfather, great-grandfather, and great-great-grandfather published newspapers in Winchester, and whose maternal grandfather published a newspaper in New Orleans, Louisiana.

VIRGINIA COMMONWEALTH UNIVERSITY

Virginia Commonwealth University is the state's largest comprehensive urban university—an institution that has distinguished itself as a special resource in Richmond and the state in the areas of teaching, research, health care and delivery, and community service.

VCU was created through the merger of the Medical College of Virginia (MCV) and Richmond Professional Institute (RPI). MCV was founded in 1838 when it was created as the medical department of Hampden-Sydney College. It became an independent institution in 1854 and affiliated with the state in 1860.

RPI opened in 1917 in an old, red brick residence across the street from the governor's mansion. The first school of its kind in the South, it was designed to train social workers and public health nurses. Located in the downtown section of Richmond, it made wide use of city resources in educating students—a tradition that has continued and grown.

VCU's sesquicentennial in 1988 marks not only the 150th anniversary

The Medical College of Virginia campus. MCV is the Health Sciences Division of Virginia Commonwealth University and is located two miles east of the academic campus.

The Student Commons, center of activity on Virginia Commonwealth University's academic campus.

of its origins, but also the 20th anniversary of the merger and the 10th anniversary of VCU's third president, Dr. Edmund F. Ackell.

VCU enrolls more than 20,000 undergraduate, graduate, and health professions students on its two campuses. It offers 134 degree programs, 40 of which are not available anywhere else in Virginia, and 65 of which can be earned in evening-only study.

The university is Virginia's fifth-largest employer with more than 11,000 faculty and staff. The Medical College of Virginia Campus includes MCV Hospitals, the fourth-largest teaching hospital in the United States.

A master plan for the MCV campus will allow the university to continue its leadership position in health care research and delivery into the twenty-first century. Known as MCV 2000, the master plan will assure even greater contributions to Virginia with a new medical sciences building and expansion of ambulatory care.

Vital signs of the university's good health are visible everywhere. Its 20-year-old heart transplant program was

one of the first two in the United States to be accredited by Medicare. And the VCU Jazz Orchestra has been named Outstanding Jazz Band in national competition four out of the past five years.

As a result of a long-term VCU study of childhood cancer, the five-year survival rate of children suffering from a type of soft tissue cancer has increased from 20 to 66 percent. VCU is one of only 20 universities in the nation that has a school in every health-related discipline.

The university embraces the challenge of the contemporary nontraditional student. Only 55 percent of VCU's student body is younger than age 25; almost 1,000 students are age 45 or older.

In November 1986 Virginia Commonwealth University kicked off a $52-million campaign—the university's first such effort. Major contributions have already been received from Mr. and Mrs. Charles G. Thalhimer, the Circuit City Foundation, Alan L. Wurtzel and the Wurtzel family and friends, the Nathan and Sophia Gumenick Philanthropic Fund, the Thomas Tabb bequest, and Philip Morris USA.

The sesquicentennial of Virginia Commonwealth University marks the coming of age of the university; it is a time to take stock of traditions, to renew pride in the present, and to ensure confidence in the future.

415

THE HENRY A. LONG COMPANY

Henry A. Long, founder and chairman of The
Henry A. Long Company.

The history of the Henry A. Long Company has long been part and parcel of the history of the world of real estate in northern Virginia and the national capital region.

Since its founding in 1979 the Henry A. Long Company has single-mindedly pursued one goal: creating value in real estate through thoughtfully planned, sensitively designed, and meticulously executed projects.

Its founder, Henry A. Long, knows the Washington, D.C./northern Virginia real estate market well. A founding partner of the Long & Foster real estate brokerage firm, he built that agency into the largest privately owned residential real estate company in the Washington region. When he left Long & Foster, he took as his mission building his new organization, the Henry A. Long Company, into the area's premier commercial real estate developer.

The Henry A. Long Company's noteworthy success has resulted from its ability to anticipate market trends and move, usually well ahead of the competition, to meet the commercial real estate

requirements of corporations and associations.

Westwood, a 37-acre commercial complex at Tysons Corner, was the first corporate campus of its kind in the northern Virginia area. The center includes more than one million square feet of office, retail, and hotel space, surrounded by landscaped courtyards, jogging trails, and other amenities.

The newest Henry A. Long development, Westfields, is a 1,100-acre corporate community that is creating an entirely new environment for corporate living. It offers a choice of selective, quality-controlled environments—each a self-contained neighborhood, yet each a part of a single, homogeneous community.

The initial development within Westfields is The Meadows, an extensively landscaped, 50-acre corporate campus where four separate buildings cluster around an internal loop road and

Pender Mill I, developed by The Henry A. Long
Company in Fairfax, Virginia.

The Meadows I Building at Westfields was fully leased to Martin Marietta Corporation.

An aerial view of The Meadows Office Park in the Westfields Corporate Center.

a scenic park. A fifth building, the new headquarters complex of American Systems Corporation, is nearby. All five buildings feature a combination of quality and flexibility unique in the northern Virginia market.

Lakeside Center is a 150,000-square-foot project in Westfields designed to suit the requirements of high-tech corporations. Extensive informal landscaping featuring transplanted mature trees provide a gracious "arrived" image and a high-quality environment.

Glenbrook will be Westfields' community of offices for smaller companies and trade associations. The master site plan incorporates several ponds along a stream that passes in front of each building.

Ridgewood, a 38-acre neighborhood, is designed for five individual corporate headquarters buildings. The site has been skillfully and carefully planned to take full advantage of the communi-

ty's clear views of Virginia's Blue Ridge Mountains; it features a naturally wooded area, carefully preserved throughout the construction process. The Henry A. Long Company is building its own new corporate headquarters as part of Ridgewood.

The Westfields International Conference Center has its own 27-acre enclave. Developed in joint venture with International Conference Resorts of Scottsdale, Arizona, MJ Property Com-

pany, and Perpetual Real Estate Services, Inc., the conference center will offer health and fitness facilities, several restaurants, television, and multimedia production and presentation capabilities, along with luxurious meeting rooms and guest quarters.

The Henry A. Long Company continues to progress as northern Virginia's premier full-service real estate developer with several exciting projects in the Washington, D.C., metropolitan area as well as elsewhere in the United States.

Westfields Corporate Center, a 1,100-acre office park in western Fairfax County, is being developed by The Henry A. Long Company.

DYNATECH CORPORATION

Dynatech Data Systems of Newington, Virginia, and Dynatech Packet Technology of Woodbridge, Virginia, are wholly owned subsidiaries of Dynatech Corporation, a worldwide system of high-technology companies based in Burlington, Massachusetts.

Dynatech is composed of many entrepreneurial-style companies, each close to its own market and quick to respond to changing customer needs. At the same time Dynatech Corporation's strict financial control and budget control give the firm a strong managerial posture. In 1987 Dynatech sales totaled well in excess of $300 million.

The two Virginia companies are both part of Dynatech's Data Communications Group, which has its own international headquarters at the Newington location. Dynatech Data Communications Group companies have maintained a well-earned image of quality and usefulness and a history of nonobsolescence of the products and services provided.

Dynatech's Data Communications Group is committed to providing the specialized products and systems necessary for organizations to reliably and economically transmit information that is vital to their operations. Dynatech

clients include governments, banks, insurance and financial institutions, leading manufacturing and retail sales companies, telecommunications companies, airlines, and public utilities. In 1986 international sales of Dynatech's Data Communications Group surpassed $36 million.

Group vice-president of Dynatech/Data Communications is R. Claude Olier. The three senior division executives are Nat Kumar, Bruce Brown, and Pierre Bretault.

Dynatech Data Systems and Dynatech Packet Technology actively design, manufacture, and market a wide range of products. Dynatech Data Systems focuses on network management and technology control systems. Dynatech Packet Technology provides products for packet networks. Together they employ more than 350 people, and each is experiencing an annual growth rate exceeding 25 percent.

Both companies trace their origins to the Nelson Cooke Engineering Company, a small electronics firm founded in the mid-1950s and purchased in 1969 by Dynatech. Cooke Engineering had two divisions, Medical Technology and Electronics.

The new Dynatech company manufactured a line of digital patch jacks that provided access to communication links for testing, monitoring, and reconfiguration. This technology evolved to include electromechanical switching, allowing users to rapidly recover from communications equipment failure.

The electronics division of Cooke Engineering, then under the leadership of Ron Wetherhogg, evolved into Dynatech Data Systems. (Wetherhogg served as group vice-president of Dynatech Data Communications until his retirement in 1985.)

Dynatech was one of the first companies to participate in the expanding data communications market, and, as the use of computers proliferated in the 1970s, more applications were developed and more networks came into use. Dynatech Data Systems played a pioneering role in this data communications revolution. Patching and electromechanical switching devices are integral components of even the largest data centers, and Dynatech continues as a leading contributor in the technology.

By 1976 the firm had expanded into international marketing activities, with sales and administration offices based in Paris and manufacturing operations in Germany. The company's American activities moved first to Alexandria, then to Springfield, and, most recently, to Newington.

Dynatech Data Systems continues to design, manufacture, and sell products and systems needed to monitor, manage, and maintain data communications networks. By responding to trends toward larger distributed networks and continuing to introduce increasingly sophisticated and powerful switching devices, the company continues to maintain its leadership role.

When people speak with each other over the telephone, static and electronic noise may be bothersome but they usually will not hinder effective communication. People also have the ability to adjust the flow of conversation so that they do not end up talking at the same time, even during conference calls. Computers, however, are not as clever,

so complex rules and management devices are necessary to control inter-network communication.

To facilitate communication between networks, data can be bound into tiny "packets." The use of this form of communication is called packet switching, an efficient and cost-effective way to transmit information over long distances. In the early 1980s Dynatech Corporation purchased a two-person company called International Packet Technology.

The subsidiary has thrived as a component of the international system created by Dynatech's Data Communications Group. Renamed Dynatech Packet Technology, it specialized in packet switching and manufactured packet assembler/disassembler (PAD) and packet switching devices used in a packet switched network. Most recently, Dynatech's Multi-PAD X.25 added new economies to the use of packet switching by providing packet assembly and data

concentration in a single unit. The result is a reduction in the number of communication lines required to support multiple connections.

The company also manufactures a variety of "gateways" that provide compatibility between private and public data networks.

Dynatech has established local manufacturing facilities in the United States, Canada, Great Britain, and Germany to serve each region. The facilities are supported by local research and development teams.

Local Dynatech sales and support companies are based in Canada, France, Germany, Italy, Japan, Norway, Sweden, the United Kingdom, and the United States. In other geographic areas, the company has established strong ties with distributors in key market segments of Europe, the Middle East, Africa, and the countries of the Pacific Rim.

THE CHARLES E. SMITH COMPANIES

Most real estate development firms think in terms of buildings. A few talk about complexes and dream about communities. The Charles E. Smith Companies are well respected for buildings—17 of them in downtown Washington, D.C., alone—but the firm is better known for its cities: Crystal City in Arlington, Skyline City on Leesburg Pike near Bailey's Crossroads, and the newest, Worldgate, neighboring Washington's Dulles International Airport.

Other major CES projects include University Center in Loudoun County, Democracy Plaza in Maryland's Montgomery County, Arlington Plaza and Courthouse Plaza in Arlington, and the Fairfax Government Center in Fairfax.

Charles E. Smith came from Russia as a child in 1911. His father became a successful New York general contractor and developer. Smith learned the business working afternoons and weekends for his father, then building his own houses in partnership with various friends and relatives. He moved from Brooklyn to Washington in 1943.

The following year Smith began building houses in Washington, financing his developments through a series of partnerships. He opened Charles E. Smith Construction in 1946. Early projects included Elmar Gardens in Riverdale, Maryland; University Manor in Silver Spring, Maryland; and the Holmead, Cromwell, and Saxony apartments in northwest Washington.

The firm built its first office building, 1717 Pennsylvania Avenue, NW, in 1961. The following year it organized Management, Inc., to handle the growing list of Charles E. Smith-managed residential and commercial properties. In 1963 it opened Crystal House I Apartments at 1900 South Eads Street, in Arlington—the first building in the area that would become Crystal City. The development and the buildings that followed soon changed the real estate business in Washington and northern Virginia.

The Charles E. Smith Companies

Skyline City on Leesburg Pike is a Charles E. Smith Companies development.

continued expanding; other projects of the early to mid-1960s included the Key Building, London House, Windsor Towers, and Normandy House in Arlington; Orleans Village South in Alexandria; 1140 Connecticut Avenue, NW, in Washington; and Rosslyn Plaza buildings "C," "D," and "E."

Crystal City construction of the mid-1960s included Crystal House II, Crystal Plaza, Crystal Towers South Apartments, and Crystal Plaza Office Buildings 2, 3, 4, and 5. The property management portfolio of CES Management, Inc., included 36 residential and 18 commercial buildings, nearly 9,000 apartments, and a total of more than 2.75 million square feet of office space.

Charles E. Smith retired from active leadership of the firm in 1967 to devote more of his attentions to philanthropic and community endeavors. He continues to serve as chairman of the board. Leadership was turned over to Robert H. Smith, his son, and Robert P. Kogod, his son-in-law, in 1967.

Crystal City, tucked between National Airport, the Pentagon, and the 14th Street Bridge over the Potomac, is the largest mixed-use project developed by a private developer on the East Coast. It has grown to include 2 complete shopping centers, 7 million square feet of office space, 3,700 luxury residential apartments, 2 Marriott hotels, 22 restaurants, and 2 fitness and recreation clubs. The residential and workday population is now approximately 60,000, and it has

The Charles E. Smith Companies Exhibit Center.

its own stop on the Washington Metro rail system. Tenants include major corporations and organizations such as USAir, the United States Patent Office, the United States Navy, AT&T, IBM, RCA, TRW, GTE, Xerox, Honeywell, Boeing, Rockwell International, and Westinghouse. A newly acquired 40-acre site will give Crystal City a continuous, 20-block stretch.

The Charles E. Smith Companies are continuing to develop other properties as well.

Skyline City's latest addition is a 26-story office tower (scheduled for completion in mid-1988) with views of downtown Washington on one side, and Virginia's Blue Ridge Mountains on the other. Like Crystal City, Skyline City is in the middle of things, easily accessible to the Pentagon, National Airport, or Tysons Corner.

The Smith Exhibit Center, an innovative center located in Crystal City, allows a visitor to see 70 office buildings in 25 minutes, and see all the Washington market of more than 30 million square feet of office space in one easy stop. Nine display rooms in the center offer videotape programs, site models, floor plans, and displays of possible office configurations.

The newest venture at CES is Worldgate, a mixed-use development now under construction on a 94-acre site

Crystal City includes 36 residential and 18 commercial buildings, nearly 9,000 apartments, and a total of more than 2.75 million square feet of office space.

next to Dulles International Airport. The complex will include a nine-plex cinema, fitness and recreation club, restaurants, retail stores, a Marriott suites hotel, and 12 office buildings. Worldgate will be a total environment, offering its tenants an outstanding image and high visibility, as well as landscaping, accessibility, and the ability to grow.

University Center in Loudoun County is a cooperative effort with George Washington University, which is to build a graduate engineering campus on land donated by CES. The balance will be a mix of office space, restaurants, residential buildings, high-

technology industry, and retail facilities.

Arlington Courthouse Plaza is a joint venture with The Artery Organization and Arlington County. With two buildings surrounding a stop on the Metro rail system, the complex will house Arlington County government, a seven-screen theater, shops, underground parking, apartments, and a hotel.

The Charles E. Smith Companies own, build, and manage its properties, developments that have come to dominate the commercial real estate world of metropolitan Washington and northern Virginia. In architecture, design, and construction technology, its developments set the style and tone for the region. Smith management offers full services, including on-site administrative and engineering personnel, certified property management personnel, computerized preventive maintenance, 24-hour emergency response center, electronic security access control system, and ongoing inspection programs for housekeeping, HVAC, roofs, elevators, concrete/structure, grounds/landscaping, energy, and fire/security.

In creating its environments for living, working, and recreation, The Charles E. Smith Companies have virtually created a life-style—an up-tempo, upscale, uptown life-style that seems ideally suited for the last decade of the twentieth century, and beyond.

The newest venture at Charles E. Smith is Worldgate, a mixed-use development now under construction on a 94-acre site next to Dulles International Airport.

SOFTWARE AG OF NORTH AMERICA, INC.

John Norris Maguire, founder and chairman of Software AG. Photo by Toby Marquez

The people at Software AG of North America, headquartered in Reston, Virginia, are actively engaged in the advanced aspects of a business that hardly existed just two decades ago. The company is among the international elite in the highly competitive business of producing computer software products that help business people find solutions for complex information management problems.

Software AG is a worldwide leader in application systems technologies, tools, and methodologies. It is an international cooperative affiliation of two organizations with offices and installations throughout the world. Software AG of North America, Inc., is headquartered in Reston, Virginia. Software AG is based

in Darmstadt, West Germany.

Originally formed in 1972 to market products developed by Software AG (Darmstadt), Software AG of North America has exclusive marketing rights for these products and for its own products in the United States and internationally. Software AG (Darmstadt) exclusively markets its own products and products developed by Software AG of North America in Western Europe and throughout the Middle East.

The founder and chairman of the board of Software AG of North America is John Norris Maguire. A graduate of the University of Rhode Island and the Massachusetts Institute of Technology, Maguire started his professional career with Raytheon, designing computer-controlled fire-control systems for missiles.

His subsequent employers included M.I.T., Lockheed Missiles and Space Company, and Consolidated

Analysis Centers, Inc., where he supervised the development of a multibillion-character socioeconomic data bank and associated software for the Department of Commerce.

Maguire founded Software AG of North America in February 1972 to introduce the ADABAS Data Base Management System to the Western Hemisphere and the Far East. ADABAS, created by Software AG (Darmstadt), is now ranked among the top one percent of all software products. Since its introduction, his company has continually produced technologically advanced software products for the integration of data base management, data communications, office automation, and applications development.

In 1976 Maguire introduced COM-PLETE, a data communications system. Within one year of its introduction, sales of COM-PLETE topped one million dollars. In 1978 Maguire introduced NATURAL, the first end-user interactive data base language.

The product mix offered by Software AG now also includes:

PREDICT, an active, on-line data dictionary that operated with ADABAS and NATURAL to organize, control, and securely store business information.

NET-PASS, a powerful session management tool for multiple on-line environments.

COM-POSE, a central communication management tool for terminal networks controlled by time-sharing systems.

SUPER NATURAL, an interactive, menu-driven application generator designed for use by end-users.

CON-NECT, an integrated office automation system with text and document processing, electronic mail, and schedule management.

Software AG's product design philosophy is strongly oriented to the requirements of end-users—providing an integrated set of information processing tools designed to meet all levels of business needs. The firm works closely with end-users, whether they be experienced data-processing professionals, executive decision makers, or production and clerical personnel.

Software AG's new corporate headquarters is planned for completion in August 1988.

The company recognized early in its history that in the software business, the service and support it provided with its products were as important as the products themselves. As a result, it created a system of project management and operations designed to help clients achieve the maximum benefits of their information resources.

Toward that end, Software AG operates customer training and support centers throughout the world to ensure successful implementation and ongoing use of its products. Simultaneously, an extensive network of active user groups provides two-way communications between users and product development teams. An annual international Software AG Users' Conference now brings together more than 2,000 of the firm's clients.

In simpler business terms, that all adds up to fiscal-year 1987 revenues exceeding $67 million. Worldwide revenues for Software AG products surpassed $200 million. The firm's base of more than 2,600 clients include many of the *Fortune* 1,000 companies representing all major industries and many state, federal, and foreign government agencies. The Software AG companies have more than 60 regional offices in North and South America, Western Europe, the Orient, the Middle East, Australia, and Africa.

Software AG's future product development plans are as ambitious as its past accomplishments. The firm is ac-tively pursuing advanced technologies including artificial intelligence systems that are not yet practical for most users, but show promise of becoming so. In many of these areas the major theoretical problems have already been solved, and the company is now seeking practical applications.

In its first 15 years Software AG has done a great deal to advance the state of software technology. In return, technology has been very good indeed to Software AG.

TECHNOLOGY APPLICATIONS, INC.

Technology Applications, Inc., is a rapidly growing firm providing professional and technical services to the Department of Defense and other government agencies. TAI was established in 1979 by James I. Chatman; from the start the company concentrated on defense engineering problems and information and management systems—knowledge work requiring technical skills and management expertise. Today TAI fulfills contracts with civilian agencies and develops, deploys, and maintains major complex military systems and related support systems for the Department of Defense. Chatman's company, like his career in the Air Force, was built on his commitment to excellence.

TAI has grown from the initiative of its founder to an organization of more than 850 employees at the start of 1988. The talent and initiative of its people are the company's strongest assets. TAI looks for talented people with enthusiasm and a desire to be involved. In return, TAI has offered opportunity and challenge in a number of career fields.

In the area of information systems, TAI personnel apply sophisticated computer resources to develop comprehensive and interactive schedules, budget and cost analyses, and various other tracking systems. Application of these systems allows enormous amounts of data to be integrated, assimilated, and manipulated to examine alternatives. One government operation that uses these services is the Army's Worldwide Military Command and Control Information System. This system is used by the president and the Joint Chiefs of Staff in directing and communicating with the nation's strategic forces. TAI engineers are responsible for many levels of technical support, including software verification and validation, communications systems design, and information system hardware and software transition planning.

TAI provides contract support to all branches of the military, not just the Army. On one contract, which affects three of these services, the firm is supporting the development of the V-22 Osprey, a tilt-rotor aircraft being developed for the Navy, Air Force, and Marine Corps for multimission applications. Company engineers assist in developing aircraft specifications, analyze support requirements, and develop computer models for scheduling program tasks, testing, and evaluation. At the Navy's Pacific Missile Test Center in California,

the firm provides engineering and data support to the Armament Systems Division. TAI engineers are engaged in performance and failure analyses for all Navy in-service armament systems.

For the fiscal year ending April 30, 1988, the company's annual revenue was $60 million, and TAI personnel were working on 150 contracts for 24 government agencies. But there were early years of struggle in getting TAI off the ground. The firm was in operation for a year and a half before it earned a profit. Initial contracts were short-term task orders; gaps between contracts created a financial burden because certain key technical staff had to be retained between tasks to assure customers that the company could start work immediately with skilled technical personnel when a new task was awarded. The firm also needed to move into larger office space as more people were hired. This was the start of TAI's expansion from one office to the 42 locations it has today throughout the United States and overseas.

The first major step in the company's expansion was made in 1983, when an operation to provide shipboard alteration and installation teams to the

James I. Chatman, president and chief executive officer of Technology Applications, Inc.

TAI's board of directors are (standing) Dale Dumas, Roland M. Brown, and (seated) Mae Morris-Chatman, James I. Chatman, and Frederick D. Cooke, Jr.

Navy was established in Norfolk. The Navy relies on contractors to help maintain its fleet at the highest state of operational and material readiness. Upgrades of combat systems, electronics, and other systems are essential to fleet operations. TAI personnel are experts in hull, mechanical, and electrical repair support; sheet-metal and pipe fitting; welding; and electronics. They are also responsible for procurement, inventory management, and material control. An example of this work is the contract the company has to install and upgrade the large shipboard nontactical computer systems.

The following year TAI opened another office in Virginia—in Hampton. The newly won contract was with NASA's Langley Research Center. TAI engineers use computer-aided design techniques to research and develop computerized schematics to document Langley's wind-tunnel system. As part of NASA's safety engineering and pressure system recertification program, the firm assesses the effects of any structural degradation and enhancements needed throughout the wind-tunnel system and provides recommendations for corrective action.

In 1985 integrated logistics support became a business area for the company. Integrated logistics support (ILS) incorporates many technical disciplines involved in maintaining and supporting complex defense systems throughout their life cycles. Developing plans, tracking spare parts, managing engineering changes and upgrades, providing critical maintenance and repair, training technicians, and documenting all aspects of weapons systems are aspects of ILS. In 1985 the firm received a contract to provide ILS support to the Air Force F-16 fighter aircraft at Wright Patterson Air Force Base in Dayton, Ohio. TAI analysts determine F-16 support and training equipment requirements, verify technical manuals, develop data packages, identify aircraft and support equipment calibration requirements, and analyze maintenance data. The Dayton operation has grown—winning additional contracts, including one under which company

logisticians are implementing a TAI-developed system to track time-compliance technical orders for the B-1 Bomber.

The Navy has also awarded TAI contracts using the firm's logistics expertise. These contracts are part of the foundation for TAI's offices in Arlington (Crystal City), Virginia. TAI logisticians assist in developing logistics support analyses and provide supply support inputs for program, technical, and budget documents for Mine Countermeasures Combat Systems and for the Auxiliary and Special Mission Ships Program.

In 1986 the company moved to its new headquarters in Alexandria. This 78,000-square-foot facility houses both the corporate staff and certain operating divisions. As TAI grew, corporate functions such as business development and human resources were expanded to serve the firm's growth.

It is essential that a federal contractor have specialized expertise in contract and fiscal areas. Accordingly, the Finance and Contracts Department

TAI develops technical manuals and documentation for major defense systems as part of its contract work with the government.

has always been an important part of the company's success. A conservative fiscal philosophy has been followed from the start. The first employee Jim Chatman hired was a financial executive who was also a certified public accountant. In the beginning, he was a part-time evening employee; today he is a member of the board of directors and the executive vice-president. By 1988, in addition to Finance and Contracts, the company is also served by a legal department and by Public Affairs and Communications.

A well-run corporation has no real growth limit except those limits imposed by the market. The professional and technical services market is of considerable size, and it is expected that this Virginia company will continue to grow and contribute to a healthy state business base.

THE JOURNAL NEWSPAPERS

The Times Journal Company's 17-acre office and printing/distribution facility in Springfield's Shirley Industrial Park. From this site, plus additional editorial offices in Maryland, the five Journal Newspapers serve the outlying suburban communities.

The Journal Newspapers and the regions they serve—the communities of Montgomery and Prince George's counties in Maryland, and the northern Virginia areas that include the City of Alexandria, and Fairfax and Arlington counties.

The Journal Newspapers and other publishing, printing, and telemarketing divisions of the parent Times Journal Company occupy a 17-acre office and printing/distribution facility in Springfield's Shirley Industrial Park. From this site, located at the intersection of interstates 95 and 495, plus additional editorial offices in Maryland, the five Journal Newspapers serve the suburban communities of Montgomery and Prince George's counties in Maryland and the northern Virginia jurisdictions of the City of Alexandria, and Fairfax and Arlington counties.

The Journals began as a response to the unprecedented growth taking place during the early 1970s in the suburban communities surrounding the District of Columbia. With this growth, the towns and cities in northern Virginia began to emerge as an independent political force and a separate, potentially lucrative consumer market. As the suburbs developed their own distinct personality, the need for and value of a newspaper totally devoted to suburban coverage became more and more obvious.

In 1971 Army Times Publishing Company was a small Washington-based independent firm producing weekly newspapers for military consumers. The management of the company was considering various alternatives for diversifying their business, and the potential for a suburban newspaper intrigued them. Editorially, the time was ripe for a newspaper that would reflect and speak to the information needs that made northern Virginians so different from Washingtonians. And, from a marketing standpoint, such a vehicle would provide a selective advertising medium for retailers to reach and sell to those big-spending families.

In December 1971 the company purchased *The Alexandria Journal,* a small weekly with about 2,000 paid subscribers. During the next four years that single newspaper was joined by *The Arlington Journal* and *The Fairfax Journal* in Virginia, and by *The Montgomery Journal* and *The Prince George's Journal* in suburban Maryland, forming a ring of editorial and advertising coverage around the nation's capital.

The growth of the suburban newspapers, coupled with the need for greater control over the production of the military weeklies, moved the firm to build its own printing plant. That facility, in Springfield, Virginia, stands today as one of the most modern, technically advanced newspaper production and distribution operations in the world.

The three eight-unit Goss Metro presses operate on a 24-hour, seven-day-a-week schedule, producing some of the finest four-color newsprint seen today. Their daily output includes not only The Journals, but an impressive list of publications for other firms as well.

By 1977 The Journal Newspapers had expanded from weekly to twice-weekly frequency. And in 1981 a significant event led to the growth stage that brought The Journals to their present size.

After years of struggling as the metropolitan area's "second daily," *The Washington Star* finally gave up the battle and ceased publication in the fall of 1981. Although it didn't exactly fit their schedule, The Journal Newspapers management viewed this as the most obvious opportunity for the suburban papers to expand and fill the void resulting from the demise of *The Star.* Experience had shown that whenever such a void was created, someone usually moved in to take advantage of it. The best way to prevent an outsider from adding new competition to the market, of course, was to fill the niche that existed. Thus, in August 1981, The Journals became suburban Washington's daily, Monday-through-Friday newspapers.

Today the five Journal Newspapers have become highly respected members of the suburban Washington

community. For more than 150,000 subscribers, The Journals fill the information void left by the world and national focus of the metropolitan dailies and area broadcast media. As these communities have grown and prospered, their residents have become increasingly aware of and concerned about their local government, their schools, their roads and zoning laws, their taxes. And they turn to The Journal Newspapers as a means of involving themselves in the decisions that affect them and their families.

In such areas as the burgeoning suburban business community, the high school and youth sports leagues, and the local political arena, The Journals have established a solid, loyal readership by offering in-depth coverage day after day, not just when the more sensational stories merit the attention of the broadcast media and *The Washington Post*. Readers count on this continuity to keep them in touch with and in control of the events that affect their daily lives.

The impressive business success of The Journal Newspapers is the result

of their having established the proper niche for themselves in a market dominated by *The Washington Post*. Although they cannot offer advertisers the mass readership and coverage of the metro newspaper, The Journals do represent an important opportunity for businesses. Advertisers can efficiently gain exposure to a very select segment of the metro Washington market. In terms of home ownership, household income, education level, investment patterns, leisure activities and spending habits, the newspapers' readers are the

The newsroom at Journal headquarters in Springfield houses the staff of The Fairfax Journal, The Arlington Journal, *and* The Alexandria Journal. *The two Maryland newspapers have separate editorial offices.*

most active and attractive consumers that Washington has to offer.

Advertisers know that because of the quality of these newspapers and the interests and life-styles of their readers, The Journals enjoy loyal, thorough attention from the suburban population they serve.

The Journal printing plant features three eight-unit Goss Metro presses. In 1988 this facility became the first commercial user of the state-of-the-art Goss Colorliner press.

DAN RIVER INC.

One of Dan River Inc.'s manufacturing facilities in Danville, Virginia.

Dan River Inc. is one of America's largest and most successful textile companies. Ever since the six founders of the corporation gathered together in 1882, the firm has been a pioneer in textile manufacturing production and innovation, and continues to be a leader in the industry more than 100 years later.

The business was chartered in 1882 under the name The Riverside Cotton Mills, producing cloth and yarn. Original equipment consisted of 2,240 spindles and 100 looms, and the first product was a plaid fabric.

As early as 1890 the company began its construction of new mills and the purchase of others, starting what has been an enormous amount of acquisition and diversification throughout its

history. In 1895 Riverside formed Dan River Power and Manufacturing Company, and in 1909 the two merged to form The Riverside and Dan River Mills, Incorporated.

The original product of the company, a 27-inch plaid fabric, was followed in the early 1900s by chambray and gingham. Dan River then experimented with just about every make of cloth during the 1920s and 1930s, and in 1940 shifted from manufacturing predominantly cotton to selling synthetic fibers such as rayon, as well as wool and worsted yarn. During World War II a

more coarse material was required for the government, and cottons and chambrays for uniforms and other military needs were produced. A shift back to finer apparel goods took place in the postwar years, emphasizing style and fashion, and today Dan River has expanded into side products such as floor coverings, beddings, velours, and polypropylene yarn.

Dan River became famous nationwide in 1919 when president H.R. Fitzgerald installed the principle of Industrial Democracy, a system modeled on the federal government and emphasizing mutual interests and better relations between management and labor. A constitution was drawn up, executive and legislative bodies formed, and bills were resolved concerning hourly wages, health benefits, and any other problems or grievances. This plan was certainly unique and provided a better way for workers to communicate their views to management.

Along with diversification and expansion, high-quality products, and current management procedures, promotional and advertising techniques also started after World War II, making Dan River more competitive and providing higher sales and major success.

Technology and machinery has evolved continually from the company's original form of equipment. Dan River Inc. has adopted the revolutionary changes in textile technology, resulting in higher productivity, greater efficiency, and lower costs.

The firm spent $190 million to improve facilities and equipment in the 1970s, and in 1979 reached the highest profit in its history, totaling more than $22 million in net earnings with a sales volume of nearly $600 million. Dan River Inc. has obtained the optimum in excellence in quality, research, productivity, and marketing, and intends to continue its earned success into its second century.

Dan River Inc.'s corporate headquarters is also located in Danville.

THE JEFFERSON SHERATON HOTEL

Start with an opulent, turn-of-the-century hotel, designed to reflect the finest traditions of southern grace and hospitality. Remodel it in the 1980s to meet the demanding expectations of contemporary business travelers. Provide it with new engineering and computerized communications. Have it managed by one of the world's finest hospitality organizations. Give every room a mini-bar, color television, and three telephones. That is Richmond's Jefferson Sheraton Hotel.

Major Lewis Ginter, a New Yorker who moved to Richmond in 1842, was a merchant, banker, newspaperman, Confederate officer, and tobacco tycoon. A world traveler (he crossed the Atlantic more than 30 times), Ginter wanted to give Richmond a grand hotel in the tradition he had experienced in European capitals. His hotel opened in 1895; it reopened, completely restored, in 1986.

His architects, Carrere and Hastings, designed a "beaux arts eclectic" structure whose twin clock towers became a Richmond landmark. Recognized both for its architectural distinction and for its place in Virginia social history, The Jefferson Hotel was elected to the National Register of Historic Places in 1969. The marble statue of Thomas Jefferson that graces the Palm Court was created by Edward V. Valentine; it stood in the Rotunda at the University of Virginia before it was brought to the hotel.

The Jefferson survived two serious fires, but then succumbed to neglect. It closed in 1980, and many Richmond residents feared its seemingly inevitable demolition. Then, remarkably, it was bought by a Richmond-based group of investors and remodeled. Now its 274 guest rooms (including 26 suites) and nearly 24,000 square feet of meeting space once again offer guests a taste of grand style and the grand tradition.

The refurbished Rotunda carries the soaring spirit of its creation, its origi-

In 1986 The Jefferson Sheraton Hotel was reopened and completely restored and refurbished. These two views of the outside of the hotel attest to its grandeur and elegance.

Major Lewis Ginter opened up this hotel in 1895 in the style and tradition of the grand European hotels of the time. Pictured here is the Rotunda as its looks today.

nal stained-glass skylight hanging 70 feet above the new carpet, custom woven in England for The Jefferson Sheraton.

Local legend has it that the grand staircase of The Jefferson Hotel served as the model for the staircase of Tara, the plantation house in *Gone With the Wind.* Certainly Rhett Butler and Scarlett O'Hara would feel at home here, although federal safety regulations required the recent installation of a hand railing down the center. Also, brass sculptures have replaced the live alligators that once lived in the Palm Court fountain, although members of the staff

repeat the hotel's legends about various encounters between guests and errant alligators.

Presidents William Henry Harrison, William McKinley, Woodrow Wilson, Calvin Coolidge, Theodore Roosevelt, and Franklin D. Roosevelt have all stayed at The Jefferson. So have countless celebrities and entertainers, including Charles Lindbergh, John D. Rockefeller, Henry Ford, Sarah Bernhardt, Charlie Chaplin, the Barrymores, Elvis Presley, and a movie actor named Ronald Reagan.

Now future generations of celebrities—and less celebrated business people and travelers—will have the opportunity to stay at The Jefferson Sheraton Hotel and share in its grace and traditions.

STATE FARM INSURANCE
EASTERN REGIONAL OFFICE

The Eastern Regional Office of State Farm Insurance is located just outside of Charlottesville, where it serves policyholders in Virginia and North Carolina.

The Eastern Regional Office of the national firm of State Farm Insurance is located just outside Charlottesville. More than 800 employees work in 4.5 acres of modern office space, providing auto, fire, life, and health insurance to State Farm policyholders in Virginia and North Carolina. Built on a 65-acre piece of land once owned by Thomas Jefferson's father, the office was designed by Ellerbe and Associates in Bloomington, Minnesota, and constructed by R.E. Lee and Son, Inc., of Charlottesville in 1979.

State Farm was founded by George J. Mercherle in 1922 in Bloomington, Illinois, and is the nation's largest auto and fire insurer. The Eastern Regional Office, one of 25 regional offices nationwide, was established in Charlottesville in 1952. At the time the 245 employees served the states of Virginia, Maryland, Delaware, West Virginia, and Washington, D.C.

In 1952 there were 119,965 policies in the Eastern Region. By the end of 1987 there were more than 2.3 million. Computers, dedicated employees, and the foresight of management, more than anything else, have helped State Farm keep up with such a large volume of business. The firm began using computers in the 1950s and continues to make machines do the work, wherever possible, to increase efficiency and improve service to its policyholders. Even the office mail is carried from place to place in the building by a robot.

Regional office employees work closely with the nearly 800 State Farm agents in the region. They underwrite applications in all four lines of insurance. They issue policies, make changes in coverages upon request, and take care of all billing. There are also departments to handle personnel, training, and management planning functions. Most claims are handled in the 34 claim offices scattered throughout Virginia and North Carolina where drive-in claim service is provided.

State Farm recently celebrated its 35th anniversary in Charlottesville and among the celebrants were 13 employees who have worked at State Farm for the entire 35 years. Many more have been with the company 20 years or longer. Despite its size and corporate status, State Farm prides itself on being a "family company." There have never been any layoffs at State Farm, even in times of recession. The current president of the firm, Edward B. Rust, Jr., took over that position when his father died in 1985. Among the employees at the regional office are husbands and wives, brothers and sisters, and parents and children.

State Farm Insurance is proud to be a good neighbor in Charlottesville and to its policyholders in Virginia and North Carolina.

SHELDON LUMBER COMPANY, INC.

Sidney Gaylord Sheldon, founder of the Sheldon Lumber Company.

Sidney Gaylord Sheldon's sons (from left) H.G. Sheldon, O.C. Sheldon, and W.E. Sheldon all helped make Sheldon Lumber Company what it is today.

Sidney Gaylord Sheldon entered the lumber business more than a half-century ago. Following his family's move to Virginia from Wisconsin, he worked a large tract of timber with his son, H.G., in Bacon's Castle for a year and a half. Two sons, W.E. and O.C., also worked directly or indirectly with their father, and by 1944 they had all decided to join forces in one company. From the Harwood Tract—site of Busch Gardens today—they cut several million feet. Two years later they moved to their present location in Toano, just north of Williamsburg, officially incorporating in 1947 as Sheldon Lumber Company.

The previous year a planing mill had been installed, with James "Jimmy" Duke supervising. Sheldon operated several small sawmills nearby, picking up and moving when the supply was exhausted.

After World War II, when most sales were to clients further north, S.G. treated himself to a shiny new Packard. In one year alone he clocked more than 40,000 miles, creating what family members recollect as a "super clientele."

Eventually the northern market pattern changed. Today's focus is on a local territory, generally within 30 to 40 miles of Toano, with some exceptions to furniture factories in North Carolina.

Even as recently as the 1950s horses were used to stack the logs to the small sawmills. This method of working the timber continued until a large stationary mill was installed in 1961. Logs were then cut on the timber tract and shipped to the central mill. Today's workers cut the timber with power saws, loading the logs on expensive machines that transport them to a loader, which sets them on trucks for the trip to the central mill. This mill produces no waste; all by-products are vital—sawdust, shavings, chips, and bark.

During the early 1960s the company played an active role in the formation of the Lumber Manufacturers' Association of Virginia, with Wesley Sheldon serving as its first president.

In 1985 the logging division was sold to brothers Robert A. and Keith A. Sheldon. The only family members currently directly employed are stockholders Wesley, Howard G. Sr., Howard G. Jr., and Keith's wife, Judy. A streamlined staff of about 70 runs the operation.

Early in the 1980s Sheldon Lumber Company expanded into the retail business, opening a store in Toano. A second store followed in Providence Forge in 1986, and a new showroom in 1987. Third-generation manager Howard Sheldon has incorporated ideas from his background in the building business, computerizing many administrative operations. The firm recently added a sales force; its previous expertise was in making lumber. Sales in 1987 were their highest to date, with the new showroom contributing to a 30-percent increase over the preceding year.

H.G. Sheldon, Jr. (center), a third-generation family member involved in the Sheldon Lumber business, stands between his father, H.G. (left), and W.E. Sheldon (right).

SPERRY MARINE INC.

Elmer Sperry, the great inventor who earned nearly 400 patents in his lifetime, began the Sperry Gyroscope Company in 1910 with one employee, no capital, and a few ideas. Several decades and a few names later, Sperry Marine Inc. is a world leader in the design and manufacture of navigation, communication, management, and control systems for defense and commercial customers in the aerospace and marine markets.

Although the company began in Brooklyn and later moved to Great Neck, New York, the world headquarters for Sperry Marine is now Charlottesville, Virginia. The firm operates district offices nationwide, facilities in Europe and Brazil, and more than 200 sales and service offices around the world.

Sperry completed the first gyrocompass in the summer of 1911. The Navy tested it on the USS *Delaware*, and soon ordered eight more.

Elmer Sperry's successful company has had many owners over the years. In 1933 Sperry Gyroscope became a part of the Sperry Corporation, along with the Ford Instrument Co. In 1955 the firm was sold and renamed Sperry Rand Corporation. Sperry Rand decided to

The Sperry Marine RASCAR Rasterscan Radar with its unique touch-sensitive screen.

decentralize the gyroscope plant and established branches in Minnesota, Arizona, and Charlottesville.

The Charlottesville branch, named Sperry Piedmont Company, opened in 1956 in a 75,000-square-foot facility with a few employees. Later that year it moved to its current location on Seminole Trail. Sperry Piedmont was renamed the Sperry Marine Systems Division in 1967. The name was modified again in 1984 to the Marine Systems Division of Aerospace and Marine Group of the Sperry Corporation. The company lost "Rand" in 1979, the same year Charlottesville built extra laboratory and warehouse space.

In 1986 Sperry Corporation merged with Burroughs and became UNISYS. The Charlottesville division, along with others, was put up for sale.

Sometimes events really do travel full circle before they come to a halt, and the most recent purchase of Sperry would seem to indicate that it has finally come home. Sperry Marine is now a wholly owned subsidiary of Newport News Shipbuilding, which built the U.S.S. *Delaware,* the recipient of the first gyro compass. Newport News Shipbuilding is a Tenneco company.

Edward J. Campbell, president and chief executive officer of Newport News Shipbuilding, said of the purchase,

Worldwide headquarters for Sperry Marine Inc. is located on Seminole Trail in Charlottesville, Virginia.

"Now we have a better shot at providing our customers with 'life-cycle' services—providing them with almost everything from a ship's design to its on-board navigational systems to its eventual deactivation."

Sperry Marine is the fourth-largest company in the Charlottesville area, with 75 percent of its 1,300 employees located at the 264,350-square-foot headquarters facilities. Its in-house capabilities range from developmental engineering to manufacturing and testing.

Twice in recent years Sperry Marine Inc. has been honored by the Defense Contracts Administration Services for quality excellence. The company continues its dedication to safety at sea, and to the national defense program with two of its newest products, RASCAR and Guardian Star. The RASCAR Radar/ARPA permits the operator to get the range and bearing on a target ship by simply touching the ship's symbol on a TV-like screen. Guardian Star is an electronic surveillance system that identifies potentially threatening vessels.

THE MARTIN AGENCY, INC.

"There's nothing like it on Madison Avenue." That is the slogan for The Martin Agency, Inc., Richmond's nationally respected communications company. With 200 employees and annual billings exceeding $100 million, The Martin Agency is the largest advertising agency in Virginia and among the top firms for creative excellence in advertising nationwide.

David N. Martin founded the company in 1965 with a staff of three and two clients. The firm's current client list includes, among others, two divisions of General Motors, Alcatel Network Systems Division/Transcom (formerly ITT Telecommunications), FMC Corporation, CSX Corporation, Barnett Banks, Life Insurance Company of Virginia, Ethyl Corporation, Virginia Power, Reynolds Aluminum Recycling, Signet Banks, and such travel and tourism accounts as Palm Beach County, Florida, Kings Dominion Theme Park, and the Henry Ford Museum & Greenfield Village.

One long-term client, The Virginia Division of Tourism, is back with The Martin Agency after several years with other firms. In 1969 The Martin Agency launched the state's "Virginia is for Lovers" advertising campaign. Widely imi-

The executive force behind The Martin Agency, Inc., are (from left) Harry M. Jacobs, chairman and chief creative officer; Donald R. Just, president and chief operating officer; David N. Martin, founder and chairman of the executive committee; and Mike Hughes, vice-chairman and creative director.

The Martin Agency developed this, one of its most successful and well-known ad campaigns, "Virginia is for Lovers."

tated throughout the nation, "Virginia is for Lovers" brought national recognition to both the Commonwealth and the agency.

In 1979 The Martin Agency moved to its specially renovated headquarters in the former Elks building on the southwest corner of Grace Street and Allen Avenue. Part of the Monument Avenue Historic District, the gracious Richmond landmark was built in 1910. In 1985 the agency expanded into the historic Shenandoah Apartment building across Allen Avenue from the Elks Building.

The Martin Agency specializes in advertising. Associated with it are Martin Public Relations; The Stenrich Group, specializing in direct-response marketing; Telmark, a Yellow Pages marketing firm; and Alan Newman Research. Together they comprise an organization that is one of the largest communications firms in the Southeast, and among the top 75 nationwide.

"This is a creatively driven organization, but features a balanced approach to marketing communications," says Martin, founder of the agency and chairman of the executive committee. "We view each ad in every campaign as an event, as an opportunity to boost attention and interest leading to sales."

The agency balances creativity with planning and strategic thinking. Other company executives include president Don Just; Harry Jacobs, chairman; and Mike Hughes, vice-chairman and creative director. Both Martin and Jacobs are members of the Virginia Communications Hall of Fame.

No longer a regional agency, The Martin Agency attracts 80 percent of its billings from out-of-state clients, and increasing attention from national publications. ADWEEK, Advertising Age, and Madison Avenue's own hometown paper, The New York Times, have tagged The Martin Agency, Inc., as among the nation's top performers. In 1987 the agency was named the Hottest Agency in the Nation by both Ad Age and ADWEEK for its unparalleled growth in 1986, the highest of any ad agency in the nation.

433

FIRST COLONY COFFEE & TEA CO., INC.

The predecessor company, James G. Gill Company, started operation in Norfolk at what was formerly Water Street and today is the Waterside Festival Marketplace.

The story of First Colony Coffee & Tea Co., Inc., is a continuing four-generation romance with quality foods. From the beginning the firm and its families have made the exotic appeal of fine coffees, select teas, and specialty foods an integral part of their business. And a sense of that family spirit runs company-wide—even in the packaging department where only three families make up some three-quarters of that part of the operation.

With an emphasis on personalized attention to its customers, whether large or small, both brokers and family members have traditionally approached their accounts as if they were friends. Headquartered in Norfolk, First Colony is the only company roasting specialty coffees on both coasts.

For the first exposure of coffee in the New World, a look back in time reveals that Captain John Smith had been introduced to the warm brew when he traveled to Arabia in the 1590s. There is speculation that he brought it to Virginia in 1607. Contention and competition for shares of the lucrative coffee-growing industry kept pace with the rapid spread of coffee drinking in Europe and America. In the eighteenth-century coffeehouses of Europe and the colonies, the brew fueled discussions of politics, religion, and the day's events. By the nineteenth century coffee had spread from aristocratic and middle-class tables to those of the working class.

Tea, meanwhile, had also become embroiled in politics in the colonies, subject to such heavy taxes that colonists dumped 342 chests of tea into Boston Harbor in 1773. Though consumption declined drastically, the first merchant ship under the U.S. flag headed for China to fill its holds with the treasured leaves.

First Colony's story actually begins roughly two centuries later, with James G. Gill, the son of a Scottish immigrant who had come to the United States in 1838. Gill's father was a naval architect who performed the redesign work on the *Merrimac* for her conversion into the *Virginia,* the famous ironclad ship of the Civil War. Born in Old Point Comfort, Virginia, Gill was the first in the family to become involved in the coffee and tea trades. During the early 1870s the family moved to Portsmouth, exporting tobacco for a living. In 1877 Gill traveled to London to make contacts in the tea business, importing tea and fancy groceries to the states.

In 1902 he founded the James G. Gill Company in Norfolk, at what once was Water Street and today is the Waterside Festival Marketplace. The firm handled specialty food items, including spices and rice. Located in a port city, the company grew naturally, thanks to access to so many international traders.

Other family members became involved over the years, and the firm prospered into the middle of the twentieth century. Gill's great-grandsons, J. Gill Brockenbrough, Jr., and Thomas J. Brockenbrough, developed a wholesale business as an outgrowth of presenting friends coffee gifts during the holidays. By 1977 they had created an independent corporation named after Virginia's status as the first English colony in the New World. First Colony Coffee and Tea Co. was founded as an independent specialty line, returning to its roots, with sales to gourmet shops, department stores, and other fine retail outlets. Gill became the company's president and Thomas its secretary/treasurer.

First Colony has traded with some of the same suppliers of select high-grown coffees for years, with roughly 50 national origins, including India, the Old Dutch houses in Indonesia, Costa Rica, Brazil, Ethiopia, the Middle East, and others. The firm purchases decaffeinated green coffees from Switzerland and West Germany in both conventional European and patented Swiss water decaffeinated forms. These beans are then roasted and blended by First Colony. To assure the freshest-possible product, there is a same-day shipment policy from both coasts.

J. Gill Brockenbrough, Jr., president of First Colony Coffee & Tea Co., Inc.

Much of the business has remained the same throughout more than 85 years of operation. The way the beans themselves are handled has changed very little, though the company now utilizes up-to-date communication systems and a computer to track orders from raw product to retailer's shelf.

Next comes the tasting process, something of a family ritual. This is the heart of developing a quality product, since machines cannot be an adequate substitute. A grinder, roaster, and coffee brewer are among the essential tools; a large, revolving table with at least six cups occupies a central position in the room. The same cupping table has been used by the family for four generations, since 1902. First the coffee beans are roasted, then ground to a powder but not to granule form, in order to expose every element of the coffee. Two or more people are involved in each testing, for both aroma and taste. Gill Brockenbrough himself personally blends and taste-tests all coffees, no matter what their point of origin.

And then, finally, the coffees are roasted on Jabez Burns roasting equipment on the fifth floor of the 1923 plant location. They are roasted until achieving just the right color, not for a fixed amount of time.

As the company grew, the brothers Brockenbrough also purchased the family firm's stock. They built a plant in San Francisco to offer national distribution of their specialty coffees. At the same time tea became second in popularity to coffee in the United States. Worldwide it is number one. In recent years, since trade has been reopened with China, First Colony has focused more attention on developing the tea trade between China and the United States. The company plans to offer the finest Chinese teas available, blended and packaged in China for marketing in America.

Tea is the firm's fastest-growing segment at present. Fine leaf teas are sold both in bulk and as packaged teas. First Colony maintains the widest selection of leaf teas stored in warehouses in this country, inventorying at least 50 different kinds at any given time.

As the interest in specialty foods has also increased, First Colony has diversified with new divisions. Its Virginia Provisions Smokehouse, situated on the banks of the James River in Lynchburg, combines traditional methods of food preparation with sophisticated technology. Smoked poultry items are the mainstay there, with all meats cured and individually processed in small batches. Each product is then hickory-smoked, slowly and naturally, with no artificial flavoring or spray. It is then flash-frozen and shipped, ready to serve.

Virginia Provisions recognizes that the state has a tradition of hospitality that is closely associated with fine foods. Thus, it produces traditional Virginia products, such as smoked Cornish hens, whole turkeys, and turkey breast, some served with sauces such as cranberry champagne, brandied apricot, chinoise, and provincial cream.

New additions for the First Colony specialty food line are the Woodson's Mill products: white cornmeal, whole wheat flour, three-grain pancake mix, old-fashioned country-style grits, apple butter, and apple cider. Woodson's Mill is a historic water-powered gristmill in Nelson County, dating back to 1780. More than 135 years ago farmers created a white-corn hybrid in this scenic area on the Piney River near Lowesville.

Little has changed in 85 years in the way First Colony handles the coffee beans. Roasting, grinding, and testing all are done at the same facility that has housed the plant since 1923.

That sweetly flavored corn became the basis for what is considered the finest white cornmeal available in the country.

Overall, this moderate-size company has capitalized on a major change in popular tastes and attitudes toward food, enabling it to move to a predominant position in the coffee industry and to increase its influence in fine foods. In modern times coffee has become second only to oil in total dollar value on the world commodities market. Meanwhile, Americans in general have acquired more sophisticated tastes than in the previous two decades, when interest in regional foods virtually disappeared. With a growing appreciation of finer coffees and other specialty foods—that often were imported items in the past—the market for specialty coffees is growing.

Though coffee consumption in the United States in general has declined for the past quarter-century, the speciality segment of the industry has soared and appears to have a vibrant future. First Colony Coffee & Tea Co., Inc., plans to assure its quality.

CENTRAL TELEPHONE COMPANY OF VIRGINIA

Central Telephone Company of Virginia, a subsidiary of Chicago-based Centel Corporation, traces its roots back to 1878—just two years after the telephone's invention by Alexander Graham Bell.

Centel Corporation is one of the nation's leading telecommunications companies. Centel provides telephone service through nearly 1.4 million customer lines in nine states; serves more than 500,000 cable television customers in seven states; operates cellular mobile telephone services; engineers, installs, and maintains advanced business telecommunications systems and networks with an installed base of nearly 1.2 million lines; provides electric service in two states; and markets a broad range of telecommunications products and services.

In March 1878 the operators of Perry's Photo Gallery in Charlottesville installed a business telephone to connect its office with the local telegraph office. Charlottesville Woolen Mills was also eager to try the new technology and in-

stalled a telephone between its plant on East Market Street and its sales room in town. The University of Virginia soon followed suit with its own line.

Charlottesville's first telephone company, Albemarle Telephone and Telegraph Company, was not formed until 1887. However, *The Jefferson Republic,* one of the town's two newspapers during this era, reported that Charlottesville actually had private telephone lines prior to 1887.

Southern States Utilities Company acquired Albemarle and a competitor in 1927, along with a number of other smaller telephone companies in Virginia. Southern States Utilities Company was, in turn, acquired in 1931, along with 20 other smaller telephone companies in Virginia, West Virginia, and North Carolina, by Central West Public Service Company of Omaha, Nebraska.

The Virginia telephone properties owned by Central West Public Service Company extended from Front Royal in the north down through central Virginia, forging a corridor that included Charlottesville, the company's largest exchange, and terminated in the southernmost part of the state. This group of exchanges formed the nucleus of what was to become Central Telephone Company of Virginia.

By 1936 Central West Public Service Company, the parent corporation, had reorganized and changed the name of its Virginia operations to Virginia Telephone & Telegraph Company. The company continued to extend its service with further mergers and acquisitions. In 1974 Virginia Telephone & Telegraph Company adopted the name Central Telephone Company of Virginia to relate more closely to the name of its parent company, which had been changed to Central Telephone and Utilities Corporation. The parent company changed its name again, to Centel Corporation, in 1982. Central Telephone Company of Virginia serves some 200,000 customers in all or part of 31 Virginia counties. It is the third-largest telephone company operating in Virginia.

Central Telephone Company of Virginia headquarters, Central Telephone's Virginia/North Carolina regional headquarters, and Central Telephone's accounting and data-processing operations for its Virginia, North Carolina, Ohio, and Florida properties are all located in Charlottesville.

Digital technology with miniaturized components and low maintenance makes enhanced state-of-the-art telecommunications available to all.

A modern-day craftsman fuses optical fiber to transmit quality information-age services to the world.

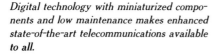

THE COLLEGE OF WILLIAM AND MARY IN VIRGINIA

The College of William and Mary's Sir Christopher Wren Building, designed by the noted seventeenth-century British architect, dates back to 1695 and is now the oldest college building in the country. It is still in use as a classroom building and is the home of the Department of Philosophy.

The College of William and Mary in Virginia, the nation's second-oldest college, is steeped in a tradition of rigorous liberal education. As a modern university, William and Mary remains prominent in the arts and sciences, yet has emerged with graduate and professional studies to prepare tomorrow's leaders for the rapidly changing, complex global business world.

Chartered in 1693 by King William III and Queen Mary II, the college severed formal ties with Britain in 1776, and became state supported in 1906. It became coeducational in 1918, and achieved modern university status in 1967 after conferring its first doctoral degrees. Since then it has become one of the top 25 national universities, according to a poll of college and university presidents. The university currently enrolls about 4,900 undergraduate students and 1,500 graduate and professional students in the College of Arts and Sciences, the School of Business Administration, the School of Education, the School of Marine Science, and the Marshall-Wythe School of Law.

For years the College of William

and Mary has been known for its role as the seat of learning for many of those who shaped the United States in its infancy. The nation's first president was its first American Chancellor, and many creators and signers of the Declaration of Independence and the Constitution, as well as other early presidents—Thomas Jefferson, James Monroe, and John Tyler—were among its alumni, as were many Justices of the U.S. Supreme Court. From those early days to the present, leadership has been a central focus. The prestigious academic distinctions of Phi Beta Kappa and the Honor System of conduct both were founded at William and Mary.

William and Mary, chartered in 1693 by King William III and Queen Mary II, is the second-oldest institution of higher education in the nation. It has become one of the top 25 national universities, and enrolls about 4,900 undergraduate students and 1,500 graduate and professional students.

In 1976 the college was the site of the third presidential debate between Gerald R. Ford and Democratic nominee Jimmy Carter. In 1983 it was the international press center for the Summit of Industrialized Nations, with leaders of the United States, Japan, and several European nations attending.

A formal degree program of business study was launched in 1919. The university now offers the Bachelor and Master of Business Administration degrees and an Executive MBA Program. Among the business school's distinctions is an accounting program ranking in the top 20 nationally by a survey of accounting professors. Recognizing learning as a lifelong process, the Center for Executive Development provides programs designed specifically for middle managers and senior executives.

The university's Bureau of Business Research publishes the monthly *Virginia Business Report,* the only monthly publication with coverage of cities throughout Virginia, including data on nine economic indicators for urban areas as well as statewide analysis.

William and Mary's contribution to Virginia business also extends to programs and research in computer science, physics, and chemistry, leading to new applied science and technological advances. Its School of Marine Science enhances environmental understanding and economic growth through estuarine studies and public policy analysis.

Since its founding nearly 300 years ago William and Mary has sought to develop critical and creative intelligence through which men and women realize their fullest potentials to shape the future of the Commonwealth and the nation.

WESTVACO

Westvaco will celebrate its centennial year in 1988.

Originally the Piedmont Pulp and Paper Company, it was founded by William Luke, a papermaker, who came to America from Scotland in 1852. The first mill was built in West Piedmont, Maryland, which has since changed its name to Luke, Maryland.

Four years after the company was founded, stockholders received their first dividend. They have received returns on their investment every year since then in one of the longest continuous runs of payments of any American company.

Common sense business principles, product innovation, continuous research, management of natural resources, and, most important, experienced, capable people have enabled the firm to evolve into the world-class competitor it is today.

Westvaco's 12 operating divisions, and four domestic and seven foreign subsidiaries in 1986 generated sales of $1.8 billion, exceeding the previous year by 5.2 percent and reaching an all-time record level for the company.

On the basis of sales, *Fortune* magazine ranks Westvaco as 196th of the 500 largest corporations in America. In the forest products industry, Westvaco in 1986 ranked as the 13th-largest company on the basis of annual sales, as well as number of employees—15,110.

The firm's mills at Covington, Virginia.

Westvaco owns a resource base of 1.5 million acres of forestlands located in the South Atlantic states, the Midwest, and Brazil. In addition, the company offers technical assistance to woodland owners who are its neighbors and represent an additional 1.1 million forested acres.

Westvaco has been part of the fabric of Virginia life for nearly 90 years. Today Westvaco's Covington, Virginia, mill and converting, printing, and customer service facilities in Richmond and Low Moor, Virginia, employ more than 2,500 people. In addition, the papermill and outlying wood-processing centers provide a market for woodland owners and some 4,000 independent loggers and sawmillers.

Located in the center of one of the largest hardwood forests in the world, the mill currently has four paper machines producing an average of 1,800 tons of product daily. The newest machine, Number One, is part of a $325-million commitment to improve and expand Westvaco's Bleached Board Division. This machine has enabled the mill to increase its capacity by 42 percent.

Number One machine began operation in February 1986 and reached nearly full capacity in record time. It produced paperboard up to 275 inches wide and is a primary source of Westvaco's major bleached board product, Hi Yield Printkote®.

Westvaco has never believed that growth in production is incompatible with protection of the environment. In conjunction with Westvaco's recent efforts to bring a new paper machine on line, the company invested some $15 million to expand and improve the efficiency of its wastewater-treatment facility, allowing it to expand papermaking operations while significantly reducing the impact on the Jackson River.

The Covington mill's wastewater-treatment plant was the first of its kind in the pulp and paper industry when it went on line in 1955. The process used to purify mill wastewater is now recognized by the U.S. Environmental Protection Agency as the "best available technology" (BAT) for treatment of pulp and paper wastewater.

Throughout the history of Westvaco's Covington mill, its location has posed special challenges that have required foresight and imagination to overcome. The difficulties of operating in a narrow valley on a small stream have made it a leader in developing environmental control technology.

Westvaco was the first company in the paper industry—nearly 80 years ago—to reduce stream pollution by recovering chemicals and wood residues from the pulping process and converting them into useful chemicals. This approach to pollution control has, for one thing, helped make Westvaco's Chemical Division operations in Covington one of the world's largest producers of activated carbon used to purify drinking water for millions of people in towns all

Located in the heart of one of the largest hardwood forests in the world, Westvaco's Covington mill has been in operation since 1899.

The cornerstone of Westvaco is, fittingly, a piece of paper. It is the certificate granted to John Luke of Aberdeen, Scotland, upon achieving his master's degree from the Association of English, Irish and Scotch Paper Makers on February 22, 1826.

across America. Westvaco is also a major supplier of carbon for automotive emissions-control systems.

Throughout its history Westvaco has invested consistently to improve and expand its pollution-control systems, utilizing the best available technology to provide practical solutions to the environmental problems that accompany growth.

Early in 1987 the firm authorized the expenditure of some $18 million to improve powerhouse emissions controls through the installation of SO2 scrubbers and a new electrostatic precipitator. Such improvements often accompany new production equipment coming on line. The SO2 scrubbers will be the first such installations in the state of Virginia.

Many of Westvaco's pioneering efforts in the environmental field have taken place in Covington and are now

Westvaco® Ovenware and paperboard with high-gloss and other coatings for cartons and commercial printing are produced at Westvaco's services and converting facility in Low Moor, Virginia.

recognized as standards for the pulp and paper industry. Replacement value of accumulated investment in systems to protect the environment exceeds $167 million at Covington. This disciplined approach to growth with a concern for the environment has enabled the company to maintain a leadership position in a world competitive industry.

Westvaco's Virginia operations make a contribution to the economy of the Commonwealth that now exceeds $180 million annually. Its forest lands grow wood and fiber, provide food and cover for wildlife, provide watershed protection, and offer opportunities for hunters, hikers, canoeists, nature lovers, and others who enjoy outdoor recreation.

Over the years Westvaco has consistently invested in new production equipment, new technology, and environmental controls. While many companies operating in the Appalachian region have long since closed their doors, Westvaco continues to serve as a driving force for progress, providing good opportunities for employees and helping plant communities grow and prosper.

PHILIP MORRIS COMPANIES INC.

In 1854 Philip Morris, Esquire, a London tobacconist with an exclusive shop on Bond Street, began producing tobacco in a new form—cigarettes—that had been popularized by dashing young British soldiers returning from the Crimean War. Philip Morris began exporting his cigarettes to America in 1872, a year before his death.

In 1902 a company bearing his still highly respected name was incorporated in New York. An American investor group acquired the firm in 1919 and incorporated it in Virginia under the name of Philip Morris & Co., Ltd., Inc. The new enterprise marketed cigarettes imported from England as well as a line manufactured in a Philadelphia factory under contract.

The major Philip Morris brands at the time were English Ovals, Oxford Blues, and Cambridge. In 1924 a marketing expert (who had just become president of Philip Morris) positioned the young company as a purveyor of premium-quality cigarettes by introducing a new line named Marlboro. Marlboro was promoted especially for sale to

The giant product tower identifies the Richmond headquarters of Philip Morris, and has become a familiar landmark to drivers on I-95 along the East Coast of the United States.

RICHMOND'S 20TH STREET FACTORY was completed in 1927, has seven floors and measures 116,517 sq. feet. Adjacent to the building is a three-story brick building which has 52,320 sq. feet; and next to this is a two-story brick building with 13,376 sq. feet. 19th Street Smoking Tobacco is joined to these three buildings which makes this operation cover the entire block, enclosed by 4 streets — Main, 19th, 20th and Cary. The Smoking Tobacco building is in the shape of an "L" and has 70,487 sq. feet.

floor space and is the world's largest cigarette factory under one roof.

women and sold for the high price of 20 cents per pack, about seven cents more than popularly priced brands.

In 1929, when Philip Morris bought the Continental Tobacco factory on 20th Street in Richmond, Virginia, the firm was welcomed by the business press of the era as "a pygmy among giants." Philip Morris still operates the 20th Street plant, though it is now one of nearly 30 corporate locations in the

The 20th Street factory in Richmond, Virginia, in which Philip Morris USA started its manufacturing operations in 1929.

Richmond area.

The upscale marketing strategy proved successful, and became a hallmark of the company. In 1933 Philip Morris introduced its English Blend, dressed in a simulated wood package and selling at the premium price of 15

cents. At the time, in the midst of the Great Depression, other cigarettes were selling at two packs for a quarter.

Lacking the huge advertising budgets of the larger, more established American cigarette manufacturers, Philip Morris searched for a distinctive way to put the new brand before the public. The inspired answer was John Roventini, a bellhop working in the lobby of Manhattan's Hotel New Yorker. One afternoon a company marketing executive gave the bellhop a one-dollar tip, and, probably as a prank, asked him to locate a "Mr. Philip Morris." Thus was born the distinctive "Call for Philip Morris" campaign that changed the course of American advertising and cigarette marketing.

The Philip Morris English Blend, later renamed Philip Morris Special Blend, was largely responsible for increasing company sales from $5.5 million in 1934 to $38 million in 1937.

The success of Philip Morris Special Blend continued through to the 1940s and World War II, when the call for Philip Morris echoed on the battlefields of Europe and the South Pacific. But tastes changed after the war, and filtered brands began gaining popularity. While sales of the Special Blend continued to be strong, the firm decided that one of its established but minor brands, Marlboro, could best help it make the transition to filters.

In 1954 Philip Morris introduced a new Marlboro made of the "Richmond recipe of fine tobaccos," packaged in a new, red-and-white, patented, crush-proof, flip-top box and sporting a cork-tipped "selectrate" filter. The rugged men who were used in the advertisements conveyed a spirit of independence. The Marlboro Man and Marlboro Country remain among the most recognizable and powerful images of American advertising.

Marlboro is Philip Morris' top-selling brand, and the best-selling cigarette in the world. Other leading Philip Morris brands include Marlboro Lights, Benson & Hedges 100's and Benson & Hedges 100's DeLuxe Ultra Lights, Virginia Slims, Merit and Merit Ultra Lights, and two popular-priced lines,

Players Lights 25's and Cambridge.

The Philip Morris Manufacturing Center in Richmond opened in 1973 as the largest cigarette-manufacturing facility in the world. Next to it is the Philip Morris Research Center, where specialists in agronomy and tobacco science seek improved ways to meet smokers' preferences. Two Richmond plants constructed earlier have been modernized to take full advantage of the latest cigarette-manufacturing technology.

With more than 11,000 employees in Richmond, Philip Morris is the largest private employer in the city. (The company's other cigarette-manufacturing facilities are in Louisville, Kentucky, and Cabarrus County, North Carolina.) Philip Morris is the largest purchaser of U.S.-grown leaf tobacco and the largest U.S. exporter of tobacco products.

Philip Morris U.S.A. is an active supporter of tobacco education programs for farmers, and supports extension agents and educators at colleges and universities in tobacco-growing states. The firm sponsors such events as the Virginia Slims tennis tourna-

The interior of the Philip Morris USA Manufacturing Center in Richmond.

ments, and the Marlboro Country Music Festival.

Philip Morris is also a generous contributor to programs benefiting cultural affairs and the humanities (including the Richmond Ballet and Virginia Museum of Fine Arts), health and welfare programs, and environmental conservation activities.

Corporate restructuring in 1967 and 1985 resulted in the creation of Philip Morris Companies Inc. as a holding company with five major divisions: Philip Morris Incorporated (the domestic tobacco company), Philip Morris International Inc., General Foods Corporation (acquired in 1985), Miller Brewing Company (acquired in 1970), Philip Morris Credit Corporation, and its subsidiary, Mission Viejo Realty Group, a California-based developer of planned communities and business properties. In 1987 Philip Morris Companies Inc. generated total sales of $25 billion.

CANON VIRGINIA, INC.

Shin-Ichiro Nagashima, president of Canon Virginia, Inc.

Canon USA's new North American manufacturing facility was among the most sought-after plant announcements in the United States during the 1980s. Several years of intense research and planning efforts brought Canon Virginia, Inc., to the Virginia Peninsula, the first major Japanese company to locate in the Commonwealth.

Canon Virginia opened in 1987, concurrent with the company's 50th anniversary worldwide. Canon USA's second U.S. plant, Canon Virginia, Inc., is housed on a 170-acre site in Newport News and is the firm's largest North American facility. The subsidiary produces NP-3000 series dual-color office copiers, with plans to produce other business products such as laser-beam printers, facsimiles, toner, and cartridges.

The Virginia plant comprises 289,000 square feet of factory and office space, representing an investment of $26 million. By 1992 that investment will reach a total of $100 million to $125 million, creating a 540,000-square-foot operation. Plans call for a second assembly building, warehouse, and toner facility, as well as a research and development center to develop new products and technologies for U.S. and export markets.

"With an affirmed commitment to internationalization," says Ryuzaburo Kaku, president of Canon Inc. and chairman of Canon U.S.A. Inc., "Canon endeavors to transcend national barriers by creating production and marketing capabilities and meeting market demands in each of the countries where we do business. Profits generated by each host country are reinvested, benefiting local economies and allowing each subsidiary to take pride in individual achievements."

Indeed, Canon's global corporate philosophy embraces a spirit of cooperation and friendship. "Canon seeks to work for the betterment of all humanity, not just the profit of one country or one company," says Kaku. Committed to quality and the excellence of its products, Canon emphasizes teamwork, focusing on people everywhere who will benefit from using its technological advances.

Canon Virginia, Inc., has been influenced by management techniques of its sister plant in Toride, Japan, which produces 90,000 copiers per month. Brief morning and afternoon exercise sessions help keep assembly-line workers alert. Participation in management is encouraged through the suggestion system. The employment projection at the Virginia plant is for 1,000 or more employees, who will eventually produce as many as 24,000 copiers and printers per month. Corporate strategy calls for parts to be sourced domestically and kept until needed for just-in-time delivery by use of a computer-aided automated warehousing system adjacent to the factory.

Tokyo-based Canon Inc. currently operates production facilities in Asia, Europe, and the United States. Worldwide revenues for business machines, photo and video products, and medical and optical equipment totaled $5.5 billion in 1986. From its headquarters in Lake Success, New York, Canon USA's sales topped $1.8 billion in 1986, representing 35 percent of Canon Inc.'s global sales.

The 289,000-square-foot Canon Virginia, Inc., manufacturing plant is patterned after parent company Canon Inc.'s Toride plant in Japan, the world's largest copier plant.

FIRST COLONY LIFE INSURANCE COMPANY

First Colony Life Insurance headquarters in Lynchburg.

In 1955 Lynchburg investment banker Edwin B. Horner organized a group of prominent Virginians to form a new life insurance company. On November 22 of that year First Colony Life Insurance Company was founded and incorporated.

First Colony would go on to pioneer impaired-risk life insurance—the practice of insuring high-risk applicants—and universal life insurance, and also be one of the first to seriously realize the potential of using annuities in tort claim settlements. Today the nationally recognized firm offers a broad line of life insurance and annuity products, and ranks in the top 5 percent of all life insurance companies in the United States.

At the close of 1964 First Colony was licensed to transact business in 12 states and could boast of nearly $100 million of life insurance in force, an industry term describing the total face amount of all outstanding policies. By the following year it had outgrown its leased space in the Krise Building and had purchased a former department store building in downtown Lynchburg. After $1.5 million in renovations, First Colony dedicated its new home in May 1966, and has since doubled the size of its headquarters building.

The Los Angeles Investment Company (LAI) was merged into First Colony in December 1971. Prior to the merger, LAI owned approximately 51 percent of the outstanding shares of the firm. The following year First Colony acquired the American Mayflower Life Insurance Company of New York, and by 1974, the company and its New York subsidiary operated in all 50 states and the District of Columbia.

The first time A.M. Best Company—the major insurance rating organization in the United States—published its letter ratings of life insurance companies, First Colony received the highest rating of "A+". That was in 1976. It has since maintained this mark of excellence every year.

In 1982 Ethyl Corporation pur-

chased all outstanding stock of the firm for some $270 million. "We are a better company because of Ethyl," claims George Stewart, chairman of the board and chief executive officer of First Colony since 1965. "They allow us almost total autonomy, provide additional capital as needed for growth, and contribute enthusiastic moral support. Ethyl has been nothing short of perfect for us." He adds that the feeling is mutual. Since the acquisition, First Colony has more than doubled in size.

It took the company 14 years to reach the billion-dollar milestone in life insurance in force. From there the firm just kept growing. Insurance in force jumped from $6 billion in 1980 to $39 billion in 1987.

First Colony Life Insurance Com-

Pictured here is the sunken garden that adjoins the First Colony Life Insurance headquarters building in Lynchburg.

pany shares its success with its community. The firm, along with Ethyl Corporation, is a major supporter of the restoration of Jefferson's Poplar Forest, and maintains a beautiful Main Street garden in downtown Lynchburg. The company sponsors the Virginia 10-Miler, which, according to road-racing officials, is one of the top races in the United States. First Colony's management is actively involved in most of Lynchburg's business, religious, and social agencies, and is proud to be a Virginia and Lynchburg corporate citizen.

WOODWARD & LOTHROP

Woodward & Lothrop celebrated its centennial in 1980. On that occasion the employee magazine cited a memoir written 50 years earlier, a memoir that itself cited a remarkable concept of the potential of the national capital region.

"Mr. Woodward and Mr. Lothrop had an unwavering faith in Washington," the memoir read. "In their vision, they saw a city constantly enlarging its population, rebuilding its structures, and becoming the center of the best life in the nation." The greater Washington area has repaid its faith and the accuracy of its foresight.

Metropolitan Washington's leading department store was founded by two natives of Maine. Samuel Walter Woodward and Alvin M. Lothrop opened their first store in Chelsea, Massachusetts. When they moved to Washington, they opened their doors as the Boston Dry Goods House. The first store was opened at 705 Market Space in the old central market, a site now occupied by the National Archives.

The founders' innovative merchandising policy intrigued the public; a bold sign advertised "one price." At Woodward and Lothrop's Boston House there would be no special discounts for volume purchasers, cash customers, friends of the management, or highly skilled bargainers. All customers would be treated alike.

With sales booming, Woodward and Lothrop decided to move their store to the popular F Street shopping district. The Carlisle Building cost approximately $100,000. It opened April 2, 1887. The proud proprietors soon found it necessary to begin purchasing and expanding into adjacent buildings.

The store's one-price policy guaranteed fair dealing. The shop featured only the finest, most popular, and most up-to-date merchandise. In 1893 the boys' department offered the Knockabout suit, "made for rough wear, but very dressy." The trousers were "double thick in the knees and seat" and, like the coat, treble sewed with silk, warranted not to be rippable. Sizes 10 to 15 years, $5. Another department offered Haviland French china, flower pattern, blue dinner plates at $4.50 per dozen.

In 1901 Woodward & Lothrop bought St. Vincent's Orphan Asylum at 11th and G streets, demolished it, and replaced it with another new building (a new home was found for the orphans). The addition gave the store almost the entire square block.

One excellent buy that year was the "Ladies Eton suit made of habit cloth in all the leading shades, large Empire revers, full sleeved, and skirt and jacket silk lined; sizes 32 to 48, $10."

Donald Woodward, son of the cofounder, became president of the company in 1917. He demolished the Carlisle Building in 1926, replacing it with a taller, more elaborate and efficient store, and merging it into the other facilities. The complex forms the core of today's Woodies Metro Center, the hub of the Woodward & Lothrop system.

Expansion beyond the downtown location began in 1937 with the construction of warehousing and service facilities at 131 M Street, NE. The 1946 purchase of Palais Royal from the Kresge Foundation brought stores at the Pentagon and in Bethesda, Maryland, and the building on the north side of G Street, across from the downtown complex. Woodward & Lothrop recently sold the "North Building," and the Bethesda facility was destroyed by fire. But the Pentagon store, Woodies' first Virginia branch, remains an active location.

Woodward & Lothrop reached out to Chevy Chase, Maryland, opening a branch at Friendship Heights in 1950, then to Alexandria, its second Virginia location, in 1952. That year's fashion news from Woodies featured a "radiant dress with minimized waist and full skirt—spring's silhouette interpreted in silk taffetized surah. In Paris Blue, Bronzine Green, and Burnished Brown, $35." Woodies opened its branch at Seven Corners, Virginia, in 1956.

The pace of construction accelerated in the 1960s, with openings in Wheaton Plaza in 1960, Eastover in 1963 (it was sold in 1972), and Annapolis in 1964. The Landmark Mall location opened in 1965, Prince George Plaza in 1966, Iverson Mall in 1967, and Tysons Corner in 1968.

Continuous expansion has made Woodward & Lothrop at Tysons Corner the largest of the suburban stores, and the most popular department store in northern Virginia.

Facilities opened more recently include the Woodward & Lothrop stores in Columbia Mall (1971), Landover Mall (1972), Montgomery Mall (1976), Lakeforest Mall (1978), Fair Oaks Mall (1980), and White Marsh, near Baltimore (1981).

Andrew Parker retired as president of the company in 1969, and Edwin K. Hoffman was elected president and chief executive officer. In 1978 Hoffman was elected chairman of the board and chief executive officer. Robert J. Mulligan is vice-chairman and chief administrative officer of Woodward & Lothrop. Tom Roach is president of the company.

"It's hard to describe the aura of this store but shopping here is part of living here," says Hoffman. "Our customers have a personal, almost a proprietary interest in us. They're as much a part of Woodies as Woodies is part of metropolitan Washington."

In 1984 A. Alfred Taubman purchased Woodward & Lothrop. A resident of Ann Arbor, Michigan, Taubman is an innovative real estate developer whose projects include Lakeforest and Fair Oaks malls. Other Taubman properties include Sothebys, the A&W restaurant chain, and a group of multi-screen movie theaters.

In October 1986 Woodward & Lothrop completed the $30-million remodeling of its downtown store, now known as Woodies Metro Center. It is a new store, designed for the metro Washington market of the 1980s; but its roots go back more than 100 years.

"The new owner appreciates and respects what this company stands for," claims Hoffman, "the way we treat our people and the way we participate in civic affairs. He's a man of tremendous principles. He understands and values Woodies' history and traditions. Nothing will change the image of Woodward & Lothrop."

JAMES MADISON UNIVERSITY

Wilson Hall and part of the Quadrangle at James Madison University.

James Madison University, founded in 1908, has been cited recently in a number of national publications as one of the finest colleges in America.

The university has been acclaimed in studies conducted by *U.S. News & World Report, Money* magazine, *Changing Times* magazine, the education editor of *The New York Times,* and several college guides.

The learning experience at JMU is designed with a global outlook. Students at the university are prepared to take their place in a world that has grown smaller through the tremendous advances that have been made recently in technology, communications, and transportation. At JMU, students are prepared for the present—but they are also prepared for the twenty-first century.

JMU is named for the fourth president of the United States. Founded in 1908 as a state normal school, JMU has operated under five different names. Its current name of James Madison University was received in 1977, when the institution was awarded university status.

A between-classes study break near the Warren Campus Center.

JMU has quintupled in size in the past 20 years.

Although the university dates back nearly to the turn of the century, JMU maintains a modern look. About half of its 80 major buildings have been constructed since 1970. The institution's greatest expansion—from 4,000 students in 1971 to 10,000 in the late 1980s—has taken place during the presidency of Dr. Ronald E. Carrier.

JMU is located in the heart of Virginia's famous Shenandoah Valley. The

university's beautifully landscaped campus contains 365 acres, including a large lake, and is adjacent to Interstate 81.

There are some 10,000 students at JMU, with the number of men and women students nearly equal. Just less than 80 percent of the institution's students are Virginians. A faculty of more than 500 scholars enables students to know their professors on a personal basis.

Academic offerings at JMU cover an extremely wide variety of courses offered in the university's College of Letters and Sciences, College of Business,

Newman Lake provides a picturesque setting for the fraternity and sorority houses at James Madison University.

College of Fine Arts and Communication, College of Education and Human Services, College of Nursing, and Graduate School. More than 100 different degree programs are available at the university, and new programs are constantly being added to meet the changing needs of students and society.

An active program of athletics at JMU provides students with a wide range of sports on the intercollegiate, intramural, and recreational levels. Some 35 intramural and club sports are offered, and 24 teams compete on the intercollegiate level—12 men's teams and 12 women's teams. JMU teams compete in Division I of the NCAA.

All of these things—and many others—have combined to give James Madison University its reputation as one of the nation's finest undergraduate universities.

WALKER MANUFACTURING COMPANY

Walker Manufacturing Company, the world's largest supplier of automotive exhaust systems to original equipment and replacement markets, started 100 years ago as a small company in Racine, Wisconsin.

One of its largest plants, located in Harrisonburg, Virginia, has greatly contributed to the growth of its hometown and has been a technological leader in the automotive industry.

Walker Manufacturing began as the Economy Spring Company, incorporated in 1888. The firm assembled and sold springs for farm wagons until the onset of the automotive age, which marked the point Walker first began to manufacture the Tire Saver—a jack used to raise cars off the ground during winter to prevent tires from rotting.

In 1916 the firm became known as Walker Manufacturing Company. The invention of the Walker Louvered Tube in the 1930s, which swirled the exhaust gases through perforated pipes inside the muffler to quiet the engine noise and had minimum back pressure, was a breakthrough in the exhaust industry. This began Walker's history of technological leadership and product innovation.

The Walker-Virginia plant was built in 1961. At that time the only business on the south end of Harrisonburg was the Belle Meade Motel. Interstate 81, which now extends from Knoxville, Tennessee, to the northern border of the United States, ended there. The plant brought hundreds of jobs to Harrisonburg. More than a quarter-century later 33 of the original 100 employees still work at the plant.

On August 30, 1967, Walker Manufacturing Company became a Tenneco company, which is a diversified industrial conglomerate. Tenneco has major operations in oil and gas, chemicals, agriculture and construction equipment, packaging, shipbuilding, and automotive parts and services.

Walker continued to grow, adding five buildings to the Harrisonburg plant by 1979, so that today it has 660,000 square feet, or 15 acres, under roof.

This growth has enabled the facility to become the major producer for replacement exhaust products to the eastern region of the United States. In 1984 Walker-Virginia introduced the Walker Pipeline to the automotive industry, heralding a new era in pipe production. The pipeline is a computer-controlled unit that combines the func-

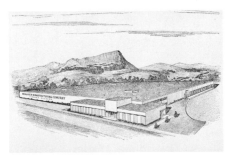

Walker Manufacturing's Harrisonburg, Virginia, plant looked like this in 1961, when it was built. In 1979 five buildings were added, and today the facility has 660,000 square feet of space.

tions of a tubing mill and a pipe bender into a compact, single-phase system. The pipeline can produce up to five different configurations of pipe at a time, with higher consistency and quality than was possible before its inception. The Harrisonburg plant now owns four pipelines—the only four in North America, and half of the existing pipelines in the world.

Due to this latest innovation in technology, Walker-Virginia currently makes more than 2,700 different models of mufflers, pipes, and accessories for the automotive aftermarket. This production schedule requires 600 people to work at the plant, making it one of the largest employers in the area.

Throughout its 25-year history, Walker-Virginia and its employees have donated more than $400,000 to the United Way. The plant has also helped build a substation for the local fire department and has contributed funds for the renovation of Rockingham Memorial Hospital. The firm continues to provide support for the local school system, numerous charities, and many community activities.

A Walker Manufacturing Company product, the Tire Saver, was used to raise tires off the ground in winter to prevent them from rotting.

447

BRIDGEWATER COLLEGE

In Bridgewater, Virginia, population 3,500, lies a private liberal arts college that has been providing a challenging and productive academic program for more than 100 years. Founded in 1880 by Daniel Christian Flory, a leader of the Church of the Brethren, Bridgewater College maintains its historic affiliation with the church, though the campus community is comprised of individuals of a wide variety of religious and cultural backgrounds.

Virginia's first senior coeducational college, Bridgewater has been coeducational since its founding. Bridgewater was also one of the first predominantly white private colleges in the South to admit students of all races. Each year students from approximately 20 states and 10 foreign countries enroll at the college.

Flory, a German Baptist Brethren educated at the University of Virginia, founded the institution as Spring Creek Normal School in Spring Creek, Virginia, in 1880. Its first session enrolled 29 men and women. Two years later the school relocated four miles to the southeast in Bridgewater as Virginia Normal School. By 1884 it had moved to its present location, and on June 18, 1886, it granted baccalaureate degrees to its first graduates.

The school changed its name to Bridgewater College in 1889 and conferred its first Bachelor of Arts degrees in the spring of 1891. Before 1919 the college conferred eight different degrees, but in 1920 consolidated all educational sequences into the traditional B.A. and B.S. degrees.

Founded in 1880 as the Spring Creek Normal School by Daniel Christian Flory, Bridgewater College is a private liberal arts college located in the Town of Bridgewater. Pictured here is Flory Hall, named after the institution's founder.

The college has been accredited continuously by the Southern Association of Colleges and Schools since 1925, having had its accreditation reaffirmed through periodic self-studies and reviews since that time.

The basic 40-acre campus is located in the Town of Bridgewater, a picturesque community nestled in rolling hills and farmlands. Contiguous to the basic campus are additional acres owned by the college. Harrisonburg (population 25,500) is eight miles from campus. The major cultural and metropolitan areas of Washington, D.C., and Richmond are within a 125-mile radius of the campus, allowing the students to enjoy the advantages of both rural and urban settings.

One of the college's greatest assets is its outstanding faculty. Students repeatedly cite the Bridgewater faculty as being comprised of extremely conscientious and concerned scholars, willing to give extra time for counseling and individualized instruction. A student/faculty ratio of approximately 15 to one facilitates the close association between faculty members and the students they teach. The focus of a strong liberal arts background for the individual student, regardless of the major field, has resulted in Bridgewater receiving a consistent ranking in the top 25 percent of the nation's colleges and universities in the number of graduates who go on to complete doctoral programs.

Bridgewater College seeks to enroll students with strong preparation who demonstrate serious attitudes toward academic achievement. Over the past five years 65 percent of the entering students have ranked in the top one-third of their high school classes.

Bridgewater has been coeducational since its founding (it was Virginia's first senior coeducational college) and was also one of the first predominantly white private colleges to admit students of all races. Today Bridgewater is a thoroughly modern college campus as seen in some of its newer buildings such as Cole Hall, pictured here.

DOYLE LUMBER INCORPORATED

Wilbur Doyle, chairman of the board of Doyle Lumber Incorporated, says that his company "started with three pieces of used equipment, one employee, and a desire to work for excellence." Since the Martinsville lumber company began in 1947, the number of employees has grown to 165, the equipment has obtained a level of technical sophistication, and the firm's success and reputation for excellence is evidence that the desire is still there.

The operation has been at its present site since 1956, occupying two other small locations before that. It began as a lumber concentration yard in 1947; it bought all of its lumber, dried it, dressed it, and then sold it as whitewood primarily for the home-building industry. In 1960 it built its own sawmill operations to accommodate its lumber quota for customers. The acquisition of Hopkins Lumber Co. in 1963 added several key people to the management of Doyle. Osmose chemical treating began in 1965 and was then updated in 1982.

Until 1985 a mix of hardwoods and softwoods (poplar, oak, and southern yellow pine) made up the primary products, but today all of the wood is yellow pine. Annually 20 million feet of board is processed through the sawmills at Doyle. However, the firm sells up to 150 million feet of board per year. An additional 130 million feet is brought in from such states as North Carolina, Texas, Mississippi, and Alabama, and is made ready to ship elsewhere.

Doyle maintains its own brigade of tractor-trailers and also uses railroad cars to transport its lumber as far west as Chicago and from North Carolina all the way up to New England.

In 1965 Doyle became an Osmose chemical licensee, and today 80 percent of the lumber is tagged with the Osmose label. Osmose is a specialized chemical procedure that involves packaging the lumber, flooding it with chemicals, pressurizing it until it absorbs the calculated proper amount, and finally letting the excess chemical moisture drip off for 36

Doyle Lumber Incorporated's Martinsville plant.

to 48 hours. Osmose chemical treating plays a major part in Doyle Lumber operations, and the company built a plant in 1987 in Henderson, North Carolina, to accommodate its quality production.

State-of-the-art technology exists in other areas of the organization as well. System 38 computers take care of everything from inventory to sorting out precise lumber stacks. David Doyle, son of Wilbur and executive vice-president, stresses the importance of keeping up with today's technology in order to continue to develop and produce the finest-quality lumber available. New devices and techniques, such as a possible device for analyzing a log and cutting it for maximum output, or a development of new particle board or strand waferboard, are always under consideration.

Careful forestry management is also practiced at Doyle, assuring an ample supply of logs, continuous production of lumber, and uniform reforestation.

Doyle Lumber Incorporated continues to emphasize quality products and to work for excellence, just as it has done for the past 40 years.

UNIVERSITY OF VIRGINIA

The Rotunda at the University of Virginia is a half-scale version of the Pantheon and the focal point of the historic Central Grounds. In 1976 members of the American Institute of Architects voted the university's Central Grounds an outstanding achievement of American architecture.

The University of Virginia was founded in 1819 by Thomas Jefferson, who outlined the institution's purpose, designed its buildings, supervised construction, planned the curriculum, and directed the recruitment of the first faculty. As the first rector of the university, Jefferson presided over the school's governing body, known as the board of visitors. James Madison and James Monroe were members of the board in early years.

When it opened for classes in 1825 with 68 students and a faculty of eight, the University of Virginia represented a dramatic innovation in American education. In an era when colleges trained students almost exclusively for teaching and the ministry, Jefferson dedicated his university to the education of leaders in practical affairs and public service. The innovative curriculum permitted the student a broader range of study than was customary, and the lecture method of instruction demanded independent thought.

Jefferson designed his "academical village" to house both teachers and students in four long rows of rooms and larger buildings that provided classrooms and dwelling space for faculty families. Selected fourth-year and graduate students still live in the original rooms Jefferson designed. The Rotunda, a half-scale version of the Pantheon, is the focal point of the historic Central Grounds. In 1976 members of the American Institute of Architects voted the university's Central Grounds an outstanding achievement of American architecture.

The original Jeffersonian buildings remain the center of the modern-day University of Virginia, situated on 1,050 acres at its primary location some 20 miles east of the Blue Ridge Mountains in Charlottesville. The university today enrolls 17,000 students. Roughly two-thirds of the students are Virginians, two-thirds are undergraduates, and approximately one-half are women. Black students make up 8 percent of the undergraduate enrollment and 7 percent of the overall student body. The bachelor's degree is offered in 52 fields and programs, the master's in 93, educational specialist in 6, first professional in 2, and the doctorate in 54.

More than 40 Rhodes Scholars have graduated from the university, which is attracting some of the very best students in the country through the merit-based Jefferson Scholars program. Established in 1980 by the University Alumni Association, the pro-

The Lawn at the University of Virginia. The original Jeffersonian buildings remain the center of the modern-day, 1,050-acre university.

The University of Virginia was founded in 1819 by Thomas Jefferson as an institution dedicated to a broader range of study and independent thought. Those academic values still apply today. Here a class is in session at the University of Virginia's Colgate Darden Graduate School of Business Administration.

gram grants full four-year scholarships and stipends to cover books and living expenses.

The institution's famous student-run Honor System was established in 1842 by Judge Henry St. George Tucker, a professor of law. The system's basic assumption is that anyone who enrolls at the university is bound by a code of honor. The sole punishment for a student found guilty by a student jury is permanent expulsion. A judicial system has the responsibility for student discipline in other areas of misconduct.

The university, presided over by Robert M. O'Neil, is supported by an enthusiastic alumni body that includes four U.S. senators, several members of Congress, and many top officials in Virginia government, as well as leaders in the business, legal, medical, and academic communities. Among well-known alumni are Edgar Allan Poe, Woodrow Wilson, and Dr. Walter Reed. There are approximately 100,000 alumni, and the Alumni Association has 60 active chapters nationwide.

The university's total endowment, supplied mostly by alumni and friends, is approximately $396 million. The annual operating budget is more than a half-billion dollars, and state revenues account for 28 percent of funding.

The university's full-time instructional faculty has grown to nearly 1,600. Among the many national and international awards faculty members have re-

ceived are the Pulitzer Prize in history, won by the late Dumas Malone in 1975 for his multi-volume biography of Thomas Jefferson, and the 1987 Pulitzer Prize for fiction, won by emeritus professor Peter Taylor.

Through their wide-ranging research efforts, faculty members are constantly developing new knowledge. Their interests include improving fuel manufacture for nuclear reactors, studying the effects of acid rain, developing better crops and vegetables through genetic manipulation, finding new ways to use computer technology in industry, and preventing infection among hospital patients. The Center for Public Service conducts research and organizes conferences on state and local government, as well as business issues. Research support from government and private sources totals some $60 million annually, and includes support arranged by the Commonwealth of Virginia's Center for Innovative Technology. The medical center provides health care for the central and western regions of Virginia.

In accordance with its dedication to prepare students for success in mainstream society, the University of Virginia has recently sought to strengthen its ties with the business world. In 1987 the institution published its first guide to university resources available to business and industry; it also named Eve Menger as its first vice-provost for industry relations.

The McIntire School of Commerce confers bachelor's degrees with specialization in accounting, finance, management, information systems, and marketing, and conducts a master of science program in accounting. The school

is ranked among the top 10 undergraduate business programs in the nation. The Colgate Darden Graduate School of Business Administration offers a highly prestigious MBA program, as well as a doctorate in business administration. The school, jointly with the Graduate School of Arts and Sciences, offers an MBA/MA in government and foreign affairs and business and an MBA/MA in East Asian studies and business. Its many seminars and workshops for managers, such as the six-week Executive Program offered each summer, help people in business prepare for advancement. The Darden School houses the Center of International Banking Studies, as well as the Olsson Center for Applied Ethics.

The Division of Continuing Education, designed to affirm that the University of Virginia's interest in serving Virginia's students is not limited by location or terminated by graduation, offers courses at seven regional centers throughout the state, including Charlottesville. It plays a major role in the operation of a satellite uplink partly sponsored by the State Council of Higher Education for broadcasting academic programming to remote locations.

In 1825 the university opened for classes with 68 students; today it has an enrollment of 17,000 students, many of whom prepare for exams at the University of Virginia's Alderman Library. Among the more well-known alumni from the university are Edgar Allan Poe, Woodrow Wilson, and Dr. Walter Reed.

McGUIRE, WOODS, BATTLE & BOOTHE

From modest local beginnings in the nineteenth century to a thriving national practice in the twentieth, McGuire, Woods, Battle & Boothe balances the character of its history with the vitality of its growth. Today the firm is among the 40 largest in the country. With more than 300 attorneys, 275 of whom are based in Virginia, the firm has more lawyers practicing in the Commonwealth than any other firm, and its reputation cuts across state, national, and international lines. From eight locations (Alexandria, Charlottesville, Fairfax, Norfolk, Richmond, Tysons Corner, Williamsburg, and Washington, D.C.), it serves the fast-growing Mid-Atlantic region and other U.S. and foreign corporate centers.

McGuire, Woods draws from the nation's top law schools, and its lawyers are experienced in virtually every aspect of civil practice. Some of the firm's strongest areas of practice are corporate finance, mergers and acquisitions, real estate finance, land use, government contracts, banking law, public finance, and tax law. Its expertise in general and special areas of litigation includes national litigation management, products liability, antitrust, labor, and environmental law.

Many McGuire, Woods lawyers have distinguished themselves through public service. Among them are two former Virginia governors, John S. Battle (1950-1954) and John N. Dalton (1978-1982). McGuire, Woods attorneys also include a former commander-in-chief of the Strategic Air Command and a former Virginia attorney general. Several members of the firm have gone on to serve as state and federal judges. The chairman of the firm, Robert H. Patterson, Jr., is well known for his many contributions to the Commonwealth in the public and private sectors.

The clients served by the firm are as diverse as its lawyers and their areas of practice. Among the industries represented by McGuire, Woods are banking, computer equipment and software, land development, health care, insurance, manufacturing, distribution, and retailing. The clientele ranges from individuals to multinational corporations. Many client relationships have lasted for decades as fledgling businesses have evolved into *Fortune* 500 companies.

The firm's distinguished reputation stems from its commitment to client service. A lawyer in the firm explains: "When clients first come to me, I make it my business to learn about their business—their vision for the future, the opportunities that they see, and the problems they face. I remember so many clients . . . who came here when they were just getting started and who have grown up with us. I'm proud to know this firm has helped them through all stages of their development."

Reflecting the growth of its clients, the firm has expanded both through internal growth and mergers. The most recent merger occurred in February 1987, when McGuire, Woods & Battle merged with Boothe, Prichard & Dudley. This merger, among the largest in law firm history, pooled a powerful industrial and corporate client base in central Virginia with real estate development and high-technology in northern Virginia and the Washington metropolitan area.

McGuire, Woods strives to represent the values that are historically associated with Virginia. Committed to the traditions of excellence—to provide all clients with quality legal services, loyalty, and established expertise—McGuire, Woods, Battle & Boothe takes pride in its heritage as it enters the twenty-first century.

One of Virginia's most popular governors, John N. Dalton, joined the firm in 1982. Until his death in 1986, Dalton engaged in the practice of corporate law and served on the boards of several major corporations.

As chairman of the firm, Robert H. Patterson heads up the executive committee, which functions in much the same way as a company's board of directors. Patterson joined the firm in 1952 and has become a prominent trial attorney and counselor to many individuals and businesses.

VIRGINIA MILITARY INSTITUTE

Regardless of his major, every Virginia Military Institute (VMI) cadet must be computer literate, and must pass the required course in academic computing. Personal computers are available to cadets in numerous areas of the post, and all academic disciplines make extensive use of them.

Steeped in a rich tradition of honor and excellence, the Virginia Military Institute has managed to preserve the high moral standards of a former time while continuing to prepare its students for success in today's society. Members of the Corps of Cadets still wear the historic gray VMI uniform, live in barracks that have housed cadets since 1851, and follow an honor code that is as old as the institute itself.

Its alumni include two commandants of the United States Marine Corps and General of the Army George C. Marshall, author of the post-World War II European Recovery Program known as the Marshall Plan and the only professional military man ever to win the Nobel Peace Prize.

Founded in 1839 to replace a troublesome arsenal guard in Lexington, Virginia, VMI was the nation's first state-supported military college and, from its inception, has stressed rigid discipline along with academic and military emphasis on leadership. VMI men have fought in every war involving the United States since the institute was founded, starting with the Mexican War just four years after VMI graduated its first class. In the American Civil War, the Corps of Cadets earned the distinction of becoming the only student body in the nation's history to fight as a military unit in a pitched battle when they helped Confederate forces win the May 15, 1864, Battle of New Market, Virginia.

Yet even with this strong military background, academics has always been VMI's principal emphasis. The founders sought to educate citizen-soldiers—men prepared for careers in civilian life but trained and ready for military leadership in time of national need. Historically only 15 percent of Virginia Military Institute's alumni pursue military careers. Civil engineering was established as the cornerstone of VMI's

The VMI Regimental Band steps off to lead the regular Friday-afternoon retreat parade at the institute. In the background are the VMI barracks, a National Historic Landmark; the entire VMI post is a designated National Historic District.

academic program, although the subject was rarely taught in higher education facilities prior to 1839. Virginia Military Institute offered the first industrial chemistry course in the South, and developed modern physics and meteorology courses in 1868.

Today the institute offers degrees in 12 fields—eight in the sciences and four in liberal arts—to its 1,300 cadets. As part of the educational process, the cadets are encouraged to develop a lifelong concept of honor, devotion to duty, and self-discipline. The program obviously works. VMI is the only state-supported college in Virginia to rank in the top 25 colleges in the nation in percentage of graduates who serve as presidents, vice-presidents, or board members of major American corporations.

In 1966 the cadet barracks, designed by Alexander Jackson Davis in the mid-nineteenth century, was desig-

A Virginia Military Institute cadet in full dress uniform.

nated a Virginia Historic Landmark by the Virginia Historic Landmarks Commission. And, in August 1974, the Honorable Rogers C.B. Morton, Secretary of the Interior, designated Virginia Military Institute as a National Historic District under the theme "Political and Military History, 1828-1860" as a significant example of the nation's cultural heritage.

BABCOCK & WILCOX

When George Babcock and Stephen Wilcox patented their water-tube boiler in 1867, it was doubtful they realized how large their company would grow and what a major contribution it would make to American technology. More than 100 years later, Babcock & Wilcox, now a McDermott International, Inc., company, is one of the nation's leading suppliers of nuclear fuel and both fossil and nuclear steam-generating systems.

The company opened its Lynchburg, Virginia, facilities in 1956. Operations have grown from a few hundred employees to nearly 4,000 today. It is central Virginia's largest employer.

America was undergoing rapid industrialization in 1867 following the Civil War, and Babcock & Wilcox met the need for an economical source of steam with the invention of a safe water-tube boiler. B&W built its first boiler at the Hope Iron Works in Providence, Rhode Island, but the new boiler did not gain national attention until 1876, when it was exhibited at the Centennial Exposition in Philadelphia.

While conducting his incandescent light experiments in 1878, Thomas Alva Edison purchased his first B&W boiler, later noting that B&W had produced ". . . the best boiler God has permitted man yet to make." In 1881, the first central station for generating electricity in the United States, owned by Brush Electric Light Company in Philadelphia, used four 73-horsepower B&W boilers for power.

B&W continued to contribute to progress in American power at the turn of the century. In 1902 the first New York City subway was powered by B&W boilers, and a year later the Commonwealth Edison Company in Chicago used 96, 508-horsepower B&W boilers to generate its electric power.

B&W supplied the U.S. Navy and Merchant Marine with more than 1,500 boilers in World War I, and in World War II equipped 4,100 steam-powered combat and merchant ships with boilers.

With the dawn of commercial nuclear power, computers, and the age of high technology, B&W has continued to be a leader in meeting the nation's energy needs. Through the firm's Defense and Nuclear Power Group, headquartered in Lynchburg, B&W is a leading producer of nuclear components for the U.S. Navy and is expanding its participation in the growing defense market. B&W products meet the exacting standards required by the Department of Energy, the Department of Defense, and the Nuclear Regulatory Commission.

B&W supplies support for commercial nuclear utilities along with supplying components for stationary and marine applications. The company is also concentrating its efforts on providing state-of-the-art maintenance, repair, and analytical services to commercial light-water reactors throughout the world.

For more than 100 years, Babcock & Wilcox has led the search for safe and economical solutions for the world's energy problems by maintaining high standards of quality and productivity as it continues to seek new business opportunities.

During the post-Civil War industrialization in the United States, George Babcock and Stephen Wilcox met the demands of the nation's energy needs with their invention of a safe water-tube boiler for generating steam power.

Today Babcock & Wilcox is a leader in meeting the nation's energy needs, supplying nuclear fuel and both fossil and nuclear steam-generating systems.

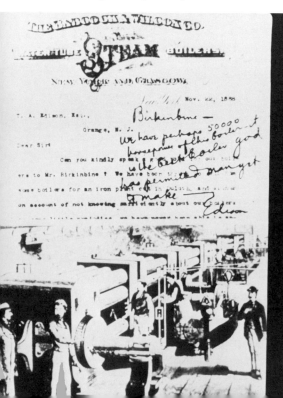

ABBOTT LABORATORIES

An aerial view of the Ross Laboratories division plant in Altavista, Virginia. The Altavista facility is the major distribution center for Ross products in the eastern United States.

In 1970 Abbott Laboratories culminated its search for a new manufacturing and distribution site for its Ross Laboratories division with the purchase of 102 acres one mile north of Altavista in Campbell County.

Ross began operating the Altavista plant in 1972 with 75 employees manufacturing Similac®, the nation's most popular infant formula.

Since its start-up this facility has expanded to manufacture more than 30 infant and other nutritional products. The plant now employs more than 650 people from Campbell and Pittsylvania counties and nearby Lynchburg. Capitalizing on its commitment to research and development and innovative engineering, Abbott retooled part of the facility in 1987 for a new high-technology production line for nutritional product packaging.

The original decision to locate in Altavista and subsequent decisions for expansions were based on the quality of the local work force, good rail and highway systems, proximity of local markets, and the commitment of government to business development. State, county, and town government, together with industrial development groups, helped Abbott locate the site. Local government and private individuals matched the company's contribution to upgrade the necessary utility systems.

Ross Laboratories manufactures more than 30 infant and other nutritional products at the Altavista facility.

Recent state initiatives in technical and secondary education and improved air and highway systems are encouraging industrial growth in Virginia. These initiatives have helped make the Altavista facility the major distribution center for Ross products in the eastern United States. This, in turn, has improved job security for employees and added stability to the local economic base.

Ross was founded in 1903 in Columbus, Ohio, when Harry C. Moores and Stanley M. Ross, brothers-in-law, joined forces to form the Moores & Ross Milk Company. Over the years the operation grew into a diversified manufacturer of nutritional products that are marketed worldwide. The Altavista facility is one of four Ross operations in the United States. Other plants are located in Columbus, Ohio; Sturgis, Michigan; and Casa Grande, Arizona. Abbott also has Ross products plants in Holland and Ireland.

The premier product in 1925 was Franklin Infant Food, the forerunner of Similac®. By 1928 the product had become so successful that Moores and Ross sold their milk and ice cream business and devoted their full efforts to developing infant and medical nutritional products.

Ross became a division of Abbott, with headquarters in North Chicago, Illinois, in 1964. A *Fortune* 100 company, Abbott is committed to maintaining leadership in infant and medical nutritionals. The firm adheres to strict standards of cleanliness and efficiency for production of Similac®, Isomil®, and Advance® infant formulas; Enrich® and Ensure® medical nutritionals for weakened adults; and other nutritional products. Employees wear company-supplied uniforms and protective clothing, and maintain sterile production conditions.

In 1988 Abbott celebrated 100 years of leadership in health care worldwide. A large measure of credit for the company's success belongs to Ross, which in 1986 became the first Abbott division to reach one billion dollars in total annual sales. Abbott's total worldwide sales that year were $3.8 billion.

Now in its second century, Abbott Laboratories plans to continue producing and distributing innovative, high-quality, affordable health care products—in Virginia, throughout the United States, and worldwide.

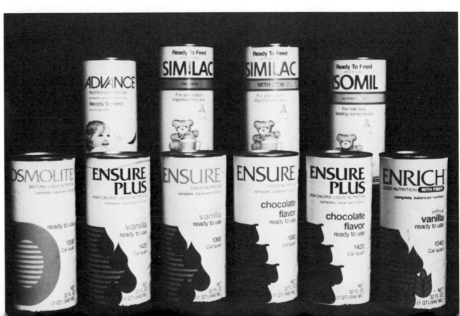

OMNI HOTELS

Omni Hotels have made their presence an integral part of several Virginia cities following the success of the flagship Omni International Hotel in downtown Norfolk.

The fortunes of this hotel have mirrored efforts to revitalize the city's central business district. Through design, and redesign, initial enthusiasm for Norfolk Gardens Amusement Park—a proposed nearby large-scale tourist development—followed by withdrawal of support for that project by the city council, Omni International Hotel has survived ups and downs, finding its niche as a convention facility, a civic event headquarters, and a dining and entertainment magnet. What has persisted through the years is a determination to make things work, whatever the time and energy required.

The first event set the pace. The Holly Ball, an annual fund raiser for Children's Hospital of the King's Daughters and major social event of the holiday season, had been booked for December 20, 1975. Though the hotel was nowhere near ready to open, ball volunteers and hotel staff took charge to make it happen. Ignoring the surrounding construction, volunteers busied themselves with elaborate decorations. The hotel sales manager swept floors; the general manager rushed pails of soapy water to the mopping crew. Mrs. Maurice Alpert, wife of the Atlanta-based developer spearheading the hotel project, oversaw the hanging of artworks she had selected.

At 7 p.m. the ballroom still was not finished; workers were still laying carpet on the stairs. An hour later, when the first Cadillac arrived at the front door, the last of the construction workers were making their way out the back door. Guests were greeted with a 20-foot Christmas tree and a ballroom filled with poinsettias and holiday greenery. Newspapers called it the "Holly Ball Miracle."

Little more than two weeks later the hotel welcomed its first guests, 15 officials of the Bank of Virginia (now Signet Bank). One month later the first convention, some 500 Virginia Jaycees, provided the Omni's first sellout

The Omni Richmond Hotel at James Center is conveniently located in the heart of the city's governmental, historic, financial, and commercial districts.

crowd. The Republican State Convention, drawing 3,000 to 4,000 representatives, filled 400 Omni rooms that June, the balance going to other downtown hotels.

Despite these early successes the Norfolk City Council's decision not to follow through with the Norfolk Gardens proposal adversely affected the hotel's convention sales program. Developer Alpert and others expressed concern that "something spectacular" was needed to attract people downtown.

With new management, though,

The lobby at the Omni Charlottesville Hotel.

Omni enjoyed a dramatic turnaround in its second year, operating at a profit. Its restaurant, Alexander's, also became a hit, and business doubled at The Esplanade, one of the region's most prominent restaurants.

In 1983 the something spectacular finally came to downtown Norfolk in the form of the city's new riverfront marketplace, Waterside, immediately adjoining the hotel. Omni added the Riverwalk Cafe to retain its own restaurant clientele.

By the beginning of the following

year virtually all of the hotel management company's assets were sold to Dunfey Hotels Corporation, a subsidiary of Aer-Lingus Dunfey Company. Through Omni International Hotels, Dunfey manages Omni hotels in Norfolk and other cities.

A $2.5-million renovation in 1985 produced a concierge floor; the plush Omni Suite, the most spectacular suite in the region; an executive boardroom for guests on the concierge floor; a mid-size ballroom on the first floor; and the first hotel dinner theater in the state. More than half of the hotel's 442 guest rooms were also upgraded.

Meanwhile the City of Charlottesville had sold its former Radisson Hotel property to Jefferson Court Associates of Arlington, Virginia. Previously under the direction of the Radisson Hotel Corporation management, the hotel had already added a contemporary flavor to the natural beauty of the Charlottesville countryside. The new owners wanted to operate the facility under the Omni name, influenced perhaps by the successful reputation of the Omni International Hotel in Norfolk. Dunfey Hotels Corporation was contracted to operate The Radisson as the Omni Charlottesville Hotel, effective December 1985.

The unique redbrick-and-glass structure literally soars above the mall site on which it sits, its design a challenge to the staid architecture of the University of Virginia's older buildings,

The 442-room Omni International Hotel in Norfolk, Virginia, sits on the city's waterfront and features a dinner theater, lobby bar, and two restaurants—The Esplanade and The Riverwalk Cafe.

eight blocks away. With a staff of 190, it serves a thriving convention business. Its Vinegar Hill Pub, a recreated colonial tavern, offers nightly entertainment. A casual atmosphere prevails in the dramatic 65-foot atrium lobby and garden. Just 15 minutes from Monticello, Thomas Jefferson's home, the Omni Charlottesville offers 209 guest rooms and a 9,205-square-foot conference center.

An elegant interior view of the Omni Richmond Hotel.

The latest addition to the Omni family in Virginia is the $43-million Omni Richmond Hotel at James Center, the largest mixed-use office, commercial, and residential complex under construction in the Southeast. Co-owned by Faison Associates and CSX Realty, the 363-room first-class hotel celebrated its grand opening in July 1987 with a lively parade through James Center and the city's financial district.

Location is everything here—in the center of Richmond's governmental, historic, financial, and commercial districts. The Omni is only six blocks from the Richmond Convention Center and directly across from the dining, entertainment, and specialty shopping amenities of historic Shockoe Slip.

The hotel's exterior, a distinctive salmon color, is drawn from Virginia quarried stone. Features include the Gallego Restaurant with gourmet food and premium wine, the White Water Cafe with a bistro atmosphere for casual dining, health and fitness facilities, two concierge floors, 12,000 square feet of meeting space, a 7,000-square-foot ballroom, and 170 king suites, 85 queen, and 94 double rooms.

TRAVELLER'S RESTAURANT

Traveller's Restaurant in downtown Richmond is named after General Robert E. Lee's horse and is the house that Lee and Traveller returned to after Lee surrendered to General Ulysses S. Grant at Appomattox in the spring of 1865. On the National Register of Historic Places, this shorttime residence of Robert E. Lee has been left intact and now serves as a warm and unpretentious restaurant.

Traveller's Restaurant may be a relative newcomer to Richmond, but it occupies a historic downtown location in the Robert E. Lee House. Businesspeople, lobbyists, politicians, and area residents have all discovered Traveller's Restaurant. So, too, have a surprising number of gourmet trendsetters throughout the country.

Traveller's occupies the basement of the house in Richmond where General Lee lived immediately after the Civil War, and fills the totally remodeled interior of a former warehouse that stands where his famous horse, Traveller, was once stabled. Richmond's revitalized downtown now surrounds the former Lee estate; Traveller's has become an oasis of gracious living amidst the commercial hubbub, a place where the past can be remembered and the present enjoyed.

Gerald Waters, founder and owner of Traveller's Restaurant, had extensive experience in both politics and restaurant operations when, in 1981, he first conceived of adapting the Lee House and grounds to its new use. Since the estate had been listed on the National Register of Historic Places, the renovation required the approval of the National Parks Service as well as the Historic Richmond Foundation that owns the property.

Virginians cherish the memory of General Lee—and while some things have had to change, much of the venerable house has survived intact. Fire codes and business needs have been satisfied with full respect for the past. Wherever possible, original interior woodwork has been preserved—including the door in front of which Matthew Brady took the last photograph of Lee in full Confederate uniform. A copy of the photograph hangs beside the door.

The menu at Traveller's is unaffected and brief. Superb prime rib, steaks, and simply prepared seafoods are accompanied by fresh rolls, crisp salads, potatoes, and fresh vegetables. The portions are generous; the quality uncompromising. The wine list includes a few selections appropriate for businessmen celebrating a successful multimillion-dollar deal, but primarily features fine American vintages of familiar varieties.

The main dining room occupies a former book depository, built in the 1920s on the site of Traveller's stable by the Virginia Historical Society. The concrete interior is covered now by dark wood paneling, and a two-story kitchen serves both the first level and balcony that fill the 18-foot interior. A reception area, lounge, and small, private dining room occupy the basement of the main house.

"We respect the memory of Lee and value the past," says Waters. Paintings and photographs of the general hang in the lounge area. A portrait of Traveller hangs in the main dining room, along with paintings of two other famous Virginia horses: Sir Archie and Secretariat. The resulting ambience reminds diners of a genteel era and tradition.

So does everything else about Traveller's Restaurant.

PATRONS

The following individuals, companies, and organizations have made a valuable commitment to the quality of this publication. Windsor Publications and the Virginia Chamber of Commerce gratefully acknowledge their participation in *Virginia: A Commonwealth Comes of Age.*

Abbott Laboratories*
Anderson & Strudwick*
AT&T
Babcock & Wilcox*
Bill's Barbecue, Inc.*
A. Smith Bowman Distillery*
Brenco, Inc.*
Bridgewater College*
Burke & Herbert Bank & Trust Co.*
The Byrd Newspapers*
The Calvert Companies, Inc.*
C&P Telephone Co.
C&P Telephone of Virginia*
Canon Virginia, Inc.*
The Cardwell Machine Company*
Carwithen Associates, Inc.
Central Telephone Company of Virginia*
Chesapeake Corporation*
Coffee Butler Service, Inc.*
The College of William and Mary in
        Virginia*
Country Squire Construction
CSX Corporation*
Dan River Inc.*
Doughtie's Foods, Inc.*
Doyle Lumber Incorporated*
Dynatech Corporation*
DynCorp*
Eck Enterprises, Inc., and Eck Supply Co.*
Electroplate-Rite Corporation*
Erkiletian Construction Corporation*
Ethyl Corporation*
The Evans Company*
Figgie International Inc.*
First Colony Coffee & Tea Co., Inc.*
First Colony Life Insurance Company*
George M. Flippen
Flow General Inc.*
Franklin Federal Savings and Loan
        Association*
GTE Southeast*
GTE Spacenet Corporation*
Guiffré Distributing Company*
Harrison and Lephoe Advertising and
        Public Relations
Hauni Richmond, Inc.*
The Homestead*
Hotel Roanoke*
Melvin Humphries
Hungerford Mechanical Corporation*
Industrial Supply Corp.

Infilco Degremont, Inc.*
Inta-Roto*
International Developers, Inc.*
Interstate Electric Supply Co., Inc.*
James Madison University*
James River Corporation*
The Jefferson Sheraton Hotel*
The Journal Newspapers*
Klann Incorporated*
Klöckner Pentaplast of America,
        Inc.
The Lane Company, Inc.*
Lillian Vernon Corporation*
The Little Oil Company, Inc.*
Lloyd Electric Company, Inc.*
The Henry A. Long Company*
Eunice Lunsford
Lynchburg College*
McGuire, Woods, Battle & Boothe*
Markel Corporation*
Marsteller Corporation*
Martha Washington Inn*
The Martin Agency, Inc.*
Marymount University*
The Mason Hirst Companies*
The Memorial Hospital of Danville
Nekoosa Packaging
Network Solutions*
Newport News Shipbuilding*
Norfolk Southern Corporation*
Norfolk State University*
Old Dominion University*
Omega World Travel*
Omni Hotels*
O'Sullivan Corporation*
Parham Scale Co., Inc.
J. Kennon Perrin Construction Company,
        Inc.*
Philip Morris Companies*
Potomac Edison Company*
Primark Corporation*
Randolph-Macon College*
Real Title Company, Inc.*
Reynolds Metals Company*
Richmond Cold Storage Co., Inc.
Richmond, Fredericksburg and Potomac
        Railroad Company*
George Edwin Russell
Schenkers International Forwarders Inc.
Scope Incorporated, A Lexicon Company*
Sheldon Lumber Company, Inc.*
The Shockey Companies
The Charles E. Smith Companies*
Smithfield Foods, Inc.*
Software AG of North America, Inc.*
Solite Corporation*
South Atlantic Coal Company, Inc.*
Southern States Cooperative, Inc.*
Sperry Marine Inc.*

State Farm Insurance Eastern Regional
        Office*
Systems Management American
        Corporation*
Taylor & Sledd*
Technology Applications, Inc.*
Traveller's Restaurant*
University of Virginia*
USAir*
Virginia-American Water Company
Virginia Commonwealth University*
Virginia Military Institute*
Virginia Mutual Insurance Company*
Virginia Polytechnic Institute and State
        University*
Virginia Port Authority*
Virginia Power*
Vulcan Materials Company Mideast
        Division*
Walker Manufacturing Company*
Ward/Hall Associates*
Wayn-Tex Inc.
Wayne Insulation Co., Inc.*
WEST*GROUP, Inc.*
Westvaco*
Williams Supply Inc.
Woodward & Lothrop*

*Partners in Progress of *Virginia: A Commonwealth Comes of Age.* The histories of these companies and organizations appear in Chapter 11, beginning on page 283.

BIBLIOGRAPHY

CHAPTER 1

Billings, Warren M., ed. *The Old Dominion in the Seventeenth Century.* Chapel Hill, N.C.: The University of North Carolina Press, 1975.

Breen, T.H. "Making a Crop." *Virginia Cavalcade* 36 (Autumn 1986): 52-64.

_____. *Puritans and Adventurers.* New York: Oxford University Press, 1980.

Bruce, Philip Alexander. *Economic History of Virginia in the Seventeenth Century.* New York and London: MacMillan and Co., 1895.

Dowdey, Clifford. *The Golden Age.* Boston and Toronto: Little, Brown and Co., 1970.

Fleming, Daniel B., Paul C. Slayton, and Edgar A. Toppin, eds. *Virginia History and Government.* Morristown, N.J.: Silver Burdett Co., 1986.

Fogel, Robert William, and Stanley L. Engerman. *Time on the Cross: The Economics of American Negro Slavery.* Boston and Toronto: Little, Brown and Co., 1974.

Hemphill, William Edwin, Marvin Wilson Schlegel, and Sadie Ethel Engelberg, eds. *Cavalier Commonwealth.* New York: McGraw-Hill Co., 1957.

Jamestown-Yorktown Foundation. *The Story of John Rolfe.* Jamestown, Va.: Jamestown-Yorktown Foundation, 1962.

Nash, Gerald D., ed. *Issues in American Economic History.* Lexington, Mass.: D.C. Heath & Co., 1972.

Salmon, Emily J., ed. *A Hornbook of Virginia History.* Richmond: Virginia State Library, 1983.

Stewart, Peter Crawford. "The Commercial History of Hampton Roads." Ph.D. diss., University of Virginia, 1967.

Ward, Harry M. *Richmond: An Illustrated History.* Northridge, Ca.: Windsor Publications, 1985.

Wertenbaker, Thomas J. *The Planters of Colonial Virginia.* New York: Russell & Russell, 1959.

Wright, Louis B. *The First Gentlemen of Virginia.* Charlottesville, Va.: Dominion Books, 1964.

CHAPTER 2

Bondurant, Agnes M. *Poe's Richmond.* Richmond: Poe Association, 1978.

Brown, Alexander Crosby. *The Dismal Swamp.* Chesapeake, Va.: Norfolk County History Society of Chesapeake, Va., 1967.

Dabney, Virginius. *Richmond: The Story of a City.* Garden City, N.Y.: Doubleday & Co., 1976.

_____. *Virginia: The New Dominion.* Charlottesville, Va.: The University Press of Virginia, 1971.

Dickinson, William Penn, Jr. "The Social Saving Generated by the Richmond & Danville Railroad." Master's thesis. University of Virginia, 1975.

Dunaway, Wayland Fuller. *History of the James River and Kanawha Company.* New York: Ames Press, 1922.

Fleming, Daniel B., Paul C. Slayton, and Edgar A. Toppin, eds. *Virginia History and Government.* Morristown, N.J.: Silver Burdett Co., 1986.

Fogel, Robert William, and Stanley L. Engerman. *Time on the Cross: The Economics of American Negro Slavery.* Boston and Toronto: Little, Brown and Co., 1974.

Harwood, Herbert H., Jr. *Rails to the Blue Ridge.* Falls Church, Va.: Pioneer America Society, Inc., 1969.

Havighurst, Walter. *Alexander Spotswood: Portrait of a Governor.* Williamsburg, Va.: Colonial Williamsburg, distributed by Holt, Rinehart and Winston, 1967.

Hemphill, William Edwin, Marvin Wilson Schlegel, and Sadie Ethel Engelberg, eds. *Cavalier Commonwealth.* New York: McGraw-Hill Co., 1957.

Keir, Malcolm. *The March of Commerce.* New Haven, Ct.: Yale University Press, 1927.

Kercheval, Samuel. *A History of the Valley of Virginia.* Woodstock, Va.: W.N. Grabill, Power Press, 1903.

Mordecai, Samuel. *Richmond in By-Gone Days.* 2d ed. 1860. Reprint. Richmond: The Dietz Press, 1946.

Morton, Richard L. *Colonial Virginia.* Vol. 2. Chapel Hill, N.C.: University of North Carolina Press, 1960.

Rice, Otis K. *The Allegheny Frontier.* Lexington, Ky.: The University Press of Kentucky, 1970.

Salmon, Emily J., ed. *A Hornbook of Virginia History.* Richmond: Virginia State Library, 1983.

Simkins, Francis Butler, Hunicutt Jones Spotswood, and Sidman P. Poole. *Virginia: History, Government, Geography.* New York: Charles Scribner's Sons, 1957.

Stewart, Peter C. "The Commercial History of Hampton Roads." Ph.D. diss., University of Virginia, 1967.

_____ . "Railroads and Urban Rivalries in Antebellum Eastern Virginia." *The Virginia Magazine of History and Biography* 81:1 (January 1973): 3-22.

Striplin, E.F. Pat. *The Norfolk & Western: A History.* Roanoke, Va.: Norfolk & Western Railway Co., 1981.

CHAPTER 3

Anderson, J.H. *American Civil War.* London: Hugh Rees, 1912.

Andrews, Matthew Page. *Virginia: The Old Dominion.* New York: Doubleday, Doran & Co., 1937.

Boney, F.N. *John Letcher of Virginia.* University, Ala.: University of Alabama Press, 1966.

Conrad, Alfred H., and John R. Meyer. "The Economics of Slavery in the Ante-Bellum South." In *Issues in an American Economic History,* edited by Gerald D. Nash. Lexington, Mass.: D.C. Heath & Co., 1972.

Crews, Ed. "Arsenal of the Confederacy Closing Down." *Richmond News Leader* (March 18, 1987).

Dew, Charles B. *Ironmaker to the Confederacy: Joseph R. Anderson and the Tredegar Iron Works.* New Haven, Ct.: Yale University Press, 1966.

Fleming, Daniel B., Paul C. Slayton, Jr., and Edgar A. Toppin, eds. *Virginia History and Government.* Morristown, N.J.: Silver Burdett Co., 1986.

Foote, Shelby. *The Civil War: Fort Sumter to Perryville.* New York: Random House, 1958.

Gates, Paul W. *Agriculture and the Civil War.* New York: Alfred A. Knopf, 1965.

Hemphill, William Edwin, Marvin Wilson Schlegel, and Sadie Ethel Engelberg, eds. *Cavalier Commonwealth.* New York: McGraw-Hill Book Co. 1957.

Hoehling, A.A. and Mary. *The Day Richmond Died.* San Diego, Ca.: A.S. Barnes & Co., 1981.

Jennings, George Wood. *The Fiscal History of Virginia from 1860-1870.* Ph.D. diss., University of Virginia, 1961.

McPherson, James M. *Ordeal by Fire.* New York: Alfred A. Knopf, 1982.

Moore, George Ellis. *A Banner in the Hills.* New York: Appleton-Century-Crofts, 1963.

Paludan, Phillip Shaw. *Victims: A True Story of the Civil War.* Knoxville, Tenn.: University of Tennessee Press, 1981.

Pond, George E. *The Shenandoah Valley in 1864.* New York: Charles Scribner's Sons, 1883.

Rubin, Louis D., Jr. *Virginia: A Bicentennial History.* New York: W.W. Norton and Co., 1977.

Salmon, Emily J., ed. *A Hornbook of Virginia History.* Richmond: Virginia State Library, 1983.

Simkins, Francis Butler, Hunnicutt Jones Spotswood, and Sidman P. Poole. *Virginia: History, Government, Geography.* New York: Charles Scribner's Sons, 1957.

Smith, James D. "Virginia During Reconstruction." Ph.D. diss., University of Virginia, 1960.

CHAPTER 4

Andrews, Matthew Page. *Virginia: The Old Dominion.* Garden City: Doubleday, Doran & Co., 1937.

Chesson, Michael B. *Richmond After the War, 1865-1890.* Richmond: Virginia State Library, 1981.

Dabney, Virginius. *Virginia: The New Dominion.* Garden City, N.J.: Doubleday & Co., 1971.

Fleming, Daniel B., Paul C. Slayton, Jr., and Edgar A. Toppin, eds. *Virginia History and Government.* Morristown, N.J.: Silver Burdett Co., 1986.

Hemphill, William Edwin, Marvin Wilson Schlegel, and Sadie Ethel Engelberg. *Cavalier Commonwealth.* New York: McGraw-Hill Book Company, 1957.

Jennings, G.W. "The Fiscal History of Virginia from 1860 to 1870." Ph.D. diss., University of Virginia, 1961.

Moger, Allen W. *Virginia: Bourbonism to Byrd, 1870-1925.* Charlottesville, Va.: University Press of Virginia, 1968.

Pearson, Charles Chilton. *The Readjuster Movement in Virginia.* Gloucester, Mass.: Peter Smith, 1968.

Ransom, Roger, and Richard Sutch. *One Kind of Freedom.* Cambridge: Cambridge University Press, 1977.

Rubin, Louis D., Jr. *Virginia: A Bicentennial History.* New York: W.W. Norton and Co., 1977.

Salmon, Emily J., ed. *A Hornbook of Virginia History.* Richmond: Virginia State Library, 1983.

Sanford, James K., ed. *A Century of Commerce.* Richmond: Richmond Chamber of Commerce, 1967.

Simkins, Francis Butler, Hunnicutt Jones Spotswood, and Sidman P. Poole. *Virginia: History, Government, Geography.* New York: Charles Scribner's Sons, 1957.

Smith, James D. "Virginia During Reconstruction." Ph.D. diss., University of Virginia, 1960.

Squires, W.H.T. *Unleashed At Last.* Portsmouth, Va.: Printcraft Press, 1939.

Stiles, Robert. "Why the Solid South? or Reconstruction and Its Results." Unpublished manuscript, Baltimore, 1890.

CHAPTER 5

Andrews, Matthew Page. *Virginia: The Old Dominion.* Garden City: Doubleday, Doran & Co., 1937.

Cocke, Karen Hisle, ed. "A Century of Leadership." *Masthead* (Winter 1985): 3-9.

Chesson, Michael B. *Richmond After the War, 1865-1890.* Richmond: Virginia State Library, 1981.

Clark, Victor S. *History of Manufactures in the United States.* Vol. 3. New York: McGraw-Hill Book Co., 1929.

Dabney, Virginius. *Richmond: The Story of a City.* Garden City: Doubleday & Company, Inc., 1976.

_____ . *Virginia: The New Dominion.* Charlottesville, Va.: University Press of Virginia, 1971.

Fleming, Daniel B., Paul C. Slayton, Jr., and Edgar A. Toppin, eds. *Virginia History and Government.* Morristown, N.J.: Silver Burdett Co., 1986.

Hemphill, William Edwin, Marvin Wilson Schlegel, and Sadie Ethel Engelberg. *Cavalier Commonwealth.* New York: McGraw-Hill Book Co., 1957.

Morton, Richard L. *History of Virginia.* Vol. III. Chicago: The American Historical Society, 1924.

Netherton, Nan, Donald Sweig, Janice Artemel, Patricia Hickin, and Patrick Reed. *Fairfax County, Virginia: A History.* Fairfax, Va.: Fairfax County Board of Supervisors, 1978.

Rubin, Louis D., Jr. *Virginia: A Bicentennial History.* New York: W.W. Norton and Co., 1977.

Salmon, Emily J., ed. *A Hornbook of Virginia History.* Richmond: Virginia State Library, 1983.

Sanford, James K., ed. *A Century of Commerce.* Richmond: Richmond Chamber of Commerce, 1967.

Simkins, Francis Butler, Hunnicutt Jones Spotswood, and Sidman P. Poole. *Virginia: History, Government, Geography.* New York: Charles Scribner's Sons, 1957.

Smith, James D. "Virginia During Reconstruction." Ph.D. diss., University of Virginia, 1960.

Ward, Harry M. *Richmond: An Illustrated History.* Northridge, Ca.: Windsor Publications, 1985.

CHAPTER 6

Addington, Luther F. *A Short History of Extreme Southwest Virginia.* Big Stone Gap, Va.: Chamber of Commerce, 1965.

Bacon, James A., Jr. "Prosperity's Just a Dream at Centennial." *Roanoke Times* (June 12, 1983): A-1.

Barnes, Raymond P. *A History of Roanoke.* Radford, Va.: Commonwealth Press, 1968.

Clark, Victor S. *History of Manufactures in the United States.* Vol. 3. New York: McGraw-Hill Book Co., 1929.

Fleming, Daniel B., Paul C. Slayton, Jr., Edgar A. Toppin, eds. *Virginia History and Government.* Morristown, N.J.: Silver Burdett Co., 1986.

Harmon, John Newton. *Annals of Tazewell County.* Richmond, Va.: W.C. Hill Printing Co., 1925.

"The Historical Pageant of Progress." Program sponsored by Southwestern Virginia, Wytheville, Va., July 4-6, 1934.

Jack, George S., and E.B. Jacobs. *History of Roanoke County.* Roanoke, Va.: Jack and Jacobs, 1912.

Jacobs, E.B. *History of the Norfolk & Western Railway.* Roanoke, Va.: Jack and Jacobs, 1912.

Lewis, Helen M. "The Changing Communities in the Southern Appalachian Coal Fields." Paper presented at the International Seminar on Social Change in the Mining Community, Jackson's Mill, W. Va., Oct. 6, 1967.

Morton, Richard L. *History of Virginia.* Vol. 3. Chicago: The American Historical Society, 1924.

Niemi, Albert W., Jr. *U.S. Economic History.* 2d ed. Chicago: Rand

McNally College Publishing, 1980.

Pendleton, William C. *History of Tazewell County and Southwest Virginia.* Richmond: W.C. Hill Printing Co., 1920.

Prescott, E.J. *The Story of the Virginia Coal and Iron Company, 1882-1945.* Virginia Coal and Iron Co., 1945.

"Roanoke Diamond Jubilee." Program from celebration, Roanoke, Va., June 14-23, 1957.

Rubin, Louis D., Jr. *Virginia: A Bicentennial History.* New York: W.W. Norton and Co., 1977.

Salmon, Emily J., ed. *A Hornbook of Virginia History.* Richmond: Virginia State Library, 1983.

Verrill, A. Hyatt. *Romantic and Historic Virginia.* New York: Dodd, Mead & Co., 1935.

Workers of the Writers' Program of the Work Projects Administration in the State of Virginia. *Roanoke: Story of a County and City.* Roanoke, Va.: Roanoke City School Board, 1942.

CHAPTER 7

Alexander, Will W. "The Negro in the New South." *Southern Workman* 50 (January-December 1921): 145-152.

Barrett, Harris. "The Building and Loan Company of Hampton." *Southern Workman* (July 1890): 79.

Blount, George W. "The Virginia State Negro Business League." *Southern Workman* 48 (January-December 1921): 599-605.

Browning, James B. "Beginnings of Insurance Among Negroes." *Journal of Negro History* 22 (1937): 417-432.

Dabney, Virginius. *Below the Potomac.* New York and London: D. Appleton-Century Co., 1942.

————. *Virginia: The New Dominion.* Garden City, N.Y.: Doubleday & Co., 1971.

Dabney, Wendell P. *Maggie L. Walker and The I.O. of St. Luke.* Cincinnati: The Dabney Publishing Co., 1927.

DuBois, W.E. Burghardt. *The Negro in Business.* New York: AMS Press, 1899.

Engs, Robert Francis. *Freedom's First Generation.* University of Pennsylvania Press, 1879.

Fitzgerald, Ruth Coder. *A Different Story: A Black History of Fredericksburg, Stafford and Spotsylvania, Virginia.*

Unicorn, 1979.

Fleming, Daniel B., Paul C. Slayton, Jr., and Edgar A. Toppin, eds. *Virginia History and Government.* Morristown, N.J.: Silver Burdett Co., 1986.

Fleming, Jesse E. "A History of Consolidated Bank and Trust Company, A Minority Bank." Thesis, The Stonier Graduate School of Banking, conducted by the American Bankers Association at Rutgers, The State University, New Brunswick, N.J., 1972.

Harmon, J.H. "The Negro As a Local Businessman." *Journal of Negro History* 14:2 (April 1929).

Heinemann, Ronald L. *Depression and the New Deal in Virginia.* Ph.D. diss., University of Virginia, 1968.

Katz, William Loren, gen. ed. *Negro Population in the United States, 1790-1915.* New York: Arno Press and The New York Times, 1968.

Lindsay, Arnett G. "The Negro in Banking." *Journal of Negro History* 14:2 (April 1929): 156-192.

Ludlow, Helen W. "The Negro in Business in Hampton and Vicinity." *Southern Workman* 33 (September 1904): 463-501.

McConnell, John Preston. *Negroes and Their Treatment in Virginia From 1865-1867.* Pulaski, Va.: B.D. Smith and Brothers, 1910.

Mordecai, Samuel. *Richmond in Bygone Days.* 2d ed. 1860. Reprint. Richmond: The Dietz Press, 1946.

Morgan, Philip, ed. *Don't Grieve After Me.* Hampton, Va.: Hampton University, 1986.

Pierce, Joseph A. *Negro Business and Business Education: Their Present and Prospective Development.* New York: Harper and Brothers Publishers, 1947.

Rich, William M. "Negro Commercial Activities in Tidewater, Virginia." *Southern Workman* 50 (January-December 1921): 138-144.

Taylor, A.A. "The Negro in the Reconstruction of Virginia." *Journal of Negro History* 11 (1926): 243-537.

U.S. Labor Department. *Bulletin.* Vol. 3. Washington, D.C.: GPO, 1898.

Washington, Booker T. *The Negro in Business.* Boston: Hertel, Jenkins and Co., 1907.

Wheelock, F.D. "A Community Asset: People's Building and Loan Association of Hampton, Virginia." *Southern Workman* 50 (January-December, 1921): 545-546.

Woodson, C.G. "Insurance Business Among Negroes." *Journal of Negro History* 14:2 (April 1929): 202-214.

Woodward, C. Vann. *The Strange Career of Jim Crow.* New York: Oxford University Press, 1955.

Work, Monroe N. "The Negro in Business and the Professions." *Annals of the American Academy* 138-140 (November 1928).

Workers of the Writers' Program of the Work Projects Administration in the State of Virginia. *The Negro in Virginia.* New York: Hastings House, 1940.

CHAPTER 8

Barnes, Raymond P. *A History of Roanoke.* Radford, Va.: Commonwealth Press, 1968.

Bottom, Raymond B. *Virginia's Record of Progress.* Richmond: Virginia State Chamber of Commerce, 1950.

Dabney, Virginius. *Virginius Dabney's Virginia.* Chapel Hill, N.C.: Algonquin Books of Chapel Hill, 1986.

_____ . *Virginia: The New Dominion.* Charlottesville, Va.: University Press of Virginia, 1971.

Fleming, Daniel B., Paul C. Slayton, Jr., Edgar A. Toppin, eds. *Virginia History and Government.* Morristown, N.J.: Silver Burdett Co., 1986.

Gottman, Jean. *Virginia at Mid-Century.* New York: Henry Holt & Co., 1955.

_____ . *Virginia In Our Century.* Charlottesville, Va.: University Press of Virginia, 1969.

Hairston, L. Beatrice W. *A Brief History of Danville, Virginia.* Richmond: The Dietz Press, 1955.

Hartig, Dennis. "Plug Tobacco: A Lucrative Home-Grown Industry." *Martinsville Bulletin* (July 4, 1976).

Heinemann, Ronald L. "Depression and the New Deal in Virginia." Ph.D. diss., University of Virginia, 1968.

Hundley, R.B. "Company Started on Town's Gamble and Founder's Nerve." *Martinsville Bulletin* (July 4, 1976).

_____ . "American Furniture Company Born as Tobacco Declined." *Martinsville Bulletin* (July 4, 1976).

Moger, Allen W. *Virginia: Bourbonism to Byrd, 1870-1925.* Charlottesville, Va.: University Press of Virginia, 1968.

Moore, John Hammond. *Albemarle: Jefferson's County.* Charlottesville, Va.: University Press of Virginia, 1976.

Niemi, Albert W., Jr. *U.S. Economic History.* 2d ed. Chicago: Rand McNally College Publishing, 1980.

Richards, Ginny. "Textiles: Industrialists Developed Natural Resources to Diversify Economy." *Martinsville Bulletin* (July 4, 1976).

_____ . "From Sawmillers to Furniture Giants." *Martinsville Bulletin* (July 4, 1976).

_____ . "Gravely Family Enterprises Date Back 180 Years." *Martinsville Bulletin* (July 4, 1976).

_____ . "Farmer's Son Builds Industrial, Political Career." *Martinsville Bulletin* (July 4, 1976).

_____ . "Fieldcrest: The Firm That Built Its Own Neighbors." *Martinsville Bulletin* (July 4, 1976).

Ritz, Wilfred J. *Industrial Progress in Virginia.* Richmond: Virginia State Chamber of Commerce, 1974.

Rubin, Louis D., Jr. *Virginia, A Bicentennial History.* New York: W.W. Norton & Co., 1977.

Sinclair, Andrew. *Prohibition: the Era of Excess.* Boston: Little, Brown and Co., 1962.

Ward, Harry M. *Richmond: An Illustrated History.* Northridge, Ca.: Windsor Publications, 1985.

Ward, H. Wesley. *The Administration of Liquor Control in Virginia.* Charlottesville, Va.: Division of Publications, Bureau of Public Administration, University of Virginia, 1946.

CHAPTER 9

Bacon, James A., Jr. "Booming Coal Port." *Roanoke Times and World News* (December 28, 1980).

Darnton, Donald C., and Charles O. Meiburg. "The Contributions of the Ports of Virginia to the Economy of the Commonwealth." Report prepared by the Bureau of Population and Economic Research, Graduate School of the Business Administration, University of Virginia, Charlottesville, Va., January 1968.

Department of Research and Statistics, Federal Reserve Bank of Richmond. *Economic Effects of the War on the Hampton Roads Area.* Richmond, Va., 1944.

Fleming, Daniel B., Paul C. Slayton, Jr., and Edgar A. Toppin, eds. *Virginia History and Government.* Morristown, N.J.: Silver Burdett Co., 1986.

Foss, William O. *The United States Navy in Hampton Roads.* Norfolk, Va.: The Donning Co., 1984.

Gottman, Jean. *Virginia In Our Century.* Charlottesville, Va.: University Press of Virginia, 1969.

Kale, Wilford. "Trials of War, Peace Challenge Yard's Creed." *Richmond Times-Dispatch* (January 18, 1987).

Knapp, John L., James Hammond, and Donald P. Haroz. "The Impact of Virginia's Ports on the Economy of the Commonwealth." Charlottesville, Va.: Tayloe Murphy Institute, 1976.

Marsh, Charles F., ed. *The Hampton Roads Communities in World War II.* Chapel Hill, N.C.: University of North Carolina Press, 1951.

Ritz, Wilfred J. *Industrial Progress in Virginia.* Richmond: Virginia State Chamber of Commerce, 1947.

Rubin, Louis D., Jr. *Virginia: A Bicentennial History.* New York: W.W. Norton & Co., 1977.

Tazewell, William L. *Norfolk's Waters.* Northridge, Ca.: Windsor Publications, Inc., 1982.

CHAPTER 10

Burton, Mary T., ed. *Picture Yourself in Fairfax County.* Dunn Loring, Va.: Fairfax County Chamber of Commerce, Spring 1987.

Center for Innovative Technology. *The Institutes.* Herndon, Va.: Center for Innovative Technology, 1985.

_____ . *Annual Report,* 1986.

Cosin, Elizabeth. "Reston Lands Space Station." *The Connection* (April 8, 1987).

Deschamps, Elizabeth M. "Reston in Space Windfall." *The Connection* (July 8, 1987).

_____ . "Space." *The Connection* (August 5, 1987).

Fairfax County Economic Development Authority, *Business Report: Construction Activity.* Vienna, Va.,

June 1987.

———. *Business Report: Association Report.* Vienna, Va., April 1986.

———. *Business Report: International Business, Fairfax County.* Vienna, Va., January 1986.

———. *Business Report: Real Estate Market Review.* Vienna, Va., Winter, 1986.

Fairfax Economic Development Authority. *Fairfax Prospectus.* Vienna, Va., September 1985.

———. *Fairfax Prospectus.* Vienna, Va., May 1985.

———. *Fairfax Prospectus.* Vienna, Va., May 1984.

———. *Economic Overview.* Vienna, Va., 1986.

———. *Population and Demographics.* Vienna, Va., nd.

———. *Labor Market.* Vienna, Va., 1986.

———. *Fairfax Prospectus.* Vienna, Va., April 1986.

———. *Fairfax Prospectus.* Vienna, Va., December 1985.

Fleming, Daniel B., Paul C. Slayton, Jr., and Edgar A. Toppin, eds. *Virginia History and Government.* Morristown, N.J.: Silver Burdett Co., 1986.

Gottman, Jean. *Virginia In Our Century.* Charlottesville, Va.: University Press of Virginia, 1969.

Governor's Task Force on Science and Technology in Virginia. *The Report of the Governor's Task Force on Science and Technology in Virginia.* Vol. 1. Richmond: 1983.

Kelly, Brian, ed. *Regardie's Regional Report: Fairfax County.* Washington, D.C.: *Regardie's,* 1986.

Malone, Roger. "Engineers Orbit Reston." *Alexandria Journal* (September 1, 1987).

Miller, Bill. "'Area Second to None' For High-Tech Firm." *Richmond Times-Dispatch* (July 24, 1983).

———. "Northern Virginia." *Richmond Times-Dispatch* (July 24, 1983).

Rhodes, Karl. "Make-Do Dulles." *Virginia Business Magazine* (April 1986): 32-44.

Rubin, Louis D., Jr. *Virginia: A Bicentennial History.* New York: W.W. Norton & Co., 1977.

Ruehrman, James C. *High Technology and Electronics.* Richmond: Commonwealth of Virginia, Department of Industrial Development, 1982.

———. *Virginia Facts and Figures.* Richmond: Commonwealth of Virginia, Department of Economic Development, 1987.

———. *High Technology, Biomedical and Related Industries.* Richmond: Commonwealth of Virginia, Department of Economic Development.

Williams, Bob. "Putting the Byte on Uncle Sam." *Virginia Business Magazine* (November 1986): 53-56.

———. "From Rats to Riches." *Virginia Business Magazine* (October 1986): 19-24.

INDEX

PARTNERS IN PROGRESS INDEX

GENERAL INDEX